D0252933

Blind Vengeance

The University of Georgia Press

Athens and London

Blind Vengeance

The Roy Moody Mail Bomb Murders

RAY JENKINS

Published by the University of Georgia Press

Athens, Georgia 30602

© 1997 by Ray Jenkins

Set in Berkeley Old Style by G&S Typesetters, Inc.

Printed and bound by Maple-Vail Book Manufacturing Group, Inc.

The paper in this book meets the guidelines for permanence and

durability of the Committee on Production Guidelines

for Book Longevity of the Council on Library Resources.

Printed in the United States of America

01   00   99   98   97   C   5   4   3   2   1

LIBRARY OF CONGRESS CATALOGING IN PUBLICATION DATA

Jenkins, Ray, 1930–

    Blind vengeance : the Roy Moody mail bomb murders / Ray Jenkins.

        p.   cm.

    Includes bibliographical references (p.   ) and index.

    ISBN 0-8203-1906-6 (alk. paper)

    1. Moody, Walter Leroy.   2. Murderers–Alabama–Biography.

    3. Mail bombings–Southern States–Case studies.   I. Title.

    HV6248.M6493J46   1997

    364.15'23'09776581–dc21   96-39577

BRITISH LIBRARY CATALOGING IN PUBLICATION DATA AVAILABLE

To my wife, Bettina

Contents

Blind Vengeance

Introduction: A Personal Odyssey

This book is based on experience, personal and professional. One of the principal subjects is a man whom I came to know in the course of observing the South as a reporter and editor for forty years. Another is a man who grew up in the small-town milieu of Georgia, not far from where I grew up, at about the same time. The third, though a bit younger than the other two, was also born in the first half of the century.

Although I never met the second and third men in this tragic triangle, as I gathered the material for this work I came to recognize that the three symbolized the South that I covered during a turbulent period. One came from modest privilege, and he might have enjoyed a comfortable life in the relative obscurity of a corporate law practice during a time of industrial boom. But he recognized the imperatives of profound social and political change, and he knew that without courageous leadership that change might degenerate into protracted violent upheaval. Another was a black man who struggled upward in a rigidly segregated society and who exercised great personal courage to challenge that order. The remaining figure was a white man who was left behind in the class conflict and became bitterly obsessed with his perception of injustice in the changing order.

It cannot be said that racial conflict directly underlay the crimes on which this book focuses. Yet, that aspect of southern society always hovered at the edges of the story—just as it has lurked in the politics of the South generally.

At the time of my birth in 1930 in Worth County, Georgia, three men who would become the dominant political figures of the state for much of my time as a journalist and sometime politician were already in place: Walter George, Richard Russell, and Eugene Talmadge—three men who were strikingly different in style and character, and yet whose politics coalesced around the overarching issue of race.

Walter F. George was a courtly, white-haired, old-style lawyer-politician who was elected to the United States Senate in 1922 to succeed Tom Watson, the enigmatic populist demagogue. A gracious gentleman who avoided coarse harangue, George became a significant figure in the state and in the nation. He was a "Southern Democrat," which meant that he was a fundamentally conservative man—and as such, generally in step with his constituency. As his seniority in the Senate grew, George gravitated toward affairs of the world, rising to become a respected chairman of the Senate Foreign Relations Committee in the 1950s.

The governor of Georgia in the year that I was born was Richard Brevard Russell. If there were such a thing as the royal blood of Georgia, it surely ran in the veins of "Dick" Russell. One of thirteen children of the chief justice of Georgia, Russell became governor at the age of thirty-two, then went on to the United States Senate where he exercised such formidable skills as a lawmaker that today a Senate office building in Washington bears his name.

In sharp contrast to these eminent public men, Eugene Talmadge was a bumptious brawler whose consummate demagoguery belied the fact that he was a Phi Beta Kappa graduate of the University of Georgia. In the heat and passion of campaign he would shed his coat to reveal his trademark red galluses, and an unruly forelock would fall across his bespectacled face. He was called "the Wild Man from Sugar Creek," but his mastery of the masses masked a secretive alignment with the conservative business interests of Georgia. Talmadge's schizophrenic political nature was best summed up in a little ditty composed by some unknown political cynic early in the Talmadge era:

The bigbugs courted the hookworms,
and their clandestine embrace,
Produced a governor of Georgia,
who raised hell all over the place.

But as unalike as George, Russell, and Talmadge may have been in style, they were linked by certain elements. Each in his own way served the privileged interests of Georgia and the nation. Dick Russell became one of the most influential figures in Washington in military matters, and he used his great skill and power to bestow upon Georgia an immense amount of federal largess in the form of military spending. George patiently shepherded through the Congress legislation that expended hundreds of millions of federal dollars on river-development projects in Georgia and other southeastern states that never could have withstood scrupulous cost-benefit analysis. Though he railed against them in his demagogic speeches, "Gene" Talmadge's public policies reflected his secret ties with the Atlanta business establishment. In 1956 Gene's son, Herman, after a term as governor, forced Walter George into retirement. But there was no break in the conservative continuity: Talmadge went on to serve for twenty-four years as the protector of federal subsidies that went in greatly disproportionate amounts to better-off landowners of Georgia—among them a peanut farmer named Jimmy Carter and, I must say, my own family as well.

Besides their basically conservative orientation, George, Russell, and the Talmadges were also linked by an adamant commitment to white supremacy. It is true, Walter George never resorted to the crude race-baiting of the Talmadges. But the fact remains that George was the principal architect of the "Southern Manifesto" of 1956, a statement signed by virtually all southern Senators denouncing—and implicitly defying—the United States Supreme Court's 1954 school desegregation decision.

In 1964, when Lyndon Johnson told his old friend Dick Russell that he intended to pass tough civil rights legislation, the Georgia senator warned the president that he might pass the bill, but the cost would be driving the South out of the Democratic Party—permanently. The ominous prediction would come to fruition before the turn of the century.

George . . . Russell . . . Talmadge—the names were household words from my earliest recollection. Like so many in his family, my father followed politics with zest and became an ardent partisan of Roosevelt's New Deal. He concocted a little skit in which I, at the age of six, was taught to mimic "Gene" Talmadge by pulling my hair across a scowling face, then Franklin D. Roosevelt by brushing my hair back and putting on a broad smile. At my father's proud urging, I happily performed my vignette dozens of times at the courthouse, in the barber shop, on the streets of our little county-seat town of Sylvester.

My forebears came to that part of Georgia early in the nineteenth century to farm land taken from the Indians. The Jenkinses of the nineteenth century held slaves and sent men to fight for the Confederacy. My great-grandfather was sheriff of Worth County at the close of the century. But mainly, my family managed to withstand catastrophes of war and economic upheaval, and that was enormously important, because in those days, ownership of land was security: as long as you could hold onto the land, you knew you would be in the same place the next year, not wandering from farm to farm like the white sharecroppers or even to the wretched industrial cities of the north, like the destitute blacks.

Two counties up, there was a similar family, the Carters, whose eldest son, Jimmy, was but a few years older than I. In an article on the op-ed page of the *New York Times* in 1976, I struggled to explain Jimmy Carter's essential southernness in the light of my own experience:

> Unless a man has picked cotton all day in August; has sat in an outhouse in 20 degrees in January and passed this time of necessity by reading last year's Sears Roebuck catalogue; has eaten a possum and liked it; has castrated a live pig with a dull knife and has wrung a chicken's neck with his own hands; has learned at least a few chords on a fiddle and a guitar; has tried to lure a sharecropper's daughter into the woods for mischievous purposes; has watched a man who succeeded in doing just that have his sins washed away in the Blood of the Lamb in a baptism in a muddy creek; has been kicked by a mean milch cow and kicked her back;

has drunk busthead likker knowing full well it might kill him; has wished the next day it had killed him; has watched a neighbor's house burn down; has drawn a knife on an adversary in fear and anger; has half-soled his only pair of shoes with a tire-repair kit; has gone into a deep dark well to get out a dead chicken that had fallen in; has waited beside a dusty road in the midday heat, hoping the R.F.D. postman would bring some long-coveted item ordered from the catalogue; has been in close quarters with a snake; has, in thirsty desperation, drunk water that worked alive with mosquito larvae called wiggletails; has eaten sardines out of a can with a stick; has killed a cat just for the hell of it; has felt like a nigger was mistreated but was afraid to say so; has stepped in the droppings of a chicken and not really cared; has been cheated by someone he worked hard for; has gone to bed at sundown because he could no longer endure the crushing isolation; has ridden a bareback mule three miles to visit a purty girl who waited in a clean, flimsy cotton dress—unless he has done these things, he cannot understand what it was like in my South.

Once when I was a teenager, my mother, a gentle woman who played the piano every Sunday at our country Methodist church, related to me, with sorrow and dismay, my grandfather's description of a lynching. It seems that after the commission of some unspeakable crime, a mob of county men seized a black man, slit his skin with razor blades, poured scalding vineger into his wounds, then dragged him along a railroad track behind a hand-pumped car until he was dead. My mother did not know whether this hapless black was in fact the one who had committed the crime. I did not ask whether my grandfather was an observer of or a participant in the lynching.

When I was growing up, virtually the entire lower quarter of the county was occupied by my relatives and blacks—the latter outnumbering the former by about two to one. These blacks for the most part worked "on halves" on our farms. I never witnessed among my family any crude "nigger-hazing"—indeed, the practice was forbidden—but there is no question that there existed a master-servant relationship that probably resembled that of the slave society in place seventy years earlier.

These blacks were fortunate if they made a hundred dollars for a year of the excruciating toil of coaxing the crops out of the exhausted soil of Worth County. Because they were perpetually entrapped in debt, they became in effect indentured retainers and were treated as childlike creatures. If these people had last names, I never heard them. Among fragments of family records that I keep, there is a canceled check for three dollars that my grandfather made out simply to "Elmo," and the check is endorsed with that single name also. My aunt Jewel, a remarkable woman who was widowed in her thirties and went on to operate a farm and raise two children, had a cook and washwoman who was called, by adults and children alike, simply Caldonia. Aunt Jewel also had Ed and Molly. My uncle Paul had O.B., who was as black as melted midnight and as strong as a mule. If a black man or woman lived into dotage, the children were taught to call them "Uncle" or "Aunt"— though in an unmistakably patronizing tone.

On our place there was a man named Lester, who was quite light-skinned—no doubt the issue of some furtive illicit coupling. Lester's wife, a tense and anxious woman named Ida, was so emaciated that my mother surmised that she suffered from the scourge of the region, "consumption." The family subsisted on pone, greens, and hogmeat Ida cooked in blackened iron pots over an open fire in a barren yard. Lester and Ida had two small children who darted about the yard half-naked, their stomachs so distended that their navels popped out. My mother fretted over their condition, and often sent me to take a bucket of fresh milk to Ida.

At that time a man named Blake lived on our farm. Blake was white, and no one knew where he came from, nor why he was not in the Army when every able-bodied man had been called into service during the Second World War. Blake lived alone in a one-room shanty that was furnished with spare necessities: a kerosene lamp that stood on an apple crate beside a mattress on the floor, and, in one corner of the room, a few pots and plates and an "oil stove." Blake was an enigmatic man who wore a dirty baseball cap and always had a faintly menacing smile, giving the impression that he knew something you didn't know.

One day as I was taking a bucket of milk to Ida I came upon Blake in her backyard. It was a taut scene: The children were frozen in apprehension, and Ida's face bespoke fury and terror as she confronted Blake with a stick of firewood. When Blake saw me, he quietly slipped away. I told my mother what I had seen, and she was indignant. She firmly told Blake that he was not to "bother" Ida.

Later that year, all the men of the farm were engaged in the grueling ritual of "picking peanuts," dragging stacks of dried peanuts across the vast dusty fields to a clattering threshing machine, which separated the nuts from the vines. It was abominable work, demanding frequent rest stops. During one of these breaks, as we sought respite from the fierce sun in the scant shade of a peanut stack, with the bulldogs lolling nearby, a mule began to wander off.

"Hey nigger," Blake snarled, "go git that mule 'fo he runs off."

Lester hesitated for a moment and murmured in a low voice, "If'n you want that mule, go git 'im yo'self, I's tired, too."

Blake exploded, "Did you hear what that nigger said?" Suddenly pandemonium prevailed, as Lester streaked across the field. A bulldog, set upon him by Blake, overtook him and brought him to the soft earth. As Lester scrambled to his feet the clumsy Blake heaved a pitchfork, javelin-like, at the terrified Negro, but the deadly implement fell far short. Lester disappeared across the crest of a low hill.

We finished the day's work in perturbed silence, and when we related what had happened that night, my mother listened in fretted interest. Early the next morning she sent me with a bucket of milk for Ida, and told me to "see if everything is all right." What I found was a shack that had, in the dead of night, been emptied of every wretched item

We never saw Lester and his family again. My mother speculated that they had spent the night in the woods, then journeyed on to the next county to seek refuge with friends or family. Wherever he may have gone, Lester forfeited the few dollars that he might have received for his part of the "sharecropping" on our farm that year.

During this time one of my occasional playmates was named Charlie, a lithe black boy, the son of Ed and Molly, who lived on Aunt Jewel's place. Charlie and I would fish together in Chalkley's Pond, and make slingshots to hurl rocks at birds or squirrels in what passed for "hunting." If we managed to kill a squirrel, Charlie would take it to be cooked for supper.

But the friendship Charlie and I enjoyed in the fields and streams did not extend to the school. Each morning I would board the garish yellow school bus, which clattered three miles over a washboard road to the school in the village of Bridgeboro. That school was the source of considerable pride within our farming community. It was a solid brick building, and its cornerstone, I soon noticed, bore the name of one of my forbears—some visionary who recognized the value of education, no doubt. There was running water, pumped by a windmill, and in the winter the rooms were heated by stoves, which burned wood that the boys were expected to gather. There was a basketball gymnasium and a little auditorium in which we could hold our school assemblies and stage plays or perhaps see a show put on by an itinerant magician. It was a good school, a place where a diligent pupil could learn not only the multiplication tables but perhaps even catch a faint hint of the beauty of poetry.

A couple of miles down the road was my playmate Charlie's school— "the nigger school." It was a drab wooden thing, unpainted, with just two large rooms, sitting atop a small, barren clay knob. There was no windmill; the children drank from a common dipper in a bucket of water drawn from the schoolyard's shallow open well. The only form of recreation was a netless ring fashioned from a rusty barrel hoop and nailed to a pine pole to make a basketball goal. The desks and books were hand-me-downs from my school.

At Charlie's school, there were just two teachers, and the grades were not formally structured. Probably there were more children assigned to this austere school than to my own, but attendance was far from equal, because there was no effort to enforce the compulsory attendance laws. Even the smallest children were kept out of school to toil in the fields.

As for buses, his school having none, Charlie walked.

In due course both my school and Charlie's school closed, their enrollments decimated by the trek of the farm people to the towns and cities of Georgia and more distant points, like Baltimore and Detroit. After this I went to a little town not far away called Camilla, where I lived with an aunt and uncle while I finished high school. After school I worked at my uncle's sawmill, which employed around sixty black laborers who toiled for the minimum wage—25 cents an hour in those days—and lived in lamplit shacks scattered around the mill. One of these was a personal servant who did odd jobs for my uncle. He was called "Ace High," and if he had any other name, I never heard it.

One night my uncle received an urgent call that something terrible had happened in one of the mill shacks, so we rushed over to investigate. The crowd in front of the hovel parted respectfully to allow the "bossman" to pass. Inside the house we beheld awful carnage. A man had been shot, point-blank, with a shotgun. Later we learned that the man who fired the deadly shot was drunk on moonshine whiskey and thought he was shooting Ace High, whom he believed to be "foolin' around" with his wife. The man was taken to the county jail, but for many weeks the normally ebullient Ace High was subdued as he went about his grunt chores.

In Camilla, I was also introduced to the casual cruelty of hazing that was a part of every black person's life in those times. Whenever the white boys of the town could wheedle the family car for an evening, they would entertain themselves by riding through "the nigger quarters" and throwing bottles against the sides of the darkened shacks. I also learned that my more venturesome schoolmates would slip away to Albany, the regional hub town that lay twenty-five miles away, for nocturnal liaisons with black prostitutes, whose services could be had for three dollars.

Some years later, when I came home for holidays from college, I encountered my childhood playmate, Charlie, lolling around Carl Smith's general store, which supplied the country people with their rudimentary needs and served as a community gathering place. Feeling a bit awkward, I engaged Charlie in idle conversation, but quickly found him to be curiously reticent—something I had not observed in our younger years. After that he "went North," and I never saw Charlie again.

When I went to the University of Georgia in the fall of 1947 to prepare for a career in journalism, the issue of race arose only one time during my four years at the venerable institution. I was serving on a committee to choose the "Big Band" that would perform at the annual Homecoming dance. Someone suggested Louis Armstrong, and the reaction was immediate: "But he's a nigger." The matter was debated for no more than a few minutes. I was among the minority who thought it was silly to think of race in this context, but I did not feel strongly enough about the matter to put up any kind of fight. In the end we chose a white band.

In marked contrast to my farm life, my only contact with blacks during my college years was through the phlegmatic janitor who cleaned our dormitory rooms. I remember him as being slightly crippled as he went about his duties in slow motion. At that time we had on our room wall a large photograph of a comely cheerleader—stark naked. The picture was, in fact, wholly fraudulent—the product of adroit air-brushing and retouching by an art student. Once my roommate caught the janitor gazing at the photograph, and told the older man in no uncertain terms that he was not to look at the picture.

During that time in our college town of Athens, there was a black boy who had an after-school job chopping onions at the Varsity, which was the leading campus sandwich shop. It is possible, indeed likely, that I may have passed him on the street, but if I did, I would have observed only a dark blur. The boy's name was Bobby Hill, and he would, twenty years later, sit in the Georgia legislature and would, in due course, become a part of this book.

On my trips home I always passed Albany State College, an institution that existed chiefly to churn out teachers for the black schools of Georgia. It never once occurred to me that any student at Albany State College would entertain the remotest wish to attend my university.

Eleven years later, the University of Georgia was briefly shut down under a state law mandating that any white school in Georgia which admitted a black student would be automatically closed. This folly lasted for only a few hours before the law was struck down by the federal court. Then, after a minor riot by white students, two black students were enrolled. One, Hamilton Holmes, subsequently graduated Phi Beta Kappa, went on to medical school, and became an orthopedic surgeon in Atlanta before his early death in 1995. The other, Charlayne Hunter, became a reporter for the *New York Times* and, later, a correspondent for the prestigious public-television program, the *MacNeil-Lehrer News Hour*. During her time at the university, she created a sensation when she married a fellow student who was white. Some twenty years after her graduation, she returned to the campus as the commencement speaker.

When I finished journalism school, I took a job on the *Columbus Ledger,* the afternoon daily newspaper published in the thriving Georgia textile city that lay on the banks of Sidney Lanier's fabled Chattahoochee River. I soon discovered that black people, who constituted a third of the town's population but only a tiny fraction of our newspaper's readership, were considered newsworthy only when they were arrested, and they were always identified as "Negro." Reporters were cautioned to take great care in this designation, because it would be libelous to identify a white man as "Negro."

It was also my newspaper's policy never to refer to a black man or woman by the honorifics, "Mr." or "Mrs." If, say, Mrs. Jones were black, she would be called simply, "the Jones woman." The absurdity of this policy came home around 1953, during the time that American prisoners of war were being repatriated after the Korean War. As it happened, among the first of these prisoners to be released was a certain Sergeant Black, who happened to be from Columbus and who also happened to be black. I was assigned to interview his family for what would be a front-page story. I interviewed Mrs. Black at some length. At the office, we were confronted with the dilemma of whether to call her, in print, "the Black woman." Faced with the prospect of publicly demeaning the wife of an authentic hero, the newspaper changed its policy; she was called "Mrs. Black."

On May 17, 1954, the United States Supreme Court rendered its historic school-desegregation decision. Like most white southerners, I simply took it as a given that no one in his right mind expected white and black children ever to attend the same schools in Georgia. After all, the great *Atlanta Constitution* editor whom I so admired, Ralph McGill, firmly supported segregation; his "liberalism" lay in the fact that he preferred not to resort to violence over the issue.

But I paid little attention to the decision, because I was preoccupied with one of the most sensational stories of the day. My assigned "beat" was Phenix City, a squalid little town that lay just across the river from Columbus. Generations of soldiers who were assigned to the vast Army training base of Fort Benning, which sprawled along the banks of the Chattahoochee River, remembered Phenix City as the place where a soldier could find merciful respite from the dull rigors of Army life, a place to get drunk, to gamble in the back rooms, to get a girl for an affordable price. Reformers who made fitful efforts to "clean up" Phenix City were attacked in the streets, and their homes were bombed at night. But the mob element that ruled Phenix City overplayed its hand: On June 18, 1954, Albert L. Patterson, a flinty old lawyer who had been elected state attorney general on a promise to purge the town of its vice-industry, was assassinated on the streets. I covered the story for a year, at the end of which our little newspaper won journalism's most coveted recognition, the Pulitzer Prize.

When this story was over, I discovered that during my preoccupation with Phenix City, the intractable race issue had come to the forefront. About this time I married a young woman who had spent her childhood in Germany during the Second World War and lost both parents. She knew, instinctively, the frightful price that a society had to pay for allowing itself to sink into the ideology of racism. Whenever she protested the folly of segregation, I would respond that she was too young and inexperienced to know about such matters; but something in my soul compelled me to acknowledge, secretly and guiltily, that she was right. Also about that time I came to know a local minister who was fired by his prominent white congregation because he became too outspoken in seeking a decent racial accommodation.

In 1957 I received a grant from the Southern Association of Nieman Fellows to spend three months in Africa, to report on the emergence of the continent from centuries of colonialism. When I returned, I began to seek out stories involving black people of newsworthy accomplishment. I heard of William Levi Dawson, who was the director of the Tuskegee Institute Choir at the fabled black college that had been founded by Booker T. Washington in the previous century. Although his name had never appeared in our newspaper, which served the Tuskegee community, Dawson by then had already attained a high reputation for his scholarly study of Negro spirituals. He had also composed "The American Negro Symphony," which was performed at Carnegie Hall under the baton of the great Leopold Stokowski. Finding this achievement newsworthy, I wrote a feature that reflected this man's gentle, dignified, thoughtful character. A photograph of Dawson was carried. Not long after that story appeared, my editor received a call from a woman who was a member of the family that owned the newspaper: She was tired of seeing "stories about niggers in my newspaper." Thereafter, blacks once again made news only when they committed crimes, or became involved in comic-opera church disputes.

One such crime story stands out vividly in my memory. One morning in the mid-1950s, I found the sheriff in Phenix City to be in an anxious state. The young daughter of one of the county's most prominent landowners had been raped by the teenage son of a black tenant farmer. I knew the scene well: It was heavy with moss and magnolia, heavy with the past. Probably the great-grandfather of the boy had been a slave, owned by the great-grandfather of the girl. Much excitement and loose talk pervaded the community, and the sheriff wanted me to put in the paper that the boy was in an unspecified but secure place, that the law would take its course.

And indeed the law proceeded with uncommon swiftness. Within days a special grand jury was assembled and returned an indictment. At arraignment, I got my first glimpse of this improbable figure who had created such public agitation. From the ill-fitting white prison frock, I could tell that he was not yet grown. And he was dumbstruck with terror as the old county judge intoned the ancient rituals of the law. He asked the boy if he were "represented by counsel." If he even understood the question, he did not respond, so the judge summoned an elderly lawyer of the community, who seemed to be waiting in the wings for a signal. Yes, the lawyer said, he would accept the appointment to represent the indigent defendant, and yes, he was ready to proceed with the trial.

Then a special session of the court was convened. Mercifully, the judge ordered the courtroom cleared of "spectators," and the girl was gently questioned. Although she was allowed to use delicate euphemisms, there was no doubt as to what had occurred. When the time came for cross-examination, the defense attorney said gravely that he had no questions, that "this little lady has already been through enough."

A doctor was called to confirm, in clinical fashion, that the rape had taken place. He identified a small garment that was stained with blood. This garment was placed in evidence. Then the sheriff testified that the boy had confessed to the crime, and the state rested its case.

The most tense moment in the trial came when the defense attorney called his only witness, the boy's mother. The woman was clearly on the edge of panic, and no one knew quite what to expect. The gist of her testimony was simply that the boy "never had been right in the head." There was a hint that the insanity defense was being raised in this oblique way, although it never became a formal plea.

The jury, twelve white men, deliberated for only a few minutes before returning the verdict: guilty, without recommendation of mercy. The judge summoned the boy, still clad in prison garb, to be sentenced to die. I looked around and saw the girl's father, his face grim and his teeth clenched. I did not see the boy's mother anywhere in the courtroom. The trial, which had begun in the morning, was over early enough in the afternoon so that the boy could be transported to the state penitentiary by nightfall.

Thereafter a certain calm returned to the county as the people awaited the appeal to the state supreme court, which was automatic in death-penalty cases. In the weeks that passed, I don't think there was even a hearing, and if there were, certainly no questions were raised about the inflamed community atmosphere, racial exclusion from the jury, improper use of confession, the draconian penalty imposed on one of such tender age—any one of which might have won a reversal. The court simply found no error in the trial. If there were a clemency hearing, it was perfunctory, and shortly after midnight on September 28, 1956, the boy was strapped into the electric chair and put to death. His body was unclaimed, so it was buried without ceremony in an unmarked grave in a potter's field.

Soon after this episode, my editor resigned when he was ordered by the publisher to tone down his editorial campaign to stop the Ku Klux Klan from staging a cross burning at the local baseball stadium. For me this heavy-handed intrusion into editorial independence signaled that it was time to move on, so I took a job in Montgomery, Alabama, in the early part of 1959.

For an eager young journalist, the languid Alabama capital city offered endless excitement: It was not only the seat of government; it was also the base of operations of the young Martin Luther King Jr., who had just guided the Montgomery Bus Boycott to a stunning success and made the civil rights movement the major story of our time.

In its editorial policy, my newspaper, the *Alabama Journal,* represented intractable resistance to social change. The editor, a courtly old Virginian named Cassius M. Stanley, had been born around the end of Reconstruction. Each morning he would arrive in a crisp seersucker suit, clutching a batch of editorials that he had scribbled out in pencil on little slips of copy paper as he sipped bourbon on the cool veranda of his antebellum home. He routinely denounced Thaddeus Stevens, the nineteenth-century "radical Republican" architect of Reconstruction. In 1961 "Cash" Stanley applauded the mob attack on the "Freedom Riders" in Montgomery, likening the episode to a spanking for a naughty child.

Soon after I arrived in Montgomery I met two remarkable people, Clifford and Virginia Durr. Born at the turn of the century into a prosperous family of southern gentry, Cliff won a Rhodes scholarship to study law at Oxford in the 1920s. He returned to America to enter government as one of the bright young idealists attracted to public service by Franklin D. Roosevelt's New Deal. In due course he was appointed to the Federal Communications Commission, where he strove for a greater commitment to noncommercial "educational broadcasting."

I was astonished to learn that one of Cliff Durr's notable victories had been at the expense of a member of my own family, Representative E. E. Cox of Georgia, who was a powerful figure in the Congress. In the course of a routine audit, FCC investigators discovered that Cox had accepted a $2,500 payment from a Georgia broadcaster for his efforts in securing a lucrative television license. Cox, whose temper occasionally got him into fistfights on the floor of the House, struck back swiftly by getting himself appointed chairman of a special committee to investigate the "nest of reds" at the FCC. But Cliff gained a valuable ally in *Washington Post* publisher Eugene Meyer. The *Post's* editorial attacks on Cox's corruption ultimately forced him to abandon his inquisition of the FCC. He escaped prosecution for bribery when President Roosevelt told his attorney general, Francis Biddle, that he could not afford to indict a powerful congressman when the nation was at war.

With the end of the Second World War and the beginning of the Cold War, Cliff watched in dismay as a panic engulfed Washington over "communist subversion." A new crop of demagogues, led first by such reactionary congressmen as J. Parnell Thomas of Kentucky and John Rankin of Mississippi, imposed a reign of terror on government bureaucrats. When Cliff was routinely offered reappointment to the FCC in 1948, he declined. President Truman called him to the White House to ask why he was refusing the appointment.

"Mr. President," Cliff told Truman, "I don't know whether you've been reading the papers lately, but I've been making some speeches that are critical of one of your programs."

"Which program?" Truman asked.

"Executive Order 9835—the loyalty program," Cliff replied, referring to Truman's creation of boards that would hear accusations of disloyalty among government workers.

"Well," Truman exploded, "I had to do something to take the ball away from that son-of-a-bitch Parnell Thomas."

Cliff respectfully demurred that he felt that Thomas's House Committee on Un-American Activities was less a danger than the loyalty boards because at least the committee had to function in public, while the administrative boards were conducting star-chamber proceedings that wrecked lives and careers.

When Cliff's replacement was announced, Truman took pains to point out that Cliff had declined reappointment and to praise his government service.

At about that time several of his young New-Deal colleagues were leaving government to organize a law firm to practice what would become the lucrative business of lobbying government on behalf of private clients. Among these were Thurman Arnold, Abe Fortas, and Paul Porter. When Cliff got the drift of their plan, he said, "It sounds to me like you fellows are going to try to undo all the things we did when we were in government." He declined to join the firm but stayed around Washington for a few years to handle cases of assorted academics and hapless government workers who were caught up in the McCarthy hysteria. In 1954, he returned to his hometown of Montgomery to enter private practice with the expectation of making a decent living handling the routine legal needs of a growing community.

This expectation was shattered in 1955 when E. D. Nixon, who then headed the Montgomery NAACP branch, called Cliff one night in a great state of agitation. Nixon related that Rosa Parks, a seamstress who had done a little sewing for Virginia Durr, had been jailed for violating the Montgomery city ordinance mandating segregated seating on municipal buses. Could Cliff help arrange bail? The two men went to the police station to rescue Mrs. Parks. This mission was duly reported in the *Montgomery Advertiser,* and thereafter Cliff never had any hope of establishing a law practice sufficient to sustain his family's modest needs. Had he not been retained to represent the family wholesale drug business, the Durrs would have had to leave Montgomery.

Virginia Foster was born in Union Springs in the Alabama Black Belt, the second daughter of a Presbyterian minister who lost his pulpit because he refused to attest his belief in the literal truth of every story in the Bible, including the tale of Jonah and the whale. Eventually the Fosters gravitated to Birmingham, where Virginia's older sister, Josephine, married a young lawyer who was considered beneath her social station but who seemed to have great promise. His name was Hugo Black.

At a time when southern women were expected to bear children and keep house, Virginia went to Wellesley, where she absorbed liberal attitudes that would remain with her throughout her life. In Washington, she rejected the role of the dutiful wife and took up controversial causes. The Durrs were neighbors and close friends of a young congressman from Texas named Lyndon Johnson. Virginia and Lady Bird developed that special relationship of women who had lost children, and the affection was to endure for life. Virginia was not one to maintain a respectful or even prudent silence; her political activities kept the Durr household in a constant uproar during periods of racial tension in Montgomery.

But Cliff and Virginia persevered, their spirit and good humor intact, and gradually their country home twenty miles north of Montgomery—a small farm affectionately called the Pea Level—became the gathering point for Montgomery's tiny liberal community and a throng of adoring friends from throughout the world.

Never in good health, Cliff died of congestive heart failure in 1975, in the little Elmore County Hospital just three miles up the road from the Pea Level. He was reading Joseph Heller's *Catch-22* when the final attack came. At a memorial service in Washington, the speakers who celebrated his life were a diverse group ranging from former Supreme Court Justice Abe Fortas and Congressman Claude Pepper to writers I. F. Stone and Jessica Mitford, but none more eloquently captured the meaning of that life than his daughter, Tilla, who said simply, "My father was a hero."

And indeed, by that time, he had been so redeemed that a memorial service was also held at the courthouse in Montgomery, and I, by then editor of the *Alabama Journal,* was among the speakers. In the presence of many who had scorned him in life, I noted that a whole generation of young southerners had come to regard Cliff as a beacon at a time when the lights of decency and honor seemed about to flicker out. I concluded my remarks: "Once you had known Cliff Durr, it meant that when you were confronted with a moral issue—as we all are—when caution and prudence of the moment would suggest that the safest course would be to take on the protective coloration of the landscape and blend into the crowd, there was a voice which kept asking, 'But what would Cliff Durr think?' The merest possibility of incurring his unexpressed disapproval was sufficient to make one examine his actions with the utmost care. And to those of us who knew him over a long period, this question— But what would Cliff Durr think?—became almost like a second conscience unto itself, even when our performance fell short of his ideal."

After I received a Nieman Fellowship at Harvard in 1964, I had opportunities to go on to larger cities and more promising jobs in journalism, but I was so captivated by the ongoing drama of Montgomery that I stayed for twenty years. The three principal actors on the political stage during that period were Martin Luther King Jr., Frank Johnson, and George C. Wallace, and the subtle symbiosis of the lives and careers of these men constituted one of the major news stories of our time. So I stayed in Montgomery, even though I developed a sense of guilt that my family, who could share only vicariously in the exciting stories I covered, paid a significant price for living in a culturally deprived environment.

Of these three men, Frank Johnson became the closest personal friend, even though Johnson's innate hill-country circumspection, coupled with a rigid judicial rectitude, made it difficult for anyone to become truly close to the man. As an editorial writer, I defended his decisions, which were bringing about a revolution at a time when the white community seethed with defiance. As a stringer-correspondent for the

New York Times and frequent contributor to its prestigious magazine and op-ed page, I wrote about the legal revolution that Johnson was bringing about—the completion of Reconstruction, no less. Once, he rendered a decision which held that merely being put in the Alabama prison system amounted to a violation of a person's constitutional right not to suffer "cruel and unusual punishment." Seeking to explain the role of the law in the South, I wrote on the op-ed page of the *Times:* "In the South the law has been an instrument of fear. The county courthouse stands there as a mighty symbol of relentless authority, a message so clear that it might as well be engraved in the marble portico over the great columns: 'Watch out, Nigger. If you get out of line, we'll send you to the chain gang. Maybe to the electric chair. And you watch out, too, white man. If you get out of line, we'll treat you like a Nigger and put you there with him.'"

In 1967 the home of Johnson's elderly mother was bombed; years later, it was learned that the bomb had been placed by a Ku Klux Klansman who thought he was attacking the judge's home. On the day after the bombing, I wrote an editorial in the *Alabama Journal* under the heading "Who Bears the Guilt?" It concluded:

> It will be argued this was the act of a deranged person, and our society cannot be held accountable. Unhappily, this argument does not hold water.
>
> Have we not for so long indulged in inflammatory emotional excesses and hate-mongering that we have brought to the surface the dangerous passions of the brute? Did not the men who threw the bomb believe that they were serving some great holy cause? Do they not this afternoon consider themselves some kind of "heroes" for bombing the home of a defenseless lady in the middle of the night?
>
> And have we not, as a state, so long countenanced violence through sluggish investigation and repeated acquittals in the face of overwhelming evidence of guilt when the perpetrators of violence have been brought to trial? Could not the bombers, in view of past history, feel reasonably assured that they would never go to jail?
>
> These are uncomfortable questions that must be asked.

I also paid a call on the judge to express my personal distress over the act and sympathy for his widowed mother. The judge smiled and simply observed, "Mama is a strong woman."

A far more difficult visit came on October 12, 1975, to offer condolences to Frank and Ruth Johnson on the day that their only son, twenty-seven-year-old James Curtis Johnson, ended a brief life in the maelstrom of southern change by committing suicide.

My relations with George Wallace were cordial although clearly adversarial. I had covered Wallace's mercurial career since 1957, when he first burst onto the political stage with his theatrical—and bogus—"defiance" of Judge Frank Johnson in one of the early tests of the Civil Rights Act of 1956, which proved to be little more than an inconvenience to southern registrars in their determination to keep black voter registration to the absolute minimum—indeed, to zero in many of the Black Belt counties with heavy black majorities.

Wallace also knew that by 1962 I was among those southerners who were quietly beginning to have grave doubts about "the Southern Way of Life," the standard euphemism for cradle-to-grave segregation. But now that Wallace had been elected governor, I felt a need to get to know the man I would be covering for the next four years. The time was the early fall of 1962, just a few months before Wallace would assume the governorship. I arranged to accompany him on an evening speaking engagement in Phenix City, the town I'd covered a few years before. Dusk was approaching on the warm, humid evening as we began the eighty-mile drive across central Alabama. There were four of us in the car—myself, Wallace, his driver, and a state legislator named Tom Bevill. I quickly discovered that there really is no such thing as a dialogue with George Wallace; there is only a monologue. As the governor-elect jabbered frenetically, we passed through the quiet little Black Belt town of Tuskegee, where blacks were about to gain the right to vote. As we drove through the darkened town, past the statue of the Confederate soldier in the town square, Wallace launched into a menacing malediction: "Mark my words, Jenkins, if the nigger ever gets in control in this town, he will mistreat the white man. That's just the way the nigger is." What struck me most was not Wallace's outburst of bald racism but the seeming approval of Tom Bevill, a sensitive and conscientious state legislator who would go on to serve for thirty years, with some distinction, in Congress.

Of the three men, my personal acquaintance with King was the briefest. Soon after arriving in Montgomery, I began to make visits to his small office in the basement of the Dexter Avenue Baptist Church, a slightly anachronistic little architectural gem amid the imposing state government buildings. King seemed to appreciate that at least one minor editor at the city's newspapers was willing to make personal contact; neither of the top editors, who had written dozens of editorials vilifying King, had ever so much as exchanged a handshake.

Our last meeting took place early in 1960. The ostensible purpose was a "backgrounder interview," although the real intent was to say goodbye to King as he was about to leave Montgomery to take the pulpit of the Ebenezer Baptist Church, which served Atlanta's black middle class.

After we had spoken for a few minutes about his plans, I noted that we were both from Georgia, and to underscore the improbability, indeed the irony, of the manner in which we became acquainted, I related an episode from my own family history as drawn from a cryptic fragment in our family Bible records. It records in the year 1853 a series of deaths in rapid succession. In the quaint patois of the time, the carefully scripted entries in the musty old book read:

> F. M. Young departed this life April 1, 1853. . . . Sara Jenkins
> and Olivia Thompson departed this life April 9, 1853. . . . James
> L. Brown departed this life April 15, 1853. . . . Alexander Daniel
> Jenkins departed this life April 27, 1853. . . .
> The above five were poisoned by a slave.

King seemed startled at this revelation. He put his hand to his brow, then said: "But now here we are, a century later, the son of former slaves and the son of former slave owners from the same red hills of Georgia, sitting here having this respectful conversation. Isn't that reason for hope?"

Yes, I replied, but we must remember that I was there in my "official" capacity as a journalist—exempted from society's rules, so to speak. I could not take him to lunch at a town restaurant, nor invite him to dinner at my home, nor go to his, even though we lived just a few blocks apart, without risking ostracism, loss of employment, even arrest. So in a sense, in seeking an integrated society King was fighting for my rights as much as for his own.

Of course, he said, he had always maintained that integration was as liberating for whites as for blacks, even more so because it lifted the guilt of carrying on an indefensible practice.

As we were about to leave, King remarked, almost perfunctorily, "If there's anything I can do for you, just call."

"Actually," I said, hesitating at the door for a moment. "There is something you can do for me. I've covered a lot of your speeches over the past couple of years and come to share your goals. What you just said, about the sons of former slaves and the sons of former slave owners holding a respectful conversation, if you'd include that in one of your speeches one day, I'd appreciate it."

He said he would, and we parted.

After that I saw King only occasionally and always in formal settings, such as press conferences. A little over two years later, in 1963, my journalistic path took me to the nation's capital on a hot August day when a huge throng of Americans joined in the March on Washington. As the late afternoon shadows began to fall across the reflecting pool that lay between the Washington Monument and the Lincoln Memorial, Martin Luther King was still waiting to speak. I remarked to my wife that I had heard him many times, so perhaps we should get a head start on our two-day drive back to Alabama. When we were far down into Virginia, I turned on the car radio, and recognized the familiar voice of Martin Luther King Jr., just beginning his speech. As we drove through the Old Dominion, past meadows where, a hundred years earlier, battles of the Civil War had been fought, King began the cadenced conclusion of his most famous speech: "I have a dream . . . that one day in the red hills of Georgia the sons of former slaves and the sons of former slave owners will be able to sit down together at the table of brotherhood." He had kept his promise, and I wasn't there to hear it.

But while King, Wallace, and Johnson were the major actors on the stage of Alabama politics, there were dozens of lesser players who performed roles in the rich and varied drama of Alabama politics. Among these were the young man whom I first encountered in the summer of 1966 when he seemed to come out of nowhere to be chosen chairman of the state Democratic Executive Committee. His name was Robert S. Vance.

Within a dozen years, Jimmy Carter, my Georgia neighbor of many years past, would be president of the United States. He would appoint Bob Vance a federal judge in 1977 and, two years later, appoint me as his special assistant for press affairs.

1 December 1989

As Christmas approached in 1989, Robert Smith Vance had every reason to be in a festive mood. At the age of fifty-seven, his political career was behind him, assuring him a modest place of honor in the history of his native state of Alabama as one who had acted with skill, courage, and integrity in navigating the treacherous waters of racial accommodation in Birmingham, the city where the gun, the bomb, and the rope had been used more eagerly to maintain segregation than in any other place in the South.

His active law practice was behind him also, leaving him comfortably well-off if not wealthy. His two sons were models of achievement, one already a lawyer following in his father's footsteps, the other about to become a doctor. Despite a family history of heart trouble, Bob Vance was in reasonably good health, and his wife of thirty-four years was a healthy and attractive woman of fifty-six. He now was completing twelve years of growing distinction as a federal judge at the level just beneath the Supreme Court, and with luck and the election of the right president, he might even hope to be elevated to that exalted high council of wise men.

Yes, life had been good to Bob Vance, and he had every reason to believe that the remainder of his life would be a happy and rewarding experience. He and Helen were already planning a leisurely trip to Europe during the coming year.

A state apart from Bob Vance, Robert Edward Robinson likewise had earned the right to pause in celebratory reflection and rumination during that Christmas season.

"Robbie" Robinson was born only a stone's throw from the very spot where, in all likelihood, his nameless forebears were brought in chains and sold in the slave market of the old Georgia seaport town of Savannah. As a black child coming of age in the 1950s, he could still see the vestiges of that ignominious heritage all about him.

What he saw stirred the impulses of freedom in young Robbie's soul. In 1963 he became one of the first black students to enter the public high school of the staid old Georgia city that dated back to colonial times. While he was still a teenager he was arrested, along with two companions, for challenging local laws that reserved Savannah's beaches for whites only.

As the edifice of the segregated South crumbled like an abandoned antebellum plantation mansion, Robbie Robinson became the first black student to graduate from that fount of prestige and propriety, the University of Georgia School of Law. He returned to his hometown to practice civil rights law and to enter the city's political life.

For the past six years he had been an alderman on the Savannah City Council—the very council that had enacted the laws which forbade Robbie, twenty years earlier, from swimming at the city's public beaches.

The Christmas season of 1989 was anything but a time of happy reflection for Walter Leroy Moody Jr. He had reached his middle fifties, and he was a bitter man, with failed marriages, failing business schemes, and a prison term in the wreckage of his spent life. His four children, one the issue of the rape of the girl who lived next door, so detested him that none bore his name. Now his long-nurtured, costly ambition to become a lawyer was slipping inexorably from his grasp.

Like generations of the children of Georgia's small-town culture, "Roy" Moody, brooding in his littered home in an Atlanta suburb, had turned to the Bible for solace from cruel adversity. His eyes fell upon the Ninety-fourth Psalm: "O God, to whom vengeance belongeth, shew thyself. . . . Who will rise up for me against the evildoers? or Who will stand up for me against the workers of iniquity?"

For a man who harbored a malignant sense of victimization at the hands of wicked and vengeful perverters of law and justice, the ancient words resonated like the voice of God Himself, sanctifying action.

Throughout that holiday season, Roy Moody worked quietly but feverishly for countless hours in a makeshift laboratory behind closed doors, even worked in the crawl space beneath his home, in the middle-class town of Rex, Georgia. He was, he told a tormented wife who was young enough to be his daughter, working on "nuclear fusion." But even this simple and subdued woman was suspicious: The strange assortment of materials with which he worked included pipes, nails, flashlight bulbs and batteries, ordinary household tinfoil—and a four-pound canister of Hercules Red Dot double-base smokeless gunpowder, which he had purchased at a gun shop called the Shootin Iron while dressed in the comical disguise of a curly wig and plastic glasses.

In the early afternoon of Saturday, December 16, 1989, Bob Vance returned from routine weekend errands to his elegant white-columned colonial home on Shook Hill Road in Mountain Brook, the exclusive residential section that lay just across the mountain from the grimy relics of Birmingham's industrial heyday. As he entered his house, Helen remarked, offhandedly, that he had just received in the mail a package from a fellow judge in Atlanta who shared an interest in horses. "It's probably some more horse magazines," said Vance as he began to open the package in the kitchen of his home. The moment he broke the seal, a powerful bomb exploded, killing Bob Vance instantly and leaving Helen Vance gravely wounded.

Two days later, Robbie Robinson sat in his law office as the early winter darkness shrouded Savannah. He had just finished an exhausting day in court, and had an hour before he was to be at a Christmas party. He took this time to open the day's mail, including a shoebox-sized package that he probably took to be a legal transcript, or perhaps a gift.

When he lifted the flap of the box, a bomb exploded with such force that his hands were blown off. A little more than three hours later, as six surgeons worked desperately at Savannah's Memorial Medical Center to save his life, Robbie Robinson died.

On June 28, 1991, Walter Leroy Moody Jr. was convicted in a federal courtroom in St. Paul, Minnesota, of all seventy-two counts of an indictment charging him with the murders of Robert S. Vance and Robert Robinson. He claimed that he had never met either of the men, and there is no reason to believe that he was not telling the truth.

2 A House of Two Swords

As the turbulent nineteenth century drew to a close, the languid central Alabama town of Talladega, nestled in the first hills of the lush green southern plateau known as the Piedmont, acquired a new resident named Frank Leslie Vance.

No one can say why a Hoosier boy would choose such an improbable place in which to seek a career, but this much is known: Frank was born on August 15, 1868, in the Indiana steamboat town of Rockport, just across the Ohio River from Kentucky. After looking over Louisville and Nashville along the way, Frank Vance arrived, with no more than the few possessions he could carry in his grip on steamboats and railroad cars, in Talladega, where a fledgling textile industry was being established to spin the cotton grown in the Alabama Black Belt into finished cloth. He was just a little over twenty when he reached Talladega around 1890, just fourteen years after military Reconstruction of the vanquished South ended with the infamous Hayes-Tilden compromise in which Rutherford B. Hayes sold out the newly freed slaves in return for the southern votes in Congress he needed to make him president. So whatever suspicions Frank Vance may have aroused among the good people of Talladega, at least he escaped the epithet of "carpet-bagger"—the reviled term applied to those who came down from the North to enter political alliance with the newly liberated blacks in the aftermath of the Civil War.

By the time Frank Vance settled in Talladega, the region was already rich in history. DeSoto had explored the area four centuries earlier, and in the early part of the nineteenth century, Andrew Jackson subdued the native Americans in a famous battle not far from the settlement that was to become Talladega. Frank also discovered that the town had been a center of antisecessionist sentiment before the Civil War, although, once the conflict began, Talladega dutifully sent its sons into battle.

Perhaps Talladegans thought Frank sprang from a family of "copperheads," a menacing term that designated Confederate sympathizers in Union states; after all, Indiana was rife with that sentiment before, during, and after the Civil War. But the fact was, Frank Vance was no more a copperhead than a carpetbagger, because his own father had served honorably as a captain in the Union army; one day Frank would come into possession of his father's sword to prove it.

Nor did Frank forsake his northern heritage in his new southern home. At a time when Republicans were viewed as opportunists and "nigger-lovers," he proudly embraced the party of Lincoln during his early years in Alabama. By day he toiled as a legal stenographer, taking down court proceedings in shorthand, and by night he "read law" in the traditional apprentice system for entering the legal profession in those days.

Whatever his motives and background, Frank Vance could hardly have chosen a less auspicious time to come to the South. The ravages of the Civil War were still visible all about him. Moreover, his arrival coincided with the panic of 1893, a depression that brought to the cities and towns the pervasive economic distress already suffered by the farmers, who groaned under low cotton prices, no access to credit, and a crop-lien system that gave the landowner first claim to everything produced by the tenants and sharecroppers.

Still, Frank Vance braved the economic hurricanes, and soon after he arrived in Talladega, he took a bride. If there were such a thing as royal blood in Talladega County, it surely ran in the veins of Annie Laurie

Harrell. On one side, she traced her ancestry to the legendary John Knott Taylor, who migrated to Talladega County from England early in the nineteenth century to establish a farm and a grist mill, which came to be designated on early maps as Taylor's Mill. On the other side, Annie Laurie descended from David Caldwell, a colonial immigrant of Scotch-Irish ancestry who had served in the Revolutionary Army.

But Annie Laurie was a frail woman and was just thirty-seven when she died in the winter of 1909, leaving Frank a young widower with two teenage boys.

Frank got into politics, and during the Republican presidencies of Theodore Roosevelt and William Howard Taft, he gained appointment to the prestigious position of United States attorney, first in the new industrial center of Birmingham, then in the state capital of Montgomery. He held those jobs until 1913, when he was summarily fired by Woodrow Wilson after the Democrats recaptured the White House as a result of the bitter break between the progressive Roosevelt and the conservative Taft. After that, Frank returned to Talladega to practice law until his death in 1924 at the age of fifty-six.

By that time Frank's eldest son, Harrell, had managed to put in a couple of years at the state agricultural college at Auburn, an educational mecca for ambitious poor boys of Alabama, and was establishing himself as a young man with a promising future in business and industry in Talladega. Harrell married Mae Smith, the daughter of William David and Leola Stewart Smith, a frugal farm family who managed to send three of their five children to college on the sale of butter, eggs, chickens, and other farm products. Mae attended Alabama College at Montevallo and for a time taught school before she married Harrell Vance in 1916.

In the fleeting false prosperity of the 1920s, Harrell Vance held a good job as paymaster in the Samoset Mill, one of Talladega's thriving textile plants. It was a valued position, which paid a salary sufficient to enable Harrell to settle his family, which by then consisted of two sons and a daughter, comfortably in the spacious white frame house that Frank Vance had built in the early part of the century at 284 North Street on a shaded lot on a hillside overlooking the town.

From their earliest days, the two boys, Harrell Jr. and William, and their sister, Martha, paid reverent homage to the pair of crossed swords that hung over the fireplace in the living room; one was passed down from their Vance forebear who had served as a captain in the Union army, the other from a great-grandfather who had served as a major in the Confederate army. "We were always told with some pride that our ancestors fought on both sides of the Civil War," Martha remembers.

The Vances became mainstays of the Methodist Church, the focus of the family's social as well as spiritual activity. Harrell served for twelve years as Sunday School superintendent, so the children were in their places every Sunday morning at 9:45, learning the ancient myths and psalms and parables of the Bible. And at eleven o'clock the family was always in their pew to hear a sermon laced with fire-and-brimstone oratory, admonishing Methodists to win salvation by strict adherence to the discipline of John Wesley, who had established the Methodist Church in Georgia a century before. On Wednesday nights, Harrell and Mae and their children had their own table at the weekly church supper, a sumptuous potluck affair that was followed by yet another sermon. Once every three months, the church would hold its quarterly meeting, an all-day affair that featured a little business and a lot of song, laughter, cake-walks, and dinner-on-the-ground.

During the 1920s Methodist clergymen became a potent force on the "dry" side of the volatile Prohibition issue, and perhaps it was this influence that led Harrell to support President Herbert Hoover in his 1928 race against the New York Irish Catholic "wet," Governor Al Smith. This small deviation in the politics of the "Solid South" might have been accepted in Talladega with only raised eyebrows, but two years later Harrell had the audacity to run for the state senate as a Republican at a time when that affiliation was viewed by most Southerners as something close to regional treason. He got few votes, and little Martha endured cruel taunts, "Your daddy's a Republican," from her classmates at the Graham Primary School just down the street from the Vance home. And it was remembered that her grandfather was a Yankee.

Harrell's political leanings were tolerated at first, but with the coming of the Great Depression, which was widely blamed on Herbert Hoover, Harrell was among the first to lose his job when the looms and spindles of the Samoset Mill began to idle. Bill Vance to this day believes that his father was fired simply for being a Republican.

For a time after he lost his job at the mill, Harrell ran a little dairy, and even delivered bottled milk himself to those who could afford that precious commodity during that time of great hardship. Unable to support his family on that meager income, he took a job as the town's agent for the Prudential Insurance Company, selling policies strictly on a commission basis. But in the thrall of the depression, there was virtually no market among Talladega's struggling seven thousand inhabitants for a luxury like life insurance; no matter how many hours a day Harrell spent trudging from house to house, his income fell.

On May 10, 1932, Mae gave birth to her fourth child, whom they named Robert Smith Vance. Arriving seven lean years after Martha's birth, Bob no doubt was an unexpected child. But soon the whole family began to dote on the new baby and his winsome nature; the gaiety he brought to the Vance home offered merciful respite from the grim depression times.

Despite the pervasive hardship, Martha and Bob felt no sense of deprivation as they grew up. "There was always food on the table," Martha recalled, years later, "and we always had decent clothes to wear." And Harrell somehow found the means to buy a bicycle for his youngest son at Christmastime in 1936. When Bob grew weary of riding his bike on the shaded streets, he would spend summer afternoons dozing in the wooden bench swings that hung on the front porch of the Vance home, or he would take long walks with his brother Bill, who would connect the houses with the families that lived in them. Sometimes Bob would go down to the town spring, which was reputed to flow at a million gallons a day, and simply gaze at this marvel of nature. Such was his idyllic life when, in the fall of 1937, he entered the first grade at the Graham School. He came home after the first day to announce, with unconcealed pride, that he had been elected chairman of his table in his first-grade class. From that day forward, his brothers, with good-natured teasing, always called him "Chairman."

But if the two younger children were sheltered from the general desperation that prevailed in Talladega during the Great Depression, the two older boys felt it keenly. By this time education had become an obsessive pursuit within the Vance family; college was viewed as the only sure way to escape the crushing poverty that the children saw all about them. It was a grim time, when boys and girls in their early teens toiled from dawn to dusk in the textile mills, when the most desperate people would slip into neighbors' houses at night to steal food, and when the blacks, often living in palpable want, could be seen picking the wild blackberries that grew along the country roadsides.

During this time Harrell and Mae Vance's second son, Bill, labored at whatever job he could get throughout his teen years, assiduously stashing away every penny he could lay his hands on, and by the time he was sixteen and getting ready to go to college, he had saved $250.

One day in the summer before Bill was to go, Harrell Vance asked his teenage son to join him for a walk. When they were safely out of earshot of the house, Harrell Vance spoke haltingly.

"Son, I know you've been saving money for college," he began. "I hate to do this more than anything in the world, but I have to ask you to let me have $150."

Bill was stunned, but he recognized the stark gravity of the situation and replied, "Of course, Daddy." The next day they went to the bank, where Bill withdrew more than half his savings and turned the precious money over to his father. But the emergency did not thwart Bill's determination to go to college; through the award of a fifty-dollar scholarship and a job in the New Deal National Youth Administration, Bill was able to enroll at Birmingham Southern College, a small but prestigious Methodist school, putting him on his way toward his goal of following in his older brother's footsteps in becoming a federal lawyer-bureaucrat.

At the end of his financial rope in Talladega, Harrell Vance heard of a more promising job open in Sylacauga, another textile-manufacturing town thirty miles down the road. There, Metropolitan Life Insurance company offered him a salaried position collecting insurance premiums by going door-to-door. Little Bob entered the second grade in Sylacauga, but the Vance family remained there for only a little over a year before Prudential Insurance lured Harrell back with the offer of a better job in Birmingham. In 1939 the Vances rented a comfortable bungalow in Birmingham's Woodlawn section.

At last settled in some measure of stability, Bob Vance grew up largely sheltered from the rough and robust side of Birmingham, which, with the coming the the Second World War, got its powerful second wind as the South's premier industrial city. Established in 1871 in a flinty valley whose red soil was too poor to farm, Birmingham lacked the gracious antebellum tradition of the proud old cities of Alabama. In Birmingham's heady atmosphere of opportunity—and opportunism— Montgomery and Mobile were regarded as relics of the past; Birmingham was a city of the future, founded to exploit the rich deposits of coal and iron that lay in the hills and valleys of central Alabama. In its first fifty years, which spanned the period roughly from the end of Reconstruction to the beginning of the depression, Birmingham exploded as the South's third most populous urban area, and many believed that it was only a matter of time before it became the region's dominant city. Birmingham was alternately called "The Magic City" and "The Steel City." On a mountaintop overlooking the teeming industrial tracts to the north and the lazy pastures to the south, a gross iron statue of Vulcan, the Roman fire god, held aloft a perpetually lit torch to proclaim the city's industrial might. Indeed, the 1940 census revealed that Birmingham had almost overtaken Atlanta in population during the depression decade.

But attentive citizens could already detect troubling fissures in Birmingham's foundations. The very name of what was to become the city's steel-making colossus, Tennessee Coal & Iron Company, bespoke absentee ownership. Indeed, TCI was owned, lock stock and barrel, by United States Steel, which dispatched managers from Pittsburgh to Birmingham like colonial administrators. Knowing they would be there but a short time, these ambitious corporate bosses were largely indifferent to the long-term social interests of Birmingham. Meanwhile, in the words of a perceptive modern historian, Virginia van der Veer Hamilton, "The majority of the people were working class, sparsely educated, economically insecure."

This combination—a rapacious, exploitive absentee-ownership class dominating ill-educated, vulnerable workers who had fled the farms when mechanization of agriculture ended the sharecropper system— produced in Birmingham a climate for violence, which would bring the city to grief and scuttle its hope of becoming the dominant regional city. The northern mill bosses tacitly nourished the city's penchant for passion by winking at Klan membership among the steelworkers—after all, if the workers spent their evenings at Klan meetings, at least they weren't attending union meetings—and never dismissing any worker found to be involved in acts of savagery against the city's disfranchised, dispossessed blacks who struggled on the economic ladder just below the poor whites. By the 1920s the Klan had up to twenty thousand members in Birmingham, among them a politically ambitious young police-court judge named Hugo L. Black. A 1926 city ordinance imposed zoned residential segregation that could well have served as the model for apartheid in South Africa two decades later; the ordinance was so flagrant that the local federal judge struck it down long before the Supreme Court began to dismantle the edifice of segregation-by-law in the South.

But if the courts would not countenance legal segregation, there was virtually no check on Klan terror. After the Second World War, dynamiting of black churches and homes became so common that the city earned a new name: "Bombingham." And by the 1960s Martin Luther King Jr. would proclaim it "America's most segregated city."

White working-class racial and economic fears found vivid expression in the person of the redoubtable Theophilus Eugene Connor, a high school dropout and itinerant railroad telegrapher who came to Birmingham in the early 1930s as a radio sports announcer. Connor's incessant booming babble soon earned him the nickname of "Bull," a colorful sobriquet that would cling for the remainder of his life. Connor entered the city's turbulent political life at about the same time Harrell Vance moved his family to Birmingham. By coincidence Connor was a Woodlawn neighbor of the Vances, although none knew him at the time, and certainly no one dreamed that little Bob Vance would become an intractable political enemy of Connor in the years to come.

Connor first ran for office as a bumptious outsider, a kind of homegrown populist and reformer. But soon after he was elected as the city's police commissioner in 1937, he became allied with the business interests as represented by the city's most prominent lawyer, James Simpson. Simpson, a front man for "the Big Mules," as the industrial corporations came to be called, became Connor's adviser, even manipulator.

Connor quickly became identified as the nation's foremost urban racial demagogue, and he enforced his will with an all-white police force in a city whose population was one-third black—and growing. In 1938 Bull sent his police to break up an integrated meeting of the Southern Conference for Human Welfare, a gathering that had attracted such notables as Eleanor Roosevelt as well as the state's progressive politicians, Governor Bibb Graves and Senator Lister Hill; as long as he was police commissioner, Connor declared in a memorable malapropism, "Negroes and whites will not segregate together in Birmingham."

Under the Connor regime, the city's voteless blacks confronted terror by day from uniformed police, terror by night from hooded Klansmen—often the same men in different clothing. A man who served for forty-two years with Connor's police force summed up Connor's policy succinctly: "Blacks had no rights whatsoever."

Harrell Vance watched all this drama from a safe distance. After he lost his job in Talladega, Harrell didn't even like to talk about politics, let alone involve himself in it. Rather, he drudged through the workaday routines of providing for his family. At the start of the Second World War, Harrell, who was already exhibiting the family propensity for heart trouble and in any event was too old to serve in the military, left his job with Prudential to take a better-paying war-production job in the electrical industry.

In this reasonably secure environment, Bob Vance grew into adolescence. He excelled in school and still had time to read mystery magazines and build model airplanes. Once, he and another neighborhood boy bought an old car, which they dismantled from bumper to bumper, only to find that they couldn't put it back together. Eventually an exasperated Mae Vance called a wrecker to remove the junk heap from her yard.

About this time Bob's oldest brother, Harrell Jr., became acquainted with Sam F. Hobbs, an influential congressman from Alabama's conservative Black Belt. Harrell saw an opportunity to secure a coveted prize for his baby brother. Not long after Bob Vance entered Woodlawn High School, he obtained, through Congressman Hobbs, appointment as a page in the United States House of Representatives.

Barely old enough to shave, the gangling teenager arrived in Washington in the fall of 1946. Mae Vance agreed to the venture only on the condition that Bob live with Harrell, who by then was a government bureaucrat residing in the Virginia suburbs of the Capital. The arrival of the bumptious kid brother was not greeted with great enthusiasm by

Harrell's wife, Jeanne, who had one small baby and another on the way. With Harrell working by day and attending law school by night, Jeanne was left with the thankless task of enforcing the household rules.

Bob was under strict orders to keep his own room tidy. One day Jeanne carried out an unannounced inspection, which revealed, stashed helter-skelter under Bob's bed, a prodigious collection of dirty clothes, wet towels, cracker boxes, half-empty Coke bottles—and a swarm of vermin. She read the riot act to her adolescent charge, only to be confronted with brazen indifference. She demanded that Harrell discipline his adored sibling, and thereafter the room was cleaner, but Jeanne still had to endure Bob's finicky eating habits.

Once Bob came home unexpectedly in the middle of the day and hurried to his room. That evening, Harrell managed to extract the reason: At the end of a morning tennis match, when Bob attempted to jump the net to shake hands with his opponent, his clumsy, overgrown feet became entangled in the webbing and he crashed to the court face first, leaving him with loose teeth that required several hours of emergency dental work.

In his job as a House page, Bob absorbed the heady lessons of major-league politics. In quiet awe he watched the barons of American political power—titans like Sam Rayburn and Lyndon Johnson of Texas, "Uncle" Carl Vinson of Georgia, and "Judge" Howard Smith of Virginia—exert their formidable skills. Because of the erratic meeting schedule of the lawmaking body, the House pages pursued their high school studies in a largely unstructured, tutorial manner, which enabled Bob to complete the high school curriculum by the time he was fifteen.

During his year in Washington, Bob grew like an Alabama pine sapling, so fast that his trousers' cuffs often revealed his garish socks as he strode softly across the floor of the House chamber, delivering arcane messages from one congressman to another. The day came when Bob topped six feet, nearly a foot taller than a young congressman from Oklahoma named Carl Albert. Albert, who was later to become Speaker of the House, seemed to resent the conspicuous height of the young page from Alabama and suggested that it was time for him to go home.

The heady experience of the Washington interlude matured Bob Vance beyond his years, and by the time he returned to Birmingham, he was ready to enter college. But the prosperity brought by the Second

World War did not fully reach the Vance family. Harrell had already suffered a heart attack; eventually he took a less-demanding job of going about the state to establish "blind stands"—little cubicles located in the lobbies of public buildings from which blind people eked out a living selling newspapers and confections. He had, no doubt, gotten the job in part through the influence of his sister, Martha Vance Snell, who had become a major figure in the state school for the blind and deaf back at Talladega.

As Bob turned sixteen in 1948, with high school diploma in hand and college ahead, it is unlikely that he paid much notice to the high political drama that played out in his state for most of that year. With the Second World War over for three years and the postwar recovery chugging along, the state's political leadership looked to the future, and most did not like what they saw. Up to that point Alabama had been a firm pillar of the "Solid South," dutifully delivering its electoral votes every four years to the Democratic candidate for president. But as Franklin D. Roosevelt's New Deal evolved into Harry Truman's Fair Deal, it grew increasingly clear that the Democratic concept of "fairness" included the black man. Truman ordered the integration of the nation's armed forces, and northern liberal politicians demanded that the federal government make good the dormant promises of the Reconstruction-era constitutional amendments. Even Alabama's own son who now sat on the Supreme Court, Hugo L. Black, joined in alarming decisions that shook the very foundations of "the Southern Way of Life."

As the nation prepared to choose its first full-term postwar president in 1948, a great sense of apprehension hung over the South. South Carolina's firebrand governor, J. Strom Thurmond, defiantly declared that there were not enough troops in America to compel racial integration in the South. Heeding such siren calls, Alabama voters in the Democratic primary of 1948 chose a slate of presidential electors who made it clear that they would not vote for the party's candidate for president in the fall elections. The complex stratagem was a daring attempt to breathe new life into the electoral college, which had become largely a powerless anachronism with the emergence of the two-party system more than a century before.

Despite the election of an unpledged slate of presidential electors, the state's Democratic Party nonetheless sent a delegation to the party's national convention in Philadelphia in the summer of 1948. Harry Truman's nomination was a foregone conclusion, but this fact did not forestall an acrimonious split in the Alabama delegation. When the convention delegates adopted a strong civil-rights plank in the party platform, fourteen of Alabama's twenty-six delegates joined other outraged southerners in a dramatic walkout from the meeting hall. Among those who marched out was Birmingham's police commissioner, Bull Connor.

Within weeks, the rebellious delegates reassembled in Birmingham, where an ad hoc political convention of six thousand cheering partisans organized the States Rights Democratic Party, which they immediately dubbed "Dixiecrat." Waving Confederate flags in a hall adorned with portraits of General Robert E. Lee, the defiant conventioneers nominated Governor Thurmond of South Carolina for president and Governor Fielding Wright of Mississippi as his running-mate. Practically no one believed the Thurmond-Wright ticket had the remotest chance of winning the election; rather, the strategy was to carry enough Deep South states to deprive *any* candidate of an electoral-vote majority. Such a result would throw the election into the House of Representatives where, the Dixiecrats reasoned, southern lawmakers would demand total state autonomy in racial matters in exchange for their votes for president—in effect, a replay of the compromise of 1876 that elected Rutherford B. Hayes as president and ended military Reconstruction.

In furtherance of this strategy, the unpledged electors chosen in the spring Democratic primary in Alabama announced their support of the Thurmond-Wright ticket. By this time it was too late for the Loyalist Democrats to assemble a slate of electors pledged to President Truman, so it became virtually impossible for an Alabamian to vote for the sitting president of the United States who was running for reelection. In November the twelve Dixiecrat electors won overwhelmingly in Alabama; three other Deep South states joined the revolt to give the Thurmond-Wright ticket a total of thirty-nine electoral votes.

But the Dixiecrats failed in their goal of throwing the election into the House of Representatives. In the rest of the country, Truman won 303 electoral votes, a comfortable sixty-two more than needed to give him a second term.

The acrimony continued in Alabama. Governor Big Jim Folsom, an unregenerate Democratic Loyalist and idolator of Harry Truman, was so indignant over having his state party machinery seized by the new secessionists that he asked a federal court to compel the Alabama Dixiecrat electors to vote for Truman on the theory that they won under the Democratic Party emblem. The Supreme Court ruled that, however anachronistic the electoral college may have become, electors were still free to vote for whomever they chose.

If politics were measured on a Richter scale, the events of 1948 would rate a nine on the Alabama landscape, and aftershocks would be felt for years to come. But there was no indication that the political upheavals caught more than passing attention from young Bob Vance. Soon after he turned sixteen in 1948 he took a job as an office clerk in the Birmingham gas company and enrolled in night classes at the newly opened branch of the University of Alabama in Birmingham. Over the next sixteen months he worked forty hours a week and took extra courses each night to enable him to become a member of the two-year college's first graduating class. By this time the managers at the gas company were so impressed at his judgment and reliability that they implored him to make a career with the company. But Bob had no intention of making such a mundane job his life's work. In the fall of 1949, he enrolled in the University of Alabama at Tuscaloosa. There, he would continue to pay all of his college expenses with an ROTC scholarship and whatever odd jobs he could find.

3 Peach County

Two hundred miles to the east of Talladega, out of the hilly Piedmont and down into the flat fecund strip of soil known as the Southern Black Belt, the languid town of Fort Valley sprawls near the geographic center of Georgia. The town is situated on a plain that resembles a valley floor, although it is not, because there are no mountains within a hundred miles. There are only a few undulating inclines, out of which little outcroppings of Georgia's fabled red clay protrude here and there like oversized bricks baked for centuries in the fierce subtropical sun.

The first settlers, arriving in the early part of the nineteenth century, called their community "Fox Valley," because it was populated by flocks of red and gray foxes, which were the bane of the farmers and the few remaining Creek Indians who struggled to scratch a living out of the stingy soil of their plain. When the early inhabitants got around to petitioning Washington for a post office for their growing community, a careless bureaucrat deciphered the handwritten request to read "Fort Valley." Well, never mind, the settlers thought; the foxes would soon be eliminated anyway. Thus the name became permanent.

The community flourished, so that by 1849 a statistical guide of Georgia could report: "Fort Valley has three stores, one Methodist church, one academy, is located thirty-two miles from the Central Railroad, and has two hundred and fifty inhabitants." This count represented the town's white populace; there is no reliable census of the slaves who lived in the area at that time, but no doubt the number was substantial, possibly even larger than the number of white inhabitants.

By the early part of the twentieth century, three prolific farm families scattered over central Georgia, the Moodys, the Hancocks, and the Parkses, began to migrate in significant numbers to Fort Valley in quest of a more promising life than the numbing toil of marginal agriculture could ever hope to offer.

Among the migrants was William Oscar Moody, a young man who, despite a formal education that ended in the third grade, possessed a fertile mind for the emerging new field of mechanics and technology. Sometime early in the century, "Oss" Moody, as he was known to everyone, set out from the family farm in Crawford County to open an automobile repair shop at Reynolds, twelve miles west of Fort Valley.

About this time Oss took a bride, Mary Lizzy Hancock. The town gossips noted that Oss "married well," the Hancocks being one of Georgia's more prominent families. A Hancock of Georgia fought in the Revolutionary War, and many Hancocks served in Georgia regiments in the Civil War, including one who fell at Gettysburg. A Georgia county bears the name of Hancock.

Oss Moody's garage did not flourish, so he was obliged to eke out a living in agriculture. Soon after he married Mary Lizzy, he got a job as an "overseer," as the straw bosses of the field hands of Georgia's farms were called in those days, on a farm around the Chula community of Tift County, some fifty miles down an unpaved road from Fort Valley. It was there, on August 14, 1909, that Mary Lizzy gave birth to a son—the first of seven children—whom they named Walter Leroy Moody.

The young family did not tarry for long in Tift County. By then Henry Ford's assembly lines in Detroit were turning out Model T automobiles by the thousands, and this industrial miracle presented a windfall opportunity for Oss Moody. By the time the First World War broke out, Oss was back in central Georgia, earning a good living as a mechanic in Roberta and Reynolds. He gained a reputation as the area's best trainer of apprentice mechanics, among them his own son, Leroy. Around 1920 Oss opened a new garage in Fort Valley.

It was a time of turmoil and tension in Georgia. Reconstruction had ended just a generation before, and living people could still remember, with burning resentment, the hateful sight of Yankee soldiers occupying Georgia soil. The Redeemers—a new political movement so named because their goal was to "redeem" the South from the humiliation of a lost war and a bitter Reconstruction—strove to establish an industrial base, the lack of which, it was universally believed, had brought defeat and ignominy to the South. Henry W. Grady, the formidable editor of the *Atlanta Constitution,* created an illusion of a "New South" in which the growing urban centers were rapidly supplanting the agrarian society of the nineteenth century. Atlanta was called "the Chicago of the South," Birmingham "the Pittsburgh of the South," Columbus "the Lowell of the South," and so on.

But the forsaken tillers and laborers like the Moodys—the overwhelming majority of Georgia's commonfolk—found their own champion in the enigmatic and charismatic Thomas Edward Watson. A gifted intellectual who had written authoritative books on French history, "Tom" Watson had been an ally of the populist giant, William Jennings Bryan—indeed, had run for vice president on Bryan's Free-Silver Democrat-Populist ticket in 1896. As an idealistic young politician Watson sought to forge an alliance between the poor blacks and the poor whites of the South; they were not, in his view, enemies of one another but rather common victims of the Wall Street barons and their bootlickers in Georgia like Henry Grady.

But the politics of race swiftly doomed Watson's ephemeral alliance. By 1900, weary of flagellating one another with the specter of "Negro domination," the conservatives and the Populists across the South reached accord: The black man would simply be removed from the political equation. Even the most eloquent and visionary of nineteenth-century black leaders, Booker T. Washington, abjectly submitted to the new order by renouncing black political aspirations in the infamous "Atlanta Compromise" of 1895. Within a short time all the states of the Old Confederacy had disfranchised the black man and imposed a system of segregation scarcely distinguishable from the slavery that had been out-lawed by the Thirteenth Amendment to the Constitution.

This general capitulation to race phobia brought about a sinister change in Tom Watson. Embittered and frustrated, he embraced racism, and gave it virulent expression in his popular political organ, *The Jeffersonian,* which almost certainly found its way into the home of the Moody family in the nether regions of Georgia. When Leroy Moody was a small boy, the principal topic of attention in *The Jeffersonian* was a dark event that took place in distant Atlanta. A little girl named Mary Phagan was murdered in the pencil factory where she worked. Soon suspicion began to focus on Leo Frank, the young plant manager. Frank became the perfect scapegoat, portrayed as the lascivious Jewish agent of rapacious Yankee exploiters of southern innocence as personified by little Mary Phagan. Although there was not a shred of credible evidence that Frank had committed the crime, Watson's *Jeffersonian* trumpeted rumor and innuendo with frenzied abandon. In that charged climate Frank was tried and condemned to die. When Governor John Slaton acted with great courage and commuted the death sentence, Watson's *Jeffersonian* thundered: "Our grand old Empire State HAS BEEN RAPED! . . . betrayed!"

Amid the hysteria, Governor Slaton fled the state, and on the night of August 16, 1915, a mob dragged Leo Frank from his cell and drove 175 miles around rural Georgia before lynching the man. The following day Frank's body was put on display before a throng of fifteen thousand, and a popular entertainer named "Fiddlin' John" Carson played "The Ballad of Mary Phagan" throughout the day on the steps of one county courthouse. This orgy of brutality was applauded by Tom Watson's *Jeffersonian* as "the triumph of justice in Georgia."

But if the Frank murder was the most notorious lynching of the time, it was but one. More than five hundred blacks were lynched during the first ten years of Leroy Moody's life—including one atrocity that would become a part of family legend.

In this time of violence, crushing isolation, oxlike drudgery, and ceaseless economic peril of Southern agriculture, Oss Moody struggled to support his growing family. He put his inventive skills to work to such an extent that he earned a reputation in central Georgia as something of a "mechanical genius." Once he designed a portable sawmill, which could be set up in the Georgia piney woods, and when a tract of timber was clear-cut, could be moved on to a new location. Although the idea would in time be widely utilized, Oss lacked the resources and connections to translate his proposal into reality in the early 1900s in a state that was mired in chronic economic distress.

These frustrations must have taken a heavy toll on Oss Moody, because about this time he began to drink heavily, and in his drinking bouts he became increasingly violent and abusive, especially to his long-suffering wife. In 1929, the year that the Great Depression hit, Oss was so addicted to alcohol—and probably syphilitic as well—that he was committed to the state insane asylum at Milledgeville, some fifty miles to the east of Fort Valley. After Oss was committed, Mary Lizzy, who still had three young children to provide for, had to return to her family at Crawford County.

As soon as he would dry out, Oss would escape and come back home. But Mary Lizzy could not keep him away from the moonshine whiskey produced by the illicit "likker stills" in the piney woods of Georgia. When Oss went on one of his violent binges, his sons would have to tie him up and take him back to Milledgeville. Once when Leroy Moody was driving the car with his father in the back seat, Oss kicked his son in the head with such force that Leroy suffered a concussion and ran into a ditch. After many commitments, Oss finally stopped drinking, and thereafter became known as the town "piddler." In 1944, he died of stomach cancer, probably induced by the "rotgut likker" he consumed during his fifty-five troubled years.

By this time Leroy Moody had already established his own reputation as the most promising mechanic in Fort Valley. When he got a secure job at Greene's Chevrolet, he decided it was time to start a family. In the late 1920s he married Foye Mozelle Watson, a pretty girl who was five years younger than Leroy and still in high school when they eloped.

Actually, Mozelle's original name was not Watson but Parks. Mozelle arrived in Fort Valley sometime around 1915, the illegitimate infant daughter of a woman named Eddie Parks, at a time when out-of-wedlock births were common among Georgia's poor whites. Eddie came to Fort Valley with her two brothers and two sisters from the community of Molena, fifty miles up the road in Pike County.

In Pike County, the Parkses were known as a clan that was not to be trifled with. Once, according to family legend, one of the Parks men had been ambushed and killed as a result of a dispute with a neighbor in the Molena community. The Parks men vowed to avenge their relative's murder, which they blamed on a man named Block. Block was not the killer—years later, it was learned that the murder had been committed by a man named Orange—but knowing the Parkses meant business when they made such threats, Block fled to Texas. But two Parks brothers, Jim and Ollie, drew straws to see who would go to Texas and kill Block. Ollie got the honor and set out on his bloody mission. He found Block plowing in his field and shot at him from a distance. The bullet only grazed Block, who fell to the ground and played dead. Ollie was caught, and served time on a Texas chain gang before returning to Georgia.

Then—again, according to family legend passed down for several generations—there was the time when the Parkses took their vengeance in a particularly brutal manner. Johnny Boy Parks got into a card game with some blacks one cold night in Molena and won all the money. On his way home just before daylight, Johnny Boy was robbed by someone who split his skull with the heavy metal bar of a cotton-scale, and the next morning he was found with his face frozen to the ground. Johnny Boy's survivors swiftly located other participants in the card game and forced them to name the stealthy attacker. Whether the identification was accurate was problematical, but the Parks men descended on the home of the hapless black man, broke down the door, placed a rope around his neck and dragged him away, while the terror-stricken man's mother wailed, "Please don't take my boy, don't take my boy." The suspect was hustled to the Parks home, where he was strung up in a tree in the front yard. For the remainder of the day the Parks men pumped bullets into the suspended corpse until there was little left but a bloody pulp. There was never any prosecution for the lynching.

Even after they reestablished themselves in Fort Valley, many of the Parks men carried on the family penchant for violence and criminality. One of Eddie Parks's brothers was said to have been a professional bootlegger. Another brother, described as "a little, dried-up fellow," shot a neighbor's wife. And one Parks man who specialized in stealing coon dogs was caught when he put a dog-for-sale advertisement in the paper, and it was answered by the very man whose dog had been stolen. A younger member of the family caused so many fights at football and basketball games with Fort Valley High School's main rival, Perry High School some twenty-five miles to the east, that the competition had to be canceled for a time.

But Eddie Parks managed to escape the family taint when she married a respectable Fort Valley man named Arthur W. Watson, who adopted little Mozelle. When Leroy Moody married Eddie's daughter in the late 1920s, she was known as Mozelle Watson.

At first the newlyweds lived with Mozelle's mother at a plain but serviceable clapboard house on Orange Street, which was not the best neighborhood in Fort Valley. But Leroy's job at Greene's Chevrolet paid him $15 a week, a salary that, during the Great Depression, enabled him to rent his own house on Bell Street, not far from the town's new high school. About that time Mozelle gave birth to her first child, a son who lived for so short a time that he was not even given a name. On March 24, 1934, a second son arrived, and they named him Walter Leroy Moody Jr. To distinguish the son from the father, they called the child "Roy."

By this time the firebrand Tom Watson had died, and his demagogic mantle had passed to an ambitious lawyer-farmer named Eugene Talmadge, whose trademark became a pair of red galluses and an unruly forelock of hair that fell across his brow as he regaled "the wool hat boys," as the yeoman farmers of Georgia were known. For them, there was no "New South." There was no market for peaches in a depression-gripped nation; the fruit simply rotted where it fell beneath the trees. There was only used-up, washed-out soil, and what little cotton could be coaxed out of the clay was usually devoured by the boll weevil.

"The poor dirt farmer ain't got but three friends on earth," the diminutive Talmadge would thunder. "God Almighty, Sears Roebuck, and Gene Talmadge."

But if the dirt farmer had only three friends, Talmadge never let his audiences forget, they had plenty of enemies: the Atlanta newspapers, the University of Georgia, and above all the brutish blacks who lurked everywhere. Almost certainly Leroy Moody would have heard speeches by "Gene" Talmadge during his twenty-year thrall over Georgia politics, and probably his son Roy heard them as well, because in towns like Fort

Valley, a visit by a leading politician.was merciful respite from life's drudgery. Talmadge made at least one visit to Fort Valley during Roy Moody's boyhood. Also, during Talmadge's last race for governor in 1946, when Roy would have been twelve, a brutal racial killing took place in Georgia that brought the opprobrium of the nation upon the state. Four young blacks, two men and two women on a date, were waylaid at random on a rural road, brutalized and murdered. There was virtually no effort to bring the killers to justice, and Governor-elect Talmadge, responding to the national outrage, called the incident "regrettable."

In Roy Moody's childhood, Fort Valley held two distinctions in addition to its status as "the Peach Capital of Georgia." One was Fort Valley State College, which had been founded just before the turn of the century, at about the same time the United States Supreme Court rendered its *Plessy v. Ferguson* decision, which gave the ultimate legal sanction to the "separate but equal" doctrine—a euphemism for cradle-to-grave segregation. Fort Valley State's purpose was to supply the black teachers for their separate schools, which by no leap of imagination could be called "equal" to the white schools, piteously deprived as they were. To a white boy like Roy Moody, Fort Valley State, lying on the outskirts of town, was simply "the nigger college."

But because white colleges were not open to any blacks at all, Fort Valley State became a tiny mecca for the most talented and promising black children of central Georgia. Among the students in the 1920s was a pretty, light-complexioned young woman with uncommonly expressive eyes who sang so beautifully that she was invited to perform at one of the Fort Valley ladies' clubs. At the time the event was considered by the town's progressives to be a milestone in race relations. The young woman's name was Lena Horne. Lena's uncle, Frank Horne, was later to leave his position at Fort Valley State to become an official of some rank in Franklin D. Roosevelt's New Deal administration.

In 1940, which was the year Roy Moody entered the first grade in the town's elementary school, the president of Fort Valley State was a black educator of growing distinction named Horace Mann Bond. Dr. Bond almost certainly was the most highly educated man in town, yet no hospital in the area would admit his wife when it came time for her to deliver her first child. Mrs. Bond had to travel more than three hundred miles, across two states to Nashville, the site of Meharry Medical College, the wellspring of most of the region's black doctors at the time. There, Mrs. Bond gave birth to her first son, Julian, who was to become a major figure of civil rights revolution more than two decades later.

Yet for all its significance, Fort Valley State remained essentially a protected enclave for a handful of privileged blacks; their less fortunate brethren labored under pervasive discrimination and the persistent peril of capricious violence. If the average white person in Fort Valley confronted hardship, the average black person lived on the edge of abject penury. Blacks constituted a majority of the population of Peach County from its formation until the twentieth century drew to a close, but they did not vote in significant numbers until the passage of the Voting Rights Act of 1965. The lack of political power translated, inevitably, into keen economic deprivation. Few black farmers owned their own land, and even these were in constant peril of losing it to the bank if they fell behind on mortgage payments, or to the state if they couldn't pay the taxes. A modest New Deal effort to foster black ownership of farms ended when forty-seven of Peach County's most powerful landowners enlisted Georgia's influential senator, Richard B. Russell, to thwart the program. Usually the only employment available for rural black males was seasonal work like picking peaches at a nickel a bushel, so their livelihood was constantly imperiled by the vagaries of the weather or the caprice of the big farmers. There was almost no work for a black man living in Fort Valley; often a family survived on the table scraps that black women brought home from their jobs as maids and cooks in the few prosperous white households in the town. In the time that Roy Moody was growing up, there was hardly a black child in Peach County who didn't suffer from hookworm or pellagra, or both.

Not even the educated or dignified women at Fort Valley State could try on dresses or shoes at the town's clothing shops, because under the unwritten rules, once the goods had touched black skin, they could not be sold to a white customer. Once after a professor objected to the rude treatment of his wife in a local store, he was stopped by the police, who demanded to know if he were "the nigger that caused the trouble." Despite such pervasive hardship and humiliation, the town's whites were confident that blacks actually *preferred* segregation. The prevailing attitude was captured in an oft-told anecdote, in which the white boss relates, with low mimicry, how his obsequious black hired hand had told him, "Lawdy, Mistah Joe, if'n you could be a nigger for jes' *one* Sat'dy night, you wouldn't *never* want to be a white man ag'in."

Because this established order was taken as a given during Roy Moody's childhood, there was virtually no meaningful contact between blacks and whites, and if race relations were discussed at all by the whites, it was summed up in a single sentence: "Our colored people are happy and carefree." To be sure, daily contact between the races was inescapable, but to the average white person, encountering a black person in the daily routines of life became an evanescent dark blur, like Ralph Ellison's "Invisible Man." Joyce Law, who knew Roy Moody best during his high school years, said she never once discussed matters of race with him. In every town in South Georgia there was a certain amount of crude "nigger-hazing," casual cruelty inflicted merely to relieve the crushing ennui of small-town life. It was common for white boys to swerve their cars toward blacks trudging along the sidewalk-less streets, sometimes lacerating their victims with green "switches" cut from trees. At night they would roar through the "nigger quarters" randomly hurling rocks and bottles against the sides of the unpainted clapboard shacks in which black families slept. But there is no indication that Roy Moody took part in such behavior.

Besides Fort Valley State, the other notable town institution of Roy Moody's childhood was the Blue Bird Body Company, the factory that produced thousands of the familiar yellow school buses that rumbled across the country roads of America.

Blue Bird was a depression miracle of sorts. During the 1920s Albert Laurence Luce established the Ford automobile agency in Fort Valley, and for a time it prospered. In 1929 he sold 107 of Henry Ford's Model Ts. But in 1930, the first full year of the depression, sales fell to 57, and the following year, to just 7 vehicles. In desperation, Luce considered closing his business and joining the throng of his fellow citizens in looking for work. Several relatives had fallen into poverty, and he had three families to feed.

But Helen Luce, a devout Methodist woman, implored her husband not to put his managerial talents under the proverbial bushel. "Laurence," she pleaded, "you must find a way to help these people to work."

Luce remembered that he had once been asked if he could install a bus body on a truck chassis to haul field workers to their toil. Perhaps, he thought, there might be a market, even in depression times, for buses to ferry rural children over the dirt trails to and from the country schools. So Laurence Luce started the Blue Bird Body Company as an act of faith in 1932.

Recalled Albert Laurence Luce Jr., years later,

> I remember hearing my father walking the floor and praying every night, trying to figure out how to meet the payroll. Everyone was having a terrible time. There were a dozen lawyers in town, and all of them were about to starve to death. The hardware store owner had to let his only paid employee go—a man with four young girls.
>
> The public schools were so hard up that they had to charge the children a fee—50 cents a month. When I was in high school in the thirties, I remember children being sent home because they didn't have the fee. My own father had trouble raising the $3.50 a month for my brothers and my cousins.
>
> Amos Murray, one of our largest peach growers, had eleven Negro families on his place. He called them all together one day and told them he couldn't carry on any more, but if they wanted to stay and try to live off the land, he'd try to give them a dollar a week. Every one of them stayed. But for eight years, Amos Murray's wife didn't have a new hat, and Amos didn't buy Coke until he had paid in full the fertilizer bill he had built up.
>
> One day my father went to the bank to get a loan—he had to have $110 to meet the payroll. But the banker turned him down— there just was no money to loan. He left the bank to tell the workers Blue Bird would have to close. He stopped on the street to say a prayer, literally. While he was standing there a friend approached and recognized my father's anguish. They spoke for a minute, and the man gave Daddy a check for $110. It saved Blue Bird.

Because no one could buy new cars and instead had to keep the old ones running, the general hardship in Fort Valley proved to be a boon for a good automobile repairman. Leroy Moody, who by this time had earned the reputation as the town's best mechanic, enjoyed a measure of security. In 1939 Mozelle Moody gave birth to another child, a girl whom they named Delores Ann.

A year later Roy Moody entered the town's white elementary school, but it was not a carefree experience. At night his mother would seat him on her lap and drill him in his reading lessons from the *Dick and Jane* books used in Georgia at the time. Whenever little Roy would make a mistake, his mother would slap him. This abuse caused the boy to cry, which annoyed Leroy Moody—not out of sympathy for the distressed tot but because it distracted him from reading the *Macon Telegraph*.

The following year a far more traumatic event occurred in Roy's life. His parents, along with the infant Delores, moved to Ohio, where Leroy underwent specialized training in military base management at the Wright-Patterson Army Air Corps Field in order to equip him for a well-paying position at the newly established military facility called Warner Robins Field, some twenty-five miles east of Fort Valley. The Moody family stayed in Ohio for two years, leaving Roy in the care of his widowed grandmother, Eddie Parks Watson. As a child of seven, Roy viewed this situation with much ambiguity. On the one hand, his grandmother was more patient and tolerant of his shortcomings in reading; on the other, he felt abandoned by parents who seemed to favor the new baby sister. With his parents far away, Roy grew sickly and missed so many sessions of school that he had to repeat a grade, so that by the time his parents returned to Fort Valley, the boy already harbored a sense of rejection, and of failure.

When Leroy and Mozelle Moody came home in 1943, Fort Valley was enjoying an unprecedented wartime prosperity. The automobile business was booming, so, instead of going to work at Warner Robins, Leroy snapped up the offer of Greene's Chevrolet to become the shop's master mechanic at the handsome wage of one hundred dollars a week, which was said to have made him the highest-paid salaried man in Peach County and which enabled the Moodys to move up from rented houses to a larger, more commodious home of their own on Calhoun Street on the town's east side.

In 1947, when Roy was thirteen and Delores a freckle-faced, red-haired girl of eight, Mozelle Moody had her last child, a boy whom they named Robert. Throughout those years the Moodys sporadically attended the Fort Valley Baptist Church, which was a notch below the Methodist Church in the social pecking order of the stratified town, but well above the fundamentalist churches that were attended by the poorest and least-educated whites of the town. From all outward appearances, the Moodys were a happy, secure family.

But Leroy yearned to have his own business, and in the postwar prosperity he was able to get bank loans and open a small garage on East Main Street, not far from the Moody home. Leroy's reputation as an honest, competent mechanic was such that the business prospered from the beginning; he could fix any model or make of car, quickly, reliably, and at cheaper prices than the dealerships charged. There was hardly a person in Fort Valley who didn't have some repair job done at Leroy Moody's Garage during the 1950s and 1960s. He became a familiar figure as he drove about the town in his immaculately polished white pickup truck, dressed in a spotless work uniform of white coveralls. "His shop was so clean you could eat off the floor," recalls one of his customers, Judge George Culpepper III. As his business prospered, Leroy bought himself a Cadillac, but he soon got rid of it because, he whispered to his younger brother, Bill Moody, his customers didn't like the idea of the town mechanic driving a better car than the ones he repaired.

When he was twelve Roy tried to earn extra money during the summers by picking peaches in the orchards that sprawled around Fort Valley, but he developed a common allergy to peach fuzz—"an unbelievable itching sensation," Roy would describe it. About this time his father began to instruct Roy in the arts of mechanics, using the Socratic method to inspire the boy's inventive imagination. When he was still in high school Roy began to formulate a new design for the internal combustion engine—work that his father encouraged.

But soon Roy began to feel that while his classmates were free to spend their after-school hours in idle chatter at the soda fountain of the Fort Valley Drug Store, he was expected to come straight to the shop, to help and to learn. He began to use tricks and excuses to avoid work so that he could spend more time alone in his room working on model airplanes. His father would not always give him the money he needed to buy the parts for the hobby, so one day he stole a tube of glue from the town dime store; he got away with his first crime. About this time Roy began to believe that his parents were arbitrary and unfair. He complained, years later, that his parents would promise him the customary childhood rewards, then dawdle in delivering them, so that when he did get them, the pleasure was destroyed by the anxiety of waiting. Increasingly he viewed his father as a domineering and unapproachable man. Asking his father for a favor, he would recall bitterly, was "just hell." He never knew whether Leroy would grant the request or would "tell me to 'shut the fuck up and just do what you are told.'"

When Roy was about twelve, Leroy decided to refinish all the furniture in the house, and Roy was given his share of assignments. When he completed the first, he thought he had done a good job and went to his room. After a few minutes his father came to upbraid him for malingering and gave him another job to do. He carried on the dusty, tedious work of sanding wood until he became so frustrated that he fled to his room in tears, but his father followed him to his room and mocked him for crying. At this time it was customary for the Atlanta-based Coca-Cola Company to give wooden rulers to schoolchildren that featured the Golden Rule: "Do unto others as you would have them do unto you." Roy came to feel the words were a hollow mockery.

Roy perceived that his little sister, Delores, was also victimized by their parents. When Delores turned thirteen, her flirtation with boys distressed her parents. One day about as she walked home from school, she was shoved by a neighborhood bully and fell onto a lawn. When she got home her mother immediately assumed Delores had been lying on the ground and berated the girl unmercifully. Roy, who had seen the shoving incident from a distance, tried to defend his sister, but despite his explanation, Mozelle refused to apologize for unjustly accusing Delores.

For years, Roy remembered these things with a bitter sense that he had been robbed of the innocent merriment of childhood.

As he grew into adolescence, Roy began to take out his frustrations on the more vulnerable ones around him. Once, his younger brother Bobby toddled into Roy's room and knocked over a model that Roy had just glued together, leaving a shamble of balsam sticks. Enraged, Roy began beating the child so unmercifully that Leroy had to intervene and admonish his elder son never to strike his brother again. Two years later, when he had begun driving, Roy Moody offered to take Bobby to

Warner Robins to watch the airplanes taking off and landing. They had barely gotten beyond the town when Roy stopped the car and gave the bewildered Bobby a severe thrashing. "That was for the model airplane you broke," Roy said. "Don't ever touch my planes again."

In Roy's high school years beginning in 1950, Fort Valley basked in a dull lazy ambience in which people went to bed at night without bothering to lock their doors. The most sensational event of his youth was a murder case. A woman of the town killed her husband with an ax one night, then secretly dragged his body to the railroad tracks that ran through the town; through miscalculation, she placed the mangled body on a rarely used side track, resulting in her swift arrest. Roy would relate the story, years later, with much merriment over the woman's stupidity.

At Fort Valley High School, Roy's teachers came to regard him as bright but lacking the personal discipline to achieve his full potential. Curiously, he had few male friends, and years later he would state flatly, "My closest friend in high school was not a child but an adult."

The person to whom he referred was James C. Stephens, who was the principal of Fort Valley High School and who also taught science courses, which tapped Roy's curiosity. Stephens took to Roy as well, and once covered up Roy's theft of a microscope from the school laboratory. Stephens was a pleasant, rotund man who wore rimless glasses that gave him a delicate appearance. Known widely as "Fess" (for "professor"), Stephens functioned in an in loco parentis role to the students of Fort Valley High.

Jeanette Wheaton, who had Roy in her study hall, remembered him as being "quiet and pensive" as he researched his assignments in the school library. But, recalls Jeanette Wheaton, who also served as the social-services officer of the Fort Valley school system, "He was a peculiar little fellow. He was never a leader in anything that I know of. He was never accepted in *the* group, and you could almost see the resentment in his face."

This resentment may have been reflected in the growing alienation from his father, whom Roy saw as a rigid and demanding man. Roy's view of his father "changed forever" on his sixteenth birthday, in 1950, when the father presented him with his own car—a 1938 Plymouth that Leroy Moody had put in mint condition, complete with fender skirts.

Most Fort Valley boys would have treasured a car of their own, but Roy saw a diabolical purpose in the gift.

"He brought it around to the house one day and he was going to present me with this present," recalled a tearful Roy Moody forty years later. "I'm sure he thought that I would be elated, but right away I knew what his motive was. And I asked him, 'Does this mean that I can't use the family car? Is that why you're giving it to me? Because if that's why you're giving it to me I'm not interested in it. I don't want this car or the family car, you know.' Because it was a situation where all my friends had free access to the family car."

If in fact this was his feeling at time, no one else knew it. The girl next door, Joyce Law, remembers, "He came roaring up to my house in his Plymouth; he was the proudest thing in the world." Moreover, Joyce Law went on, the talk about the denial of the family car, a sleek 1950 Oldsmobile 88, couldn't have been true because she rode in it many times with Roy, including once when he nearly wrecked it.

About this time the townspeople began to whisper that Roy was "spoiled." He had his own car—at a time when all the other boys had to share the family car. And he cut a handsome figure in the best clothes at a time when most school children in Fort Valley had but two outfits—"one to wear and one to wash."

These amenities won Roy Moody much favor with Fort Valley High's girls, who were captivated by the sensual persona of his slender stature, his serene chiseled features, his glistening jet-black hair, and his dreamy pale blue-green eyes, all of which evoked a hint of a pubescent Cherokee brave who might have inhabited the Fort Valley plain when the white man arrived more than a century before. He became something of a snob, avoiding the girls who came from the poorer sections of Fort Valley. He occasionally dated the brilliant, goal-oriented Margaret Howard, yet he must have known in his heart that in that class-structured society the son of the town's best mechanic could never hope to marry into one of the town's best families like the Howards, Luces, Pearsons, Dukes, or Lanes. They only married one another.

Roy saw education as the route to respectability, so he told his father that he wanted to go to college, to become a neurosurgeon. Leroy Moody interpreted this ambition as a sign of laziness. Even more disturbing, the father saw hints of dishonesty—as when Roy would fill his car from the garage gas pump without permission. And when Roy took to writing checks on the family bank account—a privilege many youngsters had in those days, so long as they didn't abuse it—Leroy perceived a sinful tendency toward profligacy in his son, which led to quarrels at home. By the time Leroy suffered a heart attack in 1953, Roy had grown to detest the grease and grime that came with working on cars, not to speak of the dreary tedium of turning wrenches all day long. When Roy announced that he had no intention of going into the garage business, "My father practically disowned me." Mozelle watched this rift with helpless resignation. But Roy's relationship with his mother was not the best, either; he complained that she would invade his privacy by reading his mail.

During this time, Joyce Law, who lived in the house just around the corner from the Moodys on Peachtree Street, adored Roy, and would follow him home from school at a demure distance. When Joyce grew more mature at around fourteen, Roy returned the attention. Although he was three years older, he took her for rides in his envied Plymouth with the fancy fender skirts.

As she got to know Roy better, Joyce noticed a perplexing quality: He would grow angry for no apparent reason and refuse to speak to her for long periods. In the middle 1950s Fort Valley didn't even have a Dairy Queen, so it was considered a lavish treat for a boy to take a girl to Macon, thirty miles away, for a malted milk shake. During the times when he was inexplicably angry with Joyce, Roy would make her sit in the back seat of the Plymouth, not saying a word during the entire trip. She would get her milk shake, but only grudgingly.

Roy and Joyce spoke of getting married, and when he was a senior he gave her his high school class ring. But one day he marched into Joyce's homeroom just before class began, and, before thirty other children, demanded that she give him back the ring. In silent humiliation she complied, whereupon Roy took the ring to the other side of the room and placed it on the desk of an astonished Margaret Howard.

At one point Roy stopped seeing Joyce and devoted all of his attentions to Margaret, who was even younger than Joyce and who was flattered, in a schoolgirlish way, to be the object of attention to a handsome older boy. Roy would go to Margaret's house, on the outskirts of town, ostensibly to study together. But Margaret, who was very studious, found out quickly that Roy really didn't like homework. He especially didn't want to spend time reading the books that were assigned in Miss Thelma Wilson's English class. Roy knew that Margaret read all of the books, so he would get her to explain the plots to him so that he could pass the tests without doing the reading.

Margaret's parents forbade their daughter to go out alone with Roy, but they allowed the youngsters to "double-date" with Margaret's older sister, Winnie, and her boyfriend, Larry Sandifer. On weekends when the weather was good, the four would drive down to Leroy Moody's cabin on the wooded shore of Lake Blackshear, thirty miles south of Fort Valley. On these aimless summer outings, Margaret began to detect an odd quality in Roy. When Larry Sandifer said something that Roy didn't like, or suggested something he didn't want to do, instead of objecting, Roy would become dolorous, his countenance darkening in silence.

About this time, the school principal, Fess Stephens, furtively called Margaret aside and cautioned her that Roy might be a bit too "experienced" for her to be going with. In any event, Roy eventually made up with Joyce, and soon disappeared from Margaret's life.

Despite Roy's penchant for humiliating her in public, Joyce adored Roy. When she was fifteen, Joyce ruefully recalled, years later, "He kept saying he wanted to 'bust my cherry,'"—using the adolescent vernacular for taking a girl's virginity. This secret rite was consummated only after several botched attempts, each of which left Roy with a frustrated sense of failure. By the spring of 1953, Roy and Joyce often would cut classes and go to Lake Blackshear alone to water ski and to satisfy Roy's insatiable sexual appetite. Joyce also remembers one terrifying episode at Lake Blackshear when Roy threw her out of a boat and she nearly drowned. He later dismissed the incident, saying he was only trying to teach her to swim.

Toward the end of her first year of high school, Joyce became pregnant, so the talk of marriage grew serious and urgent. But the adolescent lovers were too terrified to tell their parents of the pregnancy, so both the Laws and the Moodys rejected the proposed marriage out of hand and instructed the children to stop seeing each other.

At this desperate moment, Fess Stephens called Roy to his office and asked if there was anything troubling him. When Roy dissembled, Fess asked him bluntly, "Is Joyce pregnant?" Roy was astonished at the teacher's prescience, and he resented the intrusion into his personal life. Still, Roy was so frantic that he confessed all and asked Fess what he should do. The teacher said the two were obviously too young to get married, that it would "ruin your lives." Then he offered to arrange an abortion. In later years, Roy was ambiguous about who performed the abortion and where it took place, but Joyce now states emphatically: The abortion was performed by Fess Stephens himself in a room of Fort Valley High after school one day. "After it was over I hemorrhaged so bad that I almost died. For a long time Roy was real depressed. So was I."

Joyce's teachers also noticed a dramatic change in the girl at the time. Jeanette Wheaton, the "visiting teacher," remembers that Joyce missed a lot of classes because of some undiagnosed illness. Joyce had always been an A student, and had tested highly for IQ. But after she became involved with Roy Moody, she missed classes and her performance suffered so that she was constantly being counseled by her perplexed teachers.

Roy graduated from Fort Valley High in 1953. His photograph in the high school yearbook, which was called "The Vallehi," depicted him as a handsome teenager with a mane of glistening black hair, dreamy eyes, and slightly sensual lips. He was identified only as Roy Moody, rather than by his full name of Walter Leroy Moody Jr. In those days graduating seniors wrote a few parting words in the yearbook. Roy's read: "If I had the wings of an airplane." His listing of high school activities was brief: "Track: Soph., Jr., Sr." Thus, his single chosen athletic activity was the only one at Fort Valley High that was not a team sport, like the revered basketball or football. At that time it was customary to dedicate the high school yearbook to some esteemed faculty member, and the 1953 "Vallehi" was dedicated to James C. Stephens, the school principal and Roy's trusted friend and confidante, Fess.

After Roy graduated, he took a summer job at the Blue Bird Body Company, which by then was the leading manufacturer of school bus bodies in the nation. But as the business grew, Laurence Luce retained small-town habits. He retained the long-standing practice of setting aside a half an hour a week to bring a local minister to the plant to conduct an inspirational service.

One day as Roy Moody left the service, in which the sermon topic had been about the virtues of patience and hard work, he struck up a conversation with Joe Luce, who was Laurence Luce's son. In a small town like Fort Valley, it was not unusual for the factory owner's son to work alongside the son of the town's garage owner.

"I'm glad I heard that preacher," Roy said to Joe. "He helped me make up my mind about something."

"What's that?" Joe Luce asked.

"Well, I've always been determined to go to college, but my daddy won't give me the money. I was gonna get the money somehow. I was getting set up to make whiskey. Some of the fellows in the plant told me how. I already had got my equipment—a worm, and so on." A "worm" was vernacular for a coil of metal tubing, which was used to distill illicit "moonshine" whiskey, then widespread throughout rural Georgia.

"But now I know that's the wrong way to go," Roy continued. "I will just have to find another way to get the money."

Joe Luce was touched, and related the story to his father. By that time Laurence Luce had already established a certain noblesse oblige in assisting promising youngsters of Fort Valley. Laurence called Roy to his office and told him he would give him a little financial assistance if he would enroll in Mercer University, a Baptist college at Macon, thirty miles away.

It was about this time, also, that the United States Supreme Court ruled that segregated schools were unconstitutional. Revolutionary though the ruling may have seemed elsewhere, the news was received with a curious equanimity in places like Fort Valley, probably because no one seriously believed that the races would ever mix in the public schools. The state's champion of white supremacy, Gene Talmadge, had died in 1946, but his mantle had been quickly taken by his son Herman. From the state capitol in Atlanta, "Hummon," as the governor was known to his adoring constituents, darkly warned that if there were any attempt to enforce the court's ruling, "blood would flow in the streets."

But in the middle 1950s the preservation of segregation was not the uppermost concern to Roy Moody. He apparently considered Laurence Luce's offer inadequate for him to go to Mercer, especially when he could count on no support from his father.

Soon after his summer job at Blue Bird expired, on September 11, 1953, Roy Moody joined the Army.

4 Up from Slavery

In the early spring of 1875, in another part of the Georgia Black Belt not fifty miles from Fort Valley, Gus Roberson's wife gave birth to her first son, probably in a one-room cabin on a farm somewhere around the community of Linton in Hancock County. Little is known about Gus and his wife—not even her name can be found on any record—but almost certainly both were born into slavery, probably in the 1850s, and were among the half million slaves in Georgia who were officially emancipated by Mr. Lincoln's historic Proclamation of 1863.

But to someone like Gus Roberson and his wife, freedom remained a tenuous commodity at a time when Reconstruction was in its final months after a chaotic effort toward national reconciliation in the ten years following the Civil War. If the Robersons were anywhere close to typical, they found the sharecropper and tenancy system of agriculture that arose during that decade barely distinguishable from the old slave system. Moreover, the part of Georgia in which they lived still lay in devastation; Hancock County lay at the midpoint of the route General William Tecumseh Sherman took in 1864 on his famous two-hundred-mile March to the Sea, leaving only scorched earth and a legacy of hatred in his path.

So it took a measure of faith for someone like Gus and his wife to bring a new child into the world in those benighted times, and this faith and optimism was reflected by the choice of a name for their first son: They named him Joshua, for the Old Testament general who, in the words of the great spiritual, "fit de battle of Jericho, and de walls came a-tumblin' down."

Like most of the landless former slaves in the waning years of the nineteenth century, Gus Roberson and his family meandered from farm to farm in the Central Georgia Black Belt, bartering his family's toil in return for primitive shelter and a subsistence diet. The exact route of his trek is not known, but at one point he lived in the Sandersville area, so it is entirely possible that little Joshua encountered a nondescript child named Robert Poole. There is no reason Joshua would have paid any special attention to Robert, who was born in 1897, one of 13 children of parents who had also been slaves. But in the years to come, Joshua must have marveled at the irony that this little black boy he may have seen playing in the dusty alleys of Sandersville's "quarters" would join the great mass migration of blacks to the northern cities and would, in time, take the new name of Elijah Muhammad and build the Nation of Islam, which would become widely known as the Black Muslims.

Few who were born into slavery were literate—there were laws against teaching slaves to read and write—so whatever education Gus Roberson and his wife may have gained had been furtive, limited, and possibly attained after they had reached adulthood. Whatever the case, they must have inculcated some desire for learning in their children. A daughter learned to read early, and she passed on this treasured achievement to her younger brother, Joshua. This early encouragement equipped Joshua to take full advantage of such schooling as there was at a time when a modest legacy of black education still lingered from the abandoned Reconstruction era, when teachers from the North came to the South to teach the children of the emancipated slaves the basic skills of literacy.

At that time four years of education was about the most a black child in rural Georgia could hope to achieve, but apparently this amount was sufficient to enable Joshua to read the Bible, which he did with great diligence, and in due course he became a Baptist preacher, probably self-ordained. In those days few single congregations in rural Georgia could support a minister, so Joshua became a horseback circuit-riding pastor, preaching at Sandersville one week, at Wrightsville the next, then at Dublin, and so on. He might even have preached at Louisville, where his own ancestors may have been bought and sold from the slave-auction platform that still stood in the town square. More often than not, Joshua was paid not in cash but in the simple provender of eggs, chickens, cornmeal, or perhaps a slab of smoke-cured hog meat to boil with the collard greens that were the year-round staple of the rural diet.

In antebellum times most plantation owners permitted their slaves to establish their own forms of worship, and the church quickly took on its own character as the most vital force in the community life of the enslaved people. The spiritual dimension of the black church was, to be sure, of transcendent importance: It offered a promise of a world to come for a people who knew only privation and humiliation, a Promised Land across the River Jordan where there was joy and freedom and respite from the oxlike drudgery that dominated their lives. In the 1936 film, *The Green Pastures,* a gentle white-bearded ebony God strolls about Heaven in a frock coat and, when he really wants to celebrate, decrees a great fish fry. This vision of heaven was no mere fanciful fairy tale to the put-down slaves.

With Emancipation, the black church assumed even greater importance, serving not only the spiritual needs but temporal exigencies as well. Sunday gatherings became daylong affairs in which the congregants would bring copious quantities of food and drink—including, despite the prevailing religious strictures on the drinking of alcohol, copious supplies of "busthead likker"—to make a great feast at the noon hour. The church gatherings became a conduit for news of the community. Medical advice might be dispensed by midwives and self-taught "doctors." Deacons and elders of the church might function in a judicial capacity to resolve disputes. The church even served as a channel for rudimentary commerce: the exchange, say, of cottonseed for seed corn, or meal for meat. But above all, the church was a sanctuary in the most literal meaning of the word. Safely out of the sight and hearing of the white man, the black people at church could love and laugh and sing and be joyful; for a few fleeting hours they could be free from the dawn-to-dusk toil on the white man's farm.

In this setting the minister became the paramount figure of the black community, not just a preacher of God's word but an eminence, because he alone enjoyed the greatest degree of independence a black man could hope to attain in a society where blacks were being systematically stripped of basic political, economic, and legal rights. So it is safe to assume that Joshua Roberson cut an influential swath across Central Georgia as he served seventeen churches during his fifty-six years of active ministry.

The formidable demands of his ministry did not preclude Joshua from establishing a family, and on July 4, 1911, while they were living in Sandersville, his wife gave birth to a son, whom they named Robert Lee Roberson.

As a preacher's son, Robert grew up in about the closest thing to protected privilege that a black child in rural Georgia could hope to realize in the early years of the twentieth century. It was, after all, the heyday of a resurgent Ku Klux Klan, and few politicians dared seek office without proclaiming Klan membership. Even President Woodrow Wilson, who had in fact spent childhood years in Georgia, warmly praised D.W. Griffith's profoundly inflammatory 1915 film, *The Birth of a Nation,* which glorified the Klan and vilified black people. Tom Watson, the Populist demagogue, had long since abandoned his progressive visions and embraced unregenerate racism in the waning days of his mercurial political career.

Despite these prodigious impediments to the aspirations of a black boy born half a century after the Emancipation Proclamation, the value of education was deeply inculcated in the Roberson family, so Robert was among the tiny fraction of his social class who was able to complete high school, such as it was. Confronting only a bleak future in Sandersville, Robert made his way, even as the Great Depression was tightening its grip, to Savannah, the staid old colonial capital of Georgia whose history dated back to 1733, when General James Edward Oglethorpe pitched his tents on Yamacraw Bluff to shelter the weary refugees from English debtors' prisons who would become the first inhabitants of the new colony of Georgia.

Georgia was two hundred years old when Robert Lee Roberson arrived in Savannah, with what little money his father could advance him and what little he could scrape together doing odd jobs, to enroll in the Georgia Industrial College, which lay on the edge of the marshland of the state's Atlantic Coast. As the name suggests, the institution was not really a college but rather a vocational school established to train ambitious black Georgia youngsters in whatever blue-collar crafts were open to them in a time of apartheid-like segregation.

When he enrolled in Georgia Industrial, for reasons that are not known, Robert signed his last name not as "Roberson" but rather "Robinson." That version would remain with him and his offspring from that day forward.

At about the same time that Robert Robinson was establishing himself in Savannah, another depression refugee arrived in the old port city from a different direction. Edna Creech was born on April 3, 1916, on a farm near the small community of Kline in Barnwell County, South Carolina, just across the Savannah River from Georgia. Edna was one of several children of George Saxon and Savannah Cave Creech. The Creeches and the Caves had owned their own tracts of land, which made them about the closest thing you could find to "landed gentry" among black people. Ownership of land was of paramount importance, because it meant that you knew where you would be the next year, barring the calamity of bank foreclosure or forced sale of property for nonpayment of taxes. But the Creeches and the Caves were sensible, industrious farmers, and they survived not only the political convulsions unleashed by the mountebank racist politicians of the time, "Our Coley" Blease, "Pitchfork Ben" Tillman, and "Cotton Ed" Smith, but the pervasive adversity of the Great Depression with their land intact.

Despite this relative security, the comely and high-spirited Edna did not relish the prospect of drudging through life as a farmer's wife in rural South Carolina, promising only the travail of perennial pregnancy and even working in the fields when the demands of the harvest were too great for the men to meet. Besides, there had been a tragedy in Edna's family. One of her brothers had been killed in a domestic quarrel, and the event was so traumatic that Savannah Creech simply took to a wheelchair, leaving the numbing household duties largely to Edna.

Edna was barely in her twenties when she declared that she was going to Savannah, some fifty miles south of the Creech farm, in order to pursue a career as a nurse. This greatly disturbed the family, and their worst fears were soon realized when Edna married a rakish gospel singer who, between infrequent performances at local moonshine mills, took whatever jobs he could find as a laborer to provide bare sustenance for his wife and baby daughter Ruth, who was born in 1939. With the wolf of real want constantly at the door, Edna kicked out her shiftless husband and, by wit and grit, supported her baby until, in 1943, she married Robert Robinson, whom she had met while they were fellow students at Georgia Industrial College.

Robert legally adopted Ruth as his own child, and the family prospects grew bright when Robert landed a job as a Pullman car porter. This career was most prized in the black community, because it meant that the holder not only was reasonably well-paid but also cherished a measure of job security unknown to the vast majority who toiled at the whim and caprice of the white boss. Even though the job was by nature servile, the porters enjoyed a degree of pride and dignity as members of the formidable A. Philip Randolph's Brotherhood of Sleeping Car Porters. The calls for black militancy in the union's monthly newspaper, *The Messenger,* were always eagerly read in the Robinson household.

When they first married, Robert and Edna took an apartment at 416 West Duffy Street on the charring edges of old downtown Savannah. Soon the toddler Ruth was joined by a baby sister, Barbara, and then, on July 30, 1947, a healthy baby brother whom they named Robert Edward Robinson. Within the family, he would always be called "Edward" to distinguish him from his father, but to all others in the community he came to be called simply "Robbie."

Duffy Street was not the best of neighborhoods, so Robert and Edna, loving but strict parents, required their children to confine their play to the porch. The children were permitted only occasional trips as far as the little corner grocery store to purchase two-for-a-penny pieces of candy or bubble gum with the coins their doting father would give them each time he returned from the five-day run on the Savannah-to-Chicago train.

At first little Barbara was jealous of the new baby boy who intruded into her settled life, but Robbie soon became the focus of familial attention. Early on his mother and his older sisters recognized and nurtured his brightness, encouraging him to read and write when he was barely more than a toddler. When he was four, he was enrolled in the kindergarten of the Tremont Baptist Temple, a church of commanding presence on West Broad Street just around the corner from the Robinson home. Because of all this affectionate attention, Robbie was able to enter in the first grade in 1952 when he was only five. There was never any question, much less discussion, as to where Robbie would go to school: It would be the Florence Elementary School for black children, a few blocks from the Robinson home.

Edna completed the two years of training at Georgia Industrial College required to become a licensed practical nurse and worked for a brief time for a local charity clinic, which was about the only place that black citizens of Savannah could get hospital care at that time. Soon after she got a job with one of Savannah's most prominent obstetrician-gynecologists, Dr. John Hamilton Angell. Together Robert and Edna commanded an income that placed them well above that of the average black family in Savannah, and this relative prosperity enabled them to build their own house at 706 West 46th Street in Cann Park, which was then being established as the best neighborhood for Savannah's small, upwardly mobile black middle class. The location was, in reality, only a mile or two from the shabby neighborhood of Duffy Street, but to the three Robinson children it was a different universe. They had their own bedrooms for the first time, and they were allowed to go down the street to the public park, which had slides and swings and other wondrous contrivances to entertain children as they played late into the summer evenings in the cool breezes which blew in from the Atlantic Ocean. Although Robert's father, Joshua, was a Baptist minister, Edna had come from a family of Methodists, so the family became mainstays in St. Paul's Christian Methodist Episcopal Church. But at least once a month, the children would pile into the family car for a weekend visit to their grandparents. Sometimes they would head for Dublin, fifty miles to the west, to visit Joshua Roberson, who by that time had become a community patriarch and lived, in comfortable retirement, in a spacious house with a porch that curled around two sides of the house and had bench swings and rocking chairs that were so conducive to idle conversation among the adults. On other weekends, they would drive fifty miles to the north to visit Edna's relatives, the Creeches and the Caves, who still clung to sizable tracts of farmland in the South Carolina low country.

These were the passive years of the Eisenhower Administration, a time when the white people of Savannah accepted cradle-to-grave segregation of the races as a primeval natural order, and the blacks resignedly accepted the same view, even though this enforced second-class status seared their very souls. The placid tranquillity was disturbed, to be sure, when the United States Supreme Court ruled, on May 17, 1954, that legally mandated segregation in public schools was unconstitutional. But at the outset, no one in Savannah, or in most other places in the South, took the decision seriously. After all, Governor Herman E. Talmadge, defiantly carrying the banner of his late father, Gene, as an unreconstructed segregationist, assured Georgians that no decree issued by nine old men in distant Washington would ever change the settled order of racial separation in their state. So when it came time for Robbie to return to school in the fall of 1954, again there was no question about where he would go: It was to the neighborhood school for black children in Cann Park. To consider any other course would have been downright dangerous.

But if the social order in Savannah seemed immutable, ominous things began to happen in other parts of the South. In 1955 the Supreme Court rendered its first guidance as to how its historic desegregation decision was to be carried out: "With all deliberate speed." The ambiguity of the phrase was seized at once to mean local federal judges held great latitude in bringing an end to segregated education in the South. The court's equivocation also encouraged hard-line resistance. The White Citizens Council, a kind of cleaned-up version of the discredited Ku Klux Klan, formed chapters in large and small towns across the South. More than twelve thousand people turned out to hear a defiant Sen. James O. Eastland of Mississippi speak at a mammoth White Citizens Council rally in Montgomery in 1956. Candidates for public office ran at their peril if they could not claim membership in the Citizens Council. Belonging to the Council became a kind of middle-class status-symbol for doctors, lawyers, even ministers. Outwardly at least, the Council repudiated violence, relying instead on economic retaliation against any black man or woman who dared assert the newly declared constitutional right to send a child to the public schools. Anyone who did assert that right soon found himself under police surveillance and subject to jail sentence on the most trivial or trumped-up charges. Council-dominated legislatures across the South exultantly passed "interposition" resolutions declaring the Supreme Court's desegregation decision to be "null and void." And in Savannah, the all-white school board voted unanimously in August of 1955 to maintain a segregated school system.

In the face of this "massive resistance" a few courageous black families put their lives and livelihood on the line. The first major offensive against the Old Order came in 1956 in Little Rock, Arkansas. When a federal judge ordered a dozen black students admitted to the Arkansas capital's "white" high school, Governor Orval Faubus, theretofore regarded as a moderate politician who eschewed race-baiting, called out the state's National Guard to thwart the court order. Confronted with this bald defiance of federal authority, a reluctant but resolute President Eisenhower sent the 101st Airborne Division to Little Rock to enforce the order at bayonet-point.

The integrity of the federal judiciary was maintained, but rage and bitterness swept the South. The following year, when Judge Hobart H. Grooms of Birmingham ordered a single black student named Autherine Lucy admitted to the University of Alabama, rioting flared on the campus. Governor Big Jim Folsom was then in his second term—and in the advanced stages of alcoholism, which prevented him from cracking down forcefully on the rioters, even though he covertly yearned to cross the hurdle of integration. When Lucy made the insupportable charge that university authorities had conspired with the mob, she was expelled, and Judge Grooms ruled the expulsion was justified. This victory by violence emboldened the segregationists, and federal judges throughout the region took heed of the volatility of the issue now thrust into their hands. It soon became evident that the pace of desegregation depended upon the commitment of the local federal judge in a given district.

In Savannah, the white citizens assumed with much confidence that their particular federal judge would never impose a Little Rock-type order on local schools. Even by the standards of the 1950s, Frank Muir Scarlett was already a living relic of the Old South. Born in 1891 in a county immortalized by Sidney Lanier in his classic poem "The Marshes of Glynn," Scarlett was the great-nephew of the Confederate general who commanded the last embattled remnants of southern troops in Savannah before Sherman's final onslaught in 1864. Scarlett grew up in privilege sufficient to secure him a legal education at a time when that profession assured its members a life of amenity and prestige in a community like Brunswick, which lay fifty miles down the marshy Georgia coastline from Savannah. Scarlett even acquired a little railroad that he operated, on the side of his law practice. As a young lawyer, he functioned as the local political boss through his position as chairman of the Glynn County Democratic Committee. He also happened to be a cousin of Georgia's influential United States senator, Richard B. Russell, whose campaigns Scarlett managed during the 1930s and 1940s. In addition to this formidable Washington connection, Scarlett became the regional factotum of the Talmadge political machine.

Scarlett's political career ended—outwardly, at least—when President Truman, at the behest of Senator Russell, appointed him resident judge of the United States District Court for the Southern District of Georgia, covering a vast swath of the rural South that included the fabled Okefenokee Swamp but which mostly consisted of thin sandy soil and endless tracts of spindly pine trees that the impoverished blacks of the region "turpentined" under conditions little better than peonage. At his judicial investiture in 1946, one of Scarlett's law partners, in a burst of Old South rhetorical flourish, exhorted him to be "an upright and just and fearless judge, kindly and considerate and helpful to those around him, but firm, and when the occasion demands, stern and even inexorable."

The last encomium proved to be prescient when it came to the cases involving segregation that soon reached Judge Scarlett. In 1954, the local chapter of the National Association for the Advancement of Colored People brought suit in Scarlett's court charging that the city of Savannah used powers under the federal Urban Renewal program to seize and demolish squalid shotgun houses occupied by blacks in order to build a subsidized housing project exclusively for whites. Scarlett summarily threw out the NAACP's case on the ground that Savannah supplied public housing to both races on a "separate but equal" basis. The decision was, theoretically, a correct application of the Supreme Court doctrine enunciated in 1896 in the notorious case of *Plessy v. Ferguson,* and the fact that the Supreme Court had, that very year, declared school segregation unconstitutional didn't necessarily mean that segregated public housing was also unconstitutional. But Scarlett's ruling notwithstanding, the handwriting was on the wall: A year later, the Fifth Circuit Court of Appeals reversed the housing decision and ordered Scarlett to hear the case. To simplify the litigation, all but one of the eighteen black families who were initially parties to the suit dropped out. Scarlett then dismissed the suit on the ground that the sole remaining plaintiff could not demonstrate that he had ever actually applied for an apartment in the white-only housing project.

Clearly, as the NAACP and allied forces looked about the South for places to challenge segregation, Judge Scarlett's court made Savannah an unpropitious place to wage the fight. So little Robbie Robinson attended the black grade school in Cann Park.

With the advent of John Kennedy's presidency in 1961, not even Judge Scarlett could any longer shelter Savannah from the winds of change. As the decade began, the Savannah NAACP, under the vigorous new leadership of a local mail carrier named W. W. Law, enlisted a dozen of Savannah's brightest black students—nine girls and three boys—to seek admission to the all-white Savannah High School. Accompanied by their parents and NAACP officials, the students sought to enroll at Savannah High in September of 1962. When they were turned away, the group went to W. W. Law's NAACP office to initiate the federal lawsuit.

There, some of the parents were seized with anxiety over the prospect of economic reprisal. After anguished consultation with the legal titan, Thurgood Marshall of the NAACP Legal Defense Fund, a single plaintiff, the son of a local minister who felt reasonably insulated from economic retaliation, brought the class-action lawsuit demanding across-the-board desegregation of Savannah schools, and the suit reached Judge Scarlett's desk in the winter of 1962. It bore the cumbersome case-name of "Ralph STELL, a minor by L. S. Stell, Jr., his father and next friend, et al, Plaintiffs, v. SAVANNAH-CHATHAM COUNTY BOARD OF EDUCATION, et al., Defendants." The Stells lived not far from the Robinsons, and Ralph and Robbie often played together at the neighborhood playground for black children that served Cann Park.

By the time the Stell case was set for trial, the local school authorities could see massive resistance collapsing all over the South. Even in Alabama, George Wallace's inaugural-speech vow in January 1963 to maintain "segregation forever" had, by June of that year, turned into a comic spectacle with a symbolic final gesture of defiance, his "stand in the schoolhouse door," after which Wallace's own National Guard general ordered him to step aside and allow the University of Alabama to enroll two black students. Wallace's last stand was a watershed, after which communities throughout the South set about integrating the public schools through minimal compliance, the theory being that if good-faith desegregation efforts could be shown, more drastic court-ordered remedies might be avoided.

In this new atmosphere, Savannah authorities announced that the city's schools would be desegregated beginning in the fall of 1963, and for a time it was assumed that there were no longer any issues to be decided in the Stell case. Then the case took an abrupt turn: A white woman named Adrienne Roberts intervened in the case, asserting that her children, Lawrence and Daniel, would be "irreparably harmed" if compelled to attend school with black children who, she maintained, were inherently incapable of developing mentally or educationally at the same pace as white children. Mrs. Roberts's suit, moreover, was a class action brought on behalf of *all* white children in the Savannah schools. She asked Judge Scarlett to do no less than order the local school board to maintain *segregation,* not initiate *integration.*

At first the NAACP lawyers, who now included such civil rights titans as Jack Greenberg and Constance Baker Motley, considered the intervenors' request so audacious that it would be swiftly thrown out of court. After all, nine years had passed since the Supreme Court decided *Brown v. Board of Education,* and scores of lower federal courts had ordered compliance in one form or another. To the astonishment of the lawyers, Judge Scarlett declared that the white intervenors must be given an opportunity to prove their contentions about the innate mental inferiority of black children.

The hearing that followed was a bizarre spectacle, at times reminiscent of the notorious Scopes Monkey Trial in Dayton, Tennessee, in 1925, contesting the legality of teaching evolution. Mrs. Roberts was represented by the eminence grise of the Georgia legal establishment, Charles J. Bloch of Macon, along with three other luminaries of advanced years, all contributing their services *pro bono publico* to the cause of maintaining segregation. A parade of expert witnesses, most of them elderly psychologists and sociologists, took the witness stand to extol scholarly findings "proving" that black children could never hope to attain the educational development level of whites. Pseudoscientific discourses such as Carleton S. Coon's *Origin of Races* were cited as evidence and became a part of the record. One witness even borrowed a human skull from a prominent Savannah physician, Dr. Donnell Bronner, to illustrate that the brain cavity of the white person was larger than that of a black person. Dr. Bronner was, by coincidence, a partner of Dr. John Hamilton Angell, the obstetrician-gynecologist for whom Edna Creech Robinson worked as a practical nurse.

The NAACP lawyers listened in cold fury to this exotic presentation, showing scarcely disguised contempt for the whole proceeding by refusing to question the "expert witnesses." At every opportunity, they maintained that the Supreme Court had categorically declared school segregation unconstitutional, so Mrs. Roberts's claim was irrelevant and specious.

On June 18, 1963, with the opening of school just a little more than a month away, Judge Scarlett, then well into his seventh decade, rendered his decision: It was an unequivocal victory for the white intervenors.

It was a breathtaking display of judicial dexterity. Like any competent lawyer, Scarlett knew he had a serious problem with what lawyers call *stare decisis*—the bedrock judicial principle that precedent should stand unless there is a compelling case to reverse prior decisions. After all, the Supreme Court had stated emphatically in the Brown decision of 1954 that state laws mandating school segregation were unconstitutional. In one creative stroke, Scarlett cleared this obstacle by ruling that in the 1954 case, the high court had not considered scientific evidence of disparity between the races in educational development. Thus, he reasoned, the question of the scientific findings was open to new adjudication, and the "facts" presented to him by the learned experts led to the inexorable conclusion that integration of the races in public schools would cause serious harm to both black and white children.

"The congregation of two substantial and identifiable student groups into a single classroom, under circumstances of distinct group identification, and varying abilities," Scarlett declared, "would lead to conflict impairing the educational process. It is essential for an individual to identify himself with a reference group for healthy personality development. Physical and psychological differences are the common basis of group identification, indeed they compel such self-identification. To increase this divisive tendency, it has been established without contradiction, that selective association is a universal human trait; that physically observable racial differences form the basis for preferential association and that patterns of racial preferences are formed and firmly established at a preschool age."

Scarlett went on that not even "certain superior Negro children" who measured up to white standards—and this certainly would have included Robbie Robinson with his high academic performance—could attend white schools. Such "selective integration," Scarlett wrote, "would cause even greater psychological harm to the individual Negro children" because it would cheat them of "their right of achievement in their own group" by moving them into a class where they would be subject to "total social rejection by the dominant group."

So the case of *Stell v. Savannah,* which began with a demand to integrate the schools, had become the vehicle for Judge Scarlett to overrule the United States Supreme Court and require segregated schools. The decision attracted wide attention. David Lawrence, an aging conservative who was then the most widely syndicated newspaper columnist in America, warmly applauded Scarlett's judicial acuity. White Citizens Councils across the South, by this time clearly fighting a losing battle as communities across the South prepared to integrate schools, found new hope in the ruling.

The civil rights lawyers, inured to shock by the fact that Scarlett would even permit a hearing into "scientific evidence" of black inferiority, took the decision in stride and appealed to the Fifth Circuit Court of Appeals. The following spring, a panel of Fifth Circuit judges overruled Scarlett in a single curt paragraph. Soon thereafter, the U.S. Supreme Court upheld the reversal, and *Stell v. Savannah* was consigned to the lawbooks as a judicial oddity, the last gasp in the effort to maintain legal segregation. By this time, the case of *Swann v. Mecklenberg*, which sanctioned cross-district busing of children in order to achieve racial balance, was settled judicial policy.

But short-lived as it was, Scarlett's ruling allowed Savannah one more year of segregated education at a time when most schools across the South were entering the new age. Because of Scarlett's ruling Robbie Robinson resumed his education in 1963 at the Alfred E. Beach High School for Negroes not far from his home in Cann Park.

The following year, with the Stell case then resting in the dustbin of judicial history, Robbie Robinson preregistered for his final term of high school. His mother noticed that he left a little earlier than usual on the morning of registration. That night over the dinner table, Edna idly asked what courses Robbie was taking. She began to tick off the familiar names of teachers who had taught Robbie's sisters when they went to Beach High. No, Robbie said, he didn't have any of those teachers.

"Goodness," Edna exclaimed, "doesn't Beach High have any of the old teachers left?"

"I'm not going to Beach High," Robbie replied with aplomb. "I registered at Savannah High."

At this discovery, Robbie's sister Barbara recalled years later, "my mother had a fit."

5 Bull, Bombs, and Birmingham

As the summer of 1951 arrived, the University of Alabama—
"the Capstone," to generations of reverent alumni—idled
along in its languid, dog-days mode. The off-season student
body consisted of an odd mix. Some were students who had
partied too much during the regular academic year and were
now scrambling to make up credits needed for graduation.
Others were sober school teachers plodding toward masters'
degrees in the hope of increasing their penurious salaries. A
few, like Bob Vance, were in summer school to get head start
as leaders of the student body in the coming year. And a few
more were precocious youngsters, like Helen Rainey, who
were eager to get on with college.

Bob, who vaguely resembled a gangling teenage version
of Robert Taylor with rimless glasses, had just been elected
president of the Student Government Association, which made
him first among equals of the Big Men on Campus—and
marked him as a young man with a future in state politics.
He had won the coveted office in a spirited campaign against
another Birmingham boy, David Vann, in which the issues
were such mundane matters as whether to have Saturday

classes or when to hold the campus dance. The virginal civility of the campaign was illustrated by the slogan emblazoned on Bob's posters: "Don't forget the 'ce'"—a whimsical play on the similarity of the candidates' names.

One humid July day that summer, as Bob chatted with a friend in a hallway outside the student government offices in the campus union building, a petite, pixie-like coed interrupted to ask the location of the student publications office, where she hoped to do extracurricular work on the college yearbook, the *Corolla*. The friend happened to know Helen Rainey, and he introduced her to Bob.

"Well," he began, "why don't you come into my office and lie down and tell me all about yourself?"

It was the kind of mildly raffish remark that haughty upperclassmen would make to newly arrived freshman girls in those innocent times. More flattered than offended, Helen turned him down, but a few days later, on August 4, 1951, they had their first date, and Bob began to learn about Helen.

It was a tale of a quaint bit of subculture in the stultifying sameness of Alabama. Her maternal grandfather, Ernst Hauk, migrated from Germany in the middle of the nineteenth century. He landed in Baltimore, where he learned that a community of German Lutherans had settled and prospered in a place called Cullman in North Alabama, so he headed south to seek his fortune. After a stint at farming he opened the Cullman Ice Factory in 1884 to supply the townspeople with a modicum of relief from the sweltering summer heat. Ernst also took a wife from among the local *Fräuleins* and settled comfortably into Cullman life.

In the 1920s, Helen's paternal grandfather, Arthur Purse Rainey, arrived in Alabama from New York to manage one of the corporate outposts in Birmingham. The family included a son named Charles Rossman Rainey, who managed to get a little education. As a young traveling salesman, his route took him to Cullman, forty miles north of Birmingham. On one such visit he met one of old Ernst Hauk's daughters, whose name was Alberta Wilhelmina but who was known in the Cullman community simply as Tootsie.

Charles and Tootsie were married in the living room of the Hauk home in 1930. By then the Great Depression was taking hold with a vengeance, so the newlyweds lived with Tootsie's parents in their first years of marriage. They were still living in the Hauk home when, in 1934, Helen arrived; she was to be the only child of the union.

The Hauk family business prospered, selling ice in the summer and coal in the winter, so that little Helen felt no deprivation during the depression. But she saw grim hardship all about her, and especially in the stream of hungry hoboes who came to the back door of the rambling home at 612 First Avenue East. None was ever turned away, even if the fare was only a fried egg sandwich.

Uninterested in his wife's family business, Charles Rainey gravitated to state politics, aligning himself with the powerful reformist Democratic machine of Governor Bibb Graves. When Graves won a second term as governor in 1934, he asked Charles to become his executive secretary. But Tootsie, with Helen still an infant, adamantly refused to leave Cullman; Charles commuted the 130 miles from Cullman to Montgomery over unpaved country roads, which meant he could spend only weekends at home.

Too old for military service in the Second World War, Charles took a job with the Office of Price Administration. When the war ended and prosperity finally came to Cullman, Charles started a steel fabricating business in partnership with a colorful National Guard general named Walter J. "Crack" Hanna, but he continued his interest in politics. The Raineys lived only a few blocks away from the state's most promising young political figure, Big Jim Folsom, and Charles became active in Folsom's successful race for governor in 1946. Two years later Charles was elected delegate to the 1948 Democratic Convention, where he aligned solidly with the Alabama Democratic "loyalists" who refused to bolt the convention in protest over the liberal policies of Harry Truman.

Amid this heavy indoctrination in politics, Helen Hauk Rainey quietly pursued her education at Sacred Heart Academy, a Catholic school but also the only accredited high school in Cullman. Lutheran girls like Helen were exempt from the religion courses required of the Catholic girls, and there were no discernible religious tensions in Cullman in those postwar years. Helen graduated in 1951, a year ahead of the customary time, and that summer enrolled at the University of Alabama to study commerce, with the aim of going to law school when that career was still unusual for a woman.

Bob was nineteen and Helen seventeen when their courtship began, in what would have been a carefree Alabama summer but for one thing: On his weekend trips home to Birmingham, Bob observed that his mother, a quiet and imperturbable woman, suffered intense headaches. By the time he returned to Tuscaloosa for the fall semester, Bob already knew the terrible truth: His mother had a brain tumor. In the early fall she underwent surgery from which she never recovered, and on October 12, 1951, just twelve days short of her fifty-fourth birthday, Mae Smith Vance died.

Helen consoled Bob during this devastating time, and they grew closer. Their courtship consisted of the standard regimen of movies, aimless chat at the campus coffee shop, and sock-dances at the Delta Chi fraternity house. The only cloud on the horizon was the Korean War, and it was of special concern to Bob. Since he had gone through college on an ROTC scholarship, he would go immediately from law school into the military service.

On New Year's Eve of 1952, six months after he graduated and entered the Army as a second lieutenant in the quartermaster corps, Bob and Helen became engaged. The union very nearly ended before it began: Helen was almost killed in an automobile accident that kept her hospitalized, in painful traction, for a full semester. But she recovered, and on October 4, 1953, when Helen had just turned nineteen and Bob was twenty-one, they were married at the St. John's Evangelical and Reformed Church of Cullman, where the Hauks had worshiped in their Lutheran faith for three generations. Among the guests was Big Jim Folsom, who would shortly be elected to his second term as governor of Alabama.

The newlyweds honeymooned in New Orleans, then headed for Washington with all they owned packed in one car. The anxiety over the possibility of Bob's being sent to Korea, where the mortality rate for young lieutenants was frightfully high, abated somewhat when he was assigned to the Army Judge Advocate General's office. Bob and Helen established their first home in a small apartment not five minutes from the Pentagon. It was not the most challenging work for a bright young lawyer, so Bob enrolled in night classes at the prestigious George Washington University Law School to specialize in labor-law.

Bob Vance's military career might have played out uneventfully but for one thing: In 1954, Senator Joseph R. McCarthy was riding the crest of anti-communist hysteria, with all of Washington and much of the country cringing in terror of the veiled accusation, the subtle innuendo, the possibility of being hauled before a congressional committee or a loyalty board and asked the chilling question, "Are you now or have you ever been a member of the Communist Party?"

Then McCarthy overplayed his hand: He took on the United States Army, over so trivial a matter as the promotion of an obscure major in the dental corps who, by McCarthy's conspiratorial lights, had left-wing connections. In the summer of 1954 a tense and rapt nation watched the televised spectacle of the nation's top military officials testifying before a Senate committee presided over by the spidery, blue-jowled McCarthy. Suddenly the bookish officers of the Judge Advocate General's corps became the Army's front-line soldiers; among them was Bob Vance, who helped assemble the evidence and carry the brief cases to the Senate hearings. Bob was still young enough to be neither jaded nor cynical, and as an obscure junior officer he stood no risk of being crushed by the McCarthy juggernaut, so he could watch the events with detachment. From this experience, he learned that not all demagogues came from the South, nor was all demagoguery based on race. The stock-in-trade of the demagogue, regardless of region, is exploiting popular fears. Later, Bob Vance would ruefully remember the McCarthy experience when George Wallace, running for president, exploded in an interview in 1968: "I'm an Alabama Democrat, not one of those national Democrats. It's like the difference between communists and anti-communists."

The drama of the Army-McCarthy confrontation was so engrossing that Bob scarcely even noticed the Supreme Court decision of May 17, 1954, which would so profoundly affect his future—the case of *Brown v. Board of Education*, which nullified state laws requiring racial segregation in the schools.

And that summer there was another event in Alabama that would, in its own way, also alter the course of the state's politics. Bob and Helen happened to be back in their home state to attend the wedding of a friend on the weekend of June 18, 1954, when Albert L. Patterson, who had just been elected attorney general of Alabama, was assassinated by a gunman on the streets of Phenix City, a corrupt little border town whose main industry for years had been catering to the carnal desires of millions of soldiers who passed through the sprawling Georgia Army training base of Fort Benning. To Bob Vance, the murder was an appalling act of violence, but one which, he assumed, would be of little lasting consequence. As subsequent events would prove, this assumption was not accurate; the Patterson murder would resonate in Alabama politics for years to come.

With the McCarthy hearings at an end, and his work toward his master's degree from George Washington completed, Bob finagled an early discharge in order to return to Alabama late in 1954 to become law clerk to Justice James J. Mayfield Jr. of the Alabama Supreme Court. "Jimmy" Mayfield, who had just won election to the state high court at the age of forty-three, was a member of a distinguished Alabama legal family and was regarded as the court's most promising intellectual.

During their year in Montgomery, Bob and Helen Vance, still childless after two years of marriage, took a small apartment at Edgemont and Cleveland Avenue on the dividing line between Montgomery's segregated neighborhoods. Helen had no interest in the stuffy social swirl of the state capital, so she got a job as a secretary in the local office of the state's liberal Democratic senator, Lister Hill. Bob, meanwhile, spent his year of clerkship doing quiet, meticulous legal research in a musty cubbyhole of an office in the basement of the Alabama Supreme Court building, a grand edifice that stood across the street from the Dexter Avenue Baptist Church in downtown Montgomery. In his comings and goings Bob may well have encountered the church's new young minister, Martin Luther King Jr., but it is unlikely that they ever actually met. For a white man merely to shake hands with a black man in public would have been a grave affront to "the Southern Way of Life" in those times.

Bob recognized that Jimmy Mayfield was a troubled man. The justice faced a strong election challenge from a racist state senator who accused Mayfield of being "a Folsom liberal," which translated as "soft on segregation." There was an element of truth in the charge as Mayfield wrestled with the irreconcilable conflict between the Alabama Constitution, which mandated segregation, and the United States Constitution, which forbade it. But legal conflicts aside, Mayfield knew that it would be political suicide just to hint that he might support the United States Supreme Court's decision outlawing segregation in the schools. As the campaign began Mayfield tried to fight back, saying cryptically, "When I can no longer carry forth my oath of office to maintain segregation in Alabama, I shall resign." But mostly, he sought diligently simply to maintain a low profile in racially charged cases and to confine his work to matters of state law.

It could not have escaped Bob's attention that Mayfield was drinking heavily, and that there were also rumors that he was romantically involved with a young female politician of beauty and promise. Three months after Bob Vance completed his clerkship and returned to Birmingham, on April 3, 1956, Justice Mayfield, convinced that he would be defeated in the coming elections, shot himself.

"Bob loved Judge Mayfield," Helen Vance recalled, years later, "so he was terribly upset over his suicide. For months he felt a deep sense of guilt. He kept saying, 'If only I had known, if only I could have talked to him, I might have prevented it.'"

But life went on. Bob took a job as a trial lawyer with the U.S. Department of Labor in Birmingham. Two years later, at twenty-six, he entered private practice as a partner in the law firm of Hogan and Calloway, whose senior partner had married Bob Vance's sister, Martha.

Those were the days before Birmingham was glutted with lawyers, so Bob set a busy pace, handling an eclectic, workaday law practice from preparing wills to researching property titles to drawing up contracts. But he was especially gifted at the courtroom combat of litigation, and before he turned thirty he was regarded as one of the town's most promising young lawyers.

He was just getting his sea legs when personal factors intruded into his professional life: The marriage of Roscoe and Martha Vance Hogan broke up, and Bob felt that he could no longer continue as the law partner of a man who was divorced from his sister. In 1960, a new Birmingham law firm came into being under the name of Jenkins, Cole, Calloway, and Vance; Bob would remain a member of that firm, through all its permutations, until he went onto the federal bench nearly two decades later.

About this time he also gravitated to the political life of the city. Although his father and grandfather had been Republicans, Bob found no comfort in the let-them-eat-cake conservatism into which the party of

Lincoln was evolving in Alabama. In fact, he had already cast his political lot while he was in college by joining the Young Democrats, the most progressive wing of a party that was so faction-ridden, it amounted to little more than a mechanism for holding elections that claimed to meet the minimum standards of legality and decency. Besides, Helen Vance had come from a family that had been allied with progressive Democrats.

In 1958 Bob took his first plunge in the main currents of Alabama politics by sizing up the candidates for governor. Among these was George Corley Wallace, who was then an obscure state judge from Barbour County in the Black Belt of South Alabama. Wallace had been a key figure in the political machine of Governor Big Jim Folsom, once serving as Folsom's appointee on the Board of Trustees of Tuskegee Institute, the renowned black college founded in the latter part of the nineteenth century by Booker T. Washington. But by 1958 the political winds were blowing against the liberal-populist-racial moderate views of Folsom, so Wallace had broken with his mentor and was campaigning on his theatrical "defiance" of the federal government in early voting-rights cases.

In the early spring of 1958 Wallace came to Birmingham to speak to a small group of politically active young professionals. Among those in the audience was Bob Vance, whose chief interest was getting fairer representation for Alabama's large cities in a state legislature dominated by rural conservative segregationists. Wallace opposed legislative reform, so Vance gave his support to George Hawkins, a state senator from the grimy industrial city of Gadsden who was running as a labor-allied progressive in the Folsom tradition. But by this time Alabama was aflame with the politics of race, and the virtually all-white electorate was not about to choose a candidate tainted with "liberalism." Hawkins ran a poor fourth.

The winner was John Patterson, who rose from obscurity to become attorney general after his father's assassination four years earlier in Phenix City and quickly established himself as the standard-bearer for white supremacy. Wallace was the runner-up, and in the wake of his loss he told his supporters at a secret meeting that he had been "out-niggered, and I'll never be out-niggered again."

As the "Eisenhower 50s" turned into the "Kennedy 60s," with Patterson holding the governor's office and Bull Connor dominating the politics of Birmingham, and with Martin Luther King Jr. hitting full stride as the "drum major" of the civil rights revolution, Alabama was gripped by an ominous and pervasive sense of racial confrontation in which political moderates walked a perilous tight-wire. Nowhere was the tension greater than in Bob Vance's town of Birmingham, where the atmosphere was vividly captured by the *New York Times*'s eminent reporter, Harrison Salisbury, in a front-page story that carried the headline, "Fear and Hatred Grip Birmingham." Invoking his weighty credentials as a foreign correspondent, Salisbury likened the climate in Birmingham to that which he had observed in Hitler's Germany and Stalin's Russia. The article set off a firestorm of protest from the city's establishment and its dutiful voice, the *Birmingham News*. Salisbury was indicted under an obscure statute on forty-two counts of criminal libel. Assorted officials from the governor down to city councilmen also sued the *Times* for libel, and soon there was a virtual blackout of news from Alabama as out-of-state reporters shrank at the prospect of generating lawsuits that, tried before Alabama juries, could inflict financial ruin on even the most powerful newspapers.

In this grim atmosphere, Bob Vance gravitated to a group of young lawyers who recognized that the unyielding adherence to segregation would surely bring their city to grief. Moving cautiously, the group put up Tom King, a respected but low-profile young lawyer, as candidate for mayor. In the May 2 Democratic primary in 1961, King, to the surprise of many, led the cluttered field but did not attain the outright majority necessary to avoid a runoff election against Art Hanes, a former FBI agent running as the candidate of the Connor machine.

As the runoff campaign began, King called on Connor, naively hoping he might persuade the powerful police commissioner to remain neutral. Connor listened politely but noncommittally for a few minutes, and as the two men parted Connor remarked to King that an integrated group called the "Freedom Riders" had just left Washington by bus with the stated purpose of defying the segregation laws of the South but that his police would be "ready for them." As King left the City Hall, he heard someone calling from behind, "Mr. King, Mr. King." Turning with his politician's hand instinctively thrust forward, King found himself shaking hands with a large black man who would not let go of his grasp during a brief animated conversation. A few days later leaflets displaying a photograph of Tom King shaking hands with the black man saturated Birmingham's working-class neighborhoods. King complained bitterly that he had been set up by Connor, but the damage was done: King's initial lead evaporated, and Connor's puppet was elected mayor. The episode gave literal definition to the old metaphor for the inflammatory use of race in a political campaign, "laying the black hand on your opponent."

But if he suffered defeat in his first major political forays, Bob Vance found more gratification in the direction of his personal life. Helen, who had been consulting doctors about her inability to become pregnant and had even begun to think about adoption, suddenly found herself with child, and on April 10, 1961, she gave birth to a baby boy whom they named Robert Smith Vance Jr. In the meantime, Helen had come into a modest inheritance as the only child of a successful family, and Bob's income from his law practice was growing steadily, so the young couple had no difficulty in getting a sixty-three thousand dollar mortgage to purchase an elegant colonial-style home on a spacious wooded lot on Shook Hill Road in the upper-class suburb of Mountain Brook. Bob and Helen quickly melded into the affable ambience of Mountain Brook. Through Bob's friend and former law school classmate, Charles Morgan Jr., Bob and Helen joined St. Luke's Episcopal Church, thereby avoiding the necessity to choose between Helen's Lutheran church and Bob's Methodist.

Sprawling in a valley "over the mountain" to the south of Birmingham, Mountain Brook seemed a world apart from the sooty industrial metropolis. But Bob soon learned that Mountain Brook offered only nocturnal respite from the intensifying racial turmoil and violence that engulfed Birmingham and most of Alabama as the sixties began. In the spring of 1961, enraged mobs, acting in tacit concert with the police, brutally attacked the Freedom Riders in Birmingham, Anniston, and Montgomery. In 1962, George Wallace, running as a hardline segregationist, defeated Big Jim Folsom in the race for governor.

At a time when other "New South" governors were counseling moderation and compliance, Wallace, in his defiant inaugural address in January of 1963, vowed to maintain "segregation today, segregation tomorrow, segregation forever." By midsummer Martin Luther King Jr. took his civil-rights demonstrations to the streets of Birmingham, and Bull Connor responded by jailing King and turning fire hoses and police dogs on the demonstrators, most of whom were teenagers. In June Wallace fulfilled his campaign vow to "stand in the schoolhouse door" to block enrollment of two black students whom the federal courts had ordered the University of Alabama to admit; the students gained entry only after President Kennedy federalized the Alabama National Guard to carry out the court order. Birmingham's religious leaders offered no moral guidance during the growing crisis; indeed, one prestigious group of clerics, including the formidable Episcopal Bishop C. C. J. Carpenter, counseled Martin Luther King Jr. to show greater patience as he sat in a Birmingham jail.

The accumulating tension came to a soul-shattering climax just before the worship hour on Sunday, May 16, when a dynamite bomb exploded beneath Birmingham's Sixteenth Street Baptist Church, which had been a rallying point for the civil-rights marches of the summer. Beneath the rubble lay the broken bodies of four black girls, all between the ages of ten and fourteen, their white Sunday School frocks blackened by dynamite powder.

Bull Connor, reacting with astonishing insensitivity, told a White Citizens Council rally in Mobile that the bombing was "the worst thing that ever happened to Alabama," indicating that the wanton murder of four children would harm the segregationist cause. A more subdued, even defensive Governor Wallace denounced the bombing and offered a reward for the apprehension of the killers—even as his own clumsy police chief, Al Lingo, bungled the investigation into the crime to the point that no charges were brought against clearly identified suspects.

On the day after the bombing, Bob Vance's friend Chuck Morgan made an impassioned speech to the Young Men's Business Club, an organization whose membership included the town's most promising professionals, in which he declared that no matter who placed the bomb under the church, the entire community bore the guilt because of its racist past. When Morgan finished speaking, someone moved that the club open its membership to blacks; after an awkward silence, the motion died for want of a second. The Morgan speech received wide attention in the national press, but it also produced a fierce reaction in Birmingham that drove Chuck from his hometown to the refuge of more tolerant Atlanta.

Bob Vance made no speeches, but as a new father he confronted the grim reality that he lived in a community where children could be blown up in church in the name of racial values. By this time Helen had given birth to a second son, Charles, and Bob knew that he could not accept the prospect of his sons' growing up in a climate scarcely distinguishable from that of Nazi Germany. He recognized that the climate could be changed only if men like Wallace and Connor were dislodged. And he knew, further, that the challenge could not be mounted from Atlanta; the battle had to be fought in Alabama.

6 "A Lot of Get-Even Stuff"

Roy Moody entered the United States Army on September 11, 1953, six months after he had turned nineteen and six weeks after a cease-fire had been declared in the Korean War. With peace talks underway, Roy could confidently assume he would never see combat. Even so, he sought a service assignment that would assure that he not be placed "in a situation where you had to kill somebody or they would kill you." He gained a top-secret clearance and was assigned to the Army Security Agency at Fort Devens, near Boston, where he began his duties monitoring "enemy" radio traffic.

Roy saw his army hitch as an opportunity to begin college, so he looked into enrolling in Boston College. But, Roy would later maintain, his plan was "sabotaged" by his supervisor. He had to settle for taking a few night courses at the Fort Devens extension of Atlantic Union College, for which he received no credits. He reacted to the dispute with the vengeful superior by resolving to do no work without an explicit order.

After two years, he applied for flight training and on August 29, 1955, received a routine neuropsychiatric examination by Captain Robert Campbell, an Army doctor assigned to Fort Devens. In what appears to be a perfunctory evaluation, Roy told Campbell that his parents were "an easygoing compatible couple," that his home life was "a happy one in which all members of the family get along well together," and that he had many friends in high school. Campbell concluded that Roy appeared "mature and stable."

But nothing came of the application for flight school. When he grew weary of the tedious timeserving, Roy asked for an early release from his three-year commitment so that he could return home in time to enroll for the fall semester at Mercer University in Macon, Georgia. Despite his calculated goldbricking, he received the National Defense Service Medal and a Good Conduct Medal upon discharge on June 10, 1956.

On the day following his discharge, Roy enrolled as a premed student at Mercer and began commuting daily from Fort Valley, where he moved back into his parents' home. To help pay expenses for the 60-mile daily drive, he recruited other Mercer students who lived in Fort Valley. Among these was Georgeann Harris Seymour, who had graduated from Fort Valley High School three years ahead of Roy and who was taking courses toward a master's degree in order to further her career as a public school teacher. Georgeann found that her younger schoolmate had grown into a "polite, very agreeable, nice-looking young man who talked a lot about weekend waterskiing trips at his family's cabin on Lake Blackshear." Otherwise, he made no special impression on her.

But he was anything but ordinary to Joyce Law, the girl next door whom he had impregnated during his high school days. He quickly sought to reestablish the relationship, and refused to accept Joyce's insistence that she had a boyfriend now to whom she wished to be faithful. Joyce was still living at home, next door to the Moodys, so she could hardly avoid Roy. Once, she believes, he tried to run over her as she stood on the sidewalk in front of her house; Roy told her he was only playing. She thought the episode was Roy's reaction to her unwillingness to break up with her boyfriend, Loren Arnold.

Despite this disturbing episode, Roy proved to be so captivating to Joyce that they renewed the talk of marriage that had begun in high school. Joyce listened to Roy's endless personal laments. He was not doing well in school. From the outset he was on academic probation at

Mercer, and at least three times he missed a semester because of poor class performance—at a time when colleges in the Deep South were not rigorous in their demands on students largely drawn from region's poor public schools. Roy blamed his problems on his "insane" approach to college, working full time and taking too many courses in the hope of graduating in three years so that he could get into medical school. He also complained bitterly that Mercer would allow him to begin a semester with partial payment of tuition, then refuse to let him take his final examinations when he couldn't make up the difference.

Mercer was not indifferent to Roy's poor performance. In 1961 a chemistry professor noticed that Roy kept falling asleep in class; he referred Roy to Dr. J. R. S. Mays for psychological counseling. Three sessions with Dr. Mays appear to have dealt more with financial and work-schedule problems than with any attempt to discover a mental disorder; Roy stopped seeing the psychologist because he could not afford the fees.

He faced the reality that he could not graduate from Mercer in time to meet the age restrictions for enrolling in medical school. "He was devastated," Joyce Law remembers. "I busted out crying when he told me that he would never be a doctor."

Roy and Joyce would often go to their own secret place, which they called "the peach field"—an orchard just beyond the edge of Fort Valley's town limits. On one such trip in the fall of 1958 Roy began to make sexual overtures, and when Joyce resisted his advances, he raped her. After the attack Roy profusely apologized, saying he had been overcome by passion. In the weeks that followed, he kept asking Joyce if she were pregnant, and soon she discovered that she was indeed with child. Suddenly Roy grew cold on the prospect of marriage. Joyce married Loren Arnold "to give the child a name," and on June 20, 1959, she gave birth to a girl. Everyone in Fort Valley assumed that it was Loren's child, conceived before marriage.

During this time Roy grew close to his uncle, Bill Moody, who was only eleven years older and who shared Roy's inquiring mind. In the stultifying backwater of Fort Valley, Roy and Bill would often sit in the car outside Leroy Moody's home on languid summer evenings, smoking, listening to the radio, engaging in eclectic philosophical discussions. Bill Moody sensed that his nephew's superior intelligence was not accompanied by a willingness to exert the self-discipline necessary to achieve his goals in life.

About this time Roy joined the Air Force and was assigned to Warner Robins Air Force Base, 25 miles south of Macon, with the hope of continuing his studies at Mercer while training to be a pilot. But he soon resigned from the Air Force, claiming the service recruiters had misled him about the requirement of serving for five years if he accepted a commission. After leaving the Air Force, Roy moved to Macon, where he took a room in the older section of town and went through a succession of jobs. At various times he drove a delivery truck, worked in a tile factory, processed insurance claims, and recruited students for a trade school in Jacksonville, Florida. None of his jobs paid enough to keep him in school, and he began to live with a succession of women, always younger than he was, who largely supported him.

The first of these was Melba Price, whom Roy began dating in 1962. Melba soon became pregnant, and Roy moved in with her at her home at 936 Washington Avenue, on the deteriorating edges of downtown Macon. In February of 1963 Melba gave birth to a daughter, whom they named Michele.

During the five years they lived together, Roy often took Melba to meetings of the John Birch Society, an extremist anti-communist organization that found fertile soil in the South at a time when Martin Luther King Jr. was widely regarded as a "Communist agitator." The Birch Society, a kind of upscale version of the segregationist White Citizens Council that flourished in the 1950s, venerated Senator Joseph R. McCarthy, warned darkly of government conspiracies, and erected billboards urging the impeachment of Chief Justice Earl Warren. As early as 1959 Roy contacted the mother of John Birch, an American Army captain from Macon who stayed behind in China after World War II to become a Baptist missionary and who, according to the society lore, was killed in 1945 to become "the first victim of the war against Communism." During his involvement with the Birch Society, Roy bitterly complained to Melba that "the government is against us." And she saw other disturbing traits: He found excitement in secrecy and conspiracy, and he nursed a sense of victimization that engendered elaborate plans for retaliation.

Melba also learned that Roy was "obsessed with sex," and he demanded intercourse as often as seven times a day.

Roy began to write bad checks. For a while his father would cover the overdrafts, but in due course, Leroy Moody became disgusted with his son's profligate habits and put Roy on notice that no more checks would be redeemed. In April of 1965, Roy was convicted on three charges of "cheating and swindling," the legal name in Georgia for knowingly passing bad checks, and was sentenced to thirty days in jail followed by eleven months on probation.

About this time Roy began seeing Dr. Thomas M. Hall, a Macon psychiatrist to whom he had been referred by Vocational Rehabilitation, a state agency that assisted handicapped students through college. In an evaluation in January 1967, Dr. Hall wrote that Roy had given "a long and rather involved history of inadequate behavior, depressive reaction, unjust accusations which could have legally taken place like Mr. Moody described, but somehow seems unlikely to me." Roy bitterly told Hall that his father had "practically disowned me" for not taking over the garage in Fort Valley after Leroy suffered his heart attack when Roy was finishing high school. Roy told Dr. Hall that he no longer had any contact with his father, even though he remained "quite dependent on his mother."

Roy maintained that he had been depressed as a result of his "unjust" imprisonment on the bad-check charges. The psychiatrist concluded that Roy suffered "a form of ambulatory schizophrenia" that prevented self-sufficiency, and Vocational Rehabilitation authorized weekly psychiatric treatment by Hall.

Dr. Hall arranged for Roy to undergo a psychological evaluation by Dr. N. Archer Moore, a psychologist who reported that "one can make a case for sociopathic personality on the basis of his behavioral history." Moore also found that Roy showed "sexual ambivalence" and "obsessive-compulsive mechanisms," but he found nothing to prevent Roy from pursuing any vocation he chose, including his current obsession, the law.

Over two years Hall saw Roy seventy-eight times, all the while writing letters seeking to get Roy reinstated at Mercer with financial assistance from Vocational Rehabilitation. Hall found Roy to be "very persuasive— the type of individual who could sell you the Brooklyn Bridge." But eventually Dr. Hall diagnosed Roy as having a "character disorder," which he described as "inadequate personality with sociopathic adjustment to life." Hall found that Roy was motivated by "vengeful feelings" that would lead him to do things even though he knew they were wrong and could get him in trouble. "There was a lot of get-even stuff in what he always felt," Dr. Hall would say later. "He just obeys his own rules." Hall saw in Roy a tendency to file a lawsuit "for nearly everything" and, worse, a tendency to think in terms of violent solutions to his problems. Hall also observed that Roy was "constantly embroiled with women one way or another."

Despite problems with school and with the law, Roy started a business, the Associated Writers Guild of America, with one thousand dollars that Melba Price scraped together. At the outset the Writers Guild amounted to no more than a scheme in which he advertised in the out-of-state newspapers for proofreaders, then placed those who responded—and paid a twenty-five dollar fee—on a job list. No one ever got a job through Roy's enterprise. Roy didn't advertise in Georgia newspapers, he told Melba, because he wanted to avoid prosecution.

Melba found that Roy was given to braggadocio, including boasts of such fanciful criminal exploits as trying to steal an airplane when he was a teenager and outrunning a deputy sheriff in 1959 while hauling moonshine. During their five years together, Roy struck Melba on numerous occasions, once breaking her nose, and he had a number of female sexual partners during that period. Melba began to resent having to support Roy on her meager income, and one day after they had lived together for a year, she called Roy "a no-good son of a bitch." He reacted to this by becoming violent for a moment, but then he fell to his knees weeping and said, "That's all I've heard all my life."

Still, Roy yearned for the respectability of a profession. Having long since abandoned his hope of becoming a doctor, in 1966 he enrolled in the John Marshall Law School, an unaccredited but well-regarded night law school in Atlanta, seventy-five miles north of Macon. He took law courses for two years but did not graduate, nor did he ever take the Georgia bar examination.

Roy's dependence on Melba Price did not deter him from seeing other women. He continued to see Joyce Law on his frequent trips to Fort Valley. "He said he wanted to see his baby, but it was really me,"

Joyce related, years later. "He even talked again about our getting married." Joyce believes that at some time during the 1960s Roy may have lived in Atlanta, where he claimed to have driven a bread truck while suffering from amnesia that he believed resulted from a head injury in an automobile accident in the 1950s. Roy also told Joyce that he had suicidal thoughts and felt inadequate and cowardly because he was not capable of killing himself. One night someone mysteriously pumped a type of gas into the open window of the room where Joyce was sleeping with her infant daughter, and Joyce said the coughing she heard from the attacker almost certainly came from Roy. She later learned that Roy had concocted the gas, with the help of his old science teacher, Fess Stephens, from the toxic kernels of peach seeds. Joyce also believes that Roy once shot a gun into her house. "He blamed me for all his failures," she said.

During this time Roy also became involved with a nurse named Agnus Dean, who, according to Melba Price, bore Roy's third child, a boy. Joyce Law also remembers seeing Agnus Dean stalking her home in Fort Valley, with the red-haired tot in hand. About this time Roy began dating Hazel Strickland, whom he may have met at a dry-cleaning establishment where she worked as a counter clerk, even though Hazel, at eighteen, was thirteen years younger than Roy. When Hazel became pregnant early in 1969, Melba kicked him out.

When she first learned that she was pregnant, Hazel pleaded with Roy to help arrange for an abortion, which at that time was illegal in Georgia. But Roy wanted the child, and, sensing that Hazel was determined to terminate the pregnancy if he did not act, he called on an old friend, William Scarpati, whom he had met in 1956 as a fellow student at Mercer, where the two experimented with dynamite, nitroglycerin, and other explosives in the school's chemistry laboratory. Roy asked Scarpati to pose as a doctor and attempt to talk Hazel out of the abortion. When she was not dissuaded, Scarpati gave Hazel an injection of alcohol in saline which, he told her, would induce an abortion within several weeks. By the time she discovered the deception, it was too late to get an abortion.

Roy then moved in with Hazel, who, on November 9, 1969, gave birth to a son, whom they named Mark Bryan Moody.

Hazel got a better-paying job at Ralston-Purina, a growing business that dealt in agricultural supplies, and she and Roy moved into a modest house at 1360 Dublin Avenue in a white working-class section of Macon. There, Roy had a range of jobs on commission that produced little income, and he continued to operate the Writers Guild, although Hazel did most of the secretarial work at nights and on weekends.

In the spring of 1970 Roy's father, Leroy Moody, suffered a second and fatal heart attack. After that, on Sundays Roy and Hazel would take their son, Mark, and drive to Fort Valley to have lunch with Roy's widowed mother, Mozelle, who had taken a job in the purchasing department of the Peach County Hospital. But as Hazel grew weary of working day and night to support Roy, they began to quarrel and Hazel told Roy he had to pay his own bills. Early in 1972 he gave a check for $106, the final payment on a used car he had purchased from a man named Tom Downing in Atlanta. When the check bounced, Downing repossessed Roy's car, and would not surrender the vehicle even when Roy offered to make the check good. For several weeks Roy had to use Hazel's car, which meant getting up early, bundling up Mark, taking Hazel to work, delivering Mark to Hazel's mother for day care, then repeating the routine at the end of the day.

Roy complained bitterly of the injustice he had suffered at the hands of Tom Downing, and as spring arrived Hazel observed that he was spending an increasing amount of time in his office in the spare bedroom, which was declared off-limits to Hazel.

On Sunday, May 7, 1972, Hazel declared that she did not want to go to Fort Valley that day, so Roy took Mark, who was then three, for the weekly visit to Mozelle Moody. During the afternoon Roy received an urgent call from a neighbor telling him that there had been an explosion in his house and that Hazel had been taken to the hospital.

On the following day the *Macon Telegraph* carried a brief story about the episode under the headline, "Mysterious Blast Hurts Local Lady." Hazel had been seriously injured, suffering the loss of a finger as well as serious injuries to her right thigh. As soon as she had recovered sufficiently to talk, she told the investigators that she had surreptitiously gone into Roy's forbidden office and was opening a package when the explosion occurred.

While Hazel was in the hospital, Lloyd Erwin, a forensic chemist with the federal Bureau of Alcohol, Tobacco, and Firearms (ATF) in Atlanta, worked on the case for two weeks to reconstruct the exploded package to a remarkable degree. It had, Erwin found, contained a pipe bomb with two small square steel plates held to each end by threaded rods about four or five inches long. The pipe was packed with double-based smokeless gunpowder, which had been ignited by an ordinary flashlight bulb from which the glass had been removed in order to expose the filament, which grew white-hot when wired to a D cell battery. Erwin further discovered that the package contained a cryptic note composed of cutout letters from magazines pasted to form a threatening message, fragments of which read: "warning . . . of dynamite or get 43 stic . . . you will see friends and relatives go first . . . $65,000." The package was addressed to Tom Downing at his used car lot at 46 West Peachtree Street in Atlanta, and bore a label that read: "To: Tom. From: Mary."

Based on this information, on May 24 Roy was charged with manufacture and possession of an unregistered explosive and placed in jail in lieu of bond, which was set at fifty thousand dollars.

Unable to post the bail, Roy stayed in jail as he awaited his trial. During this time, between court-ordered psychiatric tests, Roy kept up a steady stream of correspondence, mostly one-way, with judges, lawyers, and others connected with the case.

He also received two cryptic, threatening pieces of mail. One of these, printed in block letters, unsigned, and postmarked from Houston, Texas, on June 15, 1972, read:

> YOU WOULD HAVE PLENTY MONEY IF YOU HAD DONE WHAT WE
> SAID   NOW ALL YOU HAVE IS A MESSED UP WIFE   YOU SCREW US
> WE SCREWED YOU   HOPE THE BITCH DIES

Ten days later Roy received a similar unsigned letter, this one postmarked in Georgia on June 26, 1972:

> HEARD ABOUT YOUR ARREST CHICKEN   YOU KNOW WE CAN
> GET YOU OR YOUR FAMILY NEXT WEEK OR NEXT YEAR   KEEP QUITE
> AND LIVE

Nearly twenty years later, Roy would acknowledge that a fellow jail inmate who was released while Roy was still in custody made harassing telephone calls to Hazel that summer, but he strenuously claimed that the man acted entirely on his own, maintaining that frightening Hazel would have made it more difficult for him to obtain pretrial release. He never admitted orchestrating the threatening letters he received, even though, curiously, he refused to turn over the mysterious messages to the FBI, because, he claimed, he was being framed by the federal authorities.

As the bomb-making trial neared in the fall term of court, Roy's distraught mother, Mozelle Moody, scraped together a few thousand dollars in an attempt to hire a lawyer named Manley Brown, a former federal prosecutor, but they were unable to reach an agreement. When Mozelle's effort fell through, with the trial at hand, Judge Wilbur D. Owens Jr., who had just been appointed by President Nixon to the federal bench in Macon, hurriedly declared Roy to be indigent and appointed Tommy Mann, a well-known Macon lawyer, to represent him. It was a curious choice, because there had been bad blood between Roy and Tommy going as far back as 1956, when Roy had accused Tommy of mishandling an insurance appraisal on Roy's car, which had been damaged in an accident. Moreover, Tommy had prosecuted Roy in 1965 on the bad-check charges even though, according to Roy, the overdrafts had been made good.

Mann got virtually no time to prepare a defense. Under Judge Owens's orders, Moody had already submitted to psychiatric evaluations in the federal penitentiary in Atlanta. The examination was conducted by Dr. J. A. Mascort, an Atlanta forensic psychiatrist, who found that Roy suffered "no mental disorder" and was competent to stand trial. Subsequently Roy underwent a second evaluation by Dr. Nelms B. Boone, a psychologist who found that Roy scored an above-average 123 on an IQ test. Dr. Boone concluded that Roy was "a somewhat egocentric individual" who tended to blame others for his misfortune and to express hostility "in indirect ways." Nevertheless, he said that Roy suffered from "no mental illness."

Still a third examination was conducted that summer by Dr. Joseph F. Alderete, another Atlanta psychiatrist, who concluded that Roy "knows what he is accused of despite the fact that he refuses to account for his movements." Dr. Alderete likewise found Roy competent to stand trial.

With an insanity defense seemingly foreclosed, and with Judge Owens out of town, Tommy Mann filed some routine motions that went to the desk of the amiable and highly respected veteran district judge of the region, W. A. "Gus" Bootle, who by then had taken senior status but was still hearing cases occasionally to help keep up with the growing workload of the court. When Owens returned, he asked Bootle to take over Moody's trial, which began in the middle of October of 1972.

At first Mann was irritated at the way Moody intruded into the trial process, almost as if he were co-counsel rather than the defendant. But Mann also recognized that Moody had a quick mind and came up with good questions for cross-examination. Indeed, Moody's scientific aptitude enabled Mann to trip up an FBI expert witness on the tensile strength of the wires in the bomb that had injured Hazel.

But with deep misgivings on Mann's part, Roy insisted on taking the witness stand on his own behalf. After all, the government's circumstantial evidence was overwhelming that the bomb had been manufactured in the Moody home on Dublin Avenue, so Roy was exposing himself to great peril in submitting to cross-examination. Once on the stand he immediately ran into difficulties in giving coherent answers to the prosecutor's questions. Sensing that he was in trouble, Roy testified that the bomb had been brought to his house by a casual acquaintance he had known in law school. When Judge Bootle demanded to know the name of this individual, Roy blurted out the name, "Gene Wallace." The gist of Roy's story was that he had met Gene Wallace, who would have been eighteen or nineteen, when they were fellow students at John Marshall Law School. Roy said that he related his problems with Tom Downing to Gene Wallace, who then concocted a scheme to "frighten" Downing as reprisal for repossessing Roy's car. After this conversation, Roy went on, Gene Wallace delivered a package to the Moody home in Macon.

Although the name would become central in Roy's future life, at that time no living person had ever heard of Gene Wallace, not even Tommy Mann. No such name could be found in the files of the John Marshall Law School. Later, it would be discovered that the same page of the *Macon News* that carried the account of the bombing, under the quaint headline "Mysterious Blast Hurts Local Lady," also carried prominently a story about how strongly Alabama Governor George Wallace was running in the 1972 presidential election. By that time Roy Moody had already begun to express admiration for the Alabama governor.

Roy evidently succeeded in planting a "reasonable doubt" in the minds of the jurors with the Gene Wallace story, because on October 19, after a four-day trial, the jury acquitted Roy of manufacturing the bomb. But he was found guilty of possession of an unregistered explosive. A week later, after reviewing the standard presentence report, Judge Wilbur Owens, who had resumed jurisdiction of the case, passed sentence of five years imprisonment, and on October 27, 1972, a manacled Walter Leroy Moody Jr. was delivered to the U.S. Federal Penitentiary in Atlanta.

7 Shaking Savannah

As an idealistic, even naive, youngster, Robbie Robinson was determined to do his small part to make integration work. One day not long after he enrolled at Savannah High School in 1964, the young black student found himself during a class break engaged in idle chitchat with a group of white students, putting forth his best effort to make the conversation seem natural and comfortable. Addressing no one in particular but well aware that Robbie could hear him, a white boy who came from one of Savannah's most prominent families regaled his gathered classmates with a "riddle."

"What kind of a 'gar' is it that smokes and stinks?" he asked.

"A *cig*-GAR," replied another white boy who obviously was a party to the mirth.

"And what kind of 'gar' doesn't smoke but still stinks?" asked the first white boy.

"A *nig*-GAR!" exclaimed the second white boy as the group roared with laughter. In a Herculean effort at amity, Robbie forced a smile. In those days Robbie endured such taunts with as much grace as he could muster in public, but when he got home he would unburden his heart to his sister

Barbara, his sense of doleful resignation that he was obliged to suffer such casual cruelty "all the time." For a boy who was by nature a happy and optimistic person, Robbie's senior year at Savannah High School thus did not prove to be a blissful and carefree experience. By the time he graduated, in the upper half of his class, in the summer of 1965, he was quite happy simply to be ignored, as most of his white classmates cheerfully did whenever they happened to encounter him.

Experiences like that of the cigar "joke" led Robbie to conclude, at an age when most high school boys were sipping sodas and flirting with girls, that blacks would never gain rights and respect in a meaningful way unless they were willing to confront the established order. To his mother's considerable apprehension, young Robbie began to take part in the civil rights demonstrations that were then sweeping the South; after all, Edna Robinson knew too well, you could get arrested, even killed, doing that sort of thing in those days. But Robbie persevered, and once he even got his picture in the *Savannah Morning News* when, one balmy summer day, he joined several of his teenage friends to plunge into the Atlantic Ocean from a beach that by law and custom had always been reserved for whites. The demonstration created an instant sensation, and some white hooligans poured heavy black motor oil into the water to drive the intruding youngsters away. The photograph in the newspaper depicted the gangling, swimming trunks-clad Robbie with two friends, all glancing anxiously over their shoulders at a group of jeering white teenagers. The police briefly took Robbie and his friends into "protective custody," and the incident ended without any charges being lodged; no doubt the authorities by that time were weary of setting up test cases of the segregation laws.

Robert and Edna Robinson took it as a given that their son would go to college. The Robinsons were, by that time, about as close as one could find to black gentry in Georgia. Their daughter Ruth had already graduated from Paine College at Augusta, a private college of high reputation in the black community, and their other daughter Barbara was by then enrolled at Paine as well. And from his earliest age, Robbie had demonstrated notable talent in the pursuit of learning.

But Robbie's experience at Savannah High had given more than he wanted of an educational environment at that moment in his young life.

When Edna approached him about his plans, he replied, nonchalantly, "I don't think I want to go to college. I want to go into the Air Force."

This greatly upset Edna Robinson, who wept at what she perceived to be her son's forfeiting a promising future for the anonymous security of military service. She even consulted the family minister, the Reverend James Hightower of the St. Paul C.M.E. Church, who listened patiently, then gently advised Edna, "Let him go. A hitch in the Air Force won't hurt him, and it probably will give him a little maturity." This advice turned out to be prescient. Robbie spent his three years in the Air Force as a military policeman, and for a time even considered making a career in law enforcement. But when he finished his service obligation in the summer of 1968, Robbie returned home, a good deal more corpulent, his family noticed, than he had been as a slender high school student; the Air Force seemed to have given Robbie a ravenous, insatiable appetite— and a weight problem that would bedevil him for the rest of his life. At least, to his mother's great delight, he had settled down now and was ready to go to college.

By that time virtually every formerly all-white southern college, public or private, had a sprinkling of black students on campus, and no doubt Robbie easily could have gained admission to one of these institutions, including the well-regarded Armstrong College, which lay on the western edge of Savannah. But the traditionally black colleges still had a powerful appeal, chiefly in meeting the special needs of the black youngsters who grew up in a sparsely populated region like the "pineywoods" of southeastern Georgia, where public education was still uniformly inferior. Even though he had no need for remedial instruction, Robbie chose to enroll in Savannah State, formerly Georgia Industrial College, which both his mother and father had attended.

Savannah State was something of a world unto itself for its two thousand students and faculty of 150, a quiet place that lay just a stone's throw from the salt water marshes that separated Savannah from the Atlantic Ocean. Robbie enrolled in the business college to study accounting, and he quickly became a popular figure on the campus. Among his friends was Clarence Martin, a gifted student who came to Savannah State from the moribund inland Georgia hamlet of Baxley. Clarence intended to go to law school after he received his undergraduate degree, and he influenced Robbie Robinson to consider the same course.

By this time Robbie had also met his first love. When he was still in high school, he would often go up for a weekend visit to his sister, Barbara, at Paine College in Augusta, sixty miles up the Savannah River from the Atlantic coast. On one of these visits, Barbara introduced Robbie to a pretty classmate from Augusta named Vivian Cook. After Robbie went into the Air Force, he continued to see Vivian over the next several years, and as Robbie neared the completion of his studies at Savannah State, he and Vivian were married.

Robbie graduated, magna cum laude, from Savannah State in 1971, completing the college regimen in three years instead of the usual four. His friend Clarence Martin had gotten a scholarship at one of the nation's top law schools, Notre Dame, and Robbie received a coveted scholarship established by the progressive Atlanta mayor of the 1970s, Ivan Allen, to attend the University of Georgia's Lumpkin Law School at Athens, some two hundred miles upstate from Savannah. In 1971 Robbie became one of the first three black students to enroll at the state university law school, which over two centuries had been the fount of so much of Georgia's political leadership.

For a bright student like Robbie Robinson, law school was a bracing intellectual challenge, especially in the areas of constitutional law and civil rights, which had loomed so large in the life of a young black boy growing up at a time when the social order was being shaken to its very foundations. But legal studies could also be a tedious regimen of mastering the arcane complexities of wills, property, contracts, and the Uniform Commercial Code if one were to hope to pass the state bar examination.

Even though classes were integrated, the social mores of the university still generally reflected the accepted patterns of the Old South. But this mattered little to Robbie because he was married now and only wanted to get on with his career as a practicing lawyer. Vivian was teaching school at the town of North Augusta, just over the South Carolina border, and they lived in a small community called Washington, about halfway between Augusta and Athens, so that both could commute. Vivian did involve herself to a modest degree in the law students' wives' club, and Robbie pursued a few extracurricular activities also. But for the most part during those three years Robbie kept a low profile and applied himself diligently to the task of learning the law. At about the time he received his law degree, in the summer of 1974, Vivian gave birth to their first child, a girl whom they named Edwina, after Robbie's middle name.

While he was preparing to take the bar examination, Robbie got a job in Atlanta with Georgia Legal Services, the agency that struggled to supply the bare essentials that the state offered to meet the legal needs of those who could not afford to hire lawyers. And Robbie soon discovered that an enormous gap existed between the needs of the poor and the resources of the agency to supply those services. After he passed the bar in the fall of 1974, Robbie remained as a staff lawyer for Legal Services, then headed by a lawyer named Steve Gottlieb. Gottlieb found Robbie's work to be competent but neither inspired nor imaginative, probably because Robbie had developed an interest in pursuing a political career.

After two years learning to navigate the legal waters, Robbie was ready to go into private practice, and he wanted to go back to his hometown of Savannah. He arranged for interviews with the new law firm of Hill, Jones, and Farrington, which by then had become established as a significant presence in Southeast Georgia by pursuing civil rights cases and generally catering to the legal needs of the long-neglected communities. In the fall of 1976 Robbie was interviewed for a position with the firm by Fletcher Napoleon Farrington Jr.

As the only white partner in the firm, Fletcher Farrington was an improbable figure for the role in which he found himself. He was born November 5, 1941, into a prominent and well-to-do family of landowners in the Black Belt of Alabama. His father, Fletcher Farrington Sr., was a politician of some note who was allied with the Farm Bureau, a powerful institution on the conservative side of Alabama politics. At first the younger Fletcher planned to follow in the family tradition; he enrolled in Auburn University to study agricultural management. But by the time he got his degree in 1964, he was captivated by the heady drama of the civil rights movement, so he went across the state to the University of Alabama to get a law degree. His first job after graduating from law school in 1967 was as a trial lawyer with the Civil Rights Division of the United States Department of Justice in Washington.

There, Fletcher was at once recognized as a gifted young advocate, and he became the government's lead counsel in a number of important cases in the South, including some before the redoubtable Judge Frank Muir Scarlett, who was then nearing the end of two decades of mercurial service as the federal district judge for southeastern Georgia. By that time, Scarlett had ceased to be the champion of the Old Order that he had momentarily become when, in the Stell case in 1963, he had held categorically that *integration* of schools was unconstitutional. In fact, by 1968 Scarlett had become quite erratic in his decisions in the growing number of racial discrimination cases that were clogging the federal courts throughout the South.

Among Scarlett's last cases was one that involved an episode in Johnson County, Georgia. Even though that happened to be the home county of a black youngster named Herschel Walker, who would subsequently win the Heisman Trophy for his dazzling football prowess at the University of Georgia, Johnson County in the late 1960s was still under the domination of an old-fashioned country sheriff named Attaway. At a time when virtually the entire South had embraced integration at least outwardly, if superficially, Sheriff Attaway still burdened black citizens of the county with casual daily humiliation, in such ways as not allowing them to drink from the "white only" water fountains in the courthouse. The Justice Department had brought a civil action against the sheriff, and the case wound up in Scarlett's court with Fletcher Farrington as the lead lawyer for the government.

There was little doubt as to the outcome of the case, even in Judge Scarlett's court. But on the day his ruling was to be handed down, Fletcher Farrington was approached urgently by Washington Larsen, a lawyer from nearby Dublin who had represented the sheriff and who had just had a conference with Judge Scarlett.

"Fletcher," said Larsen, who was pale with apprehension, "you've got to help me talk some sense into the judge."

"What's happened?" Fletcher asked.

"I've just talked to him, and he's found the sheriff innocent on all counts except on the water fountains. He's going to give him five years on probation on that count."

Amused but also concerned, Fletcher asked for an expedited conference with Judge Scarlett to make it clear that the government would prefer simply an injunction prohibiting future discrimination. He spared the old man a lecture in the most elementary principle of law: Defendants are not given sentences in civil cases.

Not long after that, Scarlett retired and returned to his more tranquil hometown of Brunswick, where he died in a nursing home at the age of eighty in 1971.

The Johnson County case was among the last Fletcher Farrington handled for the government. Soon after that episode, he quietly left the Justice Department, recognizing that Richard Nixon's rigidly conservative attorney general, John Mitchell, had no place for serious civil rights advocates among his minions.

During his travels for the Justice Department young Fletcher had gotten to know Bobby Hill, a black lawyer from Savannah. Bobby Hill's childhood had been an embittering experience. He had grown up in Athens, the home of the state university, but in that time of rigid segregation about the closest Bobby Hill could get to the University of Georgia was the kitchen of the Varsity, which was the most popular student sandwich shop of the college town. Bobby got an after-school job at the Varsity, and was assigned to chop onions, endlessly, for the hamburgers and hot dogs that the University of Georgia students wolfed down between classes.

Despite this inauspicious beginning, by wit and grit, Bobby Hill made it through law school and joined the staff of the NAACP Legal Defense Fund, which was then engaged in the final massive assault on the southern fortress of segregation. In this role Bobby came to the attention of Eugene Gadsden, a black lawyer in Savannah who, with the passage of the Voting Rights Act of 1965, became a formidable political power in Southeastern Georgia. Gadsden quickly identified Bobby's incipient talent for politics and coaxed him to make Savannah his base. In no time at all Bobby lived up to Gadsden's expectations. In the late 1960s he became among the first blacks to be elected to the Georgia House of Representatives, where, with a certain impish flair, he created great turmoil in that staid, conservative institution.

Despite their vastly dissimilar backgrounds, Bobby Hill and Fletcher Farrington liked one another, so they organized the new law firm in Savannah under the name of Hill, Jones, and Farrington—Jones being the partner who ran the Atlanta office.

Those were boom times for that kind of law firm. For all the dismay he was causing to the conservative rural legislators, Bobby Hill was considered to be among the most colorful and effective new young politicians on the scene. He possessed a politician's fine instinct for playing the media, especially television, and he had an excellent sense of pragmatic timing: He was among the first black politicians in Georgia—indeed, the nation—to throw his support to a rising political star in Georgia, State Senator Jimmy Carter of Plains. In 1968, Bobby represented an obscure defendant named Lucious Jackson Jr., a twenty-one-year-old black man who was sentenced to death in Savannah for raping a white woman. Jackson, along with William Henry Furman, another Savannah black man sentenced to die for murder, appealed the death sentence to the United States Supreme Court. The result was the controversial decision known as *Furman v. Georgia,* in which, for a time at least, capital punishment throughout the United States was suspended on the grounds that, at least as it was then administered, it was a form of "cruel and unusual punishment" that was proscribed by the Eighth Amendment of the Constitution.

Such talent and acuity made Bobby enormously successful as the firm's "rainmaker"—the irreverent name attached to high-profile partners who inveigle business to their firm—and Fletcher Farrington was equally successful as a courtroom advocate. It was a perfect combination.

On the day of the interview in 1976, Fletcher's first impressions of Robbie Robinson were mixed. Steve Gottlieb, the head of Legal Services in Atlanta, had indicated that while Robbie was a hard worker, he didn't really seem to have great interest in the workaday routines of drafting briefs and meeting court deadlines. But Fletcher was impressed with Robbie's winsome personality, so he took him on as one of the firm's three summer interns. One of the others was Clarence Martin, Robbie's old friend from Savannah State College who had by this time graduated from Notre Dame Law School. The third was William T. Coleman III, the son of a distinguished black lawyer from Philadelphia who was then serving as secretary of transportation under President Gerald Ford. Young Coleman's roommate at Yale Law School had been a bright and promising student from Arkansas named Bill Clinton. Another intern, a year later, would be a serious, quietly ambitious youngster named Clarence

Thomas, who had come from Savannah's impoverished environs but had made it through Yale Law School and who would, in 1991, become the second black man ever to be appointed as a justice of the United States Supreme Court.

Robbie performed well enough during his internship that in October of 1976 he became an associate in the firm, which by then was known as Hill, Jones, Farrington, and Friday—the last-named being Jack Friday, a young white lawyer who had developed a keen interest in civil rights while growing up in Selma, Alabama. Occasionally, when Robbie had to go to the state capital on firm business, he would use the facilities of the Atlanta branch office, and on such trips he became casually acquainted with a young lawyer there named Michael Ford who, a few years later, would become an attorney for Walter Leroy Moody Jr.

But by this time the firm was showing critical fractures. Bobby Hill had developed serious personal problems, including a cocaine habit. In Atlanta, Jones and Ford had left to establish their own practices. Jack Friday was showing emotional problems that would eventually lead to his institutionalization. As this turmoil intensified, the firm grew slipshod in financial record keeping, and began to get menacing notices from the Internal Revenue Service as well. Aware that in a legal partnership each partner is liable for the misdeeds of any other, Fletcher Farrington faced the stark reality that he might even stand to lose the large family land holdings that he had inherited in Alabama. In the wake of these accumulating troubles the firm broke up in July of 1977. Some members regrouped, but Fletcher Farrington and Robbie Robinson each went their separate ways in what is called, in the legal business, "solo practice."

Robbie rented an office at 1216 Abercorn, on Savannah's most celebrated street, just a mile or so from the historic central city with its stately colonial public squares. Robbie's quarters were in the middle of a block-long row of six pink-and-white plank townhouses with quaint arched doorways, typical of the buildings in what was called "the Victorian District." The connected houses had been converted into offices for professional people who advertised their businesses in decorous gold-and-black lettering on their front windows. Robbie's window read simply, "Abercorn Legal Associates, P.A.," the sign having been put there by a previous tenant and left unchanged by Robbie. It was a quiet block, lined with ancient oaks interspersed with little beds of palmettos and dwarf azaleas.

Maintaining a solo practice was a good deal more expensive, in terms of renting an office and advertising in the Yellow Pages, than it had been when he shared those expenses with a number of other lawyers. But even though they had split up, Bobby Hill continued to serve as Robbie's mentor, helping him get his first Cadillac, which was considered a traveling advertisement for lawyers who served poor communities. With a twinkle in his eye, Bobby also advised his young friend to get a diamond ring, which served not only as a flashy piece of jewelry but could become useful for posting as security for bail if Robbie should get arrested on some trumped-up charge. So the outlook was good that with a little diligence Robbie would build a practice that would give him the comfortable perquisites of life befitting a middle-class lawyer in Georgia's third largest city. And indeed that might have been the case had it not been for two events that took place at about that time.

In 1980 Vivian Robinson gave birth to her second child, a girl whom they named Tiffany, but soon after that Robbie and Vivian separated. The separation meant that Robbie had to pay child support while at the same time establishing his own living arrangements. Like any successful, single lawyer in his thirties, Robbie began to "play the field" among Savannah's eligible ladies, and during this time he became the father of what is discreetly called, in the black community, "an out-of-marriage child." He also was briefly remarried, to a woman named Eluisha, but she left him "cleaned out" while he was in the hospital recovering from two detached retinas.

Also about this time Robbie gravitated into city politics and began to devote more time to that interest than to his law practice. For two years he cut his teeth in the appointive position of chairman of the Savannah Transportation Authority. Then, in 1982, surrounded by doting family members as he stood on the steps of the Tremont Baptist Temple on West Broad Street just around the corner from the house on Duffy Street where he had been born thirty-four years earlier, Robbie Robinson announced his candidacy for the District Five seat on the Savannah City Council.

At this time staid old Savannah was undergoing a quiet but profoundly significant transition in its local politics. In the wake of the passage by Congress of the Voting Rights Act of 1965, the city's hitherto disfranchised black citizens began to elect their own leaders to influential positions, and most of these, like Bobby Hill, tended to be militant and abrasive in putting forth their demands to rectify the baneful legacy of two centuries of slavery and segregation. But by the start of the 1980s, with Ronald Reagan about to take over the White House, Savannah's conservative establishment followed other southern cities in confronting black political activism with a subtle strategy of divide-and-conquer. By this time it was clear that in certain districts with heavy black majorities, no white candidate could ever hope to defeat a black candidate. So the new strategy was to quietly, almost secretively, put forward an amenable—and perhaps malleable—black candidate to the liking of the establishment. The belief was that this candidate would get all of a district's white minority vote and would need only a small portion of the black vote in order to prevail. This method was advanced as "consensus politics."

By this time even the black community was exhausted from the protracted confrontation that had delineated the two decades of the civil rights revolution, so the strategy often proved to be effective. Against this background, Clarence Martin, who had become Robbie's closest confidant, tried to talk his friend out of running. After all, Clarence reasoned, the white power brokers had already settled on their candidate for the Fifth District council seat: A black banker named Joe Bell, who was certain to have more campaign money than any opponent could ever hope to match. This money no doubt would enable Bell to gain the support of virtually all of the 30 percent of the white voters in the district, plus enough of the 70 percent of black voters in order to win the seat.

But in this time of transition, Robbie Robinson did not fit neatly into any mold. As a warm, outgoing man, he did not come across as a menacing figure, the way Bobby Hill was perceived by many whites. Yet neither was Robbie viewed in the black community as an "Uncle Tom" who would kowtow to white political interests. During the campaign Bell spent forty-four thousand dollars, while Robbie struggled along on sixteen hundred dollars. But if Bell, the establishment's chosen candidate, had a thick wallet, Robbie had thicker shoe soles, and he wore them out several times over pounding the hot streets of a district that covered half of the central city and contained striking contrasts in opulence and indigence. As a campaigner the bland banker was no match for the cheery young advocate who had grown up in the heart of the district and could greet voters as former childhood playmates. Robbie won the race decisively.

Robbie had no grand agenda when he took his seat as one of three blacks on the nine-member City Council, but he set about at once making a reputation as something of the district ombudsman, addressing acute needs that had been ignored for decades. Among these was "the Lincoln Street Playground," the scornful description in the community for a heavily traveled city thoroughfare on which a number of children had been killed while playing, for want of a safe park. Robbie established a good working relationship with the town's moderately progressive mayor, John Rousakis, and pushed through ordinances setting lower speed limits and posting signs while pressing for better neighborhood recreational facilities.

And he did not abandon his roots in favor of the cocktail-party circuit. He became a familiar figure on the streets of the district, immediately recognizable by his broad grin, his ample frame, and his thick-lensed glasses. He had performed so well that when he ran for reelection in the spring of 1986, this time against Clarence "Teddy" Williams, who was described in the local press as "a 27-year-old self-employed Gospel singer," Robbie carried 82 percent of the vote. With this solid mandate in his pocket, he intensified his efforts on behalf of "the community," which, on the streets of Savannah's Fifth District, meant the black community. He pushed for "minority set-aside programs" to assure that black contractors got a larger share of city construction projects—a proposal that was coolly received and never passed by the white-majority council. He accused the council majority of conducting the real business of the city "behind closed doors," and secured a new meeting schedule to include some evening sessions for the greater convenience of citizens who worked. He sponsored legislation to name a street for Martin Luther King Jr.

The problem was, the demands of his political career meant that Robbie had to spend an inordinate amount of time on constituent service—time that had to be carved out of a paying law practice. A little city business gravitated in his direction, and he continued to handle discrimination suits for the NAACP. He took whatever personal-injury cases he could get on a contingency-fee basis, and he was appointed by judges to defend indigent criminals at the low hourly rate the state paid in such cases. But the bread-and-butter of successful law firms—business clients—did not come Robbie's way, and the city council salary of $6,400 a year barely even paid for tickets to the obligatory community testimonial dinners he attended. As a consequence, while his political profile grew, his law practice ebbed, and it became increasingly difficult to meet his personal needs, especially when, in 1988, he married for the third time.

8 Accommodation in Alabama

On the cool, sun-drenched morning of Saturday, February 18, 1961, a remarkable event took place in the capital city of Montgomery, Alabama. For a full year, thousands of the leading men of the town had worn beards, and their ladies had swished about in hoopskirts over crinoline petticoats. This odd activity reached the pinnacle of melodrama on that winter morning when a vast throng gathered in Alabama's capital city for a solemn, almost reverential, centennial celebration of the founding of the Confederacy. The *Montgomery Advertiser* published a special edition on the day that the town's most prominent lawyer, T. B. Hill, strode slowly and somberly up the steps of the gleaming white capitol on "Goat Hill" at the top of Dexter Avenue to reenact the inauguration of Jefferson Davis as the first president of the new Confederate States of America. With Montgomery's foremost citizens watching in subdued silence, Hill took the inaugural oath as he stood on a great bronze star embedded in the white marble landing to mark the place where Davis stood when the historic event first took place a century before.

The celebration was not without its moments of comic relief. During that year, the *Montgomery Advertiser*'s popular columnist, Stuart X. Stephenson, wrote a scorching commentary about the alarming number of "bearded hippies" who were now strutting the campus of the state's largest college, Auburn University; a few days after the column appeared, Stephenson wrote a contrite "clarification" that what he had seen were not hippies after all but rather, members of the Kappa Alpha fraternity who were growing beards in preparation for their annual Old South Ball. On yet another occasion, when Attorney General Robert F. Kennedy visited Montgomery in a vain effort to work out a peaceful transition to an integrated society, members of the Montgomery Chapter of the United Daughters of the Confederacy placed a huge bank of flowers over the Jefferson Davis Star in order to prevent the spot from being defiled by Kennedy's Yankee feet.

But if the Montgomery celebration was comic opera on a grand scale, the grim reality was that by 1961 much of the Deep South seemed once more on the verge of secession and civil war. White southerners at every opportunity responded to the rising black demand for equality by electing governors who were committed to holding the line on segregation at all costs, and each new confrontation produced a greater level of violence. The aborted integration of the University of Alabama in 1956 and the marginally successful integration of Central High School in Little Rock a year later had proved to be so traumatic that five years would pass before another serious attempt at desegregation was made.

But the assault on segregated public schools resumed in the summer of 1962 at a bastion of the Old South, the University of Mississippi at Oxford. After Governor Ross Barnett broke his pledge to maintain order at "Ole Miss," violence flared and President Kennedy was obliged to send in federal troops once more in order to carry out the federal court's order to enroll James Meredith at the state university. In a touch of great irony, the soldiers had to fight off an assault by a ragtag band of unregenerate segregationists led by retired Major General Edwin A. Walker— the very general who had commanded the 101st Airborne Division when it was sent to Little Rock five years earlier to enforce a similar court order to integrate Central High School.

Meredith was enrolled, but the backlash was swift and ferocious, especially in neighboring Alabama, where the state's veteran United States senator, Lister Hill, was up for reelection. Despite his record as a reliable defender of segregation during his twenty-five years as a senator, Hill nonetheless became identified in the public mind as a "Kennedy liberal Democrat integrationist." In what ordinarily would have been a walkaway election of a Democratic incumbent, Hill suddenly found himself, in the wake of the "Ole Miss" integration, confronting a serious challenge by a conservative Democrat-turned-Republican, James D. Martin of Gadsden. George Wallace, who by then had emerged as the dominant political figure of the state, did not lift a finger to help his embattled fellow Democrat, and Hill barely eked out a victory for what would be his final term in the U.S. Senate.

Hill's near-defeat shocked Bob and Helen Vance. Helen's family had long supported the Hill faction in Alabama politics, and she herself had worked on the senator's staff just seven years earlier in Montgomery. And Bob, since his years as a congressional page, had been keenly aware of the enormous influence Hill exerted in Washington. Hill's brush with defeat proved to be but a harbinger of the coming decimation of the Democratic congressional leadership in Washington.

No event more underscored the rancor of the time than one notable reaction to the assassination of President Kennedy in 1963. Upon hearing the news of the president's death, John P. Kohn, a patrician Montgomery lawyer, danced a little jig on Dexter Avenue, not four blocks down the street from the church where Martin Luther King Jr. had preached his sermons on the efficacy of nonviolence.

But the reaction of Roy Mayhall, the state Democratic chairman, was far different. A flinty old state judge from the poverty-ridden coal-mining country of northeastern Alabama, Mayhall was an indomitable Democratic Party loyalist whose allegiance to the Baptist Church and the New Deal seemed at times to be in debatable order. He had managed to cling to the party chairmanship amid the political tumult of 1962, chiefly by maintaining a low profile during the ascendancy of George Wallace. When a newspaper reporter perfunctorily called Mayhall for a comment on the Kennedy assassination, the old judge let his despair and anger pour out: This, he declared, is what you get when you practice "the politics of hate."

Mayhall did not name Wallace, but there was little doubt that he aimed the rhetorical shot at the governor. And nothing infuriated Wallace more than to be accused, however obliquely, of fomenting violence through his diatribes against "the Washington liberals."

In Birmingham, Clifford Fulford, the most influential behind-the-scenes operative of the state's Democratic Party, read Mayhall's remark in the newspapers with dismay. He knew at once that his old friend and ally would never again be elected chairman of the Democratic Party of Alabama; the only hope of avoiding a total takeover of the party machinery by Wallace zealots was to groom a stealth candidate—a loyalist who was not already identified as a hated "liberal."

Fulford had already come to know Bob Vance through St. Luke's Episcopal Church, where both families worshiped. A dozen years older than Bob, Clifford was a cheerful, outgoing man whose quiet manner belied the depth of his commitment to the political party that had guided the nation through the depression in the thirties and had crushed fascism in the forties. Fulford was born into the relative privilege of a banking family in the small south Alabama town of Georgiana in 1919, but when he was ten, his father was killed in an automobile accident. Confronting the depression with no wherewithal to support her small children, Zettie Fulford took the pittance of insurance money she received after her husband's death and enrolled in Alabama College, a "normal school" whose main mission was to prepare Alabama girls for careers in teaching. After she graduated Zettie taught in small communities like Athens and Alabaster and eventually gravitated to Birmingham. Low as her pay was, Zettie managed to save enough to enable Clifford to enroll at the University of Alabama. There, Clifford made Phi Beta Kappa, then went on to law school, finishing just in time to enter military service during the Second World War. After the war Clifford returned to Birmingham, where he moved back and forth between government service and private practice, and he drifted into politics.

At that time the Democratic Party of Alabama was entering a period of bitter division. With the unifying influence of the Second World War now behind, white Southerners returned to their ancient obsession, the position of the black man, and a great tension spread across the region with the approach of the 1948 presidential election. In Alabama, the "Loyalists"—those who favored alliance with the national Democratic Party and its policies—struggled for control of the party with the "States' Righters"—conservatives who, in any other context, would have been

Republicans. Convinced that only vigorous government action could address the intractable problems of ignorance, poverty, and ill-health that still gripped his state, Clifford Fulford aligned himself with the Loyalists, who were then led by Judge Mayhall.

Now, in the wake of the Mayhall volley at Wallace, Fulford privately concluded that the man to succeed Roy Mayhall was Bob Vance. As the violent year of 1963 drew to a close, he approached Bob, quietly and gingerly, to urge him to run for state party chairman. With the election still more than two years away, Bob told Clifford he would think about it. He had other heavy matters on his mind. His father, Harrell Vance, died on December 15 of that year, his weak heart finally exhausted. And personal considerations aside, the early 1960s were not the best of times for Loyalist Democrats in Alabama. The March on Washington in 1963 may have emboldened President Kennedy to seek a federal law to protect civil rights, but it also produced a rancorous backlash in Alabama. Governor Wallace may have lost his confrontation with the federal government over school integration, but still he emerged stronger than ever as an opponent of "federal tyranny." And violence was spreading unchecked, to the point that even the *Birmingham News,* ever sensitive to "northern insults," had to concede that Harrison Salisbury's article in the *New York Times* in 1960 about the climate of fear and hatred in Birmingham now deserved more respectful consideration.

But the agile Wallace proved to be remarkably adroit in distancing himself from the violence that flared all about him. In 1964, Wallace subtly shifted his main focus from supporting rigid segregation to opposition to the Civil Rights Bill of 1964, which held a high place on President Lyndon Johnson's political agenda. In his new role as the apostle of backlash, Wallace began to speak across the nation, and the passion he stirred among blue-collar audiences of the northern industrial regions astonished and alarmed the established political powers, especially those in the Democratic Party, which had always relied on rank-and-file labor as a vital component of the coalition that sustained Franklin D. Roosevelt through four elections, and Harry Truman and Jack Kennedy through two more.

Wallace, for whom campaigning was something akin to an addiction, began to speak not just in his narrow role as an opponent of the Civil Rights Bill but as a presidential candidate. A watershed event occurred in the late spring of 1964 when Wallace was invited to appear on NBC-TV's Sunday interview program, *Meet the Press*. Apprehensive that he might be made to look like a ignorant bumpkin by the sophisticated Washington reporters, Wallace undertook a crash course on the full range of issues that a presidential candidate was expected to discuss. This preparation included extensive briefings on foreign policy issues by his friend Grover C. Hall Jr., the influential editor of the *Montgomery Advertiser*. Hall quietly, almost secretively, briefed Wallace for the interview session.

But Wallace proved to be a nimble adversary, fully capable of fielding tough questions and obfuscating difficult issues. When the program ended, a beaming Wallace called Hall with sneering confidence, "Hell, Hall, they didn't want to know about *foreign policy*. All they wanted to know about was *niggers,* and I'm the world's leading expert on *that*."

Wallace used the *Meet the Press* appearance as a departure-point to mount a direct challenge to President Johnson for the Democratic nomination, and his swift surge of popularity among blue-collar voters set off political alarm bells across the country when he garnered more than a third of the vote in the Democratic presidential primaries in Wisconsin, Maryland, and Indiana.

In Wallace's home state of Alabama, meanwhile, there was no necessity for him to run, thanks to the intricate process the state utilized in voting for president. All Wallace needed to do in Alabama was to replicate the Dixiecrat maneuver—the very strategy he had opposed in 1948. Unlike most states, Alabama did not list the names of candidates for president on its ballot; only candidates for presidential electors were listed. Moreover, the electors were chosen before the national party even held its convention to nominate its presidential candidate. So, in the fevered climate of the spring of 1964, Alabamians chose a slate of Democratic presidential electors who were pledged to no particular candidate but who were, to the man, opposed to the one who was certain to be the party's nominee for president, Lyndon B. Johnson.

Meanwhile, the Republicans, operating in the more orderly fashion of nomination by state convention, put up a slate of presidential electors solidly committed to Barry Goldwater, the staunch conservative from Arizona. As summer approached, Goldwater, maintaining that he was acting out of political principle and not hidden segregationist tendencies, announced he would vote against Lyndon Johnson's pending civil rights bill. Since the Wallace challenge rested entirely on opposition to that legislation, Goldwater's step had the effect of cutting Wallace off at the knees. In a dramatic second appearance on *Meet the Press* on the eve of the Republican National Convention, Wallace withdrew from the race with a tacit endorsement of Goldwater.

By this time, it was too late under state law for the Loyalist Democrats to piece together an ad hoc mechanism to get a slate of electors pledged to President Johnson on the ballot. This meant that with the state Democratic Party dragooned by Wallace's neo-Dixiecrats, it was impossible for any Alabamian—black or white, liberal or conservative—to cast a vote for the reelection of the sitting president of the United States; their Hobson's choice was to vote for Goldwater—or no one. Even some of the unpledged electors running on the Democratic ticket left no doubt that they supported Goldwater.

If political events were measured on a Richter scale, what occurred in Alabama in November 1964 would go into the record books as a nine. In that watershed election Alabama shed forever its status as a Solid-South Democratic state: Goldwater carried the state so overwhelmingly that in the process he swept out of office five of the state's eight Democratic congressmen, as the voters blithely threw to the wind an immense reserve of seniority and influence in Washington.

Bob Vance was by no means a doctrinaire liberal, but he was appalled that for the second time in sixteen years Alabamians had been denied their fundamental right to vote for president of the United States—all in the name of racial values. To him, the state was behaving with the same reckless abandon that had led to secession and its ensuing grief a century earlier.

During this grim period, Bob once more was obliged to deal with a heavy personal loss. On December 4, 1964, almost exactly a year after his father's death, Bob's elder brother, Harrell T. Vance Jr., died of a heart attack. In his grief, Bob could not have failed to notice a marked predisposition of the men in the Vance family toward coronary disease.

Despite the ascendancy of Wallace, there were growing elements among white citizens of Alabama who were determined not to repeat, even symbolically, the monumental folly of secession, civil war, defeat, and reconstruction. Those who saw the need for fundamental change in the southern way of life fell into three distinct and disparate groups.

The first group consisted of those who saw the Jim Crow system as basically a moral cancer. Even in antebellum times the South had a small but intrepid band of hardy souls—writers, ministers, and intellectuals—who were willing to brave scorn and even peril to life and limb in order to assert the principle that if God created Man in his own image, then it was a form of blasphemy for mortals to diminish that creation through such pseudoscientific concepts as race, religion, and nationality. In Alabama in 1963, this group was so small that its meetings were held only in a few church basements or in the parlors of such people as Clifford and Virginia Durr of Montgomery, who came from families of gentry but who embraced the political morality of the New Deal.

The second group was made up of those Alabamians who saw segregation primarily as a legal issue. Their core belief was that fundamental social change was often difficult and disagreeable, but that in a nation of laws, Supreme Court decisions had to be accepted as the law of the land. But this group had been decimated by the apostles of massive resistance in the 1950s when it was politically dangerous for a candidate for office even to speak of "law and order," which at that fevered time was perceived as a code word for advocating compliance with decisions of the Supreme Court and civil rights acts of Congress.

The third group consisted of the Alabama business leadership, which increasingly recognized segregation not only as an artificial economic burden but also as a destabilizing influence that diverted capital investment in the state. Birmingham's captains of commerce watched with helpless dismay as other cities of the South adjusted to the new reality with varying degrees of resiliency; after all, they asked themselves, what businessman in his right mind would not choose to locate a new regional facility in progressive, stable Atlanta over reactionary, violence-prone Birmingham?

These diverse elements were brought together in common purpose by the riotous summer of 1963, especially the bombing of the Sixteenth Street Baptist Church.

And it was a fortuitous confluence for Bob Vance, who shared the values of all three groups. His old college friend David Vann, who was also now practicing law in Birmingham, had for more than a year been engaged in quiet preparations to force a change in the city's form of government, which then consisted of three powerful commissioners with Bull Connor as the first among equals. In 1962 Vann had met quietly with a group of community leaders in the office of Sidney Smyer, a real estate executive and power in the chamber of commerce, to enlist the support of the business community, which hitherto had accepted Connor's racism in the name of "stability." Vann proposed to invoke a seldom-used Alabama law that empowered voters, through petition, to put up public issues for referendum. It would require only seven thousand signatures, Vann explained, to force a referendum on replacing the antiquated three-member commission with an elected mayor and a large city legislative council with citizen-members chosen from twenty or more districts. If the change were approved, Vann went on, Connor and his cronies could be turned out of office well before their terms expired in 1965.

Smyer, by this time alarmed over the frightful price Birmingham was paying for the intractable stand of the city commissioners on segregation, eagerly embraced Vann's proposal. And the timing was perfect: Bull Connor had just been soundly thrashed in a race for governor of Alabama in which he had advocated bitter-end resistance to federal mandates to integrate public institutions. Vann offered to demonstrate the appeal of his proposal through a test-run drive to collect five hundred signatures on his petitions over the next three days. He surpassed his goal by a substantial number, and the campaign to rid Birmingham of its racist past was underway.

Vann swiftly assembled a group of young professionals, among them Bob Vance, into an ad hoc organization called "Citizens for Progress." The title was innocuous but its purpose was to take Vann's ambitious plan for restructuring city government to the voters. As a resident of an "over-the-mountain" suburb, Bob could not even vote in the Birmingham city elections, so he maintained a discreetly low profile in the Citizens for Progress as he worked to gather the necessary number of signatures on petitions to call for a special election on the Vann reform plan.

The tension-weary citizens of Birmingham responded with an outpouring of enthusiasm for change, and in no time the Citizens for Progress met the requirements to force a special election. But Bull Connor's puppet mayor, Art Hanes, steadfastly refused to call the election that he knew could result in his removal from office. Acting in the face of Hanes's bald defiance of state law, the county's probate judge, Paul Meeks, called the election for November 6, 1962. In leading the campaign against the change, Connor diligently stirred racial bugaboos, but for once the old black magic didn't work. On election day, Birmingham voted for a new form of government by a decisive margin.

Still, that was only half the battle: The men and women who would fill the new offices had to be elected, including a mayor, in a special election called for in the spring of 1963. The Citizens for Progress rallied around Albert Boutwell, a pragmatic but colorless conservative who was well known in the community as a former state senator and lieutenant governor of the state. Bull Connor, despite his repudiation in the change-of-government election the previous fall, plunged into the mayor's race carrying the banner of reaction. But the momentum for change was too great: Boutwell soundly defeated Connor, and although the lame-duck Connor would remain in office to use his fire hoses and police dogs on the demonstrators during the summer of 1963, Birmingham was on its way to making a genuine effort toward racial accommodation for the first time in its brief but turbulent history.

While the Birmingham election emboldened the moderates, the fact remained that George Wallace dominated the state with a power unrivaled since the days when Huey Long ruled Louisiana as a virtual dictator. Prohibited by law from running for a second consecutive term, Wallace, in 1965, mounted a campaign to amend the state Constitution to allow him to continue as governor. Although sentiment in the state overwhelmingly favored the change, a sturdy band of fourteen state senators killed the Wallace plan by filibuster. Wallace then quickly shifted strategy, and put his wife in the governor's race. In the May primary election of 1966, Lurleen Wallace, a pleasant little woman with no experience in and even a distaste for politics, polled a clear majority over all nine of her opponents, who included two former governors. In a stunning testimony to Wallace's power, all fourteen of the senators who had scuttled the succession plan either chose not to run for reelection or were defeated, and one committed suicide.

Amid the rich theatrics of the governor's race that year, Bob Vance quietly made his own debut in elective politics. In the early spring of

1966 Bob and Max Pope, another Birmingham attorney and stalwart Democratic loyalist, drove to the home of Judge Roy Mayhall in Jasper to file the necessary papers and pay the fees for Bob to qualify as a candidate for the seventy-two-member Alabama Democratic Executive Committee from the Birmingham district.

There was no lower-profile office than that of Democratic committeeman, yet Bob was well aware that he confronted a significant problem. At his meeting with Judge Mayhall, Bob got some bad news: Two other candidates had qualified to run for the seat Bob was seeking, which meant that if none of the three received an outright majority in the first primary, the two top vote-getters would face one another in a run-off election four weeks later. Bob was running, almost surreptitiously, as the designated candidate of the Loyalist wing of the party. This stealthy strategy to retain control of the party relied heavily on the knowledge that Loyalist candidates would receive the solid support of Birmingham's black voters, whose strength was now greatly enhanced by the Voting Rights Act of 1965. Under this strategy, it was essential for the Loyalist candidate to win in the first primary, because if he did not, the other candidate would "play the race card" in the runoff by trumpeting the fact that the Loyalist had received the black vote in the first round of voting.

As Bob and Max Pope drove back to Birmingham from the late-night meeting with Judge Mayhall, they were apprehensive. They knew Bob would get a black vote sufficient to gain a spot in the runoff, but they also knew that Bob's runoff opponent would be a States' Rights candidate who would surely have Wallace's backing and would spare no effort to "lay the black hand" on Bob, to use the crude vernacular of race-politics in Alabama. But gloomy though the outlook may have been, Bob was emphatic about one thing. "If I win this seat," he told Max Pope, "I'm going to be the chairman."

Two days later, Bob received a telephone call from Roy Mayhall, who was almost chortling with glee. "I just thought you'd like to know," the old judge related, "that the Wallace candidate gave me a bad check for his qualifying fee. I've disqualified him, so you now have just one opponent."

On May 7—the same day that Wallace's wife was elected governor—Bob Vance was elected, thanks largely to the overwhelming black vote he received, to a seat on the state Democratic Executive Committee. From that day forward he would maintain but for a $25 check that bounced, his political career would have died a-borning.

Once the new committee was in place, the first delicate order of business was to replace Roy Mayhall as chairman with as much dignity as possible. The old war horse did not want to go; he thought he could weather the storm. But his dear friend Clifford Fulford spoke to him bluntly: Wallace had just demonstrated near-total dominance of state politics through the election of his wife, and if Mayhall insisted on seeking reelection as chairman, Wallace was sure to exert his political muscle and the Loyalists would lose the chairmanship. The only way to save the day, Fulford explained, was for Mayhall to step aside in favor of Bob Vance.

The strategy worked: In the summer of 1966, Bob Vance won the chairmanship by a comfortable margin over the States' Rights faction's candidate, Arnold DeBrow of Mobile.

Bob's first exercise in official responsibility was a challenging task that was filled with the rich irony that so often characterized Southern politics: He had to help complete the process of electing Mrs. Wallace as governor of Alabama. At that point she had only won the Democratic primary, and she was being challenged by the popular Republican Congressman James D. Martin, the man who had nearly unseated Senator Lister Hill four years earlier. Bob did not shrink from his task. Among his first appearances on behalf of Mrs. Wallace was a speech to the Alabama Democratic Conference, which was the black faction of the state's party. Speaking to the organization at its Montgomery meeting, Bob stated his message as obliquely as possible: All Democrats in Alabama, black and white alike, must support the party ticket from top to bottom. This support meant voting "under the rooster"—that is, for all candidates who were running under the Democratic Party's official ballot-emblem, which depicted a crowing rooster and included the hated words, "White Supremacy for the Right." Straight-ticket voting, Bob warned, was essential to meet the growing Republican threat to local Democratic officeholders across the state. When he finished, Joe Louis Reed, the black faction's chairman, rose and ruefully said, "We understand what you are telling us, Mr. Chairman, and you can count on us."

For the blacks, about to flex their muscle for the first time since the passage of the Voting Rights Act of 1965 that Wallace had strenuously fought, it was a galling choice. But Bob Vance had made the bitter necessity somewhat more palatable by secretly promising the black leaders that his first order of business would be to remove "White Supremacy" from the party's emblem. On this basis, given the choice between Wallace's wife and Goldwater-Republican Martin, Alabama black citizens swallowed their pride and dutifully trekked to the polls in large numbers in the fall of 1966 and voted for the puppet candidate of the man who, just four years earlier, had promised to maintain "segregation forever." Backed by this incongruous coalition of blacks, white Loyalist Democrats, States' Righters, and white supremacists, Mrs. Wallace overwhelmingly defeated the doctrinaire conservative, Jim Martin.

Shortly after the election, Bob Vance called a special meeting of the state committee to fulfill his secret promise. After a spirited floor-fight that received only ephemeral attention from the press, the committee removed the words "White Supremacy" from the Democratic emblem.

The next challenge confronting Vance was, however, so complex and perilous that Machiavelli himself might have smiled with approval. There was little question that in electing Mrs. Wallace as governor in 1966 Alabamians were also giving George Wallace a resounding mandate to run for president again in 1968, and by this time the outlines of his planned campaign were becoming clear. Wallace knew perfectly well that there was no realistic hope that he could win the national Democratic Party's nomination for president, so he set out on the daunting task of organizing his vast reservoir of grass-roots support into a new third political force that he called the American Independent Party.

But Wallace also knew that there would be no need for him to organize a third party in Alabama, where he exercised near-total control over the politics of the state. All that was necessary to nail down his home state was to run a slate of presidential electors pledged to Wallace *as regular Democrats* in the party primary in the spring of 1968.

This prospect presented Bob Vance with his worst nightmare: He would be chairman of a state party that was committed not to the national party's candidate but rather to a neo-Dixiecrat who was trying to defeat the national party's candidate. Moreover, the elector finesse would place Vance, as the state party chairman, in the untenable position of having to support Wallace for president—thus placing Bob in somewhat the same bind that black voters found themselves when he urged them to support Mrs. Wallace for governor. And, even worse, it could mean that for the third time in twenty years, Alabama voters would be deprived of their right to vote for the Democratic candidate for president of the United States.

But this time the loyalist Democrats were prepared. Even though, strictly speaking, it amounted to political double-dealing, Bob Vance quietly began to work with his old friend and ally David Vann to organize an ad hoc party called the Alabama Independent Democratic Party, the sole purpose of which was to assure that Alabamians at least had the option to vote for the nominees of the national party. Of critical importance, Joe Louis Reed, the head of the black faction of state Democrats, weighed in with his formidable support for the Vann party.

There was also the problem of putting together an acceptable delegation from Alabama to the National Democratic Convention in Chicago in the summer of 1968. At that time most convention delegates in Alabama were chosen by popular election, which made it virtually certain that a heavily pro-Wallace slate of delegates would be chosen. It would be a kamikaze delegation, for certain, with the Alabama delegates going to the convention knowing they would be supporting Wallace in the November presidential election against the national party's standard-bearer. The factotums of the National Democratic Party knew this also, and in order to cut off the Wallace delegates at the pass, they demanded that all delegates who entered the convention hall take a public pledge to support the national party's nominees.

Knowing that the pro-Wallace delegates would never accept such a loyalty oath, David Vann's group, the Alabama Independent Democratic Party, sent a standby delegation to Chicago ready to take the state's allotted seats. But then the situation grew even more complicated when a splinter-group of Alabama black Democrats led by a dentist from Huntsville named John Cashin organized a *fourth* party, which was called the National Democratic Party of Alabama, and sent its own delegation to Chicago claiming to be the only authentic Democrats. Thus the national convention officials were confronted with three delegations claiming legitimacy: The pro-Wallace delegation that had been popularly elected, the Alabama Independent Democratic Party that had been put together by David Vann with Bob Vance's tacit support, and the more radical National Democratic Party of Alabama that had been organized by John Cashin with substantial assistance from Bob Vance's former liberal ally, Charles Morgan Jr.

Giving the Wallace delegates the boot was the easy part; the more delicate choice lay between the ad hoc coalition of Vann, Vance and Reed, and John Cashin's almost entirely black delegation. Cashin argued essentially that the Vann-Vance-Reed coalition was just a collection of pragmatic whites who knew that Wallace-style segregation would no longer wash and had made alliance with pragmatic blacks who were little more than "Uncle Toms." After an exercise in deft footwork accompanied by effusive rhetorical bows to the Cashin group, the national party seated the Vann-Vance-Reed delegation. For the first time in history, Alabama had an integrated delegation on the floor of the National Democratic Convention.

As head of the state party, Bob was satisfied that he had achieved all that he could at the Chicago convention. But on his way home, he made a personal confession—with fiendish glee—to his wife, Helen. Helen had gone to the convention as an alternate delegate—a standby, as it were, if she were needed in some unexpected lurch. Bob had preceded her to Chicago but had made flight reservations for her to join him. When Helen boarded the plane in Birmingham, she discovered that her ticket had been, for some unknown reason, upgraded to first class, from the economy class that the frugal Vances always traveled.

Settling into their economy-class seats for the return flight to Birmingham, Bob said, "I guess you noticed that you came up first class."

"Yes," Helen replied. "But why was the ticket changed?"

"Well," said Bob with a wry smile, "I found out that Bull Connor and his convention delegates were on that same flight, and they were traveling economy class. I was afraid if you and Bull bumped into one another, there might be an explosion."

"That," said Helen with a mischievous smile, "would have been a distinct possibility."

Despite the bewildering machinations in Chicago, no one was under any illusion that the man just nominated as the party's candidate for president, Vice President Hubert H. Humphrey, had the remotest chance of carrying Alabama. So in the November presidential election in 1968, Alabama voters had four choices: They could vote for Wallace, whose electors were running on the regular state Democratic ticket; they could vote for Richard Nixon, the Republican candidate; they could vote for Hubert Humphrey by way of the Alabama Independent Democratic Party; or they could vote for Humphrey by way of John Cashin's National Democratic Party of Alabama. In effect, Humphrey was not only running against Nixon and Wallace but running against *himself* as well. When the votes were counted, to no one's surprise Wallace's electors carried the state overwhelmingly with 691,425 votes. Hubert Humphrey drew just 196,579 running on the AIDP and the NDPA tickets combined. Richard Nixon, who won the presidency that year, came in a humiliating third in Alabama with just 146,923 votes.

Theoretically, as party chairman, Bob was bound to vote in that election for the Wallace electors; it is virtually certain, however, that in the secrecy of the voting booth, he cast his personal vote for the Humphrey-committed electors on David Vann's ticket.

Bob Vance thus had negotiated the white-water rapids of politics in 1968 with his raft afloat, but still greater peril lay ahead. His greatest fear was that the Alabama Democratic Party's history of opposing the national party's nominees would be tolerated for only so long before the national party moved to strip the state's Democratic congressional delegation, including two Democratic senators, of their party status, which would mean the loss of the seniority privilege in a system where seniority is the coin of the political realm. This danger intensified in 1968 when the wives of Alabama's two senatorial candidates ran as Wallace-pledged presidential electors—indeed, cast their electoral votes for Wallace—while their husbands would seek to claim the privileges that go with being national Democrats. But because of Vance's extraordinary efforts to assure that Humphrey would be on the state ticket, the party chose not to punish Alabama's Washington representatives.

Wallace's wife, Lurleen Wallace, died of cancer in May 1968 during the third year of her governorship. Wallace only briefly suspended his frenetic campaign for president after his wife's death before hitting the campaign trail again. In November he carried five Deep South states with a total of forty-six electoral votes—not enough to achieve his hope of deadlocking the election in a repeat of the Hayes-Tilden affair of the previous century. Now Wallace found himself out of power in Alabama for the first time in six years, and the political moderates of Alabama saw this period of transition as a chance to rid the state once and for all of the governmental neglect that characterized the 1960s while Wallace pursued the presidency with obsessive zeal.

Lurleen Wallace had been succeeded by the state's young lieutenant governor, Albert P. Brewer, who had been a classmate of Bob Vance at the University of Alabama Law School in the early 1950s. Wallace led Brewer to believe that he would not attempt to regain the governor's office in 1970. Bob Vance warned Brewer not to trust Wallace to keep his word—a warning that proved to be prescient when Wallace entered the race to unseat Brewer. In the first primary in May of 1970 Brewer actually led Wallace in a crowded field of candidates. But in the process of leading, Brewer had received the black vote, and in the runoff election Wallace used this against Brewer with a vengeance. Newspapers across the state carried full-page advertisements featuring ominous, black-bordered messages warning Alabamians that "the black block vote" was about to take over the state government. The strategy worked: Wallace came from behind to defeat Brewer by the narrow margin of thirty thousand votes out of more than a million cast in one of the highest turnouts in the state's history.

Bob Vance knew full well that Wallace's return to power meant that the governor would once more seek the presidency in 1972. In face of this certainty, the next item on Bob's agenda for the reform of the Alabama Democratic Party became all the more urgent in order to prevent Wallace from kidnapping the state party as he had done in 1968. With Wallace momentarily weakened by his narrow victory over Brewer, Bob seized the opportunity to discontinue the popular election of presidential electors. It was, after all, this pernicious practice that had fomented the Dixiecrat rebellion in 1948, the Goldwater debacle in 1964, and the Wallace revolt in 1968. At a meeting of the state Democratic Executive Committee in the summer of 1970, Chairman Vance rammed through a change in the party rules to provide for appointment instead of election of the presidential electors. From that day forward, there would be no possibility that Alabamians could ever again be denied their right to vote for the Democratic candidate for president of the United States.

Bob's single-minded pursuit of party reform had by this time identified him widely in the public mind as George Wallace's most persistent and effective adversary within the state political establishment. This enmity reached a showdown when, as everyone had anticipated, Wallace once more sought the presidency, but this time within the Democratic Party. The 1972 presidential election year began with Wallace striking terror in the hearts of national Democratic Party operatives by gaining substantial numbers of convention delegates in the early state primaries.

But the Wallace candidacy came to a sudden and violent end on May 15, 1972, when Wallace was shot by a deranged gunman as he campaigned in a shopping center in a Maryland suburb of Washington. Wallace carried Maryland in that primary, but it was a bitter Pyrrhic victory, because now he lay paralyzed from the waist down as a result of a bullet that penetrated his spine, and he would remain hospitalized for the remainder of the primary season.

Despite his grave injuries, Wallace did not officially withdraw from the race, and in July of 1972 he made a dramatic appearance before the National Democratic Convention in Miami. By the time the convention opened the nomination of George McGovern was a foregone conclusion, and this presented Bob Vance with an wrenching and perilous choice. McGovern was so pervasively detested in Alabama—the *Montgomery Advertiser* routinely called him "Goofy" McGovern—that no white politician in the state could publicly support him and hope to survive the wrath of the voters. Moreover, even though McGovern had a lock on the nomination, Wallace was still technically in the running, his name was placed in nomination, and he had strong support among Alabama's delegation.

Alabama's alphabetical status made it the first state to be called on when the convention began the arduous process of polling the state delegations to nominate the party's candidate for president. All of the black delegates voted for McGovern; all of the white delegates voted for Wallace—with one notable exception. Bob Vance, the chairman of the delegation, cast his vote for North Carolina Governor Terry Sanford.

Given the enmity between Wallace and Vance over the past six years, Vance's ploy—essentially, a face-saving cop-out—could hardly have come as a surprise to anyone. But nothing more enraged Wallace than to be upstaged by one of the "New South" governors who had come to power by advocating accommodation rather than resistance to racial equality. To Wallace, Vance's vote was an overt act of treason against the state, and he told his minions that Vance must pay for his public humiliation of the governor.

In the November election Wallace did not lift a hand to support McGovern, nor, for that matter, did Bob Vance. Presumably Vance did cast his own quiet vote for the ten sacrificial lambs he had appointed as McGovern-pledged electors, knowing it was a foregone conclusion that Richard Nixon would carry the state, which he did by the overwhelming margin of 728,701 to McGovern's 219,108. The results represented an almost total racial polarization, with Nixon taking more than 80 percent of the white vote, and McGovern drawing an even higher proportion of the black vote. John Cashin's National Democratic Party of Alabama was also on the ticket once again, but polled a paltry 37,815 votes, virtually all of them cast by blacks.

In 1974 Wallace, now permanently confined to a wheelchair as a result of the attempted assassination in 1972, launched what was widely regarded as his political Last Hurrah, his final race for governor. As Democratic chairman, Vance maintained neutrality during the primary election, although it is virtually certain that he cast his own vote for Wallace's token opponent, State Senator Gene McLain of Huntsville. In that same election Vance also had to wage his own token battle for re-election to his seat on the state Democratic Executive Committee, not only against a Wallace candidate but from a friend and neighbor as well, the redoubtable Marie Stokes Jemison, who, as the wife of a wealthy Birmingham investment banker, was the most improbable liberal in Birmingham politics. By this time Bob was sufficiently known that he won with relative ease.

As summer approached, with the primary election behind him and the contest against a yet-unnamed Republican candidate little more than a formality, George Wallace turned his attention to getting revenge against Vance for his contumacy in voting for Terry Sanford at the Democratic National Convention two years earlier. In what was an otherwise lackluster political year, this confrontation was touted in the press as a grudge-match that was sure to make great summer theater.

In his determination to purge Vance as the party chairman, Wallace devised a brilliant strategy: He would not attempt to install a States' Righter, already a dying breed by that time anyway; rather, he put forward State Senator Bert Haltom from the upstate town of Florence. Haltom had never been identified as a Wallaceite and indeed had a solid record of support for Vance's Loyalist wing. The ploy astonished just about everyone except those who knew that Haltom had, since college days, been a close personal friend of George Wallace's brother, Gerald, who was widely viewed as the Rasputin of the Wallace administration, the shadowy figure who pulled the strings of state politics while George preened on the stage of national politics.

There was a delicious sense of High Noon confrontation as the committee members gathered on a balmy June weekend at the Parliament House, a Birmingham hotel that was a popular site for political meetings. The Wallace forces were so confident that the governor's chief strategist, a cocksure young Montgomery lawyer named Mickey Griffin, was already boasting to the press of a Wallace victory. After all, the Wallace forces needed to pick up only a handful of Loyalist defections in order to elect Haltom as chairman, and it was generally thought this would be an easy feat since some committee members could always be bought off by offers of appointments, road contracts, and other benefactions which the governor's office could bestow.

But Bob Vance did not accept his defeat as inevitable. In his eight years as chairman, he had built a highly disciplined Loyalist corps, and now it was time exert all the muscle he had. Throughout the night before the election Vance trekked the corridors of the Parliament House, meeting with little knots of party faithful to shore up his support.

With uniformed state patrolmen—Wallace's shock troops, as it were—much in evidence all around the Parliament House, Vance hardly needed to point out to the committee members just how high the stakes were. "It's going to be rough," Vance told his supporters. "They're going to play every card in the deck. If they've got a financial hold on you, if there are any sexual weaknesses, I have to know. If you're vulnerable in any way, I'll understand, but I have to know which votes I can count on."

If he were not satisfied with a committee member's assurance, Vance could play hardball himself. When he sensed that Jimmy Evans, a

Loyalist committee member from Montgomery, was less than committed, Vance sent his chief lieutenant, state Attorney General Bill Baxley, to instruct Evans to draw a coded symbol—the familiar happy-face emblem—on his personal ballot for chairman.

When he felt assured of enough votes to retain the chairmanship, Vance paid a "courtesy call" on Governor Wallace, who had been so confident of victory that he had come to Birmingham for the celebration. Wallace was lying in bed when Vance called on him. The two men exchanged pleasantries. It was a civil encounter, as it always was in the infrequent meetings between two adversaries who had a certain grudging respect for one another's political talents.

Then Vance got down to business. "Governor," Vance said with aplomb, "I've got you beat. But I just want to assure you that I'm not going to crow about this, and when the voting is over, I want to leave here with as much appearance of party unity as possible."

Wallace listened with a mischievous grin and show of magnanimous civility, but clearly he did not believe Vance. So confident was he of prevailing that he took a position near the front a few hours later when he was wheeled into the meeting hall to celebrate the election of his anointed candidate, Haltom.

Vance called the meeting to order and announced that the first item of business was to elect committee officers.

Vance was nominated.

Haltom was nominated.

Suddenly a Vance partisan sprang to his feet and, speaking cryptically of the "terrible pressures" that had been brought to bear, moved that the election be held by secret ballot. This move was unprecedented, and clearly unanticipated by the Wallace forces. The hall was plunged into such pandemonium that Senator Haltom could barely be heard as he protested, with impassioned eloquence, that it would be a mockery for a party that called itself "Democratic" to choose its officers behind a veil of secrecy. "You cannot go back to your people in good conscience," Haltom implored, "if you vote by secret ballot."

Vance permitted Haltom to have his say, then without hesitation or response called for a voice vote on the question of whether to hold a secret ballot.

"All in favor of the motion vote aye."

A chorus of ayes rang out.

"All against vote no."

A chorus of nos followed.

"The ayes have it," Vance declared with a firm bang of the gavel. Then, moving through the uproar with dazzling speed and boldness, he appointed a coterie of "sergeants-at-arms" to collect the written ballots. With a flourish, Vance left the podium. A Wallace partisan seized a floor microphone. Sweating profusely, with large, bewildered eyes, the man thundered, "I rise to appeal the chair's ruling to the floor." Responding to the demand, Vance momentarily returned to the podium. "I'm sorry," he shrugged helplessly, "but the voting has already begun."

As Vance's designated "sergeants" collected the scraps of paper from the delegates, Vance wandered over to engage in amiable conversation with George Wallace and Bert Haltom, who were both looking decidedly anxious at this moment.

When the votes were all gathered, they were placed in a black satchel, brought to the front of the room, and counted as the committee members watched in quiet apprehension. Someone handed Bob Vance a scrap of paper, and he returned to the podium to announce the result: sixty-six votes for Vance, fifty-one votes for Haltom.

Amid the uproar that followed this announcement, a Vance partisan managed to get to a microphone to move that Bert Haltom be elected vice chairman, "in the name of unity and good will, by acclamation." Vance called the question, and after a chorus of ayes, declared, "Senator Haltom is elected vice chairman unanimously by voice vote."

Another Vance partisan, proclaiming himself "a liberal Democrat," rose to ask for "a standing show of support for Governor Wallace's floor manager, Mickey Griffin." It was done, but despite the gesture, Griffin looked like a whipped puppy.

As the committee went into its dull routines of business, Vance absently sifted through the chits of paper on which the members had cast their votes for chairman. One of them, he noted with a slight smile of satisfaction, was marked "VANCE"—and just beneath the letters was a caricature of the happy face. With Vance's gentle persuasion, Jimmy Evans had come through.

When the meeting ended, the delegates headed back to Sulligent, Summiton, and Sipsey Fork, to Merry, Mitylene, and Mount Meigs, the hamlets of Alabama from whence they came. But a few lingered. Late that night, on the Parliament House's bar, which was called "Once-a-Knight," a slightly tipsy committee member was heard to mutter, "If I was Wallace, I'd buy me a new crowd."

Unaccustomed as he was to losing state political battles, Wallace took his defeat at Vance's hands with good grace. After all, the party chairmanship was a position of only symbolic importance, and besides, Wallace had bigger fish to fry: He was already laying plans for yet another race for president in 1976—his fourth in twelve years.

As in 1972, this time Wallace would keep his campaign within the Democratic Party. Owing in large measure to sympathy engendered by the assassination attempt that left him paralyzed, Wallace had undergone a remarkable political rehabilitation since he first burst upon the scene as an uncompromising segregationist more than a decade earlier. Indeed, Wallace had so deftly placed himself in the political mainstream that in 1975 Senator Edward Kennedy of Massachusetts came to Alabama to be the main speaker at a Fourth of July celebration at which Wallace was presented with an "Americanism" award.

But Wallace soon found that the sympathy factor was a two-edged sword. As the 1976 campaign began in earnest, the public-opinion polls and man-on-the-street interviews began to reflect a pervasive and persistent doubt among the voters that a man who was confined to a wheelchair was not up to the job of the presidency. Wallace's strategists sought to counter this perception by pointing out that Franklin D. Roosevelt led the nation through war and depression from a wheelchair. But the comparison didn't wash: Roosevelt was perceived as a cerebral man; Wallace was a brawler. The perception of physical incapacity was underscored by the fact that Wallace was repeatedly obliged to call off campaign commitments because of the chronic pain and illnesses induced by his injuries.

If these obstacles were not enough, Wallace also had to confront something entirely new in his political career: several "New South governors" who aspired to the presidency. Two of these, Reuben Askew of Florida and Terry Sanford of North Carolina, were eliminated in the early contests for the Democratic presidential nomination, but the remaining one loomed ever larger as a formidable obstacle in Wallace's path to the presidency. That was Jimmy Carter of Georgia.

The two men, who had grown up not an hour's drive apart amid the pervasive poverty of the depression, confronted one another in a do-or-die battle in the presidential primary in Florida in March of 1976. At that point Carter still was not viewed as a serious candidate for the nomination, so the other major candidates opted to stay out of the Florida race on the theory that Carter was the best man to stop the Wallace juggernaut; after he had served that useful purpose, the conventional wisdom went, Carter could be disposed of. Despite the widespread misgivings about his physical capacity, Wallace ran a close second to Carter in the Florida voting. But when Carter replicated his thrashing of Wallace a few weeks later in the North Carolina primary, the crippled Alabama governor knew that his long quest for the presidency was at last at an end.

He could, however, still extract a measure of satisfaction—revenge, one might say—at the expense of the party establishment that had treated him with such scorn. In July 1976, Jimmy Carter came to Montgomery to secure the political blessing of George Wallace.

As a next-door neighbor and native southerner, Carter was popular in Alabama, so for the first time in their political lives, Bob Vance and George Wallace were in comfortable concert behind the Democratic Party's candidate. As state party chairman, Bob led an Alabama delegation solidly committed to Carter to the National Democratic Convention in New York in July of 1976. He took his two teenage sons, Robert Jr. and Charles, with him to savor the moment of triumph. The extraordinary political confluence was reflected at the polls in November when Alabama, which had seemingly settled solidly and comfortably into a mode of voting regularly for Republican candidates for president, delivered its ten electoral votes to Jimmy Carter by the comfortable margin of 659,170 to 504,070 for Gerald Ford. But perhaps no vote total more revealed the dramatic change that had taken place in Alabama during the past eight years than that received by Lester Maddox, the eccentric segregationist and former governor of Georgia. Running as the candidate of the surviving remnant of George Wallace's 1968 apparatus, the

American Independent Party, Maddox polled just 9,198 votes in Alabama—scarcely more than the candidate of the Prohibition Party.

Virtually all of this dramatic political movement had been taken by Wallace in the direction of Bob Vance. The governor by this time had even recanted his most fundamental positions of a decade earlier, openly conceding that segregation was "wrong" and that the policy aims of the Civil Rights Act of 1964 that he had so bitterly resisted were worthy goals. In what seemed to be the twilight of his career, Wallace was beset by an almost driven desperation to seek forgiveness for his political sins of the past. He made at least one telephone call to his old law school classmate, Frank Johnson, the federal district judge in Montgomery whom Wallace had so relentlessly vilified, begging for mercy. When the call ended, Wallace was in tears, and Johnson's eyes glistened.

Wallace's reconciliation with Vance was not so lachrymose. One night not long after the 1976 election, Wallace's second wife, Cornelia, called the Vances in Birmingham to convey Christmas wishes. In the course of the conversation, she mentioned that she had heard that Bob and Helen collected an uncommon breed of dog, called the Arabian saluki. People were constantly bestowing upon the governor all manner of unusual personal gifts, she said, and by odd coincidence someone had given him a saluki. The governor wondered if the Vances might give the animal a good home. Soon thereafter Bob and Helen Vance drove down to Montgomery to pay a call on the Wallaces. It was a slightly stilted but pleasant encounter, ending with the delivery of the saluki, a breed of dog with a long neck that makes it slightly resemble a miniature camel in white.

"Vance," Wallace said with his inimitable brand of sarcasm, "that's the ugliest dog I ever saw. Now me, I like a *po-leece* dog."

After exchanging a few more pleasantries, Bob and Helen Vance headed back to Birmingham, the backseat of their car now occupied by a handsome Saluki whom they subsequently named "Guv Ali Bama."

With Carter in the White House, it was time for Alabama Democrats to savor some of the sweets of victory that had been denied them—at least at the federal level—during the eight years of the Nixon and Ford presidencies. And the most cherished of these spoils of success were federal judgeships. Although he had never made it much of a public issue,

Bob Vance now let it be known that he wanted a seat on the United States Court of Appeals for the Fifth Circuit, the federal appellate court whose jurisdiction spread across the Southeastern United States from Florida to Texas.

In keeping with a campaign promise to minimize politics in judicial appointments, President Carter had instituted panels of distinguished citizens, made up of lawyers and non-lawyers, to recommend candidates for the appellate court posts. When the first vacancy occurred in one of Alabama's two designated seats on the regional court, the panel produced a list of four of the state's most prominent lawyers. One was Truman Hobbs, a Montgomery lawyer who had long labored in the vineyards of the Loyalist wing of the state party and whose father had been the congressman who had named Bob Vance a House page back in the 1940s. Another was M. Roland Nachman, an erudite, Harvard-trained Montgomery lawyer whose party allegiance dated back to Adlai Stevenson's races in the 1950s. A third was Pat Richardson, a former president of the Alabama Bar Association from Huntsville, who was promoted by the state's senior United States senator, John Sparkman. The fourth was Bob Vance.

Vance knew that despite Carter's best efforts, politics still played a large role in judicial selections, and he especially resented the fact that Sparkman, whom he had supported with diligence through the years, would seek to place a personal friend on the appellate court. But Sparkman was ending his long Senate service, and Vance had the support of Alabama's other senator, Jim Allen. Even Wallace put in a word for Vance.

In the fall of 1977, near the end of the first year of the the Carter presidency, the president called his advisers on legal affairs to the Oval Office to discuss nominees for a number of judicial appointments around the country. When they reached the Fifth Circuit seat, Carter was impressed by the quality of the candidates before him, but he seemed to hesitate for a moment over Bob Vance's name. It appeared, Carter said, that Vance's most notable recommendation was his service as state Democratic chairman. Wouldn't his appointment look crassly political? Charles Kirbo, an Atlanta lawyer who held no official position but was virtually a one-man "kitchen cabinet" to the president, related the special circumstances of Vance's party role, stressing his long opposition to

Wallace. Kirbo also noted that Vance had been among Carter's earliest supporters. Attorney General Griffin Bell, who at times felt that being a white male was almost an obstacle to overcome in getting a federal judgeship in the Carter administration, echoed Kirbo's recommendation.

"Okay," the president declared. "Let's nominate Vance."

On the following day Bob Vance's nomination was sent to the Senate, which gave perfunctory "advice and consent" to the nomination in the waning days of the Hundredth Congress.

Bob spent his Christmas holidays that year tying up the loose ends of a law practice and political career that had, by then, spanned nearly three decades. On January 3, 1978, surrounded by his family and a throng of friends and admirers in a flower-bedecked courtroom of the federal building in Birmingham, Robert Smith Vance was invested as a judge of the United States Court of Appeals for the Fifth Judicial Circuit.

9   "Judicial Rape"

As prisons go, the medium-security federal penitentiary in Atlanta was not the worst place in which to be incarcerated in 1972. The "Atlanta Pen," as it was known to petty criminals throughout the region, was not a "country club prison" like the ones where big-name first offenders, such as the Watergate conspirators, served their sentences. But the Atlanta Pen was a veritable paradise compared with the wretched human warehouses that the region's state prisons had become. Conditions had grown so bad in Alabama, for example, that Federal Judge Frank M. Johnson Jr. would shortly rule that merely to be placed in the state's overcrowded, underfunded, violence-ridden penal institutions violated the "cruel and unusual punishment" prohibition of the Eighth Amendment of the Bill of Rights.

Even so, Roy Moody's entry into the Atlanta penitentiary was the beginning of a traumatic experience that would profoundly change the course of his life.

At first Roy seemed to accept incarceration with a certain resignation if not equanimity. In the ample free time he found from his various assigned chores in the prison office and library, he prodigiously cranked out legal briefs and motions for himself and his new friends in prison. Mostly, though, he concentrated on a sustained but fruitless effort to have his 1972 conviction overturned.

Early in his prison experience Roy also made a close friend, the only close adult male friendship he ever formed, in his cellmate, Ted Banks.

Eight years older than Roy, Banks was born and grew up in the excruciating Appalachian poverty of Kentucky. He dropped out of school in the eighth grade and drifted to Florida, where he worked as a laborer and boatbuilder before turning to crime. His first conviction was for dealing in illegal firearms, and by the time Roy met him, Ted had become well known to federal authorities as a career "con man" who made his living cheating and swindling. He entered the Atlanta penitentiary in 1970 to serve a twelve-year sentence for counterfeiting and securities fraud.

Ted Banks soon became "like a brother" to Roy Moody, and the two would pass many hours talking about legal strategies and illegal schemes. Roy claimed to be "a better lawyer than most lawyers" and helped Ted draft legal petitions seeking to overturn his conviction. Ted, in turn, taught Roy much about building bombs and other firearms.

During his time in the Atlanta prison, Roy also became acquainted with a petty criminal from Florida named Bonnie Frank Henderson. Roy boasted to Bonnie Frank about his prowess at manufacturing chemical booby traps, such as filling a light bulb with mercury so that it would start a fire when it was switched on. Roy also admitted to Bonnie Frank that he had built the bomb his wife had inadvertently detonated, adding that Hazel wouldn't have gotten hurt if she hadn't been so "nosey" and that she was lucky she hadn't been killed.

But as his term dragged on, Roy would, he later maintained, confront the full horror of prison life. He would later relate that in 1975 he shared a cell with a man named Aponte, who came from somewhere in South America, whom Roy described as "a reserved kind of individual . . . a lot like me." One night two other prisoners burst into their cell with daggers and proceeded to stab Aponte viciously, continuing the attack even as the man lay writhing and incapacitated on the floor. "They were hollering, 'Kill! Kill!,'" Roy later maintained. "You could almost smell death. . . . I threw up, and I passed out. . . . When I came to, they were laughing . . . making fun of me because of the way I had reacted." Roy claimed to have endless nightmares about the murder.

One day as he lay dozing, he later claimed, four inmates slipped into his cell, held a pillow over his head, which nearly suffocated him, and raped him. "I never even knew who did it," he said. He did not report the incident to anyone, nor did he seek to retaliate. As a result of this episode, he said, "An awareness of that rape and the suffocation associated with it has been a part of every sexual activity I've ever engaged in since that time, including with my wife."

Despite these episodes, Roy conducted himself well during his time in prison. In a pre-parole report, a prison caseworker suspected that Roy was "sociopathic"—the term that was then used for antisocial personality disorder—and found that he was "an argumentative, manipulative individual." Still, after serving a little more than half his original sentence, Roy was paroled on August 13, 1975, with instructions that he report to a parole officer periodically until May 22, 1977.

Soon after Roy returned to Macon to pick up his life, Hazel Strickland Moody, Roy's common-law wife, filed for divorce. At the hearing Roy sought custody of their son, Mark, who by this time was six years old, even though Roy acknowledged that he was contributing nothing to the child's support. On December 8, 1975, the juvenile court of Macon awarded Hazel permanent custody of Mark but gave Roy visitation rights of one weekend each month, one week each summer, and three days during the Christmas season.

Roy did not accept this arrangement, and initiated new litigation claiming that Hazel had given perjured testimony at the divorce and custody hearing by claiming that Roy had tried to force her to have an abortion. He wrote a menacing letter to Hazel's father suggesting that his daughter might go to prison for lying under oath. He also wrote Judge O. W. McGehee of the Macon juvenile court a letter in which he claimed to belong to a group in Atlanta that sought "to expose the lucrative and common practice of unscrupulous attorneys victimizing parties to a divorce." The letter went on:

> On May 24 between 7:30 and 8:00 p.m., I appeared on a public interest program broadcast in the Atlanta area by Channel 5 TV. . . .

On this program, I sought to expand the concern to include the denial of due process by calling attention to what I consider to be abuses which I have been subjected to in your Court. Since I referred to you by name and indicated that in my opinion you had abused the powers of your office and reflected disrespect on Juvenile Court Judges in general, I assume you are entitled to equal time to defend the action or lack of action of your Court. . . . Since I plan to call public attention to this matter, I think I should be candid and advise you that if my right to appeal is not respected, I shall seek injunctive relief in the Federal District Court. If that becomes necessary, I intend to hold the functionaries that were responsible for the denial of due process accountable in a civil rights action for violation of my constitutional right to due process of law.

Roy sought, without success, to get the American Civil Liberties Union to represent him on the grounds that the court system had discriminated against him, so he pressed on acting as his own lawyer—*pro se,* in the language of the law. Still, even though he found time to keep up the barrage of litigation and insulting letters, Roy spent little time with his son, Mark, not even exercising the visitation rights he had been granted by Judge McGehee. In fact, within a year after the divorce Hazel retained a Macon attorney, William Self, in an effort to force Roy to provide monetary support for the child. On at least three occasions between May of 1976 and March of 1977 Roy was held in contempt, and on one occasion he was charged with child abandonment, which was a criminal offense in Georgia. Roy always fought back, and once threatened to call three hundred witnesses to prove that he had been unable to find a job because of physical and emotional disabilities. During this period Roy spent twenty-five days in the Macon jail, and it was more than ten years before the abandonment charge was finally dismissed on the grounds that Mark had reached the age of majority.

During this time Roy lived with whatever women would take him in for whatever period they would tolerate his sponging. In 1975 and 1976 he lived with Celeste Sproul Millen, and was reported to have slept with Celeste's teenage daughter during this period as well. Soon after Celeste kicked him out, Roy reestablished his relationship with Melba Price. During this time Roy told Melba that for several months in 1977 or 1978 he had a homosexual affair with a dentist he had met in an X-rated movie theater and that he traded sexual services for dental services. By this time Melba's daughter by Roy had reached sixteen, and Roy made passionate advances toward her before the girl knew that he was her father. Roy told others that he never really knew whether the child was his, because Melba was sleeping with other men at the time she became pregnant. When Melba became disgusted and alerted the police where they could find Roy to arrest him on the child-abandonment warrant, Roy threatened to kill Melba's children if she ever did anything that got him sent to jail.

There was, however, never any question in Roy's mind as to his paternity of Joyce Law's daughter, who by this time had reached her middle teenage years. Even though she did not bear his name, the girl was also aware that Roy was her father and even seemed to have an affection for him. But on one of her unsupervised visits, Roy showed his daughter pornographic pictures, then raped her. The event was so traumatic that the girl suppressed the memory until it was brought to the surface, years later, in psychiatric treatment.

Sometime during the late 1970s Roy established himself in the Atlanta suburb of Chamblee, where he rented a basement room from Richard Singleton for ten dollars a month, from which he operated his two mail-order scams. Soon after he arrived there he struck up a relationship with Kathy Sperry Burks, whom he met at the Po' Folks restaurant where she was a waitress. Although they dated only a four or five times, it was a tempestuous relationship. Kathy said Roy was secretive about his past, although he did speak of his "messy divorce" from "a bitch." He also spoke frequently about "niggers."

"I don't like that word," Kathy told him.

"I call 'em like I see 'em," Roy replied.

On one occasion he became so angry when a black couple entered the restaurant that he stormed out in unconcealed indignation; Kathy felt obliged to apologize to the couple.

Kathy said Roy lost his temper when she refused to go home with him after their first date, implying that she owed him sexual payment for taking her to dinner. One evening when they went to a bar, Roy became furious because someone had parked too close to his car, and he wanted to sit in the parking lot as long as it took in order to confront the offending party. Soon Kathy detected too many similarities in Roy to the abusive husband she had divorced, so she cut off the relationship.

One day in April of 1980 Roy observed a young woman checking the oil in her car at a self-service gasoline station in the Chamblee area. He approached her amiably, saying that he had always admired a woman who knew enough about cars to check their own oil, and out of this conversation developed a relationship with Karlene Shiver which lasted for more than a year. At the outset she found Roy to be "quite a charmer, a very nice-looking man."

Karlene was twenty-five at the time she began dating Roy, and she enjoyed being with him so much that she began working part time handling the voluminous correspondence with newspapers around the country in connection with his two businesses, the Associated Writers Guild of America and the North American Data and Verification Testing Service. She quickly mastered the basic elements of Roy's businesses. Small advertisements were placed in newspapers under the guise of the Writers Guild, ostensibly seeking promising writers who had manuscripts they would like to have published. When prospects responded, they were referred to the testing service, which, for a fee of twenty-five dollars, would give a rudimentary test for writing skills; every person who took the test and paid the fee was given a grade of A and encouraged to publish writings. At this point the Writers Guild would offer to publish, for a larger fee, the author's manuscript in a volume called "Authors to Watch," which was touted as a publication that was read in major publishing houses seeking promising writers. Roy was especially eager to publish stories that dealt with personal religious experience, and once he even wrote one himself as an example of the type of stories he sought. When enough manuscripts were assembled, Roy would print a few hundred copies of "Authors to Watch" and send copies to those who had submitted the manuscripts.

But Karlene noticed that many of the manuscripts were never even read, even though the fees had been paid, and she began to suspect that the whole operation was a scam. She caught him signing documents under the name of "A. W. Watson," which was his grandmother's married name, and in due course she discovered that he was in trouble with the post office over allegations of mail fraud. Once she pleaded with Roy not to take money from a disabled Vietnam veteran who had submitted a poignant but poorly crafted account of his war injuries. Roy became so angry at this that he struck Karlene so hard that her eardrum was ruptured and she had to get medical attention. She was struck on the ear again when Roy accused her of snooping by listening to an author's complaint that had been recorded on the telephone answering machine.

Karlene also found Roy to be explosive in their personal relationships. She had come to Atlanta from Alabama, and she once remarked that she was always ashamed of the image that Governor George Wallace had given her state. Roy upbraided her, saying she "didn't understand," and declared that George Wallace was one of his heroes. He constantly referred to blacks as "niggers" and maintained that "they should all be rounded up and sent back to Africa." A sensational ongoing story of the time was the systematic kidnapping and murder of black children whose bodies would subsequently turn up in the Chattahoochee River, which flowed past Atlanta. Karlene recalled a "joke" that Roy told her during this time.

"Did you hear they changed the name of the Chattahoochee River?" Roy asked.

"No," said Karlene. "To what?"

"To the Chuckanigger River," Roy replied with peals of laughter.

Karlene said that Roy once became so upset at seeing an interracial couple that he blurted out that "they should be shot on the spot." He spoke approvingly of the Ku Klux Klan and the Atlanta anti-Semitic lawyer, J. B. Stoner. Roy also made remarks like "Jew bastards" and proclaimed that "Hitler did not have a bad idea, he was just misunderstood." He railed against "the system," especially the courts, referred to policemen as "pigs," and maintained he did not finish law school because all lawyers were "crooked." He encouraged Karlene to read a John Birch Society book. He spoke scornfully of the NAACP, which he said was a front for "government Jews," and maintained that Martin Luther King Jr. was "a card-totin' communist."

In one ominous conversation, Roy spoke of getting even with "the system" and claimed to have built an explosive device while he was in high school. He related to Karlene that "the perfect" crime would be the building of "the right kind of bomb" so that when it exploded there would be "nothing would be left to investigate."

After a little more than a year, Karlene grew weary of the tedious work and of Roy's brutality and his constant involvement with other women, but when she announced her intention to break up, Roy brought a criminal charge against her, accusing her of embezzling money from him in order to bet on University of Alabama football games. Karlene was astonished at the alacrity with which Roy lied in court, including his denial that they ever had a personal relationship. Eventually the charge was dismissed.

Not long after he broke up with Karlene Shiver, in July 1981, Roy Moody struck up a conversation with Susan Kelly McBride, who was working as a waitress in an Atlanta suburban coffee shop that Roy frequented. A lithe and comely woman of eighteen who wore her long hair in a pony tail and whose sharp facial features were accentuated by large round wire-rimmed glasses, Susan was instantly captivated by the man who was clearly old enough to be her father. For Susan, this was the inauspicious beginning of what was to be nearly a decade of isolation, domination, and personal degradation.

Susan McBride was born December 3, 1962, in Hampton, Virginia. Her father was in the military, which meant that the family was constantly on the move. In her brief life Susan had lived in such diverse places as Tennessee, the Azores, and Florida before moving to Atlanta, where she still lived with her family at the time she met Roy, not long after her graduation from high school. Within a month after they met, Roy persuaded Susan to go with him for a weekend at Jekyll Island, a popular resort on Georgia's Atlantic Coast, and somehow they were stranded for four or five days. When they returned to Atlanta, Susan moved in with Roy at the Pebble Creek Apartments.

Susan came to regard Roy as intelligent, conservative, and, most of all, obsessively private. His interests were flying—he claimed to be a self-taught pilot—and sailing off the coasts of Florida. Not long after they began living together Susan found herself virtually running Roy's two businesses, the Writers Guild and the Testing Service. Roy, meanwhile, devoted virtually all of his time to his ever-growing range of legal projects, often calling on Susan to run errands to help him with his arcane schemes. Susan thought at one time that he had a dozen lawyers in retention, but he kept firing them.

Despite persistent and growing problems with the postal authorities, the businesses thrived under Susan's stewardship, at times bringing in as much as $180,000 a year. This bountiful largesse enabled Roy and Susan to move, soon after they began living together, into a commodious bungalow on a shaded lot at 6414 Skyline Drive in the pleasant bedroom community of Rex, about fifteen miles southeast of Atlanta. Soon the driveway was cluttered with two automobiles, a pickup truck, a motorcycle, two boats—all the visible accoutrement of middle-class success.

But what went on within the house was anything but ordinary. The two had no friends—indeed, Susan, in a gesture toward Roy's obsessive privacy, gave him a "house-warming" gift of a door knocker that bore the message "GET LOST." When Susan wanted to see an old high school friend, Roy told her there was too much work to do to permit her to "socialize," and he insisted on her presence, day and night. He showed displeasure even when Susan took a few hours to visit her parents, and once he became upset when Susan told him that she had friends who were black. He told her that he considered the newly established national day of recognition for Martin Luther King Jr. to be "a communist holiday."

He had virtually no contact with neighbors. When Buck Davis, the occupant of the next lot, planted flowers across the property line, Roy sent him a registered letter. He also put vegetation killer on a bush that had grown to hang over onto his lot. Roy represented himself as an attorney to Homer Drake, who lived directly behind the Moody house on Skyline Drive, and once Roy cut down some trees on Homer's property; when Homer came to Roy's house to protest the act, Roy ordered him off the property.

Business and litigation consumed all their time, and virtually every room in the house was filled with typewriters and filing cabinets that Roy used in his various commercial enterprises and legal machinations. His only outside interest was flying, which he continued to do in his Beechcraft Bonanza even after his pilot's license expired.

Soon after they began living together, Susan learned of Roy's past in bits and pieces. Sometime around 1983 of 1984 she happened to come across an old paper that indicated Roy had to be retrieved from "federal custody" in order to attend a divorce hearing. She asked if the paper meant that he had been in prison. Roy said yes, and eventually he told her that he had served time for possession of a bomb.

Through the 1980s Roy continued his interest in the John Birch Society, even though the organization had long since become so marginalized in American politics that it was scarcely ever mentioned any longer, and he contributed to the political organizations of Senator Jesse Helms of North Carolina and other right-wing politicians. He subscribed to extremist publications like *Soldier of Fortune* and *American Survival Guide,* and always had gun magazines around the house. He taught Susan how to shoot, and they each had a revolver beneath their bed.

Early on in their life together, Susan observed that Roy had a mysterious side. Whenever she did something, even inadvertently, which displeased him, he would subject her to "the silent treatment"—refusing to acknowledge her presence in any way for days at a time. Often she did not even know what offense she had committed, and she could get back in his good graces only by tearful entreaties for mercy. Once she marked the calendar with teardrops to see if she could discern a pattern to Roy's taciturn periods; she could not.

She also discovered that Roy had a tendency toward baseless jealousy, and once in a grocery store, to Susan's great embarrassment, he confronted a man whom he believed Susan was "staring at." On another occasion, he grew angry at her because he felt the T-shirt she wore for a sailing trip exposed too much of her body.

Then there was sex, for which Roy's gluttony was eclectic and insatiable. At times he videotaped their sexual relations with a home camcorder, leading her to believe that the footage might be marketed as pornographic films. He also saw other women, including his old girlfriend, Celeste Sproul, and once he said he would like to have Susan and Celeste in bed at the same time. He tried to get Susan to submit to sexual relations with his dog, and when she refused, he showed his displeasure. He frequented pornography shops, insisting that Susan accompany him, and at one such establishment they patronized on a trip to North Carolina, Susan saw him fellate another man in the peep-show booth. On another occasion he tried to get her to fellate a man through a hole between the booths.

Over the years Roy occasionally displayed a violent nature. Toward the end of their relationship, he threw Susan to the floor and pressed a tooth-brush handle against her throat so hard that it left a mark that, she later told her father, was a love-bite.

In the summer of 1982 Roy began to devote a major part of his time to the development of an auxiliary motor for use on sailboats. He placed advertisements in regional newspapers seeking design engineers to work in the company he had formed, called Superior Sail Drives, and soon after hired three men from diverse locations. Two of them, Timothy Williams and Danny Fiederer, were recent college graduates. The third, Warren Glover, was a former postal worker who, at forty-four, was seeking a more challenging career. Roy hired them at salaries of $250 a week.

When the three arrived for work in Roy's makeshift workshop in Atlanta, they found that he had already jerry-built an old lawn-mower motor into the product that he hoped to refine and market. But they received little direction from Roy, and spent most of their time sitting around playing cards and, occasionally, smoking marijuana.

In the course of hiring the three men, Roy mentioned casually that he would be taking out "key employee" insurance policies on them. This type of insurance is often taken out by businesses on employees who develop expertise in the course of their work, in order to protect the business investment. The policies, issued on December 17, 1982, by the Prudential Insurance Company, insured the three men for $750,000 each, at a total monthly premium of nearly $2,500. The beneficiary was Superior Sail Drives.

With the policies issued, Roy announced that the motor was ready for testing, and so they must go far down into the Florida Keys. On December 17 the four men set out, with Roy at the helm, for a two-hour trip out into the Florida bay from a boating town called Marathon. The three employees grew apprehensive, because the weather was cool and the waters were rough, but Roy told them he needed only to take some underwater photographs to demonstrate how the motor worked.

When they reached a location that Roy deemed suitable, the three were instructed to get out of the boat to take the pictures. Although there were life vests aboard the vessel, Roy suggested that they instead simply wear tethers in order to make their work easier.

When all three were in the chill waters and engaged in taking the pictures, Roy suddenly took off at full throttle, leaving the three men with their tethers floating free in the choppy, shark-infested sea.

What followed was a scene of desperation and confusion. At one point Roy apparently came back, but he ignored their cries for help, and when two of the men tried to reboard the craft, Roy thrust them away. Timothy Williams was nearly killed by the anchor line as Roy sped past him. The three men began desperately swimming for their lives, losing sight of one another.

Timothy Williams reached a channel marker in the Intercoastal Waterway, which runs along the southern coast. As he clung to the buoy, he saw Roy returning once more. At first Timothy tried to hide, but Roy spotted him and threw him a rope. Timothy demanded a life-preserver, but Roy refused to throw him one. When Timothy tried to get aboard the boat, Roy struck him in the head with a heavy object, leaving a gash that required sixteen stitches to close.

At some point Timothy spotted Glover and Fiederer flailing in the water. Then Roy turned the boat toward them at full speed.

"Roy, why are you trying to kill us?" Timothy shouted. There was no response. In this confusion a sailboat fortuitously appeared in the Intercoastal Waterway and picked up Williams and Fiederer. Seeing this rescue, Roy allowed Warren Glover to reboard the boat, whereupon Warren immediately knocked Roy to the deck. Warren seized a flare gun, fired one flare into air, then turned the gun on Roy, threatening to fire a flare into him if he moved. At that point Roy was, inexplicably, wearing Warren's clothes.

Soon a Coast Guard vessel arrived on the scene and took all four men to a hospital, where Roy staged what an attending physician believed was a feigned heart attack.

The following day the Florida district attorney at Marathon charged Roy with three counts of attempted murder and one count of aggravated battery, and Roy was released on bail to await trial in which conviction could result in Roy spending the rest of his life in prison.

But despite the gravity of the charges, Roy swiftly counterattacked. He took out an advertisement in a local newspaper giving his own spurious account of the events of December 17, insinuating that the three intended victims were involved in drug-dealing. He stopped payment on the last paychecks of his three employees and warned them that if they testified against him he would have them arrested on drug charges. Shortly after New Year's Day in 1983, Timothy Williams got a telephone call at his parent's home in Virginia offering to send his check if he would agree drop the charges; Williams indignantly refused. Roy accused the arresting officer of conspiring with Williams, Glover, and Fiederer to frame him. He offered James Lee Williams, an Atlanta polygrapher, one thousand dollars to provide him with a falsified lie-detector test report that lent credibility to Roy's fictitious version of what happened in Florida; Williams reported the attempted bribe to Georgia licensing authorities, who took no action because the case was being tried in Florida. Roy also threatened to take his case to the noted defense lawyer F. Lee Bailey's *Lie Detector* television program.

Despite this fierce barrage of obfuscation, Roy was brought to trial in Key West in June of 1983. The combination of an inept prosecution and Roy's relentless implication of drug-dealing resulted in a hung jury and mistrial despite the dramatic accounts of the intended victims from the witness stands. Three months later, William R. Ptomey Jr., the assistant Florida states attorney in charge of the case, announced that "while probable cause does exist as to the charges alleged, the state cannot sustain its burden of proving the defendant's guilt beyond a reasonable doubt." The case was dropped.

The case did not end there, however. In 1986 Roy brought a suit against Williams, Glover, Fiederer and a number of Florida authorities, accusing them of malicious prosecution.

The Florida prosecution seemed only to whet Roy's consuming passion for litigation and his relentless determination to manipulate the legal system. One particularly ingenious effort to obtain money by fraud grew out of a check drawn on the Writers Guild bank account that was dishonored for insufficient funds by the First National Bank of Atlanta. Out of this trivial incident Roy concocted an elaborate lawsuit against the bank alleging that the dishonored check had resulted in the loss of an opportunity to market an invention that was the work of a lifetime, costing Roy millions of dollars worth of contracts. The suit was built on a complex script involving a welter of fictitious backdated correspondence written on yellowed stationery and numerous false affidavits by Susan and his old prison buddies in Florida.

In the course of the litigation Roy arranged to see an Atlanta psychiatrist named Dave M. Davis, making it clear in his initial contact that he hoped to use Davis as an expert witness attesting to the suicidal depression he suffered as a result of the financial ruin that he claimed the bank had inflicted on him. Dr. Davis prescribed antidepressant medications that, Susan said, Roy never took. Davis also arranged to have one of his group associates, a psychologist named Dr. Howard E. Albrecht, evaluate Roy. In his initial interview with Albrecht on May 11, 1985, Roy complained of "the trauma that bitch caused me"—referring to the bank employee who had refused to honor his check. In an astonishing exercise in manipulation, Roy even drew up his own version of what he would like for the evaluation to say: "Our tests show that Mr. Moody is a genius in the area of abstract reasoning. . . . He therefore has an extremely high aptitude as an inventor. . . . When the bank refused to honor Mr. Moody's check. . . . it plunged Mr. Moody into a very severe depression [that] increased until Mr. Moody tried to commit suicide in March of 1985."

This fictitious report went on to include an explicit rejection of Dr. Thomas M. Hall's psychiatric diagnosis rendered more than ten years before, stating that Roy suffered "a sociopathic personality." From this point of departure, Roy wanted Dr. Davis to go into a bizarre discourse on the nature of socipathy and the law that would read: "A sociopath resolves problems without the normal restraints of morality, conscious [sic] or concern about the possible consequences of his or her criminal acts. If a sociopath's interest were severely jeopardized, as Mr. Moody's was, he or she would be expected to react abnormally by using force or violence without regard for the consequences of said acts. When Mr. Moody's interest was severely jeopardized, however, he reacted the way society expects normal and responsible people to react; he relied upon the judicial system to resolve his problems."

After establishing the treatment link, Roy informed the Davis group that he would not need any further services until the lawsuit came to trial. The suit lasted for eight years before it was finally dismissed in 1990.

Around 1985 Roy began to make inquiries about picking up his studies at the John Marshall Law School, where he had accumulated a few hours of credit over a twenty-year period. Apparently following up on a telephone call to the law school, Roy wrote a letter dated May 14, 1985, on the letterhead stationery of his fictitious company, Superior Sail Drives, to the registrar of John Marshall: "Dear sir, pursuant to conversation, wish to complete law degree and request transcript. Enclosed $400 as per instructions. Roy Moody, president."

Before he could enroll to resume his legal education, however, Roy discovered that a person with a felony conviction could not gain admission to the practice of law in Georgia. Thus, Roy's 1972 conviction in the Macon bombing case stood as a permanent, insurmountable barrier to his attaining his cherished goal of becoming a professional man. Upon making this vexing discovery, Roy laid aside his plans to return to law school and embarked on what would prove to be the most fateful endeavor of his complex life: He set out to expunge from the record a criminal conviction that had occurred thirteen years earlier, for which he had already served a term in prison.

The scheme began with Roy contacting Julie Ivey, a woman he had met several years earlier through David Henderson, the brother of his old prison buddy, Bonnie Frank Henderson. David introduced Julie to Roy under the alias of "Hollis," at Roy's request for unspecified reasons, but she soon learned his real name. Julie, who had just been divorced and needed money to support her young child, was put on Roy's payroll to investigate "lifestyles." Not long after she began her work, Roy told Julie that he needed her testimony in a court case, and he presented her with a script of an alleged incident about which she had no knowledge. Julie found Roy to be "a controlling man" who would tell her how to dress and how much makeup to wear as they went places together. "He exaggerated a lot," she would later recall, "but he always knew what he was doing." She remembered one occasion where he went to great pains to write a predated document with an old pencil on paper that was yellow with age. Using one of his scripts, Julie carefully prepared to testify, apparently in furtherance of his fraudulent suit against First National over the dishonored check, that Roy had become depressed and suicidal as a result of the experience—which was completely at variance with her actual observation.

Julie never testified in the bank case, but early in 1986, Roy asked Julie if she could locate someone to help him in an important lawsuit he was about to initiate. Within a few days Julie Ivey introduced Roy to Julie Linn-West, a woman she had known through occasional small-time drug-dealing.

Julie Linn-West was a truly piteous individual then in her early thirties. She was born and grew up in Des Moines, and at the age of fourteen she suffered a spinal-cord injury that left her paralyzed from the neck down. Through gritty perseverance and labored rehabilitation she managed to regain enough limited use of her arms and hands that she was able to finish high school in a wheelchair. She could even drive a specially equipped automobile. Despite her severe paralysis Julie married soon after her graduation from high school in the mid-1970s and, at the age of eighteen, she gave birth to a son.

At the time Roy met her, Julie Linn-West was living in a small apartment in Smyrna, a bedroom community half the distance around the Atlanta beltway from the Moody home in Rex. By that time she had lost her job as a telephone monitor for people who had been convicted in Georgia courts for driving under the influence of alcohol, and she was having trouble supporting her twelve-year-old son on the five hundred dollars a month she was being paid under a government rehabilitation program. So she jumped at the opportunity to earn some extra money working for Roy.

To make their arrangements, Roy drove Julie to a nearby liquor store. As they sat in the parking lot, with Susan in the back seat, Roy outlined his plan: He wanted Julie to give perjured testimony in a court proceeding to overturn a 1972 unjust conviction at the hands of corrupt judges and lawyers—a "judicial rape," as Roy put it. For this testimony he would pay her two thousand dollars. In her desperation, Julie agreed at once to say whatever Roy wanted her to say. She was given several hundred-dollar bills in partial payment and told to await instructions.

Within a few weeks Roy provided Julie with a carefully crafted text, which he called "the Gene Wallace script," for the role she was to play in court. Between January and April Roy and Susan came to Julie Linn-West's apartment countless times to coach her and refine the script. Under this fictitious account, Julie was to testify that she had known a man named Gene Wallace in 1972, and that on one of their dates in the spring of that year they drove to Roy's home on Dublin Avenue to deliver a package while she waited in the car. Gene Wallace returned empty-handed, Julie was to testify, and they had driven only a block or two when he suddenly said it was necessary for them to return to the house. But as they neared the house, there was an explosion, which led Gene Wallace to blurt out, "My God, it's exploded," and speed off back to Atlanta.

During these rehearsals Roy paid Julie, in hundred-dollar bills, promptly on the first of each month. She grew to be so impressed with Roy's cool manner and his command of legal language that she assumed that he was a lawyer. She also found Roy to be sympathetic and compassionate over her plight. Once he told her that the government wasn't doing enough to support her and that at the least she should get a new wheelchair. Julie also found Roy to be enormously skilled at lying: "He can make the unbelievable believable." In fact, at one point Julie became so absorbed in the theatrical undertaking that she expressed her anxiety that Gene Wallace might retaliate against her for implicating him in the violent act. Roy reassured her that Wallace would be afraid to take any steps that might expose him to prosecution and added, "besides, wherever he is, he's probably in a catatonic state on drugs."

But at times Julie was mystified by the arcane nature of some of Roy's demands. Once Roy had Susan disguise herself as Julie's mother— a woman named Joann Ekstrom—and go to the Washington Library in Macon to do some research on the microfiche files of news stories from the *Macon Telegraph*. Roy gave Susan and Julie a number of exercises designed to deliberately attract attention to their presence in the library. Susan was to seek instructions on how to use the microfilm to ensure that her face would be remembered, and before leaving, she was to inquire at the lost-and-found desk whether a Cross pen, monogrammed with Joann Ekstrom's initials, had been turned in following a previous visit she was supposed to have made. In due course Roy also put Joann Ekstrom on his payroll as a "private investigator," but he insisted that Julie refer to her mother as "Ann Linn."

Julie's acting lessons continued under Roy's assiduous tutelage well into the spring of 1986. Almost always Susan accompanied Roy at these sessions in Julie's modest apartment, and Susan seemed to enjoy playing with Julie's young son. At times Susan would come alone for the rehearsal sessions, and Julie observed that on these occasions Susan was warmer, less subservient, but still whenever a decision was called for, she would always say, "Let me talk to Roy and see what he wants to do. Then I'll get back with you."

When Roy was satisfied that Julie had mastered the "Gene Wallace script," he employed an attorney in Atlanta named Jake Arbes to take the formal steps toward overturning the 1972 conviction. On September 2, 1986, Arbes filed a petition for writ of *error coram nobis* asserting that the 1972 conviction was fundamentally flawed because Roy had not been allowed to present evidence of Gene Wallace's involvement in the bombing. Roy would later say that working to have his name cleared through an orderly legal process gave him a sense of relief from "a threat of imminent death."

The *coram nobis* petition is a seldom-used legal stratagem—in fact, it has since been abolished by congressional statute—and there is no record in legal literature that anyone ever pursued it with such determination as Roy Moody did in the ensuing months. But the court authorities in Macon attached no such urgent importance to the proceeding; there was enough serious new business of justice to handle without reopening old cases on dubious grounds. On December 11, 1986, Assistant U.S. Attorney Miriam Walmsley Duke made the formal response required by law to Roy's petition, basically stating that Roy had put forth no sufficient grounds to support his claim and that in any event, too much time had elapsed and the sentence had already been served. After that the matter languished for nearly a year before Roy demanded, on October 30, 1987, an expedited hearing.

With the government possibly fearing that it might lose the case by default, Roy finally got his day in court on February 2, 1988 at a hearing which featured the scripted testimony of Julie Linn-West and Joann Ekstrom testifying under the name of "Ann Linn." Roy also gave his own account of the machinations of "Gene Wallace" on the fateful day sixteen years earlier.

Although Roy had waited for more than a year for a ruling, it took Judge Duross Fitzpatrick just six days after the hearing to summarily deny Roy's petition. Over the next few weeks Roy dutifully filed the obligatory motions for rehearing and reconsideration, and when these requests were denied, Roy filed his notice of appeal to the Eleventh Circuit Court of Appeals on May 12, 1988. These maneuvers labored through the ponderous appellate procedure for the remainder of the year.

Photograph from the 1953 *Vallehi*, Fort Valley High School yearbook, showing Roy Moody surrounded by girls of the senior class. Note that all the other males are on the fringes of the photograph.

Undated photograph of Roy Moody while he was in the army in the 1950s.

Roy Moody in an undated photograph taken by Susan McBride Moody at an unidentified motel, probably in the late 1980s.

Susan McBride Moody in 1990. (Photograph by John Spink, *Atlanta Journal-Constitution*.)

House on Dublin Avenue in Macon, Georgia, where a bomb packaged for mailing exploded, seriously injuring Roy Moody's wife, Hazel. (Photograph by the author, 1993.)

The Shootin Iron Shop in Griffin, Georgia, where Moody purchased the gunpowder used in his mail bombs. (Photograph by the author, 1993.)

Old town center of Rex, Georgia, where Roy Moody lived in 1989 when he built the bombs. (Photograph by the author, 1993.)

Robert Vance at about the age of two
with his mother, Mae Smith Vance;
sister, Martha Vance (Cameron);
brothers Bill (left) and Harrell (right).
(Vance family photograph.)

Robert Vance
as a second
lieutenant in the
Judge Advocate
General's Corps
in the mid-1950s.
(Vance family
photograph.)

Helen and Bob Vance on their
wedding day, October 4, 1953,
in Cullman, Alabama. (Vance
family photograph.)

Official portrait of Robert S. Vance
as a federal judge in 1978.
(Vance family photograph.)

The Vance home on Shook Hill Road the day after the bombing in
December 1989. (*Birmingham News.*)

Undated school photograph
of Robert Edward Robinson.
(Robinson family photograph.)

Robbie Robinson and
sister Barbara as teenagers.
(Robinson family photograph.)

Robbie Robinson with
his mother and father
at his graduation
from the University of
Georgia Law School
in 1974. (Robinson
family photograph.)

Robbie Robinson with his mother, father, and other family members at his election to the Savannah City Council in 1982. (Robinson family photograph.)

Robbie Robinson with daughters Edwina (left) and Tiffany at a celebration of his reelection to the Savannah City Council in 1986. (Robinson family photograph.)

Robbie Robinson's law office on Abercorn Street in Savannah. The windows on the second floor are still boarded up after being damaged in the 1989 explosion. (Photograph by the author, 1993.)

House on Skyline Drive in Rex, Georgia, where Roy Moody built the bombs that killed Vance and Robinson. (Photograph by the author, 1993.)

Roy Moody (center) with attorneys Michael Hauptman (left) and Bruce Harvey (right) in 1990. (Photograph by Jonathan Newton, *Atlanta Journal-Constitution*.)

Edward D. Tolley, the lawyer who represented Roy Moody at his federal trial in St. Paul in 1991. (Photograph by Don Nelson, *Athens Observer*.)

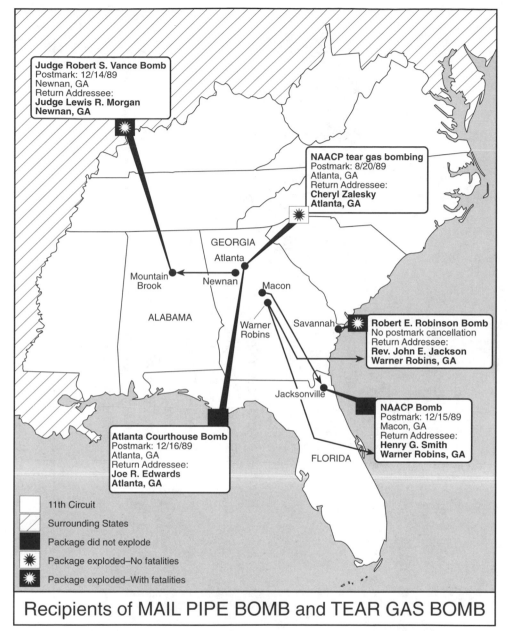

Map showing the destinations of the five bombs that were sent through the mail by Roy Moody in 1989. (United States government exhibit no. 1094 in the trial of *United States v. Walter Leroy Moody Jr.*)

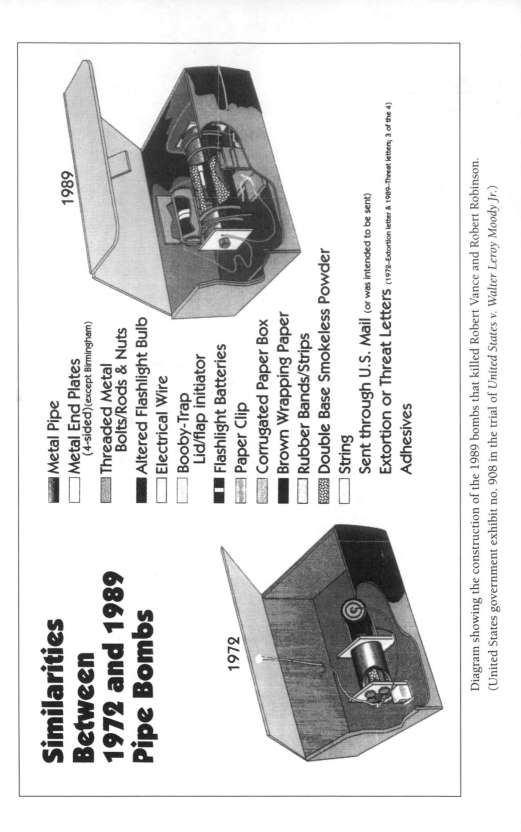

Similarities Between 1972 and 1989 Pipe Bombs

1989

1972

- Metal Pipe
- Metal End Plates (4-sided)(except Birmingham)
- Threaded Metal Bolts/Rods & Nuts
- Altered Flashlight Bulb
- Electrical Wire
- Booby-Trap Lid/flap initiator
- Flashlight Batteries
- Paper Clip
- Corrugated Paper Box
- Brown Wrapping Paper
- Rubber Bands/Strips
- Double Base Smokeless Powder
- String
- Sent through U.S. Mail (or was intended to be sent)
- Extortion or Threat Letters (1972-Extortion letter & 1989-Threat letters; 3 of the 4)
- Adhesives

Diagram showing the construction of the 1989 bombs that killed Robert Vance and Robert Robinson. (United States government exhibit no. 908 in the trial of *United States v. Walter Leroy Moody Jr.*)

10   A Second Reconstruction

For virtually all of Bob Vance's professional life, the towering figures on the federal judiciary in Alabama had been Frank M. Johnson Jr., the United States district judge in Montgomery, and Richard T. Rives, a member of the Fifth Circuit Court of Appeals whose jurisdiction stretched from Florida to Texas. From their modest chambers in the federal building in Montgomery, Johnson and Rives had rendered hundreds of decisions that changed the social and political landscape of Alabama in incalculable ways. Indeed, by the 1970s, Frank Johnson was routinely called, although much to his chagrin, "the real governor of Alabama." His jurisdiction in antidiscrimination cases had placed under his single-handed control all public schools of the state, the state police force, mental hospitals, prisons, and the state civil service mechanism. In addition, Rives and Johnson had accomplished by judicial fiat the massive reapportionment of the state legislature to break the grip of the white conservative lawmakers who represented the Black Belt.

At first bounce, they seemed an improbable pair of revolutionaries. Born in the closing years of the nineteenth century, Rives was a product of the Old South—and the poor

South. Gentle in manner, courtly in appearance, Rives was among the last judges to be appointed to the federal bench by President Harry Truman. Johnson came from the antisecessionist hill country of Alabama, the son of a man who during the depression had been the sole Republican in the Alabama Legislature. He had gained his appointment to the federal district bench under President Eisenhower after conservative Democrats lost a bitter battle to place one of their own in the coveted position.

Despite their disparate backgrounds, they moved in concert in their determination to extend the constitutional guarantees that had been largely denied to Alabama's black citizens for a century following the Civil War. In one of their first decisions as a team in 1956, they declared Montgomery's bus-segregation laws unconstitutional—the denouement of Martin Luther King's famous bus boycott.

By the time Bob Vance took his seat on the Fifth Circuit Court of Appeals, the Herculean judicial labors of Rives and Johnson—which in their massive whole amounted to the Second Reconstruction—were largely completed in Alabama and, indeed, widely accepted throughout the South. Even George Wallace now conceded that segregation mandated by law had been an evil. Bull Connor, who once proclaimed that integration would never be suffered in Birmingham as long as he lived, had died three years earlier, though he lived long enough to see his haughty boast mocked by a new social order. The fundamental guarantees of the Civil Rights Act of 1964—the right of access to hotels and restaurants, the right not to be excluded from jobs on the basis of race— were accepted as simple justice. With the unfettered access to the ballot guaranteed under the Voting Rights Act of 1965, black voters suddenly found themselves assiduously courted by white politicians; even the most obdurate segregationists of the 1950s, Herman Talmadge of Georgia and Strom Thurmond of South Carolina, added blacks to their senatorial staffs, and the redoubtable James Oliver Eastland, forced from the Senate by the rising tide of black votes in Mississippi, quietly made a contribution of five hundred dollars to the NAACP in his dying days.

Still, this superficial success in addressing the nation's most intractable social problem carried a sinister hidden side as well. Racial tensions did not melt away as the proponents of integration to confidently expected; rather, the nature of the problem only had become more subtle and complex. Soon it grew apparent that a simple absence of discrimination would not be sufficient to rectify the profound educational, economic, and social disparities that had become embedded during two hundred years of slavery and segregation. The portentous words "affirmative action" began to appear in court decisions.

Meanwhile, the segregationists devised new strategies. By 1972 George Wallace had reversed his position as a tenacious overt segregationist, but soon it became clear that the change was an adroit redefinition of the race issue. As he relentlessly pursued the presidency and the Alabama governorship in alternate election cycles, he formulated "code words" for tapping the racial fears of Americans. To blue-collar workers, the word "quota" came to mean, "Watch out, union man, the federal courts are gonna take away your job and give it to a black woman." To comfortable professionals who lived in the upscale neighborhoods of America's cities, the words "law and order" came to mean, "Watch out, rich man, a black thug's gonna break into your house, maybe rape your wife, and some bleeding-heart judge will turn 'im loose." To the religious right, the words "welfare queen" came to mean, "Watch out, Christian family, the liberals in Washington are gonna take your hard-earned money and give it to a woman who keeps having bastard young'uns." To middle-class suburban whites, "neighborhood schools" came to mean, "Watch out, neighbor, or they'll bus your children to a black school."

As the semantics changed, so did the political climate. No longer did George Wallace have the field to himself in exploiting the latent fears of white Americans of every region and every social class. By 1972, Richard Nixon had refined his "Southern Strategy" to Machiavellian perfection. It is no accident that this cynical quest for the segregationist vote through the more temperate language of the new "code words" was devised by a new Republican from South Carolina, Harry Dent, who learned his trade as a protégé of the old Dixiecrat firebrand, Strom Thurmond. By 1972 the principled if draconian conservatism of Barry Goldwater eight years earlier had been converted into an expedient ploy to win southern votes by subtly promising to ease the pressure for desegregation. This promise became an abiding article of faith for national Republican politics and delivered the South, more or less as far as the eye could see, into the hands of the party that, a century earlier, had been the hated enforcer of Reconstruction. Moreover, the "southern strategy" appealed with equal intensity in working-class neighborhoods of cities like Boston, where the federal courts were bringing increasing pressure to break down de facto segregation with such disruptive tools as crosstown busing of pupils. Playing this strategy as an accomplished violinist plays a Stradivarius, Richard Nixon swept the South and blue-collar districts of the North alike in winning a landslide reelection in 1972.

In this volatile political climate, the courts struggled to create a genuinely multiracial society. Judge Frank Scarlett's bizarre opinion in the Stell case in Savannah—the decision that stood on its head the Supreme Court's original desegregation decision of 1954—was just an aberration. Of far more far-reaching significance was the steady and systematic decisional construct that imposed on the South an "affirmative duty" to create, in the words of Judge John Minor Wisdom of the Fifth Circuit Court of Appeals, "not white schools and Negro schools—just schools." This series of decisions culminated in the supremely important 1971 case of *Swann v. Charlotte-Mecklenburg Board of Education,* in which widespread busing was ordered in order to achieve meaningful integration in the public schools of North Carolina's largest city.

By the time Vance took his seat the Fifth Circuit Court was at the end of an important period of evolution. When Vance was appointed, the Fifth Circuit covered the six southeastern states of the Gulf Coast, and the court's role in the region's development had shifted with the legal demands of the day. In the 1950s, the most challenging new issues arose from the great industrial and population expansion of Texas and Florida. The 1960s was the decade in which the legal rights of black people were inexorably established. The 1970s saw a cautious expansion of those rights to other areas.

A year after Bob Vance joined the court, President Carter elevated Frank Johnson from the district bench to the appellate court. But by 1980 the court had become so large and unwieldy, numbering more than twenty-five active and senior judges, that it became all but impossible to adjudicate appeals *en banc*—that is, for the entire court to reconsider important issues of constitutional law that had been rendered by its three-judge panels. To relieve this pressure, Congress created the

Eleventh Circuit Court of Appeals, which consisted of an even dozen judges, and Vance and Johnson soon found themselves voting together more often than not. The Eleventh Circuit covered Alabama, Georgia, and Florida, while the Fifth Circuit shrank to Texas, Louisiana, and Mississippi.

During this time Vance proved to be the kind of judge that law clerks describe as a "quick study," a man who possessed a substantial frame of reference in the law as well as an ability to grasp complex issues and reach the core of a dispute with celerity.

His workday started when he arose around dawn and began quietly pondering the day's cases as he went about the rote duties of feeding the dogs, making his own breakfast, and glancing over the *Birmingham Post-Herald* to marvel at the latest intrigues of Alabama politics. He would reach his downtown office usually before nine, and he expected all hands—his three law clerks and two secretaries—to be ready for action. He was a good office manager in the sense that he delegated assignments quickly but cheerfully, remembered birthdays and anniversaries, and knew how to stroke the egos of clever law clerks.

There was a certain disdain for other judges who seemed constantly to stew and labor to keep up with their work. Vance's docket was always clear, and often the day's tasks were completed by the lunch hour, so that the judge had his afternoons free to kibitz with other lawyers on the telephone or even receive, slightly surreptitiously, old colleagues to lament or savor political defeats and victories of the past. Despite the hint of impropriety at the spectacle of a federal judge cavorting *en camera* with grimy politicians and cagey lawyers, he kept the conversation away from pending cases, and deep down he maintained a belief that he could separate his natural inclination as an unabashed extrovert from his fastidious duty as a judge.

As Vance grew secure in his new role, oral arguments by lawyers revealed that in one important respect, he did not bring to his new work what is called "a judicial temperament." In a word, he did not suffer fools gladly. When a lawyer sought to cover his lack of preparation by playing the role of a good ol' boy country lawyer, Vance dressed the poor man down much as Henry VIII might have dealt with a clumsy footman. At times his impatience went even further: In his questioning of lawyers in oral arguments, if he sensed, fairly or not, that the law was being trifled with, he could come down on the errant lawyer with a force that was not merely intimidating but positively humiliating. Yet, no lawyer questioned his legal competence.

From the moment of its creation, the Eleventh Circuit Court confronted a number of vexing new issues in the law. The crime explosion was especially pronounced in the new circuit because the region, most notably the peninsula of Florida with its thousand-mile shoreline, was so vulnerable to penetration by drug-runners from Latin America. At the same time, the court was deluged by a tidal wave of appeals involving the death penalty, which had always been applied with greater gusto in the Southeast than in other parts of the nation. And finally, there was, ironically, a Supreme Court that was growing increasingly antagonistic toward the pattern of legal innovation that had been encouraged by the Supreme Court for nearly two decades under Earl Warren and, to a lesser extent, even under Warren Burger.

Even though he had learned his law in the age of Earl Warren, Bob Vance did not bring an inclination for judicial activism to the bench. In his earliest decisions Vance signaled a sensitivity if not deference to the intricate political and economic choices that legislators confronted in a poor state like Alabama. Still, little brush-fires continued to flare as local officials in the more benighted regions of the South continued to concoct all manner of ruses to preserve remnants of white supremacy.

When confronted with such palpable ploys, Vance did not flinch at applying the law. Typical of such cases was a significant voting-rights case that arose in the early 1980s from his home state of Alabama. A black woman named Carmen Edwards and a white man named Victor Underwood had been denied the right to vote under an obscure section of the Alabama Constitution of 1901 that allowed voter-registrars to exclude anyone who had committed crimes involving "moral turpitude." Edwards and Underwood each had been convicted of passing bad checks, and a local registrar—in an expansive definition of "moral turpitude"— had rejected them as potential voters.

The unlikely pair sued in federal court, claiming that the hoary constitutional provision was intended in its inception to exclude black voters, thus was null under the Voting Rights Act of 1965. A lower federal court ruled that the Alabama law clearly was not racially discriminatory in its application, because, after all, Underwood was white; the law had equally excluded black and white alike. Moreover, the Supreme Court, which was by then steadily narrowing the scope and impact of the civil-rights measures of the 1960s, had already ruled that states could erect obstacles to voting so long as there was no overwhelming evidence that racial discrimination was not a "substantial or motivating factor" in enacting such laws.

Edwards and Underwood appealed to the Eleventh Circuit Court, and Bob Vance drew the assignment to write the opinion. He delved deeply into Alabama history, quoting extensively from political debates of eight decades before, which showed beyond question that the very purpose of the constitutional convention that drafted the "moral turpitude" test was to establish white supremacy. Vance reversed the lower court on the grounds that the mere passage of time could not save "a purposefully discriminatory scheme whose effects still reverberate today." A year later, the Supreme Court upheld the Vance position.

In another significant voting-rights case in the 1980s, Vance once more came face to face with his old adversary, George Wallace, who was then serving his final term as governor. The case involved the operation of a dog-racing track in Greene County, an impoverished backwater region of west Alabama near the Mississippi border. In 1975 the state legislature had authorized the dog-track, which quickly became the county's principal source of public revenue through taxes on bets. The original act allowed the county's legislators to appoint members of the commission that licensed and regulated the track operations. At that time the state legislators were white—a holdover from Greene County's past. But when these legislators were about to be replaced by black representatives, the legislature hastily passed a measure that placed the power of appointment of the racing commissioners in the governor's hands. In other counties where the popular form of gambling was permitted, regulation remained in local hands.

It was, Vance concluded, a transparent scheme to deny black citizens of Greene County their capacity to regulate an important local institution, and this was precisely the kind of subterfuge the Voting Rights Act of 1965 was enacted to prevent.

But if Vance embraced a liberal attitude on civil rights for Americans, he demonstrated early in his career that he had little inclination for expanding the protective cloak of the Constitution to foreigners. In one of the most significant decisions of his twelve years as an appellate judge, Vance enunciated, in a case formally styled *Jean v. Nelson,* a rule of law that firmly shut the door on a throng of Haitian refugees seeking asylum in the United States.

For much of the twentieth century, the South Florida metropolis of Miami served as a magnet, an entry point for the human flotsam and jetsam that was churned up by the relentless social and economic problems of the Caribbean islands. Tens of thousands of inhabitants fled the dozen or so shaky states to escape persecution or penury, and in the pecking order of privation, none were more desperate than those who came from Haiti. The island-nation not only shared the general economic misery of the region but also labored under the curse of racial and linguistic isolation: The country's six million inhabitants were almost entirely of African descent, they spoke a pidgin French called Creole, and their main religion was voodoo. For more than thirty years in the second half of the century, the Haitian people groaned under ruthless back-to-back dictatorships of François (Papa Doc) Duvalier and his son, Jean Claude (Baby Doc) Duvalier.

By 1980 the repression had become so rampant that thousands of desperate Haitians took to sea in rickety boats, heading for Miami. Many perished at sea, but large numbers began to reach their destination of South Florida.

The Haitian exodus of 1980 coincided with a similar flood of refugees who set out from Fidel Castro's Cuba for the shores of South Florida. This flood of refugees created a huge political problem for President Jimmy Carter, whose administration struggled to cope with the influx and eventually applied a semantic abracadabra by classifying the Cubans as "political refugees" and the Haitians as "economic refugees." The distinction was important, because the former were entitled to asylum in this country and the latter were not.

Carter's loss of the presidency did not diminish the lure of the United States to the Haitians. By 1981 the population of undocumented Haitians in the Miami area had swollen to more than thirty-five thousand;

to stem the flow, Ronald Reagan's commissioner of immigration and naturalization, Alan C. Nelson, ordered the internment of newly arrived Haitians in large holding centers in the Miami area.

The detained refugees brought a class-action lawsuit—Marie Lucie Jean happened to be the first name on the list—charging the government deprived them of their constitutional right of due process by holding them in the camps. In a decision that was more fraught with the rhetoric of emotion than the logic of the law, Federal District Judge Eugene P. Spellman declared the refugees had been denied their constitutional rights; after all, he reasoned, they stood to be imprisoned for an indefinite period without charge.

The case was of sufficient import to command an *en banc* hearing before all twelve of the active judges on the Eleventh Circuit Court of Appeals to review the decision. On February 28, 1984, the Eleventh Circuit reversed Spellman's holding, and Bob Vance was the author of the deciding opinion.

Vance based his decision in large measure on what is known as a legal fiction—a judicially created myth or assumption to serve as the basis of a legal rule. The fiction on which Vance's decision rested was that the Haitians had *never really entered the United States*—never mind that at that very moment they were physically located in the state of Florida. Yet, it was a leap of imagination that was essential if Vance were to grant what the government sought, which was to return the refugees to the tender mercies of the tottering regime of "Baby Doc," who, within two years, would flee into exile in France.

Once he had applied the fiction that the Haitians had never "entered" the United States, Vance proceeded to bestow virtually unlimited authority on the immigration authorities in their discretion to exclude aliens, including the power to discriminate on the basis of national origin. "Aliens seeking admission to the United States," Vance declared, "have no constitutional rights with regard to their applications and must be content to accept whatever statutory rights and privileges they are granted by Congress." Vance expressly rejected such international-law considerations as the United Nations' Universal Declaration of Human Rights as having any bearing on the case. Any other holding, he went on, would inevitably result in the nation "losing control of our borders."

Within a year, the United States Supreme Court upheld *Jean v. Nelson*. Bob Vance had effectively written the law of the land in admission of refugees, and it was a law so harsh that eight of his law clerks would, in a 1991 law-review article that generally celebrated Vance's contributions to modern jurisprudence, lament the "xenophobic tenor" of his seminal decision in the Haitian refugee case.

But all Bob Vance's judicial work was not so serious or far-reaching. If a jurist stays on the bench long enough, moments of comic relief inevitably intrude into the sober and eclectic process of judging, and for Bob Vance, such was the case of *Krueger v. City of Pensacola*. The issue: Could the city of Pensacola forbid topless dancing in an establishment that served alcoholic beverages? In his opinion in the case, Judge Vance deadpanned that topless dancing had "coexisted rather uneventfully" with other forms of social life in Pensacola—until a topless bar opened too close to a church. The judge held that the city's reliance on its authority to regulate liquor sales was simply a subterfuge to clamp an unconstitutional ban on nude dancing, which, he noted, the Supreme Court had held to be "a form of expression which is protected at least to some extent by the first amendment."

In the 1980s, civil rights litigation—at least, the old fashioned 1960s variety—constituted just a fraction of the Eleventh Circuit Court's docket of appeals. With the growth of violent crime, the appeals-court judges were increasingly called on to make, literally, life-or-death decisions as the court's docket became flooded with appeals of prisoners who were awaiting execution in the state penitentiaries of Georgia, Alabama, and Florida—states that had long demonstrated an almost bloodthirsty zeal for imposing the death penalty. As the circuit's former chief judge John Godbold ruefully noted in 1987, while the Eleventh Circuit covered only three states, it generated as many death-penalty appeals as all the other ten circuits combined. "On any one day," Godbold said, "our court will have at least fifty pending death cases."

Moreover, the cases were often hideously complex in both fact and law, and almost always were accompanied by voluminous transcripts of state court proceedings. Yet they could not be handled summarily, because lives were at stake, and there was no possibility of reversing a flawed judgment, once carried out.

Bob Vance had barely taken his seat on the court before he got a baptism of fire on the death-penalty issue. As a lawyer whose practice rarely included grubby criminal cases of any kind, Vance never represented a defendant who faced the death penalty. Still, simply by reading the newspapers, and by listening to sermons at his church on Sundays, he formed his own personal opposition to capital punishment.

Indeed, for some time opposition to the death penalty had been the trend in the country and even in Vance's home state of Alabama during his own lifetime. It was not always so. In the 1930s, legal execution in Alabama had pretty much supplanted lynch-law, so that hardly a month passed that some poor wretch was not literally "burned," to use the macabre jargon of the underworld of yesteryear, in the oversized garish orange electric chair that stood in the center of a small, stark-white chamber deep behind the forbidding walls of Alabama's Kilby Prison in Montgomery. In the year 1936 alone, seventeen persons were put to death in that chamber, windowless except for a little hatch that enabled a handful of official witnesses to observe the grim midnight ritual. Multiple executions—including five in the predawn hours of February 9, 1934—were common. It could not have escaped Bob Vance's notice that virtually all of the condemned were young men from impoverished backgrounds, and 80 percent were black, in a state where blacks constituted only a little more than a quarter of the population. Most who died in the electric chair committed murders or rapes, but many had only been convicted of robbery, and one—a twenty-two-year-old black man named Frank Bass from Alabama's Tennessee Valley region—paid with his life on August 8, 1941, for the common crime of burglary.

As economic conditions improved after the Second World War, executions fell off dramatically in Alabama and the nation. In 1965, only two persons—one of them in Alabama—were put to death throughout the nation, and there followed a prolonged moratorium on capital punishment. Juries continued to mete out the death penalty, but judges, and even such hardline governors at John Patterson and George Wallace, grew increasingly reluctant to allow the execution to proceed. There had been no execution in any state for seven years by the time Bobby Hill, the Savannah black lawyer and politician, helped win the case of *Furman v. Georgia,* in which the Supreme Court, in 1972, held that the death penalty had come to be imposed so "wantonly and freakishly" as to constitute the kind of cruel and unusual punishment that was forbidden by the Eighth Amendment to the Constitution. Hill represented only one of the three defendants who brought the Furman case, but the court's decision had the effect of nullifying the death sentences of some six hundred convicts who languished on the squalid death rows of thirty-two state prisons across the country.

Even so, the Supreme Court, contrary to widespread and apprehensive public perception, had not "outlawed" the death penalty with finality. In fact, one state statute even survived *Furman v. Georgia*—Rhode Island's law that imposed a mandatory death penalty for anyone convicted of murder while already serving a life sentence. The fact that every one of the nine justices wrote his own separate opinion in the Furman case illustrated the deep division within the high court over capital punishment, and this ambivalence spurred states with strong death-penalty sentiment to draft new laws to overcome the constitutional impediments cited in the Furman case, notably the arbitrary manner in which executions had been carried out in the past.

The first state to enact a "modern" death-penalty statute was Florida, and the Sunshine State lost no time in applying its new law in the case of John Arthur Spinkelink.

Spinkelink was the perfect candidate for execution. He was so close to illiteracy that he occasionally misspelled his own name. By the time he was twenty-four, Spinkelink had already been judicially declared to be a "career criminal." He escaped from a California prison in 1972 and began a meandering flight across the country. Along the way he picked up a traveling companion named Joseph J. Szymankiewicz. Eventually the pair reached Tallahassee, Florida, where, on the night of February 4, 1973, Spinkelink shot Szymankiewicz to death in a cheap motel room. Spinkelink claimed he acted in self defense after Szymankiewicz had forced him at gunpoint to commit sodomy. But the Florida prosecutors persuaded a jury that Spinkelink had shot the sleeping Szymankiewicz in cold blood, and the young drifter became one of the first defendants to be sentenced to death under the new Florida statute.

For the next three years, Spinkelink languished on the rapidly enlarging death row at Starke Prison. Finally, in 1976, the Florida law, along with similar new death-penalty statutes in Georgia and Texas, was upheld by the United States Supreme Court in a case known as *Gregg v. Georgia.* By this time the court's composition had so changed that only two justices—William Brennan and Thurgood Marshall—continued to insist that the death penalty, under any and all circumstances, constituted "cruel and unusual punishment."

Moreover, during four years between the Furman decision and the Gregg reversal, sentiment in the nation rapidly shifted as politicians at every level made "crime in the streets" a key item on the political agenda. The eleven-year moratorium on capital punishment officially ended on January 17, 1977, when the state of Utah put to death, by firing squad, a convicted murderer named Gary Mark Gilmore, who in effect volunteered for execution by insisting that all appeals be dropped.

But while Gilmore's execution signaled a renewed use of capital punishment under more scrupulous standards of justice, other death-row inhabitants chose not to go so gently into that good night. Rather, their lawyers raged in a torrent of litigation, and nowhere were the appeals more prodigious than in the Fifth Circuit Court. Soon after he went onto the bench, Bob Vance was assigned to a panel of three judges of the Fifth Circuit to hear the appeal of John Arthur Spinkelink.

Spinkelink's appeal had already been considered and rejected by the Florida Supreme Court, as well as by Federal District Judge William H. Stafford of Tallahassee. Judge Stafford's decision reached the Fifth Circuit in what lawyers call a "kitchen-sink" appeal, in which every conceivable legal argument, no matter how outlandish, is put forward. The appeal asserted that Spinkelink's rights had been violated in more than thirty ways.

As a new judge, Bob Vance maintained a low profile, asking few questions at oral arguments in the Spinkelink case. In the summer of 1978, the panel issued a lengthy opinion that denied Spinkelink's appeal. The opinion was written by Judge Robert A. Ainsworth Jr., a respected veteran Fifth Circuit jurist from New Orleans, but neither Vance nor the other panel member, the circuit's venerable chief judge, John R. Brown, dissented from Ainsworth's measured discourse. Still, despite his subdued role, Vance must have recognized the Spinkelink case as a grim harbinger of what lay ahead.

Even though capital punishment had been reinstated in principle, the Supreme Court left many unanswered questions as to when and under what circumstances the penalty might be applied. The new death-penalty statutes of Florida, Georgia, and Texas passed muster, but others did not. In Alabama, the effort to reinstate capital punishment in 1975 emerged in a draconian form: Juries were allowed only the options of convicting the accused of capital murder, or acquitting outright. There was no provision for conviction on lesser charges such as manslaughter or second-degree murder—a principle long embedded in criminal law. When this law reached the United States Supreme Court in 1980, in the case of *Beck v. Alabama,* the justices held that such a narrow choice inevitably injected a degree of uncertainty into the trial process that could not be tolerated in capital cases.

Against this background, in 1981 Bob Vance wrote his first major decision involving the death penalty. The case involved the appeal of John Lewis Evans III, a young thug who in 1978 robbed and murdered, execution-style, a well-liked immigrant storekeeper named Edward Nassar in Mobile, Alabama.

Evans was the kind of defendant who drives lawyers and judges to distraction with bizarre and erratic behavior. At his trial in state court, Evans, against the advice of his own court-appointed attorney, took the witness stand, stated without remorse that he had killed Nassar and would kill again if he got the chance, and "very sincerely" asked the jury to give him a death sentence rather than to imprison him for the rest of his life. The jury readily granted Evans's theatrical wish.

This decision did not, however, end the matter. Evans's mother and various public-interest law groups pursued appeals, and at times Evans himself seemed to vacillate on his death wish. Once Evans's imminent execution was stayed by Justice William F. Rehnquist, probably the Supreme Court's most intractable opponent of federal-court intervention in state capital cases. In the summer of 1981 Evans's desperate appeal reached the Fifth Circuit Court, and Bob Vance was assigned to write the opinion.

It was not a long or complicated opinion. Evans had, after all, been convicted under the state statute that had been subsequently declared unconstitutional by the Supreme Court in the Beck case. Placing himself in the role of Evans's attorneys, Vance wrote that the "brooding omnipresence" of the Alabama statute without question influenced the course of action of lawyers who might have pursued a strategy of getting Evans convicted on lesser charges had the law permitted this.

When the case reached the Supreme Court a year later, however, the high court added yet another dimension of confusion to its developing death-penalty jurisprudence. Appearing to fly in the face of its own decision in the Beck case, the Supreme Court reversed the Fifth Circuit's decision and reinstated Evans's death sentence, which had been passed under exactly the same law. The court reasoned that since Evans had confessed to cold-blooded murder at his very trial, there was no possibility that the jury could have found him guilty of a lesser charge. The decision was unanimous; even Justices Brennan and Marshall, while noting their continued belief that capital punishment was unconstitutional in any and all cases, agreed that there had been no procedural defect in Evans's trial.

The decisive reversal had a profound effect on Bob Vance. He clearly was proud of his decision in the Evans case, because he conveyed this sentiment to Michael Mello during a routine interview for a clerk's position in the summer of 1981. But when the Supreme Court reversed the Evans case not long after that interview, Mello detected a dark change in the way Vance approached death-penalty cases. "He then and thereafter," Mello recalled, years later, "spoke the language of judicial restraint."

Indeed, when the Evans case drew to its inexorable grim conclusion on April 22, 1983, Vance was among the judges who rejected the final desperate appeals of the condemned man's lawyers. After a day of frantic litigation, Evans, by this time no longer eager for death, was strapped into the electric chair at a little after seven o'clock in the evening. But because of a malfunction in the electric chair, it took nearly two hours to carry out the execution, and at least one witness came away convinced that Evans was not electrocuted but was burned to death.

After the reversal of the Evans case, Bob Vance continued to labor under the curse of death-penalty cases, including the appeal of one of the most notorious murderers of modern times, serial-killer Theodore Bundy, who was ultimately put to death in Florida. But as a judge, Vance never again ruled in favor of constitutional claims that would have had the far-reaching effect of thwarting the executioner.

With the advent of the Reagan presidency in 1981, it was clear that the federal judiciary of the United States was about to undergo a major infusion of judges of a far more conservative bent than those appointed by Jimmy Carter, or even Gerald Ford and Richard Nixon, for that matter. By this time Bob Vance had settled comfortably into the relative anonymity of federal appellate judges and had begun to develop his own judicial philosophy, which sought to balance fairness and pragmatism. This philosophy found its subtle expression in the annual summer ritual of choosing law clerks for the coming year.

The law clerk is an ancient institution in the legal profession, and as the federal judiciary evolved in America, federal judges found law clerks indispensable to their labors. In earlier times, the clerks for the most part were bright and ambitious boys drawn from the local community in the hope of picking up enough practical knowledge of the law to enable them to pass the bar examination and establish their own practices. By the time Richard Rives was appointed to the Fifth Circuit in 1951, appellate federal judges were still allotted only one law clerk, but no longer did the work permit on-the-job training. Rather, a pattern had emerged whereby the clerk was chosen from the most recent graduates of the top law schools of the judge's home state.

As the law began to expand with the advent of Earl Warren's ascendancy as chief justice in 1953, law clerkships became coveted positions that, even though they paid only subsistence wages, would greatly enhance a young lawyer's resume and virtually assure employment by a major law firm at salaries that quickly surpassed those of the judges for whom they had worked. Choosing clerks—their number increased from one to three per judge by the time Bob Vance went onto the bench—became a significant summer ritual for the judges. It was vital that the clerks' view of the role of the courts be compatible with the judge's, because the growing volume of work permitted no time for arguments other than the ones put forward by lawyers for the parties in litigation. Personal compatibility was equally important, because the clerks often became like family members to their judges.

By the mid-1980s Bob Vance had sufficiently developed a judicial philosophy that his interviews had become a relaxed yet somewhat rote exercise. When he interviewed Michael Waldman for a clerkship in the summer of 1986, the judge went through the checklist of areas of the law where the clerk might encounter conflicts between duty and conscience. As always, special attention was given to death-penalty cases. Waldman said he would have no problem in applying law and precedent.

"Are there any other areas where you might have problems?" Vance asked.

Waldman, then twenty-two years of age, thought for a moment and replied with candor: "I might run into some difficulty in labor cases. My father and my grandfather were labor lawyers."

Vance nodded with understanding. Much of his practice, too, had involved labor law.

Then the judge turned slightly in his swivel chair, and pointed to a case of books that lined the wall to his right.

"Do you see those shelves?" Vance began with a slight sense of weariness. "The top four contain books that have been added in just the eight years since I came onto this court.

"Now, I don't want to add any more shelves than is absolutely necessary. The truth is, out of the dozens of cases that reach my desk each year, only eight or ten will involve serious legal principles that deserve to be examined at length. Cases that deserve to be in those books. Don't misunderstand. *Every* case is important to the parties involved, and we have an obligation to do right by them. But we don't have to make a constitutional case out of every lawsuit that comes through this office."

Impressed by Vance's candor and modesty, Waldman eagerly took the job when it was offered a few days later.

As it happened, Waldman's year turned out to be one of the most exciting and propitious of Bob Vance's dozen years on the bench. In 1986, the mercurial reign of George Wallace, who was by then a pathetic aging invalid, was at long last drawing to a close. For twenty-four years Wallace had so dominated the politics of the state, even during the two brief periods when he was out of office, that the political development of Alabama had been in a state of virtual arrest.

The 1986 governor's race attracted the customary large and diverse throng, a ragbag of eccentrics, has-beens, and serious contenders. In the first primary election, on June 3, two talented young politicians emerged as the one-on-one candidates in the June 24 runoff, offering Alabamians a clear ideological choice to lead the state in the post-Wallace years. The progressive, populist faction of the state's politics—carriers of the tradition of Hugo Black, Lister Hill, and Big Jim Folsom—found its champion in Lieutenant Governor Bill Baxley, a young lawyer from Dothan in the southeastern corner of Alabama known as "the Wiregrass." The conservative, States' Rights Democrats—in the tradition of George Wallace and Bull Connor—rallied behind state Attorney General Charles Graddick, who came from the moss-and-magnolia Old South city of Mobile.

Baxley, who had also served two terms as attorney general, had earned something of a national reputation as a young southern liberal as a result of his obsessive pursuit of unsolved or unprosecuted racial crimes in Alabama's inglorious past. In his most sensational case of this kind, in 1976 he won the conviction and life sentence of an aging Birmingham Ku Kluxer named Robert Chambless as the engineer of the notorious Birmingham church bombing in 1963.

Graddick, as attorney general during the middle 1980s, had also built his reputation as a tough prosecutor, but it was in a manner quite different than Baxley. Graddick prosecuted "common criminals" with a vengeance, which meant, in practical terms, a great many more blacks than whites. He pursued the death penalty with singular zeal, and during the campaign, his billboards across Alabama contained only the words "GRADDICK For Governor" contained in a heavy black border.

In addition to his liberalism, Bill Baxley had earned a statewide reputation as a kind of educated good ol' boy with a weakness for high cards, strong "likker," and fast women. Indeed, he had lost the governor's race eight years earlier after newspapers carried vivid accounts of an episode in which he won thirty-two thousand dollars, while inebriated, at the blackjack tables in Las Vegas. Aware of these predilections, Baxley's supporters approached the runoff election with great apprehension, and once again, the candidate's penchant for reckless behavior rose to the occasion: A female reporter who came to interview him for a campaign story wound up staying through the night, and the little dalliance was eagerly and prominently publicized in the state's obdurately conservative largest newspaper, the *Birmingham News*.

But Alabamians, amused by the antic behavior of the colorful "Kissin' Jim" Folsom, tended to be tolerant of personal high jinks if done with a flair, so despite Baxley's indiscretions the race shaped up as one of the closest in modern times.

Graddick, aware that he needed every conservative vote that could be lured to the polls, made an overt bid for Republican support. In his official capacity as attorney general, Graddick issued an opinion—which flew in the face of the law—that it was perfectly legal for those 36,448 Alabamians who had voted in the *Republican* primary on June 3 to vote in the *Democratic* primary runoff on June 24. As election day approached polling officials were bombarded with ominous warnings that they might go to jail if they attempted to prevent the Republicans from voting.

The Republicans had already chosen Guy Hunt as their candidate in the June 3 primary. Hunt was hardly the sort of fellow that the state's Republicans would want to take to The Club, which was the official name of Birmingham's swankiest social gathering-place. Indeed, Hunt had barely graduated from high school, and made his living as an erstwhile Amway salesman and part-time Primitive Baptist preacher in the upstate hamlet of Holly Pond. His political experience consisted of holding local office in a small county. But no one expected Hunt to be elected; he had run before, and lost overwhelmingly. He was just a disposable candidate, carrying the party's banner in the hope of getting voters accustomed to the idea of two-party elections in a state that continued to be dominated, at least in its home politics, by the brawling and bumptious Democrats. Being more pragmatic than principled, in the steamy summer of 1986, the Republicans knew their choice for the next governor lay between Baxley and Graddick, and Graddick was their hands-down favorite.

On June 24 thousands of Republicans who had voted to nominate Hunt in the June 3 primary returned to the polls to vote for Graddick, and the ploy worked: In one of the closest gubernatorial primary elections in Alabama history, Graddick polled 470,051 votes to Baxley's 461,295.

Baxley and his loyalist Democrat supporters lost no time in challenging the result, citing "massive illegal voting" that resulted from the Graddick-Republican cabal. Baxley demanded that the Alabama Democratic Executive Committee wrest the nomination from Graddick and give it to him. By this time, the skilled hand of Bob Vance had been

missing from the committee's helm for nearly a decade, but nevertheless, the party machinery was more securely than ever in the hands of
the Loyalists—thanks in large measure to the infusion of black political
muscle into the process that was brought about by Vance.

The party dutifully obliged and named Baxley the nominee, but the
outraged Graddick appealed the party's decision to federal district Judge
J. Foy Guin Jr. in Birmingham.

Bob Vance had watched the shenanigans with more than passing
interest, and even though the only political role permitted a federal
judge is the casting of a secret ballot, it is virtually certain that Vance
cast that ballot, on both June 3 and June 24, for his old friend and ally,
Bill Baxley. Vance's interest intensified as the bitter brawl spilled over
from the political arena into the federal courts; he sent a law clerk to
observe the proceedings in Guin's court, convinced that Guin, a Birmingham "Big Mule" lawyer who had been appointed to the bench by
President Nixon in 1973, would seize the occasion "to screw the Democrats." After two months of acrimonious haggling, Guin issued his ruling, which blocked the party from naming Baxley as its nominee and
ordered a new election.

Anticipating Guin's move, Baxley's partisans swiftly appealed the
decision to the Eleventh Circuit Court under special rules for expediting
matters of great public interest. The case was assigned to a panel consisting of all three of the state's Eleventh Circuit judges, John Godbold
and Frank Johnson of Montgomery and Bob Vance of Birmingham.
Vance was immediately challenged by Graddick's forces, who cited his
prior role in Democratic Party affairs. Judges are allowed great personal
discretion in responding to demands that they remove themselves from
cases, and Vance had anticipated the Graddick challenge. In a brief but
firm opinion, which in effect ruled on his own fitness to hear the case,
Vance said that if every judge in Alabama were to be disqualified for past
political associations, there would be virtually none left to hear such
cases. He would hear the case.

On October 1, one week after the briefs had been received and six
days after oral arguments were heard, the panel overruled Guin. In a
decision that bore Godbold's name but that contained major portions
written by Vance, the three judges held that the Alabama Democratic

Executive Committee had acted entirely within the law in giving the nomination to Baxley.

But as one who could read the Alabama political firmament with the skill of an astronomer charting the constellations, Bob Vance knew full well that he was delivering a Pyrrhic victory to his old friend. Even if the law was clear, the political waters had been so muddied, and the electorate so outraged at the spectacle of federal judges in effect naming a candidate for governor, the old political dynamic of automatic election of Democratic candidates had been reversed. On November 4, 1986, the voters of Alabama overwhelmingly chose Guy Hunt, the Reaganite Republican preacher from Holly Pond, over Bill Baxley, the bearer of the torch of Alabama Democratic populism, to succeed George Wallace as governor. Six years later, Hunt would be removed from office after being convicted, in a case prosecuted by Bob Vance's old political ally, state Attorney General Jimmy Evans, of using his office for personal gain.

Meanwhile, Bill Baxley retreated to private law practice, and when his wife gave birth to their first son, the child was named Robert Vance Baxley.

Some years later, in the spring of 1991, eight of the thirty-odd young men and women who had served as Bob Vance's law clerks drew one final assignment: The writing of an article in the *Alabama Law Review* assessing their esteemed mentor's contributions to the law during his dozen years of service on the appellate court. Paraphrasing Scripture, the clerks entitled their article "Footprints of a Just Man," and their 208-page article concluded with these adulatory words:

> He was a person who had lived a full life in the "real" world. He understood that mere words granting rights would not suffice to make rights live and breathe. He could see through legal formulations and the attempts of attorneys to plead their cases in order to gain an appreciation of the actual events behind those words (because he had been so good at the attorney's craft himself). He was passionate about making certain that all citizens have equal rights before the law, that the small and the powerless have a fighting chance against the large and the powerful. Judge Vance was a judicial craftsman who fully understood the powers

and the limitations of his position as an intermediate level federal judge. All of his passion for justice, fairness and equality was lived out with integrity in the context of his understanding that there were times when it was his job to make law while interpreting it, and other times where the limitations of precedent or the knowledge that he was making precedent prohibited his doing what the immediacy of the moment suggested was the just thing to do.

11 The Anarchist's Cookbook

By the end of 1988 Roy Moody had expended more than fifteen thousand dollars, and uncountable hours of his time, in an effort to have his 1972 bombing conviction overturned, and he had nothing to show for his Herculean labors but summary rejection by Judge Duross Fitzpatrick of the federal district court in Macon. His criminal record stood as an insurmountable barrier to his ever becoming a lawyer. Still, he pursued vindication with obsessive determination.

In February 1989 Moody's appeal of Judge Fitzpatrick's dismissal of his *coram nobis* petition reached the Eleventh Circuit Court of Appeals. The Eleventh Circuit Court was then made up of a dozen active judges, plus several "senior judges" who worked in semiretirement in order to maintain a tolerable level of currency in the court's ever-expanding case load, which was then approaching five thousand appeals each year. To deal with such a vast number of cases, the judges were assigned to sit in panels of three to hear appeals, and Moody's case was assigned to a panel consisting of two active judges, Phyllis Kravitch of Florida and Emmett R. Cox of Georgia, and one senior judge, Lewis R. "Pete" Morgan, who lived in semiretirement and raised horses in the small town of Newnan, thirty miles from Atlanta in northwest Georgia.

The case was argued in Atlanta by Michael Ford, whom Roy had hired to replace Jake Arbes, but who by this time was rapidly losing patience with his eccentric client. Ford was especially perplexed over Roy's curious ambivalence about the mysterious Gene Wallace, the putative architect of the botched bombing seventeen years earlier that had brought Roy to grief. On the one hand, finding Wallace seemed to be of paramount importance to Roy; on the other, Roy balked at Ford's suggestion that a private investigator be hired to locate the man. Still, Ford agreed to handle the case, on the condition that Roy Moody, who claimed to be "financially strapped," would do much of the legal work himself.

Roy eagerly agreed to this condition, and soon became a fixture in various law libraries in Atlanta. Now Susan McBride was running the Writers' Guild almost single-handedly as Roy spent his days poring over law books and pecking out legal briefs that increasingly took on an urgent, even apocalyptic tone. If Judge Fitzpatrick's standards of justice were accepted, Roy wrote in one brief with a certain blunt eloquence, "Human rights as we know them would be abolished. We would be living without the protection of the Constitution and government would freely subject us to whatever means necessary to achieve its ends. This court should not condone such repugnant practices."

Another of Roy's briefs was cryptic and ominous: "Whether this court elects to protect that right [to a new trial in the 1972 bombing case] will have profound social consequences. For in the absence of such protection, not only are citizens subjected to wrongful loss of freedom, but also one of the main incentives for them to be law abiding; the protection of their reputations is removed."

As the hearing date before the appellate panel approached, Roy arranged to have a court stenographer take down the proceedings—an unusual step at considerable cost. Despite the passionate entreaties of his briefs, Roy sensed as he sat in the courtroom that the judges were sullenly indifferent to his plight. He complained to Mike Ford that Judge Morgan, in particular, was "totally unprepared"—which possibly was true, since most appellate judges reached their decisions on the basis of written briefs rather than lawyers' oral arguments, which generally are perfunctory rituals that give the cloistered appellate courts an aspect of openness.

But it was Judge Cox's impatient questioning at the hearing that most troubled Roy Moody. During the oral arguments Judge Cox sharply questioned Mike Ford about the length of time that had elapsed since the 1972 conviction. "There must come a time when the criminal trial is over," Cox had remarked with evident exasperation. "You don't keep retrying it because of newly discovered evidence."

On June 13, the panel unanimously rejected Roy's appeal in a decision that was written by Judge Cox and relied heavily on the ancient doctrine of *res judicata,* as the principle of finality of judgment is called in the Latin language of the law.

Even though it was fully expected, the decision intensified Roy's choleric sense of outrage. As summer arrived Susan McBride discerned a marked change in her lover. In her eight reclusive and turbulent years with Roy Moody, she had grown accustomed to inexplicable periods of "the silent treatment," during which he refused to communicate in any way; such times always had passed, usually when his robust sexual appetite returned.

This time, it was different. Susan would later recall 1989 as "the worst year," when "the silent treatment" came two or three times every month. She felt as though she were "constantly walking on eggshells." She suspected the triggering cause of the persistent dark disposition that took hold of Roy Moody: During that summer, he at last confronted the reality that his long struggle for vindication had come to naught. He continued to pursue his appeal, asking for an *en banc* hearing before all twelve of the Eleventh Circuit's active judges to review the three-judge panel's adverse decision; and he knew there was the last resort, an appeal to the United States Supreme Court. But by the start of summer in 1989, Roy had become fatalistic; he faced the stark reality that the likelihood of gaining exoneration through the federal courts was virtually nil.

Roy was by no stretch of the imagination a religious man. He had not set foot in a church for years. Still, there was a residue of familiarity with the King James Bible, which he had read, even if perfunctorily, when he attended the First Baptist Church of Fort Valley while he was growing up, and he had often discussed religion with the succession of women in his life, going all the way back to Joyce Law. As he leafed through the pages of the Bible, seeking solace, his eyes fell upon Psalm 94.

> O Lord God, to whom vengeance belongeth, . . . shew thyself. . . .
> Lord, how long shall the wicked triumph? . . . They break into
> pieces thy people, O Lord. . . . They slay the widow and the stranger,
> and murder the fatherless. . . . They gather themselves together
> against the soul of the righteous, and condemn the innocent
> blood. . . . But the Lord is my defence; and my God is the rock
> of my refuge. And he shall bring upon them their own iniquity,
> and shall cut them off in their own wickedness.

Discovering the psalm, he would later maintain, was a transforming spiritual experience. The thrall of suicidal depression and hopelessness that hovered over him suddenly evaporated as he sensed that God was speaking *directly* to him, sanctioning any course of action to rectify the unremitting injustices that he had endured.

As the languid summer progressed, Roy Moody began to engage in studied, almost frenetic activity. In June he read with consuming interest newspaper accounts of the extraordinary feat of two scientists in Utah who claimed to have discovered "cold fusion"—an amazingly simple technique of harnessing the power of the hydrogen atom, a feat that had so long eluded the world's best scientific minds.

Roy announced to Susan he wanted to duplicate the experiment, and he started to pore over old manuals from his Army days and chemistry textbooks he had kept since his days as a student at Mercer University. He began to send Susan out on arcane missions. But now there was a new element: She was instructed to move with elaborate secrecy, to use disguises and false names, to park her car out of sight of the places where she was to make her purchases. At times she was ordered to travel great distances to purchase what seemed to be the most mundane materials, like wire brushes and paper towels and cardboard packing boxes. By habit that was now second nature, Susan never questioned these directives; she dutifully obeyed Roy's every command. Whenever she returned with her curious assortment of materials, ranging from brake fluid to scissors, Roy always demanded the original shopping list so that he could destroy it. On Roy's instructions, Susan scavenged the garage sales of the Atlanta suburbs to purchase three used typewriters. Later he informed her that he had purchased yet a fourth old typewriter while he was on his way back from one of his many trips to Florida.

During the early summer Roy and Susan made three trips to Jacksonville, a good three hundred miles away, and on one such trip Roy waited in a restaurant while Susan purchased some boxes, wrapping paper, and packaging tape.

Once, they drove a hundred miles to Chattanooga to purchase some stationery, which Roy used to type a letter while sitting in the truck, wearing gloves. Watching furtively, Susan could see that the letter was addressed to a chemical company, and she saw Roy stuff some money into the envelope. Not long after that episode, Roy received, at a mail drop he had arranged in Chattanooga for a fictitious company called "Classic Auto Paintings, Inc.," two five-pound canisters of a drying agent called "Drierite." After receiving the shipment Roy abandoned the commercial mailbox without even paying his first bill. Later he arranged to have other shipments of chemicals delivered to an abandoned business in Chattanooga. On another trip to Chattanooga, Roy waited in a suburban branch library while Susan purchased rubber bands, mail supplies, a wire brush, a tube cutter, a twenty-inch length of faucet tubing; she was unable to locate a large metal pipe he wanted.

Roy called his obsessive labor simply "the chemical project," for which he needed a never-ending mixture of the odd and the ordinary: kitchen scales, Clorox bleach, distilled water, rat poison, baking soda, a pizza cutter, acrylic tubing, and dry ice, to name just a few items on his eclectic lists. He set up a laboratory in the front bedroom of the ranch-style home on Skyline Drive, which they had occupied for the past five years, and warned Susan never to enter the work area. Later, he would take his peculiar tools and materials into the cramped crawl space beneath the house itself, and Susan began to hear strange noises, and smell unusual odors drifting up through the floors. Once, when Roy took a weekend off to attend a flying show in Oshkosh, Wisconsin, Susan took a furtive look beneath the house, and even her untrained eye detected something most unusual: The water pipes had all turned green, like long-weathered copper. She mentioned this to Roy, who told her not to worry about it. Later, she saw him working feverishly to clean the corrosion off the pipes—without much success.

As summer waned, Susan detected an increasing frustration in Roy; "the chemical project" simply was not working. Around the end of July Roy seemed to abandon the project and packed up two footlockers with an exotic aggregation of weapons, ammunition, bottles of poison, electronic surveillance equipment, instruction manuals for assembling booby traps, pseudoscientific treatises on perversions and sex crimes, and pornographic magazines depicting women engaged in sexual relations with animals. Among the manuals was something called *The Anarchist's Cookbook*, which gave recipes for making assorted devices of terror. Then he delivered the two trunks to his old prison buddy, Ted Banks, for safekeeping in a storage warehouse in Florida. Roy told Banks that he needed the secret stash because he was "having trouble" with Susan.

When he came back from Florida, Roy turned his attention to another project that involved what he called "the smoke grenade," a device he had obtained from Ted Banks. He told Susan that she would no longer be required to go out and make purchases, that he had all the materials he needed to finish his work. Susan continued to run the business while Roy devoted all of his attention to his secret labors. Each evening they would watch the local television news, and among the stories that received great attention in early August 1989 was the rejection by the Eleventh Circuit Court of Appeals of the anxious request of a local teachers' organization to overturn a court-mandated reassignment of many white teachers to black schools in the middle-class Atlanta suburbs of DeKalb County.

Shortly after lunch at home on August 20, Roy asked Susan to give him enough stamps to mail "a two- or three-pound package." He put the stamps in his pocket and left, with a wrapped package in hand, on his motorcycle, clad in heavy rain gear, even though the day was hot and clear. Later that evening he returned, without the package.

The following day, some twenty miles away from the Moodys' home in Rex, work went on as usual in the regional office of the National Association for the Advancement of Colored People on Martin Luther King Drive in the southwestern section of Atlanta. Around midday the postman brought the day's mail, which included something unusual: a package about the size of a shoebox. Murlene Murray, who had been a secretary in the NAACP office for more than thirty years, read the return address from the standard mailing label:

CHERYL ZALESKY, ATTORNEY AT LAW
100 PEACHTREE ST. NW
ATLANTA, GEORGIA

Perhaps it was a transcript, Murlene Murray thought, as she tore away the wrapping paper. Suddenly the package exploded, and the entire office was filled with tear gas. "I thought my face was on fire," Murray recalled later. "I was sure I had been blinded." Six other people in the office at the time suffered burning sensations to the skin and eyes, some requiring hospital treatment.

On the same day the tear-gas bomb was delivered to the NAACP office—August 21—the following letter, unsigned and with no return address, was mailed from an Atlanta area postal station to Eleventh Circuit Court of Appeals and to fourteen television stations in states as distant as Pennsylvania and Wisconsin:

DECLARATION OF WAR
THE UNITED STATES COURT OF APPEALS FOR THE ELEVENTH
CIRCUIT DOES DELIBERATELY AND WRONGFULLY REFUSE TO FULFILL
ITS OBLIGATION TO PROTECT THE INNOCENT.

THE COURT'S FAILURE TO RENDER IMPARTIAL AND EQUITABLE
JUDGMENTS IS DUE TO RANK BIAS AND THE MISTAKEN BELIEF ITS
VICTIMS CAN NOT EFFECTIVELY RETALIATE.

THEREFORE, CITIZENS OF DENSELY POPULATED CITIES SHALL
BE SUBJECTED TO HIGH CONCENTRATION LEVELS OF CARBONYL
CHLORIDE AND CYANODIMETHYLAMINOETHOXYPHOSPINE OXIDE.
THE ATTACKS SHALL CONTINUE UNTIL WIDESPREAD TERROR FORCES
THE COURT TO ADOPT THE IMPARTIAL AND EQUIABLE TREATMENT
OF ALL AS ITS HIGHEST PRIORITY.

THE MEDIA IN TARGET CITIES HAVE BEEN NOTIFIED OF THE
TERRORIST ATTACKS AND THAT THEY CAN OBTAIN GAS SAMPLE DATA
BY CONTACTING THE COURT.

SUBSEQUENT TO EACH ATTACK, THE MEDIA SHALL BE REMINDED
THE COURT'S CALLOUS DISREGARD FOR JUSTICE MADE THE ATTACK
NECESSARY.

Despite his obsession with his secretive projects Roy Moody still found time to pursue the other preoccupation of his life: He routinely filed legal documents necessary to carry on the dozen or so lawsuits he had going at the time. He even sued his sister and brother, whom he accused of plotting to cheat him out of his inheritance from their mother. He received notice that the Eleventh Circuit Court of Appeals, in a perfunctory order, had rejected his request for a rehearing on the decision of the three-judge panel that had ruled against his *coram nobis* proceeding, and he prepared to appeal this last rejection to the United States Supreme Court. During this time Roy continued to show up with great regularity at law libraries, and, according to the librarians, demonstrated an especially keen interest in the current "slip opinions"—pamphlet-style texts of recent court decisions. Thus it is almost certain that Roy's eyes would have fallen on a decision of the Eleventh Circuit on September 15 in the case styled *Jacksonville Branch, NAACP v. Duval County School Board.* In this case a panel of Eleventh Circuit judges overruled a district judge in Jacksonville who had held that the Jacksonville public school authorities had acted in good faith in seeking desegregation over many years, and that the time must come when courts got out of such cases. Not so, said Judge Robert Vance in his opinion in the appeal case. "The remoteness in time of the school authorities' intentionally discriminatory actions," Vance bluntly declared, "is irrelevant."

The words struck in harsh discordance with Judge Cox's almost flippant dismissal of Roy's appeal on grounds of "finality." What greater proof, Roy asked Susan, that "the niggers" get justice while the white man got the shaft in the federal courts?

Two weeks after the Jacksonville decision was handed down, on September 29, another panel of the Eleventh Circuit Court issued an opinion in a Savannah school desegregation. The "slip opinion" in the case prominently identified Robert E. Robinson of Savannah as the attorney of record. Given Roy Moody's close attention to the latest court actions during that time, it is virtually certain that the "slip opinion" in the Savannah case also passed through his hands.

Amid all this frenetic activity, Roy also found time to place a classified advertisement in the personals column of the *Atlanta Journal* soliciting female companionship. At least two women responded to the ads.

Linda Aycock Spires began corresponding with Roy sometime in October, but she was disturbed when his first letter to her asked too many personal questions. Still, even though she refused to meet Roy, she continued to receive letters, some fifteen or twenty altogether. In these letters Roy claimed to be divorced, and said that he was doing research on a secret government project involving a silent submarine engine. Once they had a telephone conversation, during which she brought up the subject of civil rights, adding that some of her best friends were blacks. At this Roy became quite agitated and called Linda a "nigger-lover." A few days later he wrote her a letter of apology, saying that she would have to know his family background to understand his bitterness toward blacks.

Also among those who responded to the classified advertisement was Jackie Stanford, who began to meet Roy at coffee shops in the Atlanta area. Once, on the spur of the moment, they drove to Chattanooga and spent the night in a motel.

But while Jackie found Roy to be an exciting conversationalist, she also observed a disturbing quality: He seemed to be obsessed with the courts, and in one moment of great agitation he complained bitterly to her that the Eleventh Circuit Court judges were "all crooked, in cahoots. There is no fairness, no justice." Once, Roy sent Jackie a photograph of Susan and suggested a sexual encounter among the three of them. The charming man seemed to turn into a smooth operator, even a con artist, so Jackie dropped Roy a note saying that she had reconciled with her boyfriend and wanted to break off any further contact.

As fall arrived and the leaves began to cover the wooded lot of the Moody home on Skyline Drive, Roy announced to Susan that he was shifting his work to "the other project." As with "the chemical project," he instructed Susan never to enter his makeshift laboratory in the front bedroom of their house. Once more Susan began to receive shopping lists for such odd things as metal wash tubs, heavy-duty scissors, rubber bands, shower-caps, rain suits, plastic bags, faucet tubing, black paint, and flashlight batteries and bulbs. Once he instructed her to steal something from beneath a car, but she could never grasp just what he wanted; later, she surmised, he got the item from Ted Banks. Susan was also told to scour the house to gather all the threaded rods she could find. Sometime in November, Roy shoplifted two packages of two-and-a-half inch nails from the hardware shelf of a Kroger's supermarket in the Atlanta area.

As Roy worked in taciturn intensity, Susan began to hear muffled explosions coming from Roy's secret room. Around Halloween, close to midnight, Roy instructed Susan to drive him down a country road some distance from their house. When no other cars were in sight, he held something out the window and told Susan not to look; she heard what she thought was a gunshot. Some weeks later he had Susan drive him to an even more secluded area, where he instructed her to leave him for fifteen minutes while he headed into a woods carrying a metal pail that contained an object covered by an old towel. When she returned, Roy had the pail in hand, but now it was empty, and the bottom had been blown out. Roy fretted that a vehicle had passed several times on the road, and someone may have heard "the explosion."

About that time Roy made an urgent visit to his old friend Ted Banks at the Whitehouse Marina in Titusville, on the Atlantic coast of Florida, where Banks had found a job as a night security guard. Roy told Banks he needed some welding done to make some parts for a boat engine he was working on, and they arranged to meet at night. In the dim light Roy collected the materials he needed from around the marina's repair shop—nuts, bolts, threaded rods, and a piece of two-inch pipe about a yard long.

Under Roy's supervision Ted Banks cut a length of pipe with the shop's electric band saw. Roy inspected it closely and declared it unsuitable for his needs. Another length was cut, but this, too, was unsatisfactory. Finally the correct cut was obtained for Roy's needs, and Banks duplicated the cut to produce several more pieces of pipe, each about six inches long. Then Roy directed Ted to weld flat plates of metal, cut from scraps lying on the shop floor, onto the ends of the pipes. Each of the plates were drilled with several holes, giving access to the interior of the capped pipes. At this point Ted became apprehensive.

"Roy, we aren't making bombs, are we?" Ted asked.

"No, we're not making bombs," Roy assured him.

When the welding was completed, Roy had one more task: He asked Ted to cut several lengths of threaded rods, each slightly longer than the pipes with the welded plates. When the work was done, late in the night, Roy placed the pipes and rods in a plastic bag and told Ted he was going back to Atlanta. Before leaving, he asked Ted to purchase a large quantity of gunpowder, which he would pick up later.

One day in early October, when "the other project" was well under-way, Susan approached Roy hesitantly and said she would like to have her name legally changed to Susan McBride Moody. They had, after all, lived together for more than eight years, she reasoned, and most people thought they were married. To Susan's astonishment, Roy said it would be simpler just to get married. So after nearly a decade of turbulent life together, Susan, who was then twenty-six, and Roy, who was going on fifty-six, were married in a quiet civil ceremony. Before the wedding they fulfilled the usual requirements of Georgia law, filling out the proper forms, securing blood tests and the like. But there is no indication that at any time Susan was told one salient fact: Under Georgia law, a woman cannot be compelled to testify against her husband in a criminal trial. As an accomplished guardhouse lawyer, Roy Moody almost certainly knew this fact.

There was no wedding trip, because Roy was deeply involved in his secretive laboratory work as well as his numerous pending lawsuits, which kept him in the area's law libraries for many hours during the fall of 1989. Among the "slip opinions" that almost surely came to his at-tention was one issued by the Eleventh Circuit Court on November 3, in which Judge Robert Vance summarily rejected yet another fervent plea from the white teachers of DeKalb County seeking to avoid reassign-ment to black schools. At about that same time, Roy wrote the United States Supreme Court seeking an extension of time to file his appeal in his *coram nobis* case. Justice Anthony Kennedy signed a routine order granting an extension until January 18, 1990.

On November 21 Roy sent Susan a distance of some three hundred miles to the northern hump of Kentucky to purchase the most common-place items. Wearing such an elaborate cloak-and-dagger disguise that she inevitably attracted special attention from anyone she dealt with, Susan moved furtively about the small town of Florence, Kentucky, pur-chasing packing boxes, photocopying materials that she took pains to shield from view with her body, and, finally, purchasing more than twenty dollars worth of stamps at the local post office. Throughout the trip she wore a pair of gloves that Roy had given her as "an early Christmas present."

When she returned home late in the evening, Roy was not there. Within a few minutes Roy called and said, with evident relief, that he would be home shortly. When he arrived, he explained that he had become alarmed that she had been arrested en route and the documents she was carrying had been seized. If she had not answered his last call, he told her, he would have left at once for Florida.

As November drew to a close, Roy's behavior became increasingly eccentric and mysterious. On Thanksgiving Day he took his camcorder to photograph cars in the driveway of the mother of his old nemesis, Tom Allen. Six days later Susan paid for some carpeting that Roy had arranged to have installed in his secret workroom on December 8; later, he changed the date for the installation to December 12.

In late November or early December Roy called Ted Banks at Titusville to inquire about the gunpowder he had requested. Banks, by now certain he was being drawn into a bomb-making scheme, told his friend he was afraid to make the purchase.

Shortly after this conversation, Roy went to a hardware store in Griffin, Georgia, some fifteen miles from Rex, and asked the store manager, Warren Phillips, where he might purchase some materials for making ammunition. Phillips referred him to a gun store not far away, called the Shootin Iron.

Soon afterward Roy turned up at the establishment wearing cheap tinted glasses with pink plastic rims and an orange wig that didn't quite cover his thick black hair. If this outlandish get-up were not enough to assure that Roy's image would be indelibly engraved in the memory of James Paul Sartain, a part-time clerk at the Shootin Iron, the order that Roy placed added an even greater element of the extraordinary: Roy wanted four thousand CCI handgun primers and a four-pound canister of Hercules Red Dot double-base smokeless gunpowder.

Never before had Sartain sold such a large quantity of gunpowder to a single customer; the preferred quantity of powder by most sportsmen who reloaded their own ammunition was the one-pound canister.

"Why don't you buy it in four one-pound cans?" Sartain asked. "The powder starts to go bad when the can's opened."

"No," Roy replied. "I'm going to use it all at one time."

The bill came to $122.72, which Roy paid with a hundred-dollar bill and a fifty-dollar bill.

Susan noticed that the pace of work on "the other project" intensified during the first two weeks of December, although Roy always found the time to keep up with his legal affairs, and even to engage in petty harassment of Tom Allen.

On December 4, Roy sent Susan out for a few more items. She was instructed to go to Kroger's supermarket, where the high volume of customers would make her less likely to be recognized or remembered, to purchase some plain brown wrapping paper. And she was to obtain a cardboard box with a large flat surface free of printing. In accumulating these materials, Roy ordered, Susan was to wear gloves at all times.

Susan got the impression that Roy completed work on "the other project" on December 6, when he began an elaborate cleanup operation. He carefully collected all of the materials with which he had worked so laboriously in the forbidden room, placed them in pails and washtubs, and had Susan drive him to carwash dumpsters or to secluded woods where he would dispose of the refuse, instructing her not to watch. When he completed the cleanup, he went to Wheeler's Building Supply and purchased, with Susan's credit card, several sheets of plywood, which he placed on the floor of the laboratory room with a heavy adhesive glue and more than six hundred nails; Roy told Susan that the flooring was necessary to provide "extra support" for his projects. On December 12, Randy Forrester arrived to lay the carpet that Roy had ordered just after Thanksgiving. After the carpet had been laid, Roy sent Susan to Sears to purchase, under an assumed name, a vacuum cleaner that he used to thoroughly clean the room once more; Susan then returned the vacuum cleaner for a refund. About this time, Susan also rented a heavy-duty vacuum cleaner from a janitorial supply firm to clean gravel in the backyard where Roy had been burning a large amount of receipts, shopping lists, and other records that he had accumulated since June.

Even the most routine activities during that period drew close attention from Roy. Once, when Susan purchased some ordinary brown paper to wrap family Christmas presents, Roy had her return it because it was too similar to the paper that she had bought a week earlier at Kroger's.

Susan remembers that during this period Roy asked her where he might find a zip code directory. She told him there was one on the counter at the post office at Briarcliff, an Atlanta suburb some distance from where the Moodys lived.

In the middle of December, Roy took several trips to unnamed locations. He would leave in the afternoon, driving Susan's car, and not return until late at night or the following day. He told Susan, cryptically, that he wanted to arrive at his destination after dark.

12 "The Mail's Come"

With the winter solstice just five days away, dawn broke well after seven o'clock on the morning of December 16, 1989, in Birmingham, Alabama. By the habit of many years Bob Vance had already been up for an hour by the time the first gray light began to appear behind the spindly pines and hickories that grew, higgledy-piggledy, in the four acres of woods that surrounded his home on the city's elegant Shook Hill Road, over the mountain and safely distanced from what little air pollution still spewed forth from the smokestacks of the decrepit foundries and steel mills that had been the city's economic mainstay throughout its turbulent first century as the South's premier industrial city.

Bob Vance was, as usual, singing in his robust if untrained voice as he went about his morning routine. It was a habit that had, in earlier years, annoyed the boys, especially on Saturdays when they were trying to sleep late, and that made Helen envious. "He woke up happy," Helen would say. "I wish I could do that."

Bob made his coffee and paid his customary morning visit to the kennels of the Arabian salukis that he and Helen bred and exhibited in the better dog shows across the country. The animals, six of them altogether, happily greeted their master with a raucous chorus of howling and barking. He adored the dogs, an interest that he acquired from Helen, and he especially enjoyed the trips to dog shows where he was increasingly in demand as a judge, although he would complain, good-naturedly, that he found it odd that he was confined to judging salukis when in his professional life he could judge *any* human who came before his court.

It was a gray, overcast morning, just cool enough to require a light denim jacket as Bob Vance began spading the soft red earth in preparation for the vegetable garden he would plant in the spring—"therapy," he often told his law clerks, from the rigors of the legal conflicts over which he presided throughout the week as a judge of the United States Court of Appeals for the Eleventh Judicial Circuit. By now he had held the prestigious judgeship, at a level just beneath the Supreme Court, for a dozen years. He found the work intellectually challenging, and rewarding in terms of public service.

He worked in the yard throughout the morning, taking occasional breaks to go back into the expansive house where he had lived for the past twenty-seven years, to share coffee and small talk with Helen, who always arose later than her husband. By now they had become accustomed to the absence of the boys, who had grown up there. Robert Jr. had already established himself as a promising member of one of Birmingham's leading law firms; Charles, the younger son, was a medical student and Ph.D. candidate in psychology at one of the South's pre-eminent institutions of higher education, Duke University in North Carolina.

Just two days earlier Bob Vance had completed four days of on-the-bench hearings in Atlanta, listening to oral arguments by the region's best lawyers in pending cases before his court. Although he would continue to drop in from time to time at his office in the federal building in downtown Birmingham, there would be no more serious court work for the remainder of the holiday season.

Bob and Helen Vance spoke of seasonal activities. They had hosted the annual Christmas party for the Birmingham Kennel Club a week earlier, and it had gone well. On the previous evening they had attended a fund-raising event of the Birmingham Humane Society, on which

Helen had served, off-and-on, as a director. Animal welfare was becoming an office affair as well as a home interest; Bob's longtime secretary, Mary Nell Terry, had sold them the tickets to the dinner.

"Isn't this our year to have the Christmas dinner?" Bob idly inquired. It was a long-standing custom for the far-flung Vance families to gather at one member's home, on an alternating basis, each year.

"I can't remember when we last had it," Helen said. "But we need to check it out, I guess. Christmas is just ten days away. I'll find out today."

They ruminated over plans for the coming year, when they would take another trip to Europe with their close friends, Frank and Dawn Lee. It was an old friendship that had, in years past, led to much good-natured adversarial banter. Frank was a top executive in Luckie and Forney, a leading Birmingham advertising firm that had often handled the ballyhoo for Governor George Wallace's campaigns at the time when Bob Vance was a leading figure in the anti-Wallace political faction in Alabama.

Helen prepared an early lunch, soup and a sandwich, which they ate at the kitchen table. Then Bob got into his Cadillac, still dressed in his gardening clothes, to run some errands—a stop by the hardware store, a visit to the liquor store to replenish supplies for assorted visitors who might drop in, unannounced, during the Christmas season.

Helen busied herself with the mundane chores of the season, wrapping presents, addressing Christmas cards. At a little after noon, there was a knock at the door. It was the mailman—one she did not recognize. Probably a holiday substitute, she thought.

"A couple of packages, Mrs. Vance," he said cheerily. "They were too big to go in the box down by the road. And here are the letters, too."

Helen Vance thanked him and took the packages. One was about the size of a shoebox, and bore the return address of Bob's brother Bill, who lived in Washington and was getting ready to retire from the Central Intelligence Agency. The other parcel was somewhat larger, about the size and weight of a four-inch stack of magazines. The package wrapped in plain brown paper, secured by twine. It was postmarked "Newnan, Ga." and the neatly typed red-bordered return-address label, she noted, bore the name of Lewis R. Morgan, a senior judge on the Eleventh Circuit Court of Appeals. Helen knew that "Pete" Morgan shared her husband's interest in horses, and that he occasionally sent Bob old issues of equine magazines.

Helen deposited the mail on the kitchen table and returned to her Christmas tasks upstairs. Around two in the afternoon she heard her husband come in the back door, returning from his errands. She went downstairs to greet him.

"The mail's come," she said, gesturing at the letters and two packages that lay on the circular table where they had just had lunch. "One of them looks like a Christmas present from Bill. The other one is from Pete Morgan."

Helen took a seat across the table while Bob Vance, standing, leafed absently through the letters first. Then he picked up the larger package.

"I guess Pete's sent me some more of those horse magazines," he said, as he began to tear away the heavy sticking tape that secured the package. She watched as he pulled open the flap of the box.

Suddenly everything went blank and ominously silent. She could remember no sound. The next thing she recalls, she was lying on the kitchen floor, staring at the ceiling. The light fixture had vanished.

Oh, the light blew, she thought. *And then I realized, no, that wasn't what happened. It was an explosion.*

Helen Vance struggled to her feet and stared in bewildered horror at the stark devastation around her. Across the room, in a corner of the kitchen, her husband rested in a sitting position on the floor, against the wall.

He made a couple of noises, like you make when someone hits you in the stomach and knocks the breath out of you—not groans or not grunts, just a noise. He did not say anything. And I—it took me, I don't know, seconds or a minute or so to realize what had happened, and I realized it was a bomb.

Bob Vance lay motionless. Helen knew that she was injured. She was bleeding in several places, but she felt neither pain nor immobility, so she did not believe her injuries to be serious. Later, she would learn that a nail, two and a half inches long, had penetrated her right breast, gone through her lungs and liver and almost exited her back. Of eighty nails in the package, traveling at the bullet-speed of thirteen thousand miles per hour, only that single one had struck her.

But I knew if my husband was alive that I had to get help.

The houses on Shook Hill Road are far apart, and Helen Vance had it fixed in her mind that the explosion had not made much noise. And in fact it hadn't. Jim White, a neighbor of twenty years who lived in the next house, remembers that his dogs started barking around 2 P.M., as if they'd heard something suspicious; but he heard nothing.

Helen Vance picked up the telephone to call for help. Unaware that she had been temporarily deafened by the blast, she heard no dial tone. She assumed the phone lines had been broken by the blast.

She went upstairs and gathered some towels, which she then gently placed against the gaping wounds in her husband's chest and stomach.

I did not feel for a pulse or anything I just—I just kept thinking I've got to get out and get help. . . I think he was already dead, but I knew—I knew in my head he was dead but in my heart I kept hoping, well, maybe if I can get somebody here quick we can do something.

She went outside the wrecked house and got in the large gray Dodge van that the Vances had just bought to ferry their beloved Salukis to dog shows and veterinary clinics. In confusion she began to turn toward Highway 280, a main traffic artery that runs south from Birmingham. *There are always some people selling firewood out of pickup trucks along the roadside down there this time of year. They will help me.*

Suddenly she was seized by panic. *I thought, well, if they see me and find out I'm not dead, they may kill me. And I was thinking they would be sitting down toward 280.*

She turned the van back and drove up the long driveway to the home of her next-door neighbors, the Jim Whites. She blew the horn, got out and banged on the door, but was unable to make herself heard. When no one came, she got back into the van and drove on to the home of the next neighbors, the Charles Ashbys, blowing the horn steadily as she approached. Margaret Ashby rushed out.

"Well come in, Helen . . ." Margaret Ashby began, stopping in mid-sentence as it became apparent that her neighbor and old friend was seriously hurt.

"A bomb's gone off," said Helen Vance. "I think Bob's dead. Will you call for help?"

"Of course," murmured Margaret Ashby in shock, as she rushed back into the house.

As soon as Margaret left, Helen, still in a daze, started the van again and drove back to her home, a quarter of a mile back down Shook Hill Road. She had been there for only two minutes or so, and was sitting motionless in the van when Charles Ashby, Margaret's husband, roared up the driveway. There he found Helen, staring forward emptily, but completely lucid.

"Are you all right?" Ashby asked.

"Yes, I'm all right," Helen said. "But I'm afraid Bob's dead. It was a letter-bomb."

"Don't you want to go back to the house?" Ashby asked.

"No," said Helen. "I think I'll just sit here."

"Well, you just sit still and wait for help," he replied. "I'm going to see about Bob."

Ashby, a semiretired representative of an electrical equipment company, had known Bob Vance well. They had for many years attended St. Luke's Episcopal Church together. Ashby also regularly took part in a cardiac rehabilitation class that Bob had attended at Birmingham's St. Vincent's Hospital since he had undergone angioplasty, a type of surgery to widen arteries supplying blood to his heart muscle. The Ashbys, in fact, were planning a Christmas party that the Vances were to attend.

Inside the house, Charles Ashby gazed in stunned horror at the wreckage. The room was filled with the acrid smell of gunpowder, and among the debris he could see bloody footprints—obviously those left by Helen after she had placed the towels against her husband's wounds an hour earlier. In the corner of the room he saw Bob Vance; Ashby knew at once that it would be fruitless to administer aid.

Ashby rushed back to Helen to find police and paramedics converging on the scene with lights flashing and sirens wailing. One paramedic dashed into the house, another began to attend Helen, who still remained unaware that she had suffered injuries that would keep her in surgery for late into the night and hospitalized through Christmas.

"How is my husband?" she asked the paramedic who was attending her. He replied that he did not know, he had not been in the house.

After a few minutes the other paramedic came out of the house and ordered, "Let's get her to the hospital."

At that instant, cold logic muscled its way through all the confusion that swirled in Helen Vance's head.

Now I know, she said to herself. *They wouldn't be putting me in this ambulance if Bob weren't dead.*

13 "Priority Mail"

The news of the Vance murder led virtually every television newscast and was prominently featured on the front pages of the Sunday newspapers across the nation on December 17, 1989, including the *Savannah Morning News*. As a politician who followed the news closely and as a lawyer who had cases before the Eleventh Circuit Court of Appeals, Robbie Robinson almost certainly would have taken note of the mysterious murder if it had been a routine weekend.

As it happened, Robbie and his new wife, Ann, were holding their annual Christmas party on the Saturday that Bob Vance was killed. Birmingham was more than three hundred miles to the west of Savannah, and it was a city known for bombings and other violence for years. Besides, the early focus of suspicion was the drug trade that so clogged the dockets of the Eleventh Circuit Court of Appeals, so there was no reason, even if he had seen the story, for Robbie Robinson had no reason to believe that he was in any special danger in the aftermath of the Vance assassination.

The Robinson home was a spacious brick-and-cream stucco bungalow at 1420 Vassar Street in a section of Savannah where many of the city's black middle class lived in secure and comfortable suburban seclusion. Ann Robinson had decorated the house festively, even stringing lights in the shrubbery. Both liked to entertain, and they'd invited everyone they knew just to drop in as early as they wished on the balmy late-fall Saturday.

Throughout the day and far into the night people drifted in and out, probably a hundred or more altogether. Among these were Ann Robinson's brother and his wife, who noticed that Ann didn't quite seem to be herself. When Ann's brother asked if anything were wrong, she shuddered and said, "I just feel real strange. I guess I'm not in the mood for socializing." A little later, Robbie also sensed that something was bothering Ann, and he interrupted his duties as a busy host to go to her.

"Let's dance," he said. "You're my wife, and I love you."

They danced, but the perplexing anxiety continued to hover over Ann.

Throughout the night guests drifted in and out, and it was five o'clock on Sunday morning before Robbie and Ann were alone again. They talked about the party, but Robbie's conversation took a curiously ominous turn when he mentioned that he wanted to talk to her about what she should do "if anything happens to me."

"Let's talk about it later," Ann said wearily.

The first streaks of dawn were visible when the exhausted couple tumbled into bed.

They had slept for only a few hours when Herman Allen dropped by, around nine. Allen was a Savannah policeman who had been assigned to the night shift and hence couldn't come to the party. Robbie answered the door, then roused Ann to ask her to fix Herman a sandwich from the party leftovers.

"I'll make the sandwich," she said, "but I'm not going to church this morning." From lifelong tradition, they went to different churches except on special occasions, like Easter.

The TV was on, but no one was paying special attention. If there were any news reports about the Vance murder, they registered on neither Ann nor Robbie. The Savannah paper was still in the box on the outer edge of the lawn when Robbie left for regular Sunday services at St. Paul Christian Methodist Episcopal Church.

He got back home around two, and spent the rest of the cool, breezy afternoon helping Ann clean up from the party. Robbie turned in around ten o'clock because he had to get up early Monday morning to prepare for a routine criminal case to which he had been appointed.

"See you later," Robbie said as he hurriedly gave his wife a perfunctory kiss. Then he added, "by the way, your car is nearly out of gas. You need to get some on your way to work."

Robbie arrived around nine at his office on Abercorn Street, as he had done for the past twelve years. But by this time, it was problematical just how long Robbie would remain there. The rent was $1,500 a month, far higher than the amount he had been paying when he was with Bobby Hill's firm a few blocks further south, on 34th Street. This cost, coupled with the $770 a month he was spending on the half-page display advertisement in the yellow pages of the Savannah telephone directory, was too great a strain on a law practice that wasn't doing all that well. Besides, he had another office in Hinesville, some forty miles east of Savannah. Robbie faced some hard business decisions as the new decade approached.

During the morning he made a few telephone calls and dictated the day's letters for his secretary, Joyce Tolbert. Around 10:30 he headed for court. By this time, court appointments to represent indigents had grown to be a major part of Robbie's law practice, along with discrimination suits, personal injury cases arising out of fender-bender automobile accidents, and routine legal affairs of the City of Savannah.

Robbie disposed of the case fairly quickly by plea bargaining with the state's attorney. Shortly before noon he placed a call to Clarence Martin. In addition to being old friends, Robbie and Clarence served as one another's personal lawyers. Clarence had helped get an appointment for Robbie as a "special master"—a kind of administrative overseer—in a lawsuit, and Robbie wondered if he might get an advance on his fee. Clarence was not there, so Robbie left his request on the answering machine and said he would get back later in the afternoon.

While Robbie was in court Joyce Tolbert handled the routine morning office affairs as she had done for the past three years as Robbie's legal secretary. At a little after eleven o'clock, Bernard Johnson, the cheery mailman who had become a familiar figure on the Abercorn Street route, arrived with the day's mail. The delivery included, in addition to the usual stack of bills, payments, and communications with other lawyers, a shoebox-size parcel wrapped in plain brown paper. The package bore a priority mail sticker, and a red-and-white paste-on label neatly typed, with a return address that read:

REV. JOHN E. JACKSON

100 RAVENWOOD WAY

WARNER ROBINS GA 31088

Joyce Tolbert had never heard of the Reverend Jackson, and Warner Robins was halfway across the state from Savannah, but she had no reason to be suspicious of the package. She logged mail according to established procedure, then took the letters, unopened, and the package up the narrow flight of stairs that led to Robbie's office on the second floor and placed it all in a neat stack in the seat of the large leatherette desk chair. By long-standing instruction, the secretaries were not to open Robbie's mail.

Meanwhile, Ann, forgetting Robbie's parting advice, ran out of gas. Not wanting to endure Robbie's good-natured taunts about her absent-mindedness, she called her father, who brought her a can of gas. She got home around one o'clock, and found Robbie chatting with Hal Jenkins, a neighbor and close friend who had dropped by.

Robbie lingered around the house until around 4:30, when he put on his coat to go to the office.

"Do you really need to go?" Ann asked. "It's so late."

"I have to see a client," Robbie replied, apparently fibbing to cover his real purpose, which was to see if Clarence Martin had arranged for the advance on his fee.

"Well, in that case, you might be getting home late," Ann replied. "So you can just drop me off at Mama's house."

The evening shadows were falling by the time Robbie let Ann out of the car in the front of her mother's modest home on Milfrey Street. He said he would pick her up in an hour or so.

Robbie stopped by the office of his old friend and mentor, Bobby Hill. "Hey, Bubba," Robbie said, using the vernacular for "friend" in the Savannah black community, "come over to the office for a drink." Bobby made such sociable visits with some regularity, and he often sat on the side of the desk as Robbie sifted through papers. But on this day Bobby had some other things to do and said he would drop by a little later.

Robbie told Bobby to get a bottle of liquor, and added, "be sure to get some matches." It was a small joke. Even though he knew that Bobby detested smoking, Robbie was constantly asking him, absentmindedly, if he had any matches. Bobby chuckled, and said he would get the liquor and the matches and would see him later.

It had begun to rain by the time that Robbie finally got back to the office just before 5:00, entering from the rear alley where he parked his Cadillac. As he paused at Joyce Tolbert's desk to pick up the letters that needed to be signed, his secretary reminded him that he had a Christmas party to attend that evening at St. Paul's Church—the sort of obligatory social occasion that every politician attends. Robbie remarked that he probably would get there late, then he lumbered up the narrow staircase to the second floor. As always, Joyce could hear him walking heavily about the spacious room above, could even hear the muffled sounds as he talked on the telephone. One of the calls he made was to Clarence Martin, who told him he still hadn't heard from the client about the advance on the special-master fee.

At a little after five o'clock Robbie called for Joyce to pick up the signed letters, and when she went into the room she saw the package, still unopened, sitting on Robbie's desk. She took the day's letters back to her desk and was getting ready to go to the post office, the last chore of the day, when a thunderous explosion shook the building. The smoke detectors went off, and Joyce could hear the sound of shattered glass raining onto the street from the windows of the second floor. In the din she thought she heard someone "gasping for air." Instinctively, she started to go upstairs, but once she reached the steps, she hesitated. She returned to her desk, where she called the 911 emergency number to report the explosion. Then she called her mother, then her pastor to relate the terrifying sound she had just heard; each told her to be calm, and to pray.

Aubrey McDonald, a nineteen-year-old neighborhood resident, was getting off the bus at that moment. "I heard this boom and this shatter and I didn't know where it came from," he later recalled. "The bus moved and I saw all this glass and I started running." After he collected his wits, Aubrey returned to stand in the rain and watched as the police removed bags of evidence from the gutted office.

Meanwhile, Clarence Martin lingered in his law office ten blocks away, waiting for the return call about Robbie's advance. Clarence turned on the office television to watch the early evening news, and discovered that there had been an explosion at the Robinson law office. It was not known whether anyone had been hurt. At about that same moment, Bobby Hill received a call from someone whose name he doesn't remember, telling him "Your friend has been hurt."

Back at the scene of the bedlam on Abercorn Street, Dr. Emerson Brown, who operated an optometry shop in the two suites of townhouses adjoining the Robinson law offices, had also heard the explosion and felt the building shake. Thinking that a leaking gas main must have ignited, he rushed outside to find the sidewalk covered with shattered glass.

"What happened?" he asked Joyce Tolbert, who was sitting, in a dazed condition, at her desk.

"I don't know." She murmured. "There was just this loud explosion."

Dr. Brown crept gingerly up the stairs. The office was in shambles, and behind what remained of the desk he gazed in horror at the ghastly spectacle of Robbie Robinson, on his knees, his right arm blown off just below the shoulder, his left hand mangled beyond recognition as a human body part. But Robbie, moaning incoherently, clearly was still conscious.

Dr. Brown, who had little formal training in medicine, rushed to Robbie's side, but he saw at once that he could not even stop the bleeding, much less treat injuries of such gravity. He put his arms around the wounded terror-stricken man and kept softly repeating, "Just hold on, help is on the way." But he could tell that Robbie's pulse was growing weaker.

About ten minutes later, Christopher Scalisi, a paramedic with the City of Savannah emergency services, burst into the room but froze at the door as soon as he saw the carnage.

"Is it safe to come in?" Scalisi yelled.

"For God's sake," Dr. Brown responded. "This man needs help."

In his semiconsciousness, Robbie emitted alternately low moans and high-pitched wails as he knelt on the floor, with Emerson Brown's arms around him. Scalisi saw at once there was nothing he could do, so he and his paramedic partner prepared to take Robbie to the hospital.

But getting him there proved to be a grim ordeal. In his delirium Robbie flailed with his mangled left arm and kicked as the two men tried to place him on the stretcher. Once they subdued him sufficiently to get him onto the gurney, they had great difficult in maneuvering the narrow staircase because Robbie's bony stump of a right arm kept getting caught in the slatted banister. Robbie was still struggling so much when he reached the Savannah's Memorial Medical Center that it took six people to get him into the emergency room. By this time Mayor John Rousakis was at the hospital to inquire about his friend and city alderman.

At eight o'clock in the evening, a distraught and bewildered Joyce Tolbert still lingered in the office, watching the horde of federal and state investigators sift through the rubble. When the telephone rang, she answered apprehensively, thinking that the call might bring news about Robbie's condition. But it was not the police or the hospital; it was Ann Robinson.

"Robbie hasn't gotten home," she said. "I was wondering if he's still at the office?"

Joyce Tolbert hesitated for a long moment, then said:

"You need to go to the hospital."

"Why?" Ann Robinson asked.

"Something has happened to Mr. Robinson," Joyce Tolbert replied. "You need to go to the hospital."

Not knowing how long she would have to stay, Ann hurriedly changed into a blouse and pants she borrowed from her daughter, who was then living with Ann's mother.

When she reached the hospital, she was astonished to find several of Robbie's close friends and associates, including Mayor Rousakis, gathered in the waiting room. They all wore grave, troubled expressions.

Paula DeNitto, the duty surgeon assigned to the emergency room, approached Ann and told her that Robbie had to undergo urgent surgery. Ann insisted on seeing her husband, and reluctantly, Paula DeNitto took her into the operating room.

As she gazed upon her comatose husband, covered with blood, she gasped, "What in the world's happened to him." Then she fell backward, into the arms of someone who was standing behind her.

When she recovered, Ann was taken to another room, where she found Robbie's daughter Edwina also waiting. In her shock and panic, she still believed that Robbie would be all right.

In the operating room, Paula DeNitto and other doctors worked feverishly on Robbie, now subdued by massive doses of sedatives.

But the frantic efforts were all in vain. Three and a half hours after he had opened the deadly package at his office on Abercorn Street, Robbie Robinson died. Paula DeNitto looked up at the clock, and made a mental note that it was 8:35 P.M.

Paula went to the room where Ann and Edwina were waiting.

"He's passed," she murmured softly.

"Oh my goodness," Ann Robinson blurted out. Then the two women—wife and daughter—dissolved in tears in one another's arms.

14 "He Might As Well Have Put His Signature on Them"

Numb with grief and disbelief, Bob Vance's closest friends gathered in the early twilight of December 16, 1989, on the expansive lawn at 2836 Shook Hill Road. Janie Shores, an Alabama supreme court justice and so dear a friend that she asked Bob and Helen to be the godparents to her daughter Laura, spoke for all as she murmured over and over, "Who could have done such a thing; Bob didn't have an enemy in the world."

In their groping bewilderment, a few associates ventured to speculate that the vile deed must have been the work of "the drug cartels." Such suspicion was inevitable, because for much of the decade the nation had been fixated on drumfire reports of rich and powerful gangs of drug lords who held such power in Latin America that they could even topple governments that dared to challenge their vast traffic in cocaine, heroin, and marijuana to the United States. The Reagan Administration's efforts to stem the illegal commerce were fitful and largely ineffectual, but whenever cartel minions were snared, they usually wound up on trial, and later on appeal, in the courts of the Eleventh Circuit. Bob Vance had handled many such appeals in his dozen years on the bench.

Meanwhile, the news of the assassination swiftly reverberated in distant points. In Washington, Attorney General Richard Thornburgh called President Bush late in the afternoon to relate the grim details of what Thornburgh called "the most direct assault on the rule of law imaginable, the assassination of a judge." Thornburgh got the impression that Bush may have known Vance. This was not the case; more likely, a Washington political operative named Vic Gold, who knew both Bush and Vance well, had at some time spoken admiringly about the judge to the President.

"Mr. President, this is the kind of case the FBI will solve," Thornburgh said. "It may take time, but the case *will* be solved."

That same afternoon Thornburgh repeated his emphatic avowal to FBI Director William S. Sessions, who scarcely needed any special encouragement to go all out to arrest Bob Vance's killer. Before he was named by President Reagan to head the FBI in 1987, Sessions had served for twelve years as a federal district judge from Texas, so he had known Bob Vance personally and professionally. Moreover, Sessions had presided over the trial that resulted in the conviction of a man accused in one of only two assassinations of federal judges in the nation's history.

Meanwhile, in the sprawling, lazy metropolis of Jacksonville, on Florida's upper Atlantic coast, Judge Gerald Bard Tjoflat, the tall, silver-haired chief judge of the Eleventh Circuit Court of Appeals and a legendary figure for his exuberant nature, received the stunning news by telephone as he was getting dressed to go to a Christmas party on the balmy evening. Tjoflat's lawyerly logic told him at once that since appellate judges routinely sat in panels of three, there could be at least two others, and maybe many more, who were unaware of their peril if the Vance murder was carried out by a vengeful defendant who had lost his appeal.

As he made his first call, Tjoflat was appalled to discover that federal budget cutbacks under his close personal friend, Ronald Reagan, had so diminished the United States Marshal's Service that the mechanism on which judges relied for routine protection had diverted its weekend telephone calls to what he quickly discerned to be "a mom-and-pop answering service." When the person who answered asked Tjoflat how to spell his unusual name—it is pronounced, "CHO-flot"—the veteran jurist threw up his hands in vexation and spent much of the remainder of the night calling judges of the circuit to warn them not to open any packages they may have received in the mail. Attorney General Thornburgh, in Washington, issued urgent protective orders, and by Sunday every federal judge in the three-state circuit had been assigned a detail of marshals as bodyguards.

At the scene of the crime in Mountain Brook, scores of law enforcement agents from federal, state, and local levels combed the Vance home and the leaf-covered hillside in search of the tiniest clues. Al Whitaker, the FBI's special agent in charge of the Birmingham office, strove to give some coherence to the diverse throng of lawmen who swarmed about the scene.

Whitaker, a twenty-year veteran of the FBI who was by then already looking to retirement, had been out buying a Christmas tree on the gray, chilly afternoon and was pulling into the driveway of his house in suburban Birmingham when his message beeper sounded.

He deposited the tree on the lawn and went inside to telephone the message center. "Please call Marty Keeler"; it was urgent, the message said.

Chester Martin Keeler was the police chief of Mountain Brook, and while his job of enforcing the law in the upscale bedroom community didn't bring him into a lot of contact with the FBI, he had gotten to know Whitaker during his two years as special agent in charge of the Birmingham FBI office.

"It looks as if there's been a bombing," Keeler said in a tremulous voice. "Judge Vance has been killed."

Whitaker felt a little awkward. "Who's Judge Vance?"

The knowledge gap was understandable. FBI agents, after all, worked for the most part in the district federal courts where cases were tried. They rarely had any contact with the appellate judges who roamed the three-state district and conducted their quiet work largely in the anonymity of panels of three. Few other agents in Whitaker's office had heard of Vance, either.

"Well, he's a federal judge," Keeler replied, "so there's definitely FBI jurisdiction."

From his home phone, Whitaker set into motion the procedure for calling out the troops. He had sixty-five agents, and fifty-five more support personnel, under his command, and many of these were in distant places. But he wanted every agent within quick driving distance to report for duty, at the downtown office or at the scene of the crime.

With the Christmas tree still lying on the damp lawn, Whitaker headed for Mountain Brook. As he drove, he picked up his car telephone and spoke with FBI Director Sessions, who at that point had not heard the news.

Smoke was still in the air, acrid and visible, when Whitaker arrived at the Vance home on Shook Hill Road. He conferred quickly with Marty Keeler and determined that there was no question that the federal crime of assaulting a federal office had been committed, and the FBI had jurisdiction. Keeler, whose work mostly consisted of investigating burglaries and keeping the traffic flowing, happily deferred to a man he knew to be experienced in investigating bombing cases.

Whitaker's first order was to keep the growing coterie of reporters and camera crews at the foot of the hill. "Keep them informed," he said, "but don't let them get underfoot."

Al Whitaker silently recalled his frustration in another bombing, having worked the notorious Unabomber case in Seattle—so named because the terrorist's first targets seemed to be United Airlines. "I am bound and determined," he told his agents, "that we will not wind up with another unsolved case here." And from his experience, he knew that in bombing cases, it was crucial to comb the scene with great care to recover every shred of material that had not been destroyed in the bomb, even little scraps of paper the size of confetti. Whitaker hastily organized his assembled men and gave each an area to cover.

Within minutes an agent came scurrying back to Whitaker. He had found something weird on a computer screen in a basement office: a picture of a row of tombstones. Could it be, Whitaker thought, a kind of perverse message left by a deranged cultist? As it turned out, it was just one of the computer games that Bob Vance would play when he needed respite from his legal labors.

Whitaker remained in command at the scene until late in the evening, speaking to William Sessions at least once more to make certain that bomb specialists were being sent from Washington. At around eleven that night he and his agents gathered in the headquarters office in downtown Birmingham for a "talkaround"—an end-of-the-day discussion that would become a permanent feature of the investigation in the coming weeks.

By that Monday morning the dim outlines of "VANPAC"—the hastily assigned acronym for "Vance package bomb task force"—had begun to emerge when an x-ray screening device hastily installed at the Eleventh Circuit Court's headquarters in downtown Atlanta detected, unmistakably, a bomb inside a package that had arrived by mail over the weekend. The package was addressed only to the "clerk's office," and bore the return address of an Atlanta attorney named Joe R. Edwards, listing an office address on Atlanta's renowned Peachtree Street just a few blocks from the court headquarters. Incredibly, the jittery security squad allowed the package to fall three feet off the end of a conveyer belt as half a dozen men watched in frozen terror. FBI bomb specialist Peter MacFarlane and his squad "suited up" and removed the deadly device in a five-thousand-pound reinforced steel bucket. Later they would learn that their protective suits were wholly inadequate to the peril; if the bomb had exploded, anyone near it would have been killed, no matter what they wore. But it did not explode, and at an unspecified location far out in the Georgia countryside, through methods that still remain secret for security reasons, McFarlane carried out RSP—render safe procedure—and defused the bomb intact.

The discovery of the Atlanta bomb reinforced the suspicion that the terrorism was the work of someone with a burning, unrequited grudge against federal judges. But the investigation was once more thrown into turmoil when, fifty hours after Bob Vance was killed, another mail-delivered bomb exploded at 1216 Abercorn Street in Savannah, fatally injuring Robbie Robinson.

Earlier in the same day Robinson was killed, Willye Frank Dennis, the longtime chapter executive of the NAACP field office in Jacksonville, Florida, also received a mysterious package, about the size of a shoebox, which was addressed with unusual precision in detail:

LEGAL COUNSEL
JACKSONVILLE BRANCH NAACP
5410 SOUTEL DR.
JACKSONVILLE, FLORIDA 32219

The return address bore a name which Willye Dennis did not recognize: Henry G. Smith Jr., who listed a Warner Robins, Georgia, address.

Because of a busy schedule and a car breakdown, Willye Dennis never got around to opening the package on the day it arrived. At 5:30 A.M. the following morning Mrs. Dennis got an urgent call from a colleague alerting her to Robbie Robinson's murder on the previous evening in Savannah, just one hundred miles north of Jacksonville. Without even getting out of bed, she first called to warn a staff member to stay away from the package, then alerted the Jacksonville sheriff's office that she had received a suspicious box.

Her suspicion proved to be deadly accurate. Bomb specialists sped to the scene and, using x-ray devices, determined at once that the package contained an explosive. When the device was defused, the investigators found inside four copies of a neatly typed message that read:

TO THE OFFICER WHO OPENED OUR SMOKE BOMB:

YOU ARE HEREBY ORDERED TO NOTIFY ALL OFFICERS OF THE NAACP THAT THEY HAVE BECOME TARGETS FOR ASSASSINATION BECAUSE OF THEIR FAILURE TO PROPERLY STRIVE FOR A COMPETENT FEDERAL JUDICIAL SYSTEM.

AMERICANS FOR A COMPETENT FEDERAL JUDICIAL SYSTEM SHALL INDICATE CREDIT FOR EACH ASSASSINATION BY PROVIDING YOU WITH THE NAMES OF THE DECEASED FOLLOWED BY THE SECRET CODE, 010187. THE CODE SHALL NOT BE MADE PUBLIC.

FAILURE TO COMPLY WITH ORDERS OF AMERICANS FOR A COMPETENT FEDERAL JUDICIAL SYSTEM SHALL RESULT IN YOUR ASSASSINATION.

010187

In addition to the bomb and the cryptic message, the new bomb-box contained what promised to be the bomber's first major mistake: Two identifiable fingerprints on a piece of paper.

By this time Attorney General Thornburgh was convinced that the terror was the work of a white-supremacy group, a dying spasm, perhaps, of the racist violence that had pervaded the South until just a few years earlier.

In Washington, James T. Thurman, a taciturn Kentuckian who headed the FBI's explosives unit, by now had his five-member staff working full time, and they soon identified enough fragments of the two exploded bombs to indicate with fair certainty that they resembled the two intact devices. The explosives specialists also quickly determined that all four bombs originated at a common source.

Back in Atlanta, Lloyd J. Erwin, a lanky north Georgia mountain boy who had managed to escape the region's intractable poverty with a degree in chemistry and who by then was comfortably settled in the midpoint of a rewarding career as a forensic analyst with the Bureau of Alcohol, Tobacco, and Firearms, knew that sooner or later he would become involved in the case.

That involvement came swiftly but in an unexpected way. Erwin was a member of an obscure professional club known as the Atlanta Metro Bomb Intelligence Organization, which by coincidence had scheduled its monthly meeting on Tuesday, December 19, at Ryan's Steak House in a suburb of Atlanta. Needless to say, the mail bombs were the exclusive topic of conversation as the assorted agents exchanged arcane tidbits of information and passed around sketches of the bombs. Putting together what he already knew and what he heard that night, Erwin was seized by a flash of memory and intuition. On a restaurant paper napkin, he sketched out a rough diagram of the bomb that had brought about Roy Moody's conviction in 1972. Erwin had been the principal expert witness at that trial seventeen years earlier, and the four new bombs, he told his Atlanta ATF colleague, Richard Rawlins, were so similar to the earlier one that Moody "might as well have put his signature on them."

The following day, Rawlins passed on Erwin's sketch to Brian Hoback, the Atlanta ATF agent designated to coordinate his agency's investigation. The ATF unit, unlike the massive FBI task force that spilled over into three states, was small enough that the group could assemble at the close of each day to compare findings and give some coherence to the investigation. On December 20, Hoback told his men to begin assembling a file on Walter Leroy Moody Jr.

As it happened, Roy Moody had already been doing some work of his own. On December 18, two days after Vance's death, Roy Moody dispatched a letter by Federal Express to the clerk of the United States Supreme Court. He requested an extension of time for preparation of his appeal in his *error coram nobis* case, which had now been firmly decided at the appellate level. The letter read:

I had planned to file my pro se motion for an out of time en banc hearing together with a motion seeking an expedited hearing on same in the Eleventh Circuit Court of Appeals this morning.

Yesterday, however, I learned of the tragic news about one of the judges. Under the circumstances I do not feel it would be proper for me to seek an expedited hearing.

Consequently, I must request that the time within which I may file a petition for a writ of certoiari [*sic*] be extended from January 18, 1990, to February 18, 1990.

Meanwhile, in the week that followed the Vance attack, twenty federal judges across the three states of the circuit received, in plain envelopes, copies of the cryptic messages that had been found in the bombs that were mailed to Vance, Robinson, and the Jacksonville NAACP. In addition there was an even more puzzling document— found intact in the unexploded Jacksonville bomb—which read:

> MR. MARTELLE LAYFIELD, JR.
>
> YOU ARE ORDERED TO NOTIFY ALL FEDERAL JUDGES AND ALL ATTORNEYS IN THE UNITED STATES THAT THEY HAVE BECOME TARGETS FOR ASSASSINATION BECAUSE OF THE FEDERAL COURTS' CALLOUSED DISREGARD FOR THE ADMINISTRATION OF JUSTICE.
>
> AMERICANS FOR A COMPETENT FEDERAL JUDICIAL SYSTEM SHALL INDICATE CREDIT FOR EACH ASSASSINATION BY PROVIDING YOU WITH THE NAMES OF THE DECEASED FOLLOWED BY THE SECRET CODE, 010187. THE CODE SHALL NOT BE MADE PUBLIC.
>
> FAILURE TO COMPLAY WITH ORDERS OF AMERICANS FOR A COMPETENT FEDERAL JUDICIAL SYSTEM SHALL RESULT IN YOUR ASSASSINATION.
>
> 010187

Layfield had been a prominent Georgia lawyer who was long active in Republican Party politics, as well as in American Bar Association activities. The letters that went to the twenty judges all were addressed with the words, "THE LATE," before their names. The letter to Layfield did not, even though he had died, of natural causes, nearly four months earlier.

More than a week passed before the next bizarre development. On December 27, Brenda Wood, a popular black news anchorwoman at the WAGA-TV station in Atlanta, received an envelope that bore the return address: "AMERICANS FOR A COMPETENT FEDERAL JUDICIAL SYSTEM, ALABAMA, FLORIDA AND GEORGIA." Inside Wood found a letter with a bewildering message, claiming that a secret meeting of the "officers" of the putative organization were ordering her to provide Martelle Layfield with the names of Vance and Robinson along with the code number 010187. The message ordered Wood to prepare a news report and send copies to major news organizations for broadcast on Christmas Day. "FAILURE TO COMPLY," the letter read, "SHALL RESULT IN YOUR ASSASSINATION." The letter continued:

THE UNITED STATES COURT OF APPEALS FOR THE ELEVENTH CIRCUIT
HAS BEEN QUICK TO STRESS THE IMPORTANCE OF CIVIL RIGHTS
FOR BLACKS BUT SLOW TO STRESS THE IMPORTANCE OF BLACKS
TO DEMONSTRATE CIVIL RESPONSIBILITY. THIS FAILURE CREATED A
CLIMATE THAT HAS SPAWNED AN ALARMING NUMBER OF SAVAGE ACTS
OF VIOLENCE BY BLACK MEN AGAINST WHITE WOMEN. JULIE LOVE,
FOR EXAMPLE, A YOUNG INNOCENT WHITE LADY WAS ROBBED, KID-
NAPPED, GANG RAPED, SODOMIZED, MURDERED AND DISMEMBERED
BY A GROUP OF BLACK MALES. HER REMAINS WERE CONCEALED FOR
AN EXTREMELY LONG PERIOD OF TIME, LEAVING HER LOVE ONES IN
EXCRUCIATING ANGUISH. JULIE LOVE WAS AN INNOCENT PERSON,
AN INNOCENT PERSON WHO ALSO HAD CIVIL RIGHTS. SHE IS ONLY
ONE OF THOUSANDS OF INNOCENT WHITE WOMEN WHO HAVE BEEN
RAPED AND MURDERED BY INHUMAN BLACK BARBARIANS. PROTECT-
ING THE INNOCENT WARRANTS A HIGHER COURT PRIORITY THAN
GRANTING THE BLACKS' DEMAND FOR WHITE TEACHERS FOR THEIR
CHILDREN. THE MESSAGE AMERICANS FOR A COMPETENT FEDERAL
JUDICIAL HAS FOR THE JUDGES IS SIMPLE, IF YOU WANT TO LIVE,
YOU SHALL MAKE PROTECTING THE CIVIL RIGHTS OF THE INNOCENT
YOUR HIGHEST OBLIGATION AND YOU SHALL FULFILL THAT OBLIGA-
TION. THE MESSAGE AMERICANS FOR A COMPETENT FEDERAL JUDI-
CIAL SYSTEM HAS FOR ATTORNEYS AND THE BLACK LEADERSHIP IS
ALSO SIMPLE, IF YOU WANT TO LIVE, YOU SHALL TAKE THAT ACTION

REQUIRED TO PREVENT BLACK MEN FROM RAPING WHITE WOMEN.
AMERICANS FOR A COMPETENT FEDERAL JUDICIAL SYSTEM ASSASSI-
NATED JUDGE ROBERT S. VANCE AND ATTORNEY ROBERT ROBINSON
IN REPRISAL FOR THE ATROCITIES INFLICTED UPON JULIE LOVE. TWO
MORE PROMINENT MEMBERS OF THE NAACP SHALL BE ASSASSINATED,
USING MORE SOPHISTICATED MEANS, AS PART OF THE SAME REPRISAL.
ANYTIME A BLACK MAN RAPES A WHITE WOMAN IN ALABAMA, FLO-
RIDA OR GEORGIA IN THE FUTURE, AMERICANS FOR A COMPETENT
FEDERAL JUDICIAL SYSTEM SHALL ASSASSINATE ONE FEDERAL JUDGE,
ONE ATTORNEY AND ONE OFFICER OF THE NAACP.

The new missive gave the investigators significant leads. The Julie
Love rape-murder case had been heavily publicized in the Atlanta area,
so the implication was clear that the writer of the menacing letter most
likely lived within the WAGA-TV broadcast area, which included most
of Georgia as well as portions of four neighboring states. The targeting
of NAACP operatives, coupled with the obsession with race-tinged violent acts, reinforced the suspicion that the bombs were being sent by a
violent white-supremacy group.

Moreover, as Judge Tjoflat pointed out to the FBI, all the messages
now contained a legalistic tone—such as the repeated use of the word
"shall" rather than "will"—which suggested that the author of the letters might be a lawyer. This confluence led some agents to focus on J. B.
Stoner, a sinister crippled lawyer in Atlanta who had for years been directly or indirectly connected with violent racist elements. But the agents
soon concluded that Stoner was too old and too broken by the time he
had spent in prison to be a credible prime suspect; besides, he had been
involved in no practices or movements of recent weeks that would suggest he had a role in the rash of bombings.

As the investigators struggled to make sense out of the burgeoning
confusion, on Wednesday, December 20, the small picturesque St. Luke's
Episcopal Church in Mountain Brook overflowed as the great and the
humble gathered for Bob Vance's funeral service. Among those attending were Attorney General Thornburgh, representing the President, and
FBI Director William Sessions. Also present was former President Jimmy
Carter, who, just a dozen years before, had appointed Vance to the federal

bench. But mostly the congregation consisted of grieving relatives, and a throng of admiring friends of a lifetime. Helen Vance, however, was not present; her grave injuries would not allow her to leave St. Vincent's Hospital.

Robbie Robinson's funeral was held four days later. A snowstorm, something that almost never happened in Savannah, prevented the high and mighty of the land from attending the funeral. But a great throng of local friends, relatives, and political dignitaries gathered at the venerable St. Paul's C.M.E. Church to pay final tribute to a beloved son who had been born and lived for most of his forty-two years within a few blocks of the church.

As Birmingham and Savannah settled back into the holiday season, it passed without public notice that Robert and Charles Vance gathered at Helen Vance's bedside in St. Vincent's Hospital for a solemn Christmas dinner. A few days later, after Helen was released, she called the old family friend, Clifford Fulford.

"Cliff," she said, "something's wrong. I can't cry."

"Don't worry," Fulford said with infinite gentleness, "the day will come when you will. And we will all cry with you."

By the arrival of the new year, the mysterious bomber had spread his terror over three states and into the jurisdictions of six FBI field offices, but there was still no overall coordinator assigned to the case. Each special agent in charge—as the FBI field commanders are called— reported directly to Washington. There, the reports were combed daily by Bill Baker, the assistant director of the FBI's criminal investigation division, and his boss, Oliver "Buck" Revell, whose title was associate director for investigations. Not a day passed that Revell and Baker did not brief Sessions, the FBI director, on the VANPAC investigation, but the fact was, they had many equally pressing matters on their plates as well, including the bombing of Pan-American Airlines Flight 103 in 1988 over Lockerbie, Scotland.

Almost by default, the investigation increasingly came to be concentrated in the hands of William L. Hinshaw II, the special agent in charge of the Atlanta office. Hinshaw knew his region well. A North Carolinian by birth, he went to The Citadel, the prestigious military academy located at Charleston, South Carolina. A standout student in athletics and academics alike, he was commissioned as a lieutenant in the infantry upon graduation in 1963, and served a tour of duty with the Rangers in Vietnam before assignment as an ROTC instructor at the University of Alabama. He took advantage of the assignment to get his master's degree in public administration, and in 1968 he left the military service to join the FBI. He demonstrated wide-ranging skills and won rapid promotion. In 1989, still two years short of his fiftieth birthday, he was named special agent in charge of the Atlanta FBI field office, one of the busiest in the nation.

Bill Hinshaw had not even unpacked all of his boxes from his previous assignment as special agent in charge of the Mobile office when the Christmas mail bomb cases hit the front pages of the nation's newspapers. The case instantly became the top item on his agenda—after all, the president of the United States had promised the American people that no effort or expense would be spared in tracking down the killer or killers of Bob Vance and Robbie Robinson.

With the investigation spread over three states and an even larger number of agencies, Hinshaw called for a summit of the heads of all the regional law enforcement units in Atlanta on January 17, to assess the progress of the investigation in the month that had passed since Bob Vance was killed.

Hinshaw was astonished when Robert Mueller, the young assistant attorney general from Washington, showed up with a dozen or more attorneys in tow to attend the meeting. He did not like this development. He knew Mueller by reputation as a privileged product of an Ivy League college and a top law school. In Hinshaw's eyes, Mueller lived up to his reputation as a brash, on-the-rise young man with a penchant for intimidating everyone he dealt with. Mueller simply told Hinshaw he was there to help solve the case.

There is an old admonition that seasoned FBI agents use when they want to caution United States attorneys about turf-invasion: "You prosecute, we investigate." At this point VANPAC was still clearly in the investigation stage, but it had also spilled over into at least four separate U.S. district attorney's jurisdictions. As with the FBI, there was no central coordinating office. The regional district attorneys were each reporting to Washington, independently, to Mueller. Like his counterparts at the FBI, Mueller had many other matters to command his attention, including not only the Pan-Am 103 bombing but a host of banking and Wall Street scandals as well.

Based on what he had learned so far—and he did not know about Lloyd Erwin's suspicions—Attorney General Thornburgh, the one man with authority over both the FBI and the district attorneys, grew increasingly fixated on his belief that the bombings had to be the work of white supremacists. This certainty was reinforced in early January of 1990 when FBI analysts, who had been painstakingly scouring court files in search of documents that might offer clues, made a breathtaking discovery. An eccentric junk dealer and self-ordained Baptist preacher in South Alabama named Robert Wayne O'Ferrell had typed out his own appeal in a personal-grievance lawsuit against former employers that he had lost in the federal district court in Montgomery; *the typewriter that O'Ferrell used was, unmistakably, the same one that had written the death threats contained in the package bombs mailed in December.*

O'Ferrell, whose family had connections to racist organizations, instantly became the prime suspect in the murders of Bob Vance and Robbie Robinson. For several tense days the information was closely guarded, because clearly the matter was no longer merely in the investigative stage; it commanded the close attention of the most skilled lawyers in drawing up search warrants that would not later endanger a subsequent prosecution.

The search warrants authorizing a raid on O'Ferrell's junk store on the outskirts of Enterprise, Alabama, were issued on January 17. The three FBI special agents in charge in Atlanta, Birmingham, and now Mobile—Enterprise was in that district—agreed the raid should begin the following morning. But that night, the chagrined field officers got instructions from Washington to postpone the raid until the following Monday, January 22. The reasons for the delay were ambiguous, but gradually the field agents learned that Attorney General Thornburgh wanted the raid delayed until Monday in order to coincide with his scheduled meeting with President Bush and a group of civil rights leaders, including the Reverend Joseph Lowery, who had succeeded Dr. Martin Luther King Jr. as president of the Southern Christian Leadership Conference; Ben Hooks, the NAACP's national director; and Earl Shinhoster, the director of the Atlanta regional office of the NAACP where a mailed tear-gas bomb had exploded the previous summer.

At 9:30 A.M. on that day Thornburgh strode into the Roosevelt Room of the White House and announced with a sense of triumph that "federal agents" were at that very moment closing in on the prime suspect in the mail bomb cases. As an experienced prosecutor, Thornburgh was subtly careful not to make his claim too extravagant, but nonetheless the participants got the firm impression that "something big was happening."

And indeed, at precisely that moment, Robert Wayne O'Ferrell, with his dog Lassie beside him in the front seat of his pickup truck, drove up to his place of business on the edge of the languid South Alabama town that was the nearest community to the Army helicopter training facility at Fort Rucker. O'Ferrell parked in front of the garish, barnlike structure, which bore a crudely fashioned sign that read, "Old & New Dept. Store," and at once observed an unfamiliar car parked in front of the building. As O'Ferrell got out of his truck, two men stepped from the car and, flashing badges, identified themselves as FBI agents.

"How can I help you?" O'Ferrell asked apprehensively.

"We want to know what you know about the bombs that killed Judge Vance in Birmingham and Attorney Robinson in Savannah," one of the men replied.

"Well, I heard about it on TV and on the radio and read about it in the papers," O'Ferrell replied. "My wife Mary Ann and I were at work that Saturday when we heard about it, and we talked about how bad it was to kill somebody like that."

The two men then showed the bewildered O'Ferrell several photographs of himself surreptitiously taken at a number of locations, including his parents' home, over the past several days, and informed him that his telephones had been "bugged."

"Why?" O'Ferrell implored. "I can't imagine why you would do that? I don't have anything to hide."

The two men did not respond, but asked O'Ferrell to "ride with us down to the city hall." He readily complied, but added that he hoped he would not have to stay for long, because he needed to open the store.

When they reached the Enterprise City Hall, O'Ferrell was hustled into a room that clearly was a makeshift command headquarters for the FBI.

"We are going to open your life like a book," one of the agents began. "Everyone will know about you."

Then the interrogation immediately turned to a typewriter, and was followed by a flurry of questions about bombs, pipes, nails, and gunpowder. At one point someone thrust before the horrified O'Ferrell a photograph of Bob Vance's body, gaping with wounds, slumped against a kitchen wall in which many nails were embedded.

After more than an hour of questioning, O'Ferrell was photographed and fingerprinted and shown search warrants that authorized a massive raid on his home, store, and small farm. He was directed to get back into the FBI car to return to his store. As he approached, he saw a horde of reporters, including television film crews, mingling with what appeared to be scores of investigators, with the initials of their agencies emblazoned on the backs of their coats. The entrance of his property had been sealed off by barricades and heavy tapes.

"I'm so embarrassed I could crawl into a hole," O'Ferrell said as he got out of the car. "If you think I had anything to do with those bombings, and when you realize what a mistake you've made, I want an apology from y'all."

"We don't apologize to nobody," an unidentified man responded.

A throng of news reporters shouted questions, but O'Ferrell, heeding the FBI's admonition, ignored every inquiry as he went about unlocking doors of various buildings on his property. Once inside, the agents demanded that O'Ferrell give them any pistols he might have. He gave them two. The agents removed the cartridges, and returned the firearms to their owner.

Around midmorning, the store telephone rang. It was Mary Ann's employer, in a great state of agitation.

"Wayne," the man began, "there are two FBI agents here, and they want Mary Ann to go with them."

"That's nothing," replied O'Ferrell, who by this time had recovered his wits and wit. "There are about a hundred FBI agents standing around my counter. Let me talk with Mary Ann."

The husband and wife were permitted to speak only after agents on the respective ends of the line had discussed the matter.

"Wayne, what in the world is going on?" Mary Ann O'Ferrell asked.

"Are you sitting down?" Wayne O'Ferrell asked. "They think I had something to do with the bombs that killed Judge Vance and that lawyer from Savannah."

Mary Ann laughed nervously. "Wayne, are you kidding me?"

"No," he replied, "I'm not kidding."

At a little after one o'clock, in a somewhat bizarre display of congeniality, four FBI agents took O'Ferrell to Gran's Place, a popular local eatery, for lunch. A throng of reporters hovered outside. The agents repeatedly told O'Ferrell not to speak to the reporters, and even advised him to cover his face with his hand as he moved about. Later his family members asked him why he did this, saying that it gave an impression of guilt.

O'Ferrell asked if he could take a lie-detector test "to clear up this whole thing." An agent replied that such a test would require permission from Washington. When the five men left Gran's Place, they did not return to the O'Ferrell complex; they went straight to City Hall, where O'Ferrell was spirited into the building through the Fire Department door. Despite the ploy, the reporters saw him and continued to shout questions. The agents once more told him to keep silent.

At around 4:30, he began the six-hour ordeal of a polygraph test. At one point, he would later claim, the polygraph operator yelled at him and threatened to electrocute him if he didn't tell the truth. They told him Mary Ann had already confessed to their role in sending the bombs. "That's a lie," O'Ferrell protested. "She didn't tell you anything like that, because all we know about the bombings is what we saw on TV and read in the papers."

Throughout the examination the questioners kept coming back to the typewriter. O'Ferrell readily acknowledged that he had owned many second-hand typewriters—he bought them often at sales of salvage goods at the nearby Army base at Fort Rucker—and that in fact he'd used whatever typewriters he had for sale to write business and personal correspondence, including letters to the federal court in connection with the case he had brought against the Gulf Life Insurance Company. But he steadfastly insisted that he had sold the typewriter, although he could give no details as to the purchaser.

At around 10:30 O'Ferrell demanded that he either be charged or released so that he could go home. The agents acceded, but insisted on sending a detail with him for "protection," once more warning him not to talk to the media.

When he reached home he found his two daughters and son-in-law distraught from the day's events, including, around 9:30 P.M., an anonymous telephone call to the O'Ferrell home in which the caller warned "You'll be the next to get a bomb."

Mary Ann O'Ferrell's ordeal coincided with that of her husband's. It began in the morning when federal agents approached her at her part-time job caring for an invalid woman, in addition to her regular job; she refused the FBI's request to go in for questioning until she had completed her cooking and cleaning duties. The agents followed her from room to room as she worked, and once even followed her to the bathroom, keeping close watch as if she might attempt to escape through the window.

When she finished her job, Mary Ann still refused to go in for questioning and instead drove to the O'Ferrell complex, only to freeze when she saw the horde of reporters, camera crews, and police teams swarming about her home. At this point she agreed to accompany Enterprise policewoman Cindy Dunway back to the ad hoc operational headquarters at City Hall. Around 10:30 that night, she agreed to take a polygraph test, during which she was told that her husband had admitted his involvement in the bombings and "you might as well admit, too."

"You're lying," she replied. "Wayne did not tell you that."

Her ordeal had lasted for nearly twelve hours, during which she got vivid descriptions of how Bob Vance's body was ripped to pieces by the bomb. As they had done with her husband, the interrogators raised the specter of the electric chair. She was told that her husband had confessed, and that her only chance of staying alive was to make her own confession "so we can get the whole thing over with."

Shortly before midnight, Mary Ann called her distraught family to say that she was leaving City Hall.

"Stay there," O'Ferrell said. "I'll come and get you."

"No," his wife replied, "I ain't staying here another minute." Mary Ann reached home at 12:15 accompanied by an FBI agent who told them not to discuss the case with anyone—not even among themselves. When the agent left, O'Ferrell looked outside and found his home virtually encircled by reporters, including one who had his ear pressed against a windowpane.

Nearly eighteen hours after "the longest and worst day of my life," Robert Wayne O'Ferrell spent a sleepless night in bed.

The following morning he arose early to find the siege still in full force. He drove six miles over to New Brockton, where he bought two "no trespassing" signs. He returned and started to nail the signs onto a fence post when a reporter approached him and began asking questions.

"If you step across that line," O'Ferrell said, pointing to the ground, "I will have you arrested."

Around noon several FBI agents came to him and asked him to go back to City Hall for more polygraph tests. O'Ferrell agreed, only to find himself peppered with insistence to "go ahead and admit that you did it." At one point, an agent spoke of "when you are walking your last walk down those halls to the electric chair" and suggested that the authorities might "go easy on you" if he confessed.

"Thank you," O'Ferrell replied, "but I'll stick to the truth. You can stay with me for twenty years and you won't find anything, because there are two people that know I don't know anything about the bombing."

"Who are they?" an interrogator asked.

"Me and Jesus Christ."

With all polygraph tests strongly indicating that O'Ferrell was not responding truthfully, the FBI intensified its investigation. In addition to the lie-detector tests, O'Ferrell acceded to the demands of the agents to give blood and hair samples to be used to seek out any DNA elements that might be found in the bombs. Acting under the assumption that the missing typewriter might have been broken into tiny pieces and flushed down the toilet, agents in waterproof suits dug up O'Ferrell's cesspool and sifted its contents; nothing resembling typewriter parts were found.

Over the next days and weeks O'Ferrell's parents, including a mother who was suffering from Alzheimer's disease, were questioned at their rural home in nearby Conecuh County. His church and elements of the community stuck by him; someone even wrote a sympathetic country-music tune, "The Ballad of Wayne O'Ferrell," which chronicled the ordeal of an innocent man bedeviled by vengeful inquisitors. But his business, which had provided a marginal living even in the best of times, collapsed entirely when his customers were questioned by federal agents. His daughter, Danielle, was taunted at her local high school as "the bomber's daughter." Wayne and Mary Ann, who were already having marital problems, separated. O'Ferrell began to develop health problems, which required visits to the local emergency room, and soon he was confronted with ten thousand dollars in medical bills—and no insurance. He hired a lawyer, whom he could advance only a modest down payment for services.

But if he had support in his narrow circle of church and community friends, O'Ferrell was widely viewed beyond the environs of Enterprise as the prime suspect in the bombing. President Bush made several general statements about the bombings that kept the issue on the front burner, even alluding to the crime in his State of the Union address to Congress on January 31. FBI agents in Enterprise told O'Ferrell flatly that Bush was talking about him; they even warned him not to attempt to harm any agents, because he was kept in the crosshairs of sharpshooters virtually all the time. The president clearly had bought into Attorney General Thornburgh's dogged certainty that the mail bombs had been made and sent by some fanatical white-supremacy group with a lingering bitterness at the federal courts and civil rights organizations that had redrawn the social and political map of America over the previous quarter of a century.

But gradually the raid on O'Ferrell's complex began to peter out as no solid evidence was forthcoming. At a meeting of top FBI agents in Birmingham in early February, Al Whitaker asked the assembled men to jot down on a scrap of paper, in secret-ballot fashion, whether they believed O'Ferrell sent the mail bombs. Eleven of the twelve answers were "no," and the remaining one read "not sure." Despite the collective certainty of the agents that O'Ferrell had been drawn into the case only through bizarre coincidence, the frenetic and unproductive searching went on for six weeks, and in early March Wayne and Mary Ann O'Ferrell received separate, identical letters from the federal district attorney in Birmingham, Frank W. Donaldson, formally notifying each that "you are the target of a Federal Grand Jury investigation into the murder of Judge Robert S. Vance and other matters." The purpose of the letter was to "invite" the O'Ferrells to appear before the grand jury in Birmingham that was investigating the Vance assassination. The letter was accompanied by a document entitled "Advice of Rights," which, in somewhat technical terms, made it clear that the O'Ferrells could not be compelled to testify.

They declined the invitation.

15 "I Bought Three Typewriters for Roy"

While the FBI focused its vast resources and manpower on Wayne O'Ferrell, the Atlanta task force of the Bureau of Alcohol, Tobacco, and Firearms quietly pursued Lloyd Erwin's identification of the striking similarities between the bomb that exploded in Roy Moody's house in 1972 and the four bombs that were mailed during the week of December 10, 1989. The ATF team, which consisted of only a handful of agents in the Atlanta office, was a far cry from the army of FBI agents assigned to the case. But this very smallness made the effort more manageable; the ATF agents could gather in a single office at the end of the day to assess their findings and give a degree of coherence to the investigation. Moreover, the ATF was not under the Department of Justice but rather under the Treasury Department. The task force quietly began to assemble a file on Roy Moody, who had no known connection to any white-supremacy organizations—the chief focus of the FBI's investigation.

Using Lloyd Erwin's description of eleven technical similarities between the 1972 bomb and the 1989 bombs, the ATF conducted a computerized database "signature" search of ten thousand bombs and found that no others bore such a striking resemblance as these two sets.

When Probate Judge William Self arrived for work at the Bibb County Courthouse in Macon on January 10, 1990, he was told by an anxious office clerk that two "federal men" wanted to speak with him. By this time an experienced lawyer of fifteen years, Bill Self was seized by a moment of apprehension over the fact that the agents had not called beforehand to relate their purpose. But since he always got to the office well in advance of the workaday hearings that constituted the bulk of his work, he set aside the routine morning chores and invited the agents, Joe M. Gordon of the ATF and David Kirkland, an inspector with the U.S. Postal Service, into his spacious, book-lined office in the heart of the old Georgia city.

"What can I do for you?" Self asked as they took their seats.

"I guess you have read about the bombs that killed the federal judge in Birmingham and the city councilman in Savannah," Gordon began.

Self smiled knowingly. "Now I know why you are here."

He excused himself for a moment, and got his file on the divorce case in which he had represented Hazel Strickland Moody more than a decade earlier. What had begun as a routine divorce proceeding that should have taken no more than a few pages of documents now consisted of four thick file-folders, an eclectic mix of legal documents, most of them filed in response to Roy Moody's inventive legal ploys to contest the divorce, to gain custody of Mark Bryan Moody, and to avoid making court-ordered child support payments.

The following day the ATF began the first surveillance of Roy Moody's home on the quiet suburban street in Rex, Georgia, but because of limited manpower, the stakeout was sporadic. Bill Hinshaw, the FBI's special agent in charge of the Atlanta office, believed the ATF was on the right track in focusing on Moody, but over the next few weeks his views got short shrift in Washington. Hinshaw was told bluntly that Attorney General Thornburgh remained adamant in his view that the bombings were the work of white-supremacy groups—never mind that the O'Ferrell investigation produced no solid leads.

Still, Hinshaw quietly put his own agents on the Moody trail. On January 30, a little more than a week after the O'Ferrell raid began,

Hinshaw sent agents to the suburban Atlanta office of Michael Ford, the attorney who had once worked with the Bobby Hill law firm in Savannah but who had subsequently represented Roy Moody in some of his legal battles. Ford was staunch in his belief that Moody had nothing to do with the bombings.

A week later, Hinshaw secured a search warrant, based largely on Lloyd Erwin's identification of Moody's "signature bomb," authorizing a raid on the Moody home in Rex. On February 7 Roy Moody's name first appeared in the Atlanta newspapers as a potential suspect in the mail bombings, even though the principal focus at this time was still on O'Ferrell. Several items were seized at Roy's house, but nothing that would directly link him to the bombings. Hinshaw's agents also began to interview former associates and acquaintances of Moody, including erstwhile girl friends, business associates, and attorneys who had represented or opposed him in his myriad court forays.

One of these associates was a man named Richard Singleton, who had rented an apartment to Roy in the 1970s. He continued to rent to his former tenant, for ten dollars a month, some basement storage space. The Singleton home was in Chamblee, a residential community northeast of Atlanta. As the agents sifted through the odd collection, a young ATF agent named David Hyche noticed a device that looked remarkably similar to the drawing that Lloyd Erwin had made of the pipe-bomb that exploded in Roy Moody's house in Macon in 1972. The apparatus was taken to Erwin, who immediately identified it as a more sophisticated device than the 1972 bomb, yet less so than the 1989 bombs. It was, as it were, the missing link in the evolution of the bombs.

This evidence was enough for Hinshaw to gain court authorization, around the middle of March, to place a wiretap on Roy Moody's telephone line.

By this time Moody's extensive history of litigation had been thoroughly examined, and the *coram nobis* lawsuit seemed especially promising since it had involved the federal courts over a protracted period. Miriam Walmsley Duke, the assistant district attorney in Macon who had represented the government in resisting Moody's effort to have his 1972 conviction set aside, told agents she was certain that the "Gene Wallace" tale was an elaborate tissue of perjury. Little or no thought had been given to prosecuting Moody after he lost the case, however, because harried government prosecutors have enough to do without seeking out crimes where no large issues were at stake or where no significant damage had been done.

But suddenly in the spring of 1990 the *coram nobis* caper took on a new life as a potential way for the federal authorities to get their hands on Moody even if they couldn't prove that he had mailed the bombs. In late March of 1990 ATF agent William Grom located and confronted Julie Linn-West, the paraplegic woman who had been Roy Moody's principal witness in his obsessive effort to get the 1972 bomb-possession conviction overturned. In almost no time the telephone taps picked up Linn-West's panic-stricken call to Roy Moody. The agents scurried back to Linn-West's small, sparely furnished apartment in the Atlanta suburb of Smyrna. The terrified woman, sensing that she faced a perjury prosecution, swiftly caved in under the gentle persuasion of Grom's questioning: She admitted her testimony about the mysterious Gene Wallace leaving the bomb at Moody's house in 1972 had been a lie from start to finish, concocted and scripted in its entirety by Roy Moody and Susan McBride.

By this time Moody's every move was being monitored, and soon he was seen entering Linn-West's apartment. The purpose of these visits was to cajole her not to cooperate with the agents, to offer her more money to maintain her silence. Roy not only told Julie Linn-West that she stood to be prosecuted for perjury if she collaborated but also went on to hint that he had Mafia connections that would target the woman's mother if Roy should go to jail.

Linn-West was shaken, especially by the implied threat of violence against her mother, but still she agreed to allow the investigators to install a secret video-camera in her apartment to record Roy Moody's visits.

Fully aware by then that his telephone was tapped and his every move observed, on some of these visits Roy insisted on communicating with Julie Linn-West with written notes passed from hand to hand, then burned over the kitchen sink. On other occasions, Roy insisted that Julie go with him and Susan for rides in his car. Still, the cameras were able to pick up enough to show conclusively that the *coram nobis* proceeding had been a scam based on perjured testimony.

With the O'Ferrell investigation clearly going nowhere, FBI Director Sessions in Washington found himself increasingly under pressure to take new actions. Among those who were bringing pressure was Judge Tjoflat, the Eleventh Circuit chief judge who was functioning as the court's liaison with the investigation and, in the view of some of the agents, making a nuisance of himself—acting, as one put it, "a bit like a college professor who tells the football coach how to run plays."

For several weeks Sessions's aide, Buck Revell had been pressing for the appointment of a single inspector in Atlanta to be placed in overall charge of the VANPAC investigation. Revell's assistant, Bill Baker, had been hesitant to take such a step, which would mean supplanting local field agents who were jealous of their independence on their own turfs.

In late March Revell persuaded Sessions that with an investigation that spilled over into three states and twice that number of FBI field offices, it was essential to have a ranking figure to coordinate VANPAC.

"The director has okayed sending in an inspector," Revell told Bill Baker one morning in late March.

"Who do you want to send?" Baker asked.

"Larry Potts."

"Well, he's the perfect one."

At forty, Larry Potts was already widely regarded as one of the most promising agents in the whole vast apparatus of the FBI. His college degree—from the University of Richmond—was not in law or accounting, the standard disciplines required of FBI agents, but rather history and psychology.

In his sixteen years with the FBI he had performed with skill in a wide range of jobs across the country before coming to headquarters as chief of the highly sensitive public corruption unit. After that he had one more field assignment—as assistant special agent in charge of the Boston office, one of the FBI's major outposts—before returning to Washington as chief of the white-collar crimes section. In this role he paid only passing attention to the VANPAC investigation and, in fact, was hoping to get an assignment as special agent in charge of the FBI's Charlotte office.

On March 28 he got a call asking him to come to the office of his immediate boss, Bill Baker. Up to that point Potts had maintained only a peripheral interest in the VANPAC investigation, concentrating instead on his own jurisdiction. But often he would ask, as he passed through Baker's office, how the mail bomb investigation was going. Baker would only shake his head and say, "This is one we've got to solve."

On that cool Wednesday morning, Baker got right to the point: "The decision has been made to appoint an inspector in the VANPAC case."

"Good idea," Potts replied. He knew, from Bill Sessions, that Buck Revell had been urging that course for some time.

"Well, I'm glad to hear you say that," Baker continued with a smile, "because you're going to be the inspector."

Potts asked if he could consider it overnight. It would mean, he told his wife that evening, being away from home, probably for several months. But such assignments came with the job. She agreed.

Larry Potts spent the next two days delegating unfinished jobs to others in the white-collar crimes section and, in between, dashing across the street to the Department of Justice to confer with Assistant Attorney General Robert Mueller, who had worked with the FBI agent on other cases in the past and was close enough to call him by his chummy nickname of "Pottsy." Potts especially wanted to concentrate on telephone wiretaps, and he knew that this kind of surveillance was a legal minefield that required the attention of skilled lawyers. He also knew that at some point the case would require the service of a full-time lawyer, and he wanted to start the process of getting one assigned.

With his personal and professional affairs in reasonable order, Potts left Washington on Sunday, April 1. Two hours later he was met at the Atlanta airport by Bill Hinshaw, who by that time was discouraged over the fact that the attorney general continued to be obsessed with the idea of a racial conspiracy when, in Hinshaw's mind, the enigmatic, solitary figure of Roy Moody was the prime suspect.

Even though Potts was supplanting Hinshaw as the director of the most important criminal investigation currently underway, the two men hit it off right away. As they headed to Atlanta to check Potts into his hotel, Hinshaw suggested they might drive by Roy Moody's house at Rex, which was only fifteen minutes from Atlanta's sprawling Hartsfield International Airport. Potts readily agreed, and as the two men drove slowly down Skyline Drive, the afternoon shadows had begun to fall.

Roy Moody, wearing a large straw hat, emerged from his house and appeared to do some work on one of his automobiles in the cluttered driveway. In all likelihood, Moody saw the surreptitious visitors and wanted to greet them in his own arrogant manner. The hunter and the hunted had come face-to-face.

Early the next morning Larry Potts called his first meeting of the VANPAC task force. A hundred or more people crowded into the cramped quarters hastily carved out for him in the Atlanta FBI suite. The scene was taut with anxiety, and no one knew better than Larry Potts that his task demanded not just competent detective skills but a mastery of bureaucratic politics as well. The people he would be supervising included not just FBI and Justice Department people, but ATF agents, postal inspectors, U.S. marshals, and state and local police.

"I know that you are apprehensive about this arrangement," he began candidly, "but I want to assure you that we are all in this thing as full partners. I intend to win your confidence."

Potts swiftly proved to be up to the daunting task of building the partnership he promised. Gentle in manner and appearance—he gives the impression of a slightly balding college student who has to watch his caloric intake—Potts came with a solid reputation for competence rather than career-building, and his performance justified that reputation. Beyond that, the agents knew that he could command attention in Washington.

The agents learned that the 8:30 meeting was to be an every-morning affair. Involving scores of agents from close to a dozen agencies, the meetings would sometimes last until ten o'clock, which caused some grumbling at the outset that the agents were spending too much time hobnobbing in the office and too little doing the grunt work of running down every lead that offered the remotest promise of shedding new light on the crime.

In addition to the morning meetings, Potts also paid special attention to the top figures in the FBI's rival agencies. He had an agreement with Tom Stokes, the head of the Atlanta ATF office, that anytime a problem arose, they would meet quietly for lunch at a nearby Georgia barbecue restaurant to work out the problem and smooth ruffled feelings of agents who felt aggrieved for one reason or another.

Potts hit it off especially well with Bill Hinshaw, the resident FBI chief, primarily because from the outset he shared Hinshaw's view that Roy Moody, not Wayne O'Ferrell, was the prime suspect. Washington had promised Potts all the manpower he needed to carry out his job, and Hinshaw made it clear that his agents were at Potts's disposal anytime he needed them.

Potts first major initiative was to formulate areas of specialization in assignments and end the previous scattergun approach in which agents in effect claimed their own assignments, sometimes covering the same ground that had already been explored by other agents in other agencies.

His next order of business was to intensify surveillance of Roy Moody through telephone wiretaps, electronic bugging, and observation of his every movement. Within days after Potts arrived in Atlanta, Roy Moody couldn't go to the country store in Rex without having an entourage in tow, and for the first time news stories began to make guarded, cryptic links between Moody and the mail bombings. At first Moody even seemed to relish the attention he was getting, and would frequently issue statements professing his mystification at why the authorities should be so interested in his activities.

And indeed Moody's in-your-face stance was well-founded. After all, Erwin's identification of Moody's "signature bombs," while highly persuasive to the investigators, did not come close to making a case to convict. But Potts's new, efficient organization of the investigation quickly reaped a rich dividend. On April 3, two ATF agents, William T. McFarland and Marnita E. Hoggatt, were scouring the area gun stores when they struck paydirt. Warren Phillips, who ran a hardware store in Griffin, thirty miles south of Atlanta and fifteen miles from Rex, identified a photograph of Roy Moody as the man who had come in to inquire if the store sold gunpowder. Phillips said he didn't, but he had referred Moody to the Shootin Iron on the seamy edge of town. The next day McFarland and Hoggatt went to the drab cinderblock gunshop, where a part-time clerk named James Paul Sartain also identified Moody as the man who, almost comically attempting to disguise himself with an orange wig and pink glasses, had purchased an unusually large amount of Hercules Red Dot double-base smokeless gunpowder the previous winter.

For the first time, Moody was linked directly to a major component of the four mail bombs, each of which contained about a pound of gunpowder.

With this discovery, Potts recognized that the investigation had reached the point where a skilled, full-time special prosecutor was required. The investigation overlapped five jurisdictions, and he knew there was no way he could work with five separate district attorneys, politically appointed lawyers who were, as a breed, not disposed to take orders from an FBI agent, even one with the exalted rank of inspector. Moreover, the local district attorneys had plenty of other cases to command their attention besides VANPAC. But each time Potts broached the subject of a special prosecutor with his main contact at the Justice Department, Bob Mueller, he only got assurances that the matter would be looked into.

After he had been in Atlanta for more than a month, Potts made an urgent trip back to Washington on May 4 to meet with Attorney General Richard Thornburgh. Throwing bureaucratic caution into the wind, Potts made his plea directly to the attorney general of the United States: "We just have too many prosecutors involved in this case. We need to have a special prosecutor."

Thornburgh turned to Mueller and said, "Get him a special prosecutor." Mueller cast a resigned, respectful glance at Potts as if to say, "Okay, you've got your special prosecutor."

Before he left Washington, Potts stopped by Mueller's office once more to see when he could expect the appointment to be made.

"I have a list of possibilities," Mueller said, and he began to read.

"Louis Freeh—"

"Stop right there," said Potts. "He's the best."

Mueller moved swiftly, because that same evening Freeh called Potts to discuss the case. The assignment would, Potts candidly told Freeh, involve an open-ended commitment of time—time that would have to be spent in lonely hotel rooms away from family. But he also appealed to Freeh's sense of duty, not to speak of ego. "It will be a great opportunity," said Potts, clinching the argument.

Larry Potts's enthusiasm for the appointment was well founded. Louis Joseph Freeh was born January 6, 1950, in Jersey City. His father,

William Freeh Sr., had been a real estate broker in Brooklyn who recognized that the New Jersey suburbs of New York not only offered a better social climate for raising a family but more opportunities for a successful career as well. The 1950s were a time when J. Edgar Hoover was a godlike figure in the eyes of innocent American boys, and Louis was still a teenager when he first thought that he might want to be a "G-man," as FBI agents were called in those days. A bright and serious student, he enrolled in Rutgers, New Jersey's state university, where he won his A.B. degree, Phi Beta Kappa, in 1971. He immediately enrolled in the Rutgers Law School, and while still a student got his first taste of politics, working part time as a clerk in the Newark office of the New Jersey liberal Republican United States Senator Clifford P. Case.

He had also dabbled in his father's real estate business, and for a time after finishing law school he did real estate legal work. But within a year he fulfilled his childhood dream by becoming an FBI agent. He quickly gained a reputation for unraveling complex cases. His investigation of New York waterfront racketeering led to the conviction of some of the area's most powerful union bosses, shipping executives, and organized crime figures. After six years with the FBI, Freeh moved to the United States attorney's office, where he continued to focus on organized crime. In 1987 he led the team of federal prosecutors in a sensational case that came to be known as "the pizza connection." After a fourteen-month trial, sixteen top figures of a worldwide Mafia drug ring who used pizza parlors as fronts for their illegal operations were convicted and sentenced to long prison terms. Still in his thirties, he was widely regarded as an investigative genius.

Freeh had been elevated to associate United States attorney, supervising a staff of 180 lawyers on the criminal side of the federal prosecutors office in Manhattan, when he received the call from Attorney General Thornburgh in the second week of May 1990 asking him to take over the legal side of the VANPAC investigation. It was a tall order, and Freeh ended the conversation with two conditions: First, he must talk it over with his wife, Marilyn, to see how she would react to being left with four small boys while he was down in Atlanta for an indeterminate period; second, he wanted to take with him a young associate in the Manhattan federal attorney's office named Howard Shapiro.

The long shadows of the skyscrapers were already falling on Foley Square—the center of the federal justice mechanism in New York—when Freeh called Shapiro out of a staff meeting on an impending drug prosecution.

"Can't this wait until tomorrow?" Shapiro asked Freeh.

"No," Freeh replied stonily, "I have to give the attorney general an answer tomorrow."

Louis Freeh was not a man given to flamboyant name-dropping, so Shapiro knew right away that important work was at hand. When Freeh put his request on the table, Shapiro smiled to himself; he had followed the mail bomb case from a distance and it stirred his competitive instincts. "That's the kind of case I'd love to work on," he thought as he read about the abortive raid on the O'Ferrell farm in Alabama. Now that the opportunity fell onto his desk, he told Freeh that he would have to talk it over with his wife.

"Just give me an answer early in the morning," Freeh said.

From brief association Freeh knew that Howard Shapiro was as bright as they come. He was a magna cum laude graduate in political science from the prestigious Williams College. At Yale Law School, not only was he on the *Law Journal* staff but was teaching assistant to the eminent legal scholar, Owen Fiss. He was still in his twenties when he joined the United States attorney's office in New York soon after he finished law school, and was well on his way to becoming his own generation's Louis Freeh.

Shapiro's wife, Shirley, was pregnant with their first child, but she knew that the assignment, even though it meant long periods of separation, was exactly the sort of case that had led her young husband into public-service law. She said only that she hoped he could get home frequently and would stay in touch daily on the telephone.

The next morning, May 11, Shapiro told Freeh he would take the assignment. There would be some grumbling, to be sure, within the bureaucracy of the district attorney's office, which was comparable to a midsized Manhattan legal partnership. The departure of two of the office's most effective prosecutors would only add to the heavy case loads of those lesser lights left behind. They moved swiftly, and on May 13, 1990, Louis Freeh and Howard Shapiro took their places in a corner of the VANPAC office of the Atlanta FBI suite. Realist that he was, Shapiro was well aware that his assignment might not end in glory. By this time Potts and his investigators were convinced that Roy Moody had sent the bombs. Within hours after their arrival Freeh and Shapiro came to share this view, but they also knew the evidence needed to convict him remained elusive. Shapiro fretted that he and Louis Freeh might be going to Atlanta to put the investigation into inactive status within a month or two.

About the time that Freeh and Shapiro were getting their sea legs, Roy Moody was also getting an infusion of legal talent. For two years Michael Ford had represented Moody in several of his lawsuits, including the *error coram nobis* case that by this time had been abandoned by Jake Arbes.

Ford had established his own law practice with his wife, Diane, but early in his career he had operated the Atlanta branch of the Bobby Hill law firm at the same time that Robbie Robinson was getting his start with the firm in Savannah. Whenever Robinson had some business in Atlanta, he would use Ford's office facilities, but they never got to know each other well.

Ford's representation of Moody began in the fall of 1987, focusing chiefly on Roy's vexatious lawsuit against the First National Bank in Atlanta. Ford found Moody to be a winsome figure but a highly unusual client. Moody insisted on taking an active role in the process. Ford recognized at once that Moody had a rudimentary understanding of the law, and he especially liked to do research. In preparing litigation, Moody could always explain any inconsistency in his position, and given a day or two could come up with a document that would support his story. From the outset Ford made it clear that he would work for Moody only on a fee-for-service basis, rather that a contingency-fee arrangement in which lawyers share in the proceeds of any monetary damages they might recover for a client. Given Moody's litigious nature, this agreement meant a good deal of income for a fledgling law firm, and the bills were always paid on time. Ford was well aware that Moody's business enterprises, even if constantly under scrutiny by the postal authorities, produced good fees. Moody spent a great deal of time around the office, and often brought Susan McBride with him because she was, in effect, the manager of Roy's businesses. But Ford noticed that Susan was always subdued, and at every opportunity would get away from the legal conferences to make paper airplanes and play with the Fords' ten-year-old son, who often came to the office after school.

Ford was astounded when, in January of 1990, federal agents came to his office to ask him if he knew of any activities by Moody that might shed light on the mail bomb cases, which were still dominating the local news in Atlanta. Mindful of his ethical obligation of confidentiality to his client, Ford was circumspect, but he told the investigators he could not believe that Moody was involved in such a violent act.

But over the next few weeks, as Moody seemed to relish the attention he was getting from the entourage of agents and reporters who followed him, Ford grew apprehensive. In the early spring Ford was representing a defendant in a drug case in Newnan, a small town thirty miles west of Atlanta, when he encountered another Atlanta lawyer, Bruce Harvey, who was representing another defendant at the Newnan case.

"I've got a case that I'd like to get you in on," Ford said softly to Harvey during a break in the trial.

"What's that?" Harvey asked.

"Roy Moody called me and wants me to represent him in these search warrants they're serving on him in this mail bomb investigation. This sounds right up your alley."

Harvey's competitive instincts were aroused. From what he'd read in the press, it looked as if the government was acting in a heavy-handed manner in carrying out searches of Moody's house and Susan's car.

Bruce Harvey is that special breed of lawyer that exists in most cities of any size in America. He was, in a curious way, a relic of the 1960s. He grew up in Massachusetts but came south as a teenager when his father, a college professor, joined the faculty of the University of Georgia's School of Business and Finance, eventually becoming dean. In the early 1970s Bruce entered law school, but by this time campus radicalism had pretty much passed, especially at places like the University of Georgia. So Bruce, who developed a keen interest in civil-liberties issues, pretty much stayed to himself in law school. He didn't even know Robbie Robinson, who was in law school at the same time.

After graduation Bruce Harvey established a practice in Atlanta and quickly gained a reputation as a no-holds-barred advocate who would take the seamiest of criminal cases and often win them on technical points, such as defective search warrants. He was especially effective in representing defendants in drug cases. On the wall immediately behind him was a picture of Clarence Darrow, autographed by the great defense attorney of the early part of the century. He made a good deal of money and drove a spidery black Porsche sports car, which bore a license plate that read: ACQUIT. He let his jet black hair grow to thirty inches, and wore it in a ponytail, which, together with his intense deep-set eyes made him an intimidating, even slightly sinister, presence in a courtroom. Newspaper reporters seldom wrote about him without using the all-inclusive description, "flamboyant."

Little strands of gray had already begun to appear in the ponytail by the time Bruce Harvey became associated with Roy Moody. Despite their disparate backgrounds and interests, the two men seemed to hit it off well. Harvey found Moody's denials of involvement in the mail bombings every bit as convincing as Mike Ford had. Moody always arrived at the Harvey law office neatly dressed and carried on his business in a calm, articulate demeanor.

Moody's visits to Harvey's office grew to be almost daily, and now he was always followed by a horde of police agents and TV news crews. Moody seemed to relish talking about the latest news leaks and devising a responsive strategy. Up to this point the FBI investigation had been foundering, with most of the attention focused on the O'Ferrell farm some two hundred miles away in South Alabama. But once the investigation was taken over by Louis Freeh, Harvey knew the focus was about to change. Suddenly there was such a blizzard of search warrants, postal restrictions, and the like that Harvey soon felt as if he were a lone fireman fighting a four-alarm fire with a garden hose.

Because much of his legal efforts dealt with challenging search warrants, Harvey enlisted an attorney named Michael Hauptman to help in the case. Hauptman outdid even Harvey in flamboyance. He handled the work of the American Civil Liberties Union in a state where many people thought the ACLU was synonymous with the Communist Party, and was married to a former prostitute he'd once represented in some legal battle; the two even appeared together on the Phil Donahue show.

The team of Harvey and Hauptman guaranteed a large press contingent at any courtroom appearance on behalf of Moody. But Harvey was always what judges called "lead counsel."

Recognizing that they were waging, among other things, a public-relations battle, Harvey and Hauptman, in their dealings with the press, always referred to Moody as "Wally"—a shortening of their client's first name, Walter. They felt that such a name, which Moody had never used in his life, would make him sound like an everyday, next-door-neighbor kind of guy.

In due course reports began to filter back to Harvey that the FBI was questioning Julie Linn-West about her testimony in the *coram nobis* proceeding three years earlier. Harvey knew then that the government was aiming for an indictment for obstruction of justice with the idea of getting Moody in jail in order to pursue the main investigation with less distraction.

About this time Louis Freeh made an unusual call to Harvey.

"Look," Freeh began guardedly, "we don't have enough to arrest him yet, but we know this guy sent those bombs, and I'm very worried that he's the type of person who would plant bombs anywhere he could, maybe even hold hostages."

Freeh then asked Harvey to allow an FBI team to sweep his law offices. "We won't look for any papers or anything," Freeh assured the astonished Harvey. "We just want to make sure he hasn't left any bombs in your place."

The warning was unsettling enough to overcome Harvey's skepticism and instinctive distrust of federal prosecutors so he allowed one sweep of his office.

Freeh focused ever more intensely on the *coram nobis* proceeding, reasoning that an indictment would not only get Moody out of circulation but would drive home to Susan that she was in deep trouble. On July 10 a federal grand jury in Macon indicted Roy and Susan on thirteen counts of obstruction of justice.

Hours after the indictment was returned, the young ATF agent David Hyche and a coterie of colleagues from other agencies entered Roy Moody's house. They even took an emergency medical technician because they knew of Roy's history of feigning heart attacks.

Moving gingerly toward the rear of the house, Hyche opened a workroom door and found Roy on the telephone, frantically trying to call Bruce Harvey. Hyche looked around and found that he was alone with a man with a long history of violent reactive behavior. The boyish agent swallowed hard and said, "Come on, Roy, you're going with me."

Moody remained serenely calm, but taciturn. On the trip to Macon, where Roy would be jailed to await a bail hearing the next day, Hyche tried to engage him in conversation, but the arrested man would respond only in single-word answers.

Susan Moody was arrested at the same time, and placed in a separate car for the ninety-minute drive to Macon. But for her, the indictment brought an immense sense of relief; even though she was being incarcerated, at last she was out of the clutch of the enigmatic and diabolical man she had lived with for eight troubled years.

In the ordinary course of criminal-law proceedings, defendants who are indicted for non-capital crimes are entitled to gain release on bail while they await trial. But federal statutes and case law permit denial of bail in cases where a defendant is deemed likely to flee before trial or where there is compelling evidence that his release might constitute a danger to the community. On the surface, Roy Moody fit neither criterion and, in addition, his alleged crime was non-violent. But Freeh's young assistant, Howard Shapiro, found an obscure provision in the Federal Bail Reform Act that placed obstruction of justice in a special category: On the theory that a person charged with that crime would likely continue his illegal activity if he were released on bail, a judge could deny bond to defendants so charged.

At a tense hearing before Judge Wilbur Owens on July 13, Bruce Harvey asked that Moody be released on bail pending trial. But Owens, taking his cue from Shapiro's citation of the Bail Reform Act, ruled that Roy "is a danger to the community and if not committed could be expected to attempt to retaliate against or tamper with witnesses against him." Owens ordered Moody to be held in the federal penitentiary in Atlanta. At the same hearing, the judge set Susan's bail at $250,000. A few days later her family posted their home as security, and she was allowed to go free on the condition that she at all times wear an electronic monitoring anklet that emitted radio signals to alert the authorities if she moved beyond the confines stipulated by the court. Clearly a double-standard was applied—after all, Susan was as deeply implicated in concocting perjury as was Roy—but there was a method in the strategy. Releasing Susan would separate her still further from Roy and would enable family and friends and possibly even federal agents to persuade her that her only hope of extricating herself from the prospect of a long prison term was to cut a deal and testify against Roy Moody.

At about the same time as he was indicted, Moody suffered another major setback. The United States Postal Service revived its long-standing if somewhat neglected case against Roy for defrauding people by mail. The service ordered that all mail that came to Moody's business boxes be returned to the sender. This order had the devastating effect of abruptly shutting off Moody's cash flow.

Despite this development, Bruce Harvey, Moody's flamboyant lawyer, still represented Roy at the bail hearing before Judge Wilbur Owens in Macon. When he lost his bid to get Roy released on bail, Harvey filed a motion asking Owens to appoint him to continue to represent Roy as an indigent client. Owens rejected the request on the grounds that Harvey did not maintain a practice in the Macon federal district. Harvey was convinced that the stern, efficiency-obsessed Owens simply did not want a legal gunslinger in his court. Nonetheless, Harvey by then recognized that an insurmountable conflict of interest had arisen: In the past he had represented both Roy and Susan, and now their interests were about to sharply diverge. This fact made it impossible for him to continue, and, with a tacit sigh of relief, he withdrew from the case.

An hour's drive east of Atlanta, in Athens, the seat of Georgia's venerable state university, Edward D. Tolley was following news reports of the Moody case with more than passing interest. He was intrigued by the enigmatic man who by now was clearly the prime suspect for sending the mail bombs that had killed two prominent public men. In addition, as a young attorney who had made a name for himself as a skilled courtroom advocate, he was equally intrigued by the legal challenges the case presented.

Ed Tolley was born in San Antonio in 1950, the son of a mother who was a secretary and a father who was a salesman. The family moved to

Atlanta in 1963, the year that Ed entered high school. It was a time of considerable tension throughout the South—when the first cautious, tentative steps were being taken to desegregate public education. But Atlanta, with its legacy of moderate political leadership and its boast of being a city that was "too busy to hate," made the transition with more grace than most cities, and as a youngster Ed Tolley got along well with the handful of black students who were his football teammates at Atlanta's prestigious North Fulton High School.

After graduation he made the natural migration to the University of Georgia, where he entered on an ROTC scholarship to pursue a degree in English, hoping for a career as a high school teacher and football coach. But before long he switched to business. He graduated in 1971 with a coveted honor, Distinguished Military Graduate, and immediately enrolled in law school. In the class just ahead of him was Robbie Robinson of Savannah, but their paths barely seemed to cross. After he got his law degree in 1975, Ed Tolley served his obligatory hitch in the Army. When he was discharged four years later as a captain, he returned to Atlanta to take over the practice of a retiring attorney. Before long, however, he was offered a partnership in a leading firm in Athens, the town where he had spent most of his learning years. Among his first criminal cases was defending a man accused of a highly publicized Mafia-style hit murder. The man was convicted, but he escaped the electric chair so popular with Georgia juries, and Ed Tolley emerged with a solid reputation as a principled young lawyer who represented his client "zealously within the bounds of law," as the code of ethics demands of all lawyers. Shortly after that Judge Wilbur Owens, whose federal jurisdiction included Athens, appointed Tolley to represent an indigent man accused of bank robbery. Again, Tolley lost the verdict, but he got as good a sentence as could be hoped for for his client.

In July 1990 Tolley was in court, defending a man accused of murder, when, during a break, his secretary delivered him a pink telephone memorandum slip that read: "Call Claude Hicks ASAP."

"Oh hell," Tolley told his secretary. "I think I know what this is about."

He was right. Claude Hicks, the federal magistrate for the Middle District of Georgia, informed Tolley that Judge Owens was appointing him to represent Walter Leroy Moody Jr., who by now had been declared indigent.

Tolley had mixed feelings. Based on what he had read in the news accounts, he knew the case would be arduous and probably winless and that it would probably involve several months' time in preparation and trial—time that would have to be carved out of his lucrative law practice, and time that would be compensated at the stingy standards of the federal bureaucracy. He also sensed that even though he was being appointed only to defend Moody against the obstruction of justice indictment, the path inevitably would lead to the mail bombings. And yet there was something deep inside him that said this case would be the ultimate test of a lawyer's commitment to the ideals of his profession—to defend the rights of a terrorist who had literally declared war on the American judicial system by striking violently at the very symbol of equal justice under law, the impartial judge. In his first formal act in the case—his letter formally accepting the appointment—Ed Tolley told Judge Owens he intended "to do my very best in this unique case."

When he cleared his desk of the immediate pending tasks and distributed less urgent other ones to his partners, Tolley recruited a young lawyer from his firm and together they drove to Atlanta for the first formal interview with Walter Leroy Moody Jr., who by then was ensconced in the high-security unit of the sprawling federal penitentiary on the outskirts of the Georgia capital city.

Tolley mentally sized up the man he would be defending. He certainly did not look or act the part of a stealthy, cold-blooded killer. Rather, the man Tolley met was polite and cordial, and displayed a sense of humor. Tolley had faxed his resume to Moody in advance of the meeting, and in their first face-to-face encounter, Moody seemed very pleased with Tolley's credentials. But mostly, Tolley was struck by Moody's intense interest in the technical procedure in the case: He asked for elaboration on every detail of Tolley's proposed defense strategy. One topic, however, was explicitly excluded from that first conversation—Ed Tolley wanted to hear nothing at all about the mail bombings.

With Moody now out of circulation and his income source shut down, Louis Freeh and Howard Shapiro could adopt a more methodical approach to the tasks that lay ahead, preparing for the trial in the obstruction-of-justice cases while also pursuing indictments in the murder case.

Still, new information came grudgingly. By midsummer the main evidence still consisted of the similarity of the bombs Moody had built in earlier years to the four mailed in December 1989, and James Paul Sartain's identification of Roy as the man who, in absurd disguise, had purchased a large amount of gunpowder a few weeks before the terror began.

The O'Ferrells were still under scrutiny—indeed, still "targets" of the grand jury investigation—even though the massive raid on their farm had produced no significant evidence: The mysterious typewriter was still missing. But as fall arrived, the O'Ferrells signaled a willingness to cooperate. On October 9, Howard Shapiro mailed to Robert Wayne and Mary Ann O'Ferrell identical letters advising them that they were "no longer considered to be the target of the Grand Jury investigation into the murder of Judge Robert S. Vance." The letter asked that they "not disclose this communication to anyone other than your attorneys or your family." Even though the letter constituted a measure of exoneration after their arduous ordeal, the O'Ferrells nonetheless complied with Shapiro's request. More importantly, Mary Ann O'Ferrell agreed to go to Birmingham to see if she could identify, from a police lineup, the person who bought the missing typewriter from O'Ferrell's junk store.

Around the middle of October, Susan Moody consented to go to Birmingham to take part in that lineup, and she was identified by Mary Ann O'Ferrell as the person who bought the typewriter in the summer of 1989.

This major break enabled Louis Freeh to go to the Atlanta federal grand jury, which, on November 7, returned a seventy-one-count indictment charging Walter Leroy Moody Jr. with the murders of Bob Vance and Robbie Robinson. Attorney General Richard Thornburgh announced the indictments at a full-dress press conference in Washington. In the course of the press conference, he was asked if the O'Ferrells were still under investigation. Despite Shapiro's secret letter a month earlier stating flatly that they were not, the attorney general replied: "I have no comment on that."

Thornburgh had good reason for his celebratory mood. Despite his early indication that the case would be solved promptly, almost a year had passed since Bob Vance and Robbie Robinson had been killed, and federal agents had expended more than 140,000 hours on the case. After an eleven-month investigation, which at times bordered on the comical, the prestige of the FBI and the Justice Department emerged intact.

A thousand miles south of Washington, Joyce Law Arnold Sweeting watched Thornburgh's announcement on the evening television news in her cramped and untidy apartment in a drab housing project south of Macon, not far from Fort Valley, where she and Roy had grown up. Although the news came as no surprise by this time, Joyce, now fifty-five and incapacitated with diabetes, watched in dumbstruck silence. The daughter Joyce had borne to Roy Moody thirty years before, happened to be visiting her mother as the news was announced. Through clenched teeth, Roy's daughter murmured, "I hope he gets what he deserves. . . . I hope he gets what he deserves."

Despite the triumphant fanfare that accompanied the announcement of the indictments, misgivings still lurked in the meticulous legal mind of Howard Shapiro. After all, the case rested perilously on three pieces of circumstantial evidence: Lloyd Erwin's "signature bombs," James Paul Sartain's testimony that Roy had purchased four pounds of gunpowder, and Mary O'Ferrell's highly dubious identification of Susan as the person who bought the missing typewriter. No one had come close to placing the fatal bombs in Moody's hands. Shapiro knew that a lawyer of Ed Tolley's skill, not to speak of an adroit perjurer like Roy Moody, could quite possibly implant sufficient "reasonable doubt" in the mind of jurors to win an acquittal in the murder case.

But even in his brief experience as a prosecutor, Shapiro had also learned that an indictment changes the whole dynamic of a prosecution, so he was banking on the realistic hope that the prospects for conviction would improve before trial.

Meanwhile, the obstruction-of-justice case against Moody was docketed for trial in the fall term of federal court, and Shapiro had no misgivings about the strength of the government's evidence in this prosecution. Nor, for that matter, did Ed Tolley. Tolley's first act as the appointed defense counsel was to file a motion to disqualify Judge Owens on the basis of his links with Roy Moody's legal problems in the past. In effect Tolley was suggesting, as delicately as possible, that Owens might not be able to render impartial justice. Probably Owens could have rejected the motion without risking being reversed on appeal—self-recusal of a judge on grounds of bias is a highly discretionary matter, and rarely exercised. Nonetheless, Owens appeared to welcome the opportunity to shunt off the trial of a man whom he knew from experience could be a maddeningly troublesome defendant. Moody's case was shifted to Georgia's southern district, under the jurisdiction of Judge Anthony Alaimo, and set for trial in December in the sleepy Georgia coastal town of Brunswick—the very place from where Alaimo's predecessor, Judge Frank M. Scarlett, had come.

Due process requires that the prosecution in criminal cases disclose to the defendant's lawyer all major evidence it expects to present at trial. As Ed Tolley grew more acquainted with the government's case against Moody, he recognized the futility of prevailing. Any alert person could tell from cursory perusal that the "Gene Wallace" episode was a fabrication from start to finish, and besides, Julie Linn-West had now cut a deal with the prosecution to testify that the whole affair was a construct of lies. If this were not enough, the government would introduce telephone wiretap recordings and secretly made videotapes in which Roy candidly talked about his crime. Early on, Tolley recognized that Moody had only one chance to win acquittal, and even that was a long shot. At arraignment Tolley entered a plea of not guilty by reason of insanity. Once this decision was made, Tolley promptly arranged to have Moody evaluated by Dr. Sheldon Cohen, an Atlanta-based forensic psychiatrist.

Cohen wasn't the only person who was listening to Roy during his incarceration. When the FBI first installed secret listening devices at the Moody home on Skyline Drive in Rex, they quickly discovered that Roy had a habit of mumbling to himself. Based on this awareness the investigators secured judicial authority to install a microphone in his cell. What this device picked up was mostly incomprehensible jibberish, but one statement came through with clarity: "Robert," Roy Moody mused, "I meant you no harm." There was no way to tell whether he was referring to Robert Vance, Robert Robinson, or some other person named Robert.

At the same time that Ed Tolley was methodically getting a grip on Roy Moody's case, Susan McBride Moody strove to pick up the pieces of her shattered life. She had moved back in with her parents, who had put up their modest Atlanta home as security for Susan's bail. The strict conditions of her release allowed her to work, but she quickly discovered that she was now notorious: the moment a prospective employer discovered her involvement with Roy Moody, she was shown the door. She didn't need the money so much as she needed something to occupy her days, so she enrolled in DeKalb College to take basic freshman courses.

For at least five years Susan had recognized that she was a virtual captive of Roy Moody, a man easily old enough to be her father, but she could find no way to extricate herself. She was all too aware of Roy's vengeful nature, and she reasoned that if she simply packed up and left, he would surely come after her. As the 1980s drew to a close she was increasingly aware that Roy was engaged in something secret and sinister and that she was being drawn inexorably into his web of intrigue. But never once did it occur to her that he might be plotting murders.

After the Vance and Robinson murders, not even a sheltered and naive young woman like Susan could fail to make the terrifying connection between the bombings and the perplexing tasks that Roy had given her over the past few months. If there were any doubt at all, that doubt dissipated when she and Roy were watching the evening TV news a few days before Christmas of 1989. Roy's attention perked up visibly when a reporter began to relate that a state judge in Maryland had been gravely injured by a bomb that had been mysteriously delivered to his house.

"That one," Roy said cryptically, as if speaking to himself as much as Susan, "wasn't mine."

By this time Susan was so certain of what had happened that she did not even ask him to elaborate; she simply listened in cold, terrified silence. Under the circumstances, it was little wonder that Susan McBride Moody experienced an immeasurable sense of relief when she was indicted for obstruction of justice and removed from the horror of her imprisonment in the placid ranch-style bungalow in Rex, Georgia, to the relative safety of the federal penitentiary in Atlanta fifteen miles away.

As an experienced prosecutor, Louis Freeh knew that Susan could become the most important figure in the prosecution of Roy Moody, not only in the obstruction-of-justice case but in the mail bombings as well.

What he did not know, at that point, was the extent of Susan's involvement in the murders. Her profile as a frightened, subdued young woman who was dominated by an older man certainly suggested that she might have been an innocent party who was merely doing Moody's Machiavellian bidding. On the other hand, she just as easily might have been a knowing conspirator in the murders.

If she fell into the first category, then she was potentially the critical witness needed to convict Moody. In fact, fairly early on when the investigation was beginning to come together, the FBI made some tentative overtures toward securing Susan's cooperation by sending some agents to talk to her father. But the meeting did not go well, possibly because McBride was afraid the agents were there seeking information to use against his daughter. After her indictment in July, however, another meeting with McBride was arranged, and this time Larry Potts himself took part in the discussions. Nothing was resolved, but the clear message got across to McBride that his daughter was in deep trouble and the only hope of extricating herself was to tell the whole truth and nothing but the truth.

The federal judge, Wilbur Owens, had also recognized the possibility if not virtual certainty that at some point Susan's legal interests would diverge from Roy's. At the same time that Owens appointed Ed Tolley to represent Roy, he designated a young Macon attorney named Sandra Popson to represent Susan.

Sandra Popson quickly developed a great pity and even affection for the unpretentious young woman as she prepared to go to trial. Popson remembered having seen television pictures of Patty Hearst, the West Coast newspaper heiress who was captured in the 1970s by a gang of political terrorists and had seemed to convert to her captors' extremist ideology. Susan seemed to greatly resemble Patty Hearst as a haunted young woman who didn't know where to turn. Popson knew that Susan had also been indicted, along with Roy, on federal mail-fraud charges in Atlanta, and that the public defenders' office, in preparation for that case, had arranged for a psychiatric evaluation of Susan with the view of asserting the new and slightly risky legal defense known as "the abused-woman syndrome." If the case should come to trial, Popson would use the same defense in the obstruction-of-justice case.

In her preparation she had occasional contact with Louis Freeh and Howard Shapiro, but there was no discussion of a plea bargain at the outset. There is a certain unwritten code, akin to a ritual dance, that governs the negotiations between prosecutors and defense attorneys over plea bargains. Each must bring something to the table to get the negotiation started. But by the beginning of fall neither Popson nor Freeh had made a move that the other could consider a starting offer.

Around the first of October, during a routine meeting with Sandra Popson to discuss the case, Susan haltingly suggested that she would like to get a divorce from Roy Moody. Popson at once recognized this as a major development, but she had to explain to Susan that the appointment to represent her in the criminal case did not include representation in a civil divorce proceeding. Even so, Popson quietly arranged to get some legal forms that would enable Susan to file for a divorce on her own. With discreet on-the-side advice from several individuals who had come to like her during the investigation, Susan McBride Moody on October 19, 1990, filed her petition in the Clayton County Courthouse at Jonesboro.

At about this same time Sandra Popson happened to be defending a criminal case in federal court in Macon. During a break, Popson called aside the United States attorney, Sam A. Wilson Jr., aside for a furtive conversation.

"You know," she said in a whispered tone that could have been a mere casual comment, "we're getting pretty close to trial on that Susan Moody case, and nobody's called me."

"Why don't you call Louis Freeh?" Wilson responded without a pause.

"Sam," she replied, "Louis Freeh needs to call me."

When Popson got back to her office, there was a message on her desk that Freeh had called, and the following day the special prosecutor, along with a team of lawyers and assorted agents, drove from Atlanta to Macon for a meeting with Susan in Sandra Popson's office. Susan watched, almost indifferently, as the team of prosecutors, all men, darted in and out of conferences with Sandra. Toward the end of the day the group had produced a draft of a "proffer agreement," which is legal jargon for the working paper that starts the plea-bargain process. Now, they wanted a sign of good faith from Susan.

Already coached by Popson, Susan murmured: "I bought three type-writers for Roy."

Soft as they were, Susan's words struck with such force that even the jaded federal prosecutors were stunned with silence for a moment. Then Louis Freeh said, with a palpable sense of relief, "I think we have a deal." On November 10, in an unannounced, almost secretive court session, Susan Moody pleaded guilty to obstruction of justice. The sentencing was delayed, pending her testimony at Roy Moody's trial, which was soon to begin. In the first week of December, her divorce was quietly granted and she legally resumed her maiden name.

Around this time, Ed Tolley, who by now was convinced that Susan had been cooperating with the federal authorities for many weeks, made a regular visit to Roy Moody at the Atlanta penitentiary.

"Roy," Tolley said. "I have some bad news. Susan is going to testify against you."

Without speaking a word, Roy Moody blanched and passed out.

16 "He Just Obeys His Own Rules"

The more Ed Tolley explored Roy Moody's bizarre past, the clearer it became that his only recourse was the criminal-defense lawyer's last line of defense: He would have to plead that Roy was insane at the time he committed the crimes.

Tolley knew the peril in such a course. Pleading insanity would tacitly concede at the outset that illegal acts were indeed committed, and once made, the concession could never be wholly revoked. Moreover, he knew that the moment the insanity defense was invoked, he would forfeit a large measure of control of the case and enter the murky world of psychiatry; once he opened Roy Moody's mind to that inexact science, he could not predict where the trail of inquiry would lead. And at the end of this perilous path, Moody's "sanity" would be determined by twelve jurors applying their own instincts and impulses of law and psychiatry. Finally, even if he won acquittal by pleading insanity, Roy almost certainly would face an indeterminate period of incarceration in an institution for "the criminally insane."

Any understanding of the insanity defense must begin with "the M'Naghten Rule." Like generations of law students before him, Ed Tolley learned the rule in his criminal-law classes at the University of Georgia. This judge-made principle of law came into being in 1840 when a deranged young man named Daniel M'Naghten shot and killed a man he believed to be the prime minister of England. At his trial, M'Naghten became the first person in the history of English law to be found "not guilty by reason of insanity." Needless to say, in Victorian England the verdict created a sensation, and out of this debate emerged the renowned "M'Naghten Rule," a harsh legal dictum that stated in effect that a person practically had to be a manifest lunatic in order to win acquittal on grounds of insanity.

As the law and psychiatry evolved, judges over the next century expanded the rule gradually, gingerly, even grudgingly, so as not to alarm a citizenry that remained largely suspicious of claims that unseen demons could drive people to commit wicked deeds. Still, American jurisprudence cautiously began to incorporate such vague and malleable psychiatric hypotheses as "mental defect" and "irresistible urge" as potential defenses against seemingly irrational heinous crimes.

This evolution came to an abrupt halt, at least in the federal courts of the United States, when Congress passed the Insanity Defense Act of 1984, largely in reaction to public indignation over a jury's finding John Hinckley not guilty by reason of insanity following an attempted assassination of President Reagan in the early spring of 1981. So by the time Roy Moody went on trial for perjury and obstruction of justice in the languid South Georgia coastal town of Brunswick, the M'Naghten rule had been codified so that Tolley, in order to prevail, was required to prove that Roy suffered "a severe mental disease or defect" that rendered him "unable to appreciate the nature or quality of the wrongfulness of his act."

Ed Tolley was acutely aware of all these formidable considerations, but still he had little recourse but to enter an insanity plea when Roy Moody went on trial on December 11 of 1990. After all, confronted with those devastating secretly recorded videotapes, and with Susan Moody now prepared to acknowledge the web of lies on which the "Gene Wallace" hoax rested, Tolley came to court almost defenseless. He knew, further, that in making the insanity plea in the Brunswick trial he was, for all practical purposes, committing Roy Moody to make the same plea in the murder case that now lay ahead.

If he had any hope of proving insanity, Tolley needed the best "expert witness" he could find. With court approval and at government expense, Tolley arranged for a psychiatrist to evaluate Roy Moody. Knowing that insanity-defense cases often come down to one psychiatrist's word against another's, Louis Freeh prudently arranged for a psychiatrist of his own choosing to conduct a separate evaluation.

Psychiatric interviews were not a new experience for Roy Moody. Over the years, he had already encountered numerous psychologists and psychiatrists.

The first was Jeanette Wheaton, the school "guidance counselor" at Fort Valley High in the early 1950s. Wheaton had little formal training in psychology, but she possessed a certain street-smart instinct, and in a small town like Fort Valley, she knew all the secrets as well. And she saw in Roy Moody a vain, selfish young man inclined to cut corners to achieve his goals. Jeanette Wheaton cautioned Joyce Law to beware of Roy—advice that, Wheaton would later lament, came too late.

In 1955, an Army captain named Robert J. Campbell examined Roy for neuropsychiatric clearance in connection with Roy's application for flight training. From the sparse available accounts, the examination was perfunctory and unremarkable. Roy described his childhood home life as "a happy one in which all members of the family get along well together." He claimed to have had many friends as an adolescent. Campbell found no indication of neuropsychiatric disease, and wrote that Roy appeared "mature and stable"—a fit candidate for flight training.

But fit or not, Roy proved to be so indolent in his work that his immediate service superiors were not about to recommend him for flight training, and he left the Army soon after his encounter with Campbell.

Not long after he left the service Roy soon encountered another psychologist. According to Roy's own account, he developed a habit of falling asleep in class—because, he maintained, he was having to work so hard in order to earn money to stay in school. During this time a sympathetic chemistry professor arranged for Roy to see Dr. J. R. S. Mays. But the counseling consisted of no more than two or three interviews, and ended, according to Roy, with Mays suggesting sources of private financial help to enable to help Roy stay in school.

By the end of 1966 Roy had already been jailed at least once for giving bad checks, and had also developed a pattern of difficulty in his personal relations with women. His *modus operandi* was to seduce, then sponge off younger women, working only sporadically while continuing to take college classes. The school authorities apparently recognized that Roy had problems that might be considered a disability under the federal-state Vocational Rehabilitation program, and in January 1967 a Mercer University counselor arranged for Roy to be evaluated by Dr. Thomas M. Hall, a Macon psychiatrist.

Hall's earliest notes indicate that Roy recounted his treatment by Dr. Mays but added that he had stopped seeing the psychologist because of lack of funds and because "some emotional barriers" developed. In his file notes, Dr. Hall went on that Roy gave him "a long and rather involved history of inadequate behavior, depression reaction, unjust charges which could have legally taken place like Mr. Moody described, but somehow seems highly unlikely to me." Roy also complained bitterly about his father's rigid and demanding nature, claiming this relationship, along with "unjust charges," was probably the source of his depression. In these sessions Roy often spoke to Hall of his fantasies about suicide. Hall made a tentative finding that Roy suffered from "a form of ambulatory schizophrenia" and arranged, through Vocational Rehabilitation, to see Roy once a week on an ongoing basis.

File records indicate that Dr. Hall enlisted a psychologist named Dr. N. Archer Moore to evaluate Roy. In his report on that evaluation, Moore wrote that "one can make a case for sociopathic personality on the basis of [Roy's] behavioral history," and he made cryptic observations that Roy demonstrated "sexual ambivalence" and "obsessive-compulsive mechanisms." Nonetheless, Moore noted no serious psychopathology, and even concluded that Roy's IQ, measuring 125, made him suitable to pursue any vocation he chose.

Hall's involvement continued for nearly two years, totaling seventy-eight office visits, with the psychiatrist writing various letters seeking to get Vocational Rehabilitation assistance for Roy to continue his fitful attendance at Mercer University. But by this time Roy was already in his early thirties and continued to go from one unsatisfactory job to another. The relationship with Dr. Hall appears to have ended on October 21, 1968, when the Vocational Rehabilitation funding of the treatment expired, but Hall would surface again in a more significant way five years later when Roy was about to go on trial for the 1972 bombing in Macon that nearly killed his wife, Hazel.

On August 30, 1972, Judge Wilbur Owens called Dr. Hall to give a deposition to determine Roy's mental capacity to stand trial. At that hearing Hall repeated his early diagnoses of "ambulatory schizophrenia," but went on to say that Roy was "very persuasive . . . the type of individual who could sell you the Brooklyn Bridge." Still, Hall cautioned that Roy would do things even though he knew they were wrong and could get him into trouble, and "there was a lot of 'get-even' stuff in what he always felt." Hall went on:

> He was constantly in some sort of difficulty . . . on the edge of trouble and acting out. He was constantly embroiled with women in one way or another, alcohol sometimes at that point. . . . He was attempting to get back into Mercer. He had been thrown out . . . because of poor grades and nonpayment of bills, and he was trying to get some justification for that.
>
> I felt that he was extremely self-destructive, but not in a suicidal sense, but was simply self-destructive in the terms of his inability to judge adequately situations that would wind him up in trouble. . . . He was continually failing . . . in any endeavor. . . . For instance, one of the incidents that I just happen to remember had to do with Lamar Pontiac. I think they repossessed a car . . . and since he felt that he had made his payments adequately he filed some sort of suit against them. Maybe it was justified, maybe it wasn't, I don't know, but it was the sort of litigious response that he had for nearly everything that made me feel that he was constantly going to be embroiled in something unless I could persuade him in some way to think more cautiously about what he did. . . . He just obeys his own rules.

Hall testified he also noted, in the sessions in 1967 and 1968, a dark tendency in Roy Moody toward violent reprisal, especially toward his father, who by now would have nothing to do with him. Yet, Hall went on, Roy still seemed to hope somehow to get back into Mercer in the hope of becoming a lawyer.

In the end, Hall testified, he diagnosed Roy has having a "character disorder" that he characterized as "inadequate personality with socio-pathic tendencies."

Two weeks after Hall related these findings in testimony at the competency hearing in 1972, Roy struck back with his own motion: He claimed that virtually everything he had told the psychiatrist during nearly two years of treatment had been feigned in order to give "the appearance of mental disability" necessary to get the Vocational Rehabilitation service to pay his college tuition.

Then Roy dropped a bombshell: The relationship was abruptly discontinued "because of homosexual advances made by the Doctor." Years later Roy would repeat the charges that Dr. Hall had engaged in sexual aggression not only against him but another unnamed patient as well.

Based on Hall's testimony, Judge Owens ordered additional tests to determine Roy's sanity. Dr. J. A. Mascort, a psychiatrist, interviewed Roy at the Atlanta penitentiary in June 1972 and concluded that Roy was competent to stand trial and that he had been "most possibly mentally and legally competent" around the time the bomb exploded at his home on Dublin Avenue some six weeks earlier.

A second evaluation was conducted about the same time by Dr. Nelms B. Boone, a psychologist, who gave Roy the standard battery of tests that confirmed Roy's native intelligence with an IQ score of 125. Boone said Roy tended to be "vague and somewhat rambling" about his life, so that it was impossible to get a clear picture on why he was unable to hold a steady job or why he was still working on his college degree at the age of thirty-eight. Boone concluded that Roy was "a somewhat ego-centric individual who is consistently attempting to present himself in a favorable light" and who "tends to resist self-disclosure and to minimize faults in himself." Boone also thought it likely that Roy "expresses hostility in indirect ways" and is "less socially responsible than most men of his age." Nonetheless, he went on, his evaluation found "no mental illness."

Apparently in an abundance of caution, Judge Owens ordered yet a third evaluation, this one conducted by Dr. Joseph F. Alderete, a psychiatrist. On August 2 Alderete reported that Roy seemed to be "in a big hurry to get back to Macon" to stand trial and even threatened to go to the media if his psychological testing were not completed by the deadline he imposed. But threats aside, Alderete, like the others, found no overt manifestations of mental illness such as hallucinations, delusions, or psychosis. "He knows what he is accused of," Alderete wrote, "despite the fact that he refuses to account for his movements. He knows the court views the act with which he is charged as a crime no matter what his own views may be."

Clearly there was little in this early psychiatric history that offered Ed Tolley much hope of prevailing by pleading insanity. But then Tolley discovered something a bit more promising in Roy's past. It seems that in the spring of 1985, not long after he had filed his bogus litigation against the First National Bank of Atlanta, Roy contacted an Atlanta psychiatrist named Dave M. Davis, possibly on the recommendation of Susan McBride's mother. With the First National case approaching, on April 11 Roy wrote to Dr. Davis:

> My attorney, Mr. Charlie Tanksley, has advised me that a trail [sic] date of June 17, 1985 has been set. Consequently I need to determine if I can afford your services.
>
> Essentially the case involves a situation where a manager of a branch bank wrongfully denied me access to funds on deposit for some forty days. As a result I was unable to fulfill previously contracted obligations that resulted in a contract being voided for my non-performance. Lost [sic] of the contract resulted in extensive loss of financial support for the development and marketing of an invention I had worked countless hours on for fifteen years.
>
> The personal effect on me has been just as devastating . . .
>
> I would appreciate it if you would advise me of the cost of having you appear as a witness on my behalf.

A deal was struck quickly: Davis not only took the case as a forensic expert but also in a treatment role. Davis's clinic was an all-purpose facility, with Davis prescribing medication, a social worker named Tom Dixon providing psychotherapy, and a psychologist named Howard Albrecht performing testing. Albrecht turned out to be Tolley's most propitious hope, however faint, for persuading the jury that Roy was insane.

In his initial interview with Albrecht on May 11, 1985, Roy made it clear that his purpose was to prove "the trauma that bitch caused me"—

a reference to the bank employee who had refused to give him the disputed money from his account. Roy also made it clear in that interview that he hoped to dictate personally the conclusions of his tests and treatment reports.

After initial testing and a single interview, Albrecht gave Roy what he was seeking: diagnoses of "dysthymic disorder"—a technical term for chronic depression—along with a mixed personality disorder involving tendencies toward narcissism, infantile manifestations, and obsessive-compulsive behavior. "He will not commit suicide at his own hand," Albrecht wrote, ". . . rather will contrive for circumstances to produce it as through an accident or disease. In the same way that the patient does not see himself as being responsible for his own life, he will attempt to not be responsible for his death."

Despite these findings, Albrecht's testing determined Roy's IQ to be 127; Albrecht lamented that "it appears that the patient does not apply his abilities for judgment to social situations."

Following further testing Albrecht found that Roy fit into a group of individuals whose profiles "tend to show a pattern of chronic psychological maladjustment and frequently have histories of acting-out behavior, including outbursts of anger." Albrecht went on:

> Apparently emotionally immature, he is dependent and demanding and tends to become hostile when his demands are frustrated. He appears to be suspicious of, and irritable toward, the professional staff [of the Davis clinic]. . . .
>
> He appears to be rather dependent in interpersonal relationships, demanding and manipulative, and may act aggressively if frustrated. . . .
>
> Individuals with this profile often have a long-standing personality disorder, with substance use and abuse a prominent feature of their clinical pattern. . . . They may also show elements of anxiety or depressive disorder. . . .
>
> Since these individuals typically have difficulties controlling anger they usually experience relationship problems that need to be dealt with in therapy. They also tend to blame others for their problems and see no need for personal change. Major long-term changes are not likely to occur.

Yet there were contradictory findings that indicated Roy yearned to dominate situations and people around him. He said there were times when he felt like "smashing things," and he admitted that as a youngster he had stolen things and had been disciplined for "cutting up." He also conceded that he had been in trouble with the law and that his "unusual sex practices" had caused him problems.

Albrecht's files also contained a remarkable document that could only have been produced by Roy in an effort to tell his evaluators precisely what he wanted them to report. The undated document reads in part: "Our tests show that Mr. Moody is a genius in the area of abstract reasoning. . . . He therefore has an extremely high aptitude as an inventor. . . . When the bank refused to honor Mr. Moody's check . . . it plunged Mr. Moody into a very severe depression. . . . The severity of the depression increased until Mr. Moody tried to commit suicide in March of 1985. . . . Experiencing this high level of depression will be harmful to Mr. Moody for the rest of his life."

Subsequently Roy even went so far as draft a report that would have Albrecht refuting the earlier findings of Dr. Hall. This extraordinary document reads:

> I disagree with Dr. Hall who diagnosed Mr. Moody as having a sociopathic personality. A sociopath resolves problems without the normal restraints of morality, conscious [sic] or concern about the possible consequences of his or her criminal acts. If a sociopath's interest were severely jeopardized, as Mr. Moody's was, he or she would be expected to react abnormally by using force or violence without regard for the consequences of said acts. When Mr. Moody's interest was severely jeopardized, however, he reacted the way society expects normal and responsible people to react; he relied upon the judicial system to resolve his problems.

The Davis clinic's psychotherapy notes pulsate with Roy's fabrications of his heroic struggle to build a better engine and the suicidal depression that followed the bank's frustration of this lifelong "dream." But the Davis file also suggests that Roy disclosed his 1972 conviction only after he had been in treatment for several months, and even then he minimized the nature of the charge. The file contains a notation that Roy said, "Gene Wallace did it." During this time the Davis clinic group was in contact with Roy's attorneys in the First National Bank case, as well as with the bank's lawyer.

Roy stopped going to the Davis clinic in the final weeks of 1986, when trial of the First National case was postponed, but he told the doctors that he might need their testimony later. And indeed on January 6, 1988, Dr. Davis gave a deposition in which he concluded that Roy's depression resulted from the "unsuccessful business transaction" that was blamed on the bank and that Roy could well have committed suicide had he not received treatment. In the course of that treatment, Dr. Davis said, Roy was given a prescription for a antidepressant medication called imipramine, which, Susan McBride observed, Roy only pretended to be taking. Davis also prescribed that Roy take a mild sleeping aid called Vistaril.

By 1990 Judge Wilbur Owens knew enough about Roy's background that he felt it prudent to order new psychiatric evaluations to be carried out at the Atlanta penitentiary to determine whether Roy was competent to stand trial—a critical but wholly different issue from whether he had been legally sane at the time the murders were committed. These tests were carried out in the early fall of 1990 by Dr. Scott A. Duncan, a staff clinical psychologist with the federal prison system. Duncan quickly concluded that Roy was not only competent to stand trial but that he was a highly intelligent person, whose 130 IQ score placed him in the top 3 percent of the population. Duncan said Roy gave no indication of serious mental illness in the past, although he did express a possibly paranoid concern that the FBI might fabricate evidence to be used against him. At the most, Duncan believed, Roy had a "personality disorder." As a precautionary measure, Duncan placed Roy on a "suicide watch" after the episode in which Roy fainted after being told that Susan was turning against him.

Clearly Duncan's findings did not help Roy, so Ed Tolley arranged to have his own evaluation performed, at court expense, by Dr. Sheldon Cohen, a young Atlanta psychiatrist with a growing reputation as a forensic expert. In November and December of 1990 Cohen conducted more than six hours of interviews in which Roy intoned his eclectic litany of diatribes encompassing the familiar themes of parental abuse, prison rape, "judicial rape," prison murder, and "Gene Wallace." Roy also quoted from John Locke and the Bible.

There was a contrived and rehearsed tone to Roy's rambling discourses, suggesting that he might be attempting to create a a psychologically sympathetic if not exculpatory version of his personal history. Roy's obsession about what others were doing to him and his preoccupation with revenge led Cohen to conclude that Roy was indeed paranoid, although he was uncertain whether the paranoia was accompanied by delusions. Roy's cynicism emerged in unalloyed form when he told Cohen of his own variation of the Golden Rule: "Do unto others before they do unto you; or do unto others what they have done to you." This quotation he cited to justify not only his tacitly admitted fabrication of the "Gene Wallace" tale but all of the deceptive practices that had become the main characteristic of his personality.

Cohen summed up his findings with a colorful analogy: "In a sense, this man was sort of like Don Quixote, tilting against windmills, except that what he was doing was just . . . creating more and more problems for himself, as he felt he was justified in taking any kind of action similar to what had been taken against him. He felt if they could fabricate evidence against him, then he could do likewise."

Ed Tolley was not reassured by Cohen's findings. But as it happened, possibly at Roy's suggestion, Cohen had engaged Dr. Howard Albrecht, the clinical psychologist with the Davis group, to perform routine testing on Roy. Based on these tests, in a letter to the court on December 5, 1990, Albrecht advanced a "preliminary" diagnosis that Roy could be delusional as a result of a "persecution complex" that was caused by child abuse. Albrecht went on that because of poor relations with his parents, "It was very clear that Mr. Moody cannot distinguish reality from fantasy." The psychologist concluded that Roy's thinking was "essentially schizophrenic."

Albrecht's sketchy notes taken during more than eleven hours of testing and interviews indicate that Roy seemed to be making the bizarre claim that his preoccupation with pornography, including filming of his own sexual relations with Susan, was a form of self-treatment to help him "get over the trauma of rape"—meaning the attack he claimed to have suffered in prison.

Ed Tolley knew this was a slender legal reed, but it was all he had to cling to as Roy Moody's trials approached.

17 The Mind of Roy Moody

Meanwhile, Louis Freeh, acutely aware of the huge stakes in the trial, not to speak of Ed Tolley's reputation as a skilled defense advocate, was not about to rely solely on the evaluation of a single prison-staff psychologist, Dr. Scott Duncan, as his expert witness. Freeh quietly arranged to have Moody evaluated for the government by Dr. Park Elliott Dietz. As the specialist who had evaluated John Hinckley, the man who shot President Reagan in March of 1981, Dietz had come to be regarded by some as the foremost forensic psychiatrist in the country.

Dietz, who was by then a professor of psychiatry and biobehavioral sciences at the University of California at Los Angeles, interviewed Roy for thirteen hours on the weekend before the trial opened in Brunswick on December 10. It was the beginning of more than twenty-five hours of interviews that would, at times, take on an eerie real-life resemblance to the fictional interrogation of the consummate criminal, Rodion Raskolnikov, by the St. Petersburg police detective, Porfiry Petrovitch, in Fyodor Dostoyevsky's great nineteenth-century psychonovel, *Crime and Punishment.*

While Roy seemed to relish intellectual jousting with Dietz, his co-operation was always precarious. On the afternoon of December 9, with the trial only hours away, Roy testily accused Dietz of conducting not an evaluation but a charade that was predetermined to undermine the insanity plea, formally entered at arraignment before Judge Alaimo on December 5. The basis of Roy's accusation seemed to have been a news story in the *Atlanta Journal-Constitution* in which government sources were quoted as saying they would refute any insanity claims Roy might put forward. "Why should I cooperate with you?" Roy seethed, the moment Dietz sat down for an interview. Dietz had no ready answer. Roy demanded to know the extent of Dietz's forensic practice, how much money he was being paid by the government to conduct the evaluation. Dietz gave only vague answers or no answers at all. After a tense fifteen minutes, Roy abruptly terminated the session.

The following morning, December 10, the trial began in the old federal courthouse building in Brunswick. In his opening statement Ed Tolley made it clear that Roy was pleading both not guilty *and* not guilty by reason of insanity—a seemingly contradictory position, but routine in criminal trials of this kind. Standing before the jury, Tolley put forward his best country-lawyer, good-old-boy form, which had proved so effective in his growing number of successful defenses. In his opening argument he said he intended to prove that Julie Linn-West and her mother, Joanne Eckstrom, were just a couple of drug-dealing "gals" who had fabricated the whole "Gene Wallace" episode to lure a guileless Roy Moody into a diabolical plot of blackmail and extortion. It was a classic Moody defense: casting Roy as the victim. Almost as an aside, Tolley told the jurors he intended to call "expert" witnesses who would show that if Roy did commit any crimes, he did so at a time when he was legally insane.

Despite his confident assertions in opening argument, Tolley knew that he could never undermine the credibility of the two women, especially when their stories were so chillingly confirmed by the secret tape and video recordings of Roy's own words and movements. As the trial progressed, Tolley placed all his hopes on the insanity defense, and even in this he had to rely entirely on the frail reed of Dr. Howard Albrecht's testimony.

Albrecht dutifully testified that Roy showed signs of "disturbed thinking consistent with a psychotic process." But in the end Albrecht proved to be a poor witness. In his direct testimony he clearly gave the impression that he had seen Roy Moody for the first time just a few weeks before the trial began, but under Louis Freeh's tough cross-examination he was obliged to admit his prior involvement in the First National matter nearly five years earlier.

Moreover, Dr. Sheldon Cohen's testimony did not support Albrecht's conclusions. Indeed, Cohen's conclusions were practically the same as those of Park Elliott Dietz, the government's expert witness.

As the trial reached its fifth and final day, Roy abruptly took over his own defense. Over Ed Tolley's objections, Roy withdrew his insanity plea. In a daring and complex strategic move, Roy sought to retain a fragment of the insanity defense by arguing that the psychiatric evidence showed him to mentally ill only to the extent that he was unable to form the requisite *mens rea*—the legal term for guilty intent—to commit the crimes of which he was accused. The reason for the unexpected withdrawal, Tolley speculated to himself, was Roy's fear that the jury might actually find him not guilty by reason of insanity, an outcome that inevitably would send him to a mental institution for an indeterminate period.

Whatever the reason, after a close examination of Roy Moody, Judge Alaimo overruled Tolley and allowed the insanity plea to be at least partially withdrawn.

Roy's theatrical action in effect cut Tolley off at the knees. The lawyer was obliged to argue, in face of "smoking-gun" evidence, that the government had not really proved "beyond a reasonable doubt" that Roy made up the "Gene Wallace" hoax out of whole cloth and had bribed Julie Linn-West and her mother to commit perjury. Tolley also weakly argued that even if the jurors accepted the government's case, Roy still had not formulated in his own mind an intent to commit a criminal act.

The argument got the short shrift Tolley expected; after an hour of deliberation, the jury found Roy guilty on all thirteen counts on December 14, 1990—two days shy of the first anniversary of Bob Vance's death. Following standard practice in the federal courts, Judge Alaimo postponed passing judgment pending the compilation of a presentence report by court case workers. In early January, Alaimo sentenced Roy to fifteen years in prison—less than a quarter of the maximum that could have been given on the conviction.

Louis Freeh and Ed Tolley emerged from the Brunswick trial with an undisguised respect for one another as accomplished professionals who played tough but always by the rules. Even though no date had been set for the murder trial, the two men knew what lay ahead. They knew that the trial almost certainly would be held at some distant point, because every judge of the Eleventh Circuit had known Bob Vance personally. Freeh also knew that Tolley's remotest hope of prevailing was to plead the insanity defense again—and hope for better cooperation from his erratic and unpredictable client this time.

Anticipating this defense, Freeh asked Dr. Park Elliott Dietz to resume his psychiatric evaluation of Roy Moody to determine Roy's mental state at the time of the bombings as well as his capacity to stand trial in the coming months. Indeed, even though Roy had angrily terminated his dialogue with Dietz on the day before the trial began, the two men met again on the day before Roy's conviction. This meeting, which lasted for two hours, took place in the federal courthouse at Brunswick.

With the trial over, Dietz approached his quarry with more deliberation. On May 8, 1991, he spoke for two hours with Susan McBride. That same day Dietz also interviewed Roy's doltish friend from prison days, Billy Sproles, and on the following day he interviewed Jackie Davis, one of the women Roy had snared with his newspaper "personals" advertisements. Then on May 14, Dietz held a three-hour session with Roy in the Atlanta federal penitentiary. Aware that the sessions were being videotaped, Roy arrived at the Spartan cinderblock-walled white interview room well-coiffed and looking even a little elegant in his bright orange prison jumpsuit.

At the outset Dietz gave Roy what might be called a psychiatric "Miranda warning." Anything he said, Dietz told Roy, might be used against him in the forthcoming prosecution. Roy understood. He asked if he would be supplied with a copy of the videotapes. Dietz assured him a copy would be sent to his lawyer.

Two days later, on May 16, Dietz and Moody held a marathon seven-hour session, and by the time the exhausted men completed the ordeal, the videotapes contained a remarkable record of the mind of Walter Leroy Moody Jr.

If there were a consistent theme to Roy's revelations to Dr. Dietz, it was the burning sense of aggrieved victimization, with the federal courts cast as his most fiendishly persistent tormentor. As he confronted Roy, Dietz had the marked advantage of a record replete with expressions of hostility toward lawyers in general and federal judges in particular. For twenty years Roy had single-mindedly sought to obtain "justice" by rewriting his personal history with Orwellian ingenuity, but at virtually every turn his effort was frustrated by guileful federal judges. No individual more embodied his persecutors than Wilbur D. Owens Jr., the federal district judge in Macon.

Soon after his indictment for obstruction of justice in July 1990—an indictment that routinely might have been tried by Judge Owens—Roy filed a *pro se* motion announcing that he intended to call Judge Owens as a witness "to establish the facts and circumstances of his 'off the record actions' that denied defendant adequate legal representation in 1972 thereby resulting in his wrongful conviction for constructive possession of a pipe bomb."

In his interview with Dietz in December 1990 Roy elaborated on his hostility toward Owens. Roy maintained that early on in his 1972 trial he recognized that his court-appointed lawyer, Tommy Mann, was not taking seriously the defense of his case.

"I started writing letters to the judge to try to let me get rid of this guy," Roy said. "I filed a motion, a *pro se* motion to dismiss him. It was received, stamped 'Received,' in the clerk's office, but never filed.

"Somebody, and it was Judge Owens, didn't want me screwing around with his hand-picked attorney, so this motion—I didn't even realize that he had not ruled on it or that it had never been filed until after I had been convicted and [was] in prison. I found out through correspondence with the clerk's office that—I'm assuming—Judge Owens never allowed this motion to be filed.

"I don't know whether you know it or not," Roy went on, "Judge Owens has the distinction of having the worst record of any federal judge in the United States on decisions. He's the bottom of the barrel when it comes to federal judges, and going back and reviewing this case I can understand why. He is responsible, I think, for a lot of the failure regarding Tommy Mann, so I can't put everything in Tommy Mann's lap. I think it's a combination of things. I think it's Tommy Mann, and the judge, and probably the prosecutors and the agents who would misrepresent the facts."

Roy went on that Owens was "notorious" for taking improper actions in off-the-record methods that could not be challenged.

In addition to the long paper trail, Dietz also had, prior to the interviews, studied Roy's jail-cell mutterings, which were picked up by electronic surveillance. In their totality these statements amounted to a virtual admission of the fatal bombings. On April 7, 1990, for example, the microphones picked up a fragment of Roy's self-conversation that said: "Anytime you're dealing with a court you're dealing with a goddamn crook." On April 19, he said: "Now you've killed two . . . now you can't pull another bombing." On August 5 Roy said: "I'll assassinate you, I'll blow you . . . up." And, on September 14, Roy muttered the cryptic words: "Robert, I didn't want to do you harm."

Many times the microphones could pick up Roy's musings only in such fragmentary fashion that the words were nearly incomprehensible, but yet a consistent paranoid theme clearly pervaded his thoughts. A sampling of some of the intercepts, over a three-month period, include the following cryptic remarks:

"Two . . . got rid of the people. Whew . . ."

"You screwed me one time, in secret. You put the screws . . . a judicial rape at one time, in secret, it will never happen again! You . . . judicial raping could be one time? And see? I'll guarantee you, it will never happen again. Now you, you don't believe me, you're in for a rude awakening."

". . . he and the devil leaned back and did us a mail bomb. Man, if you hadn't delivered the mail bomb, what the heck would the government expect fella? Someone to . . . take one out without a gun?"

"That's why if you find out that the person who was shot in the face has a pistol and is punishing the man that shot him in the face—then it is a different story. It's natural under the circumstances. The circumstances in this case is, I was subjected to a judicial raping by the court and bomb jury. . . ."

Once he appeared to have been banging on his cell table as he muttered: "You express your intention to hurt . . . that's your solution. I intend to hurt. . . . That's the solution, I intend to hurt. . . ."

Despite these self-implicating statements, Roy initially refused to answer any questions relating to the bombings or the threatening letters when he resumed his interviews with Dietz in May 1991. Roy claimed that his attorney had told him not to respond to such questions.

Pressing on, Dietz reminded Roy that the entire dialogue rested on an assumption that Roy would assert an insanity defense—a step which, Dietz pointed out, ordinarily implied that the crime had been committed. To this Roy responded obdurately: "There'll be no such admission."

"I can't really say what the attorneys are going to do," Roy went on. "The only thing I can say is that I'm not guilty of the charges and so if that precludes a . . . any kind of defense, then it will have to be precluded."

"You're saying that for this [insanity plea] to have merit, I first have to admit guilt, and that's not the case," Roy went on. "So, really I . . . I'm wondering if it would be of any advantage. Didn't you indicate that in order to pursue an insanity plea you'd have to say I'm guilty, but I did it because the devil made me do it?"

Roy laughed nervously over his witty turn of phrase; Dietz maintained his stony countenance.

"Something of that sort would be the ordinary defense of insanity," the psychiatrist replied.

"Yeah," Roy said absently.

"Now, from time to time people do try creative ways to have their cake and eat it, too. But certainly the ordinary way is to acknowledge one did it and explain what the crazy reason was. And that, I take it, you're not prepared to do."

"To acknowledge that I did something that I didn't do?" Roy asked incredulously. "I'm not prepared to do that, no."

Dietz shifted his ground. "What will happen if we spend time going through particular evidence that would seem to point to your guilt?"

"I would not comment on any of it other than to tell you my attorney has advised me not to do so."

"So any particular evidence that I might bring up to you, you're not gonna comment about if it relates to the crimes you're charged with?"

"Right."

"And what is it that you are prepared to do during the court-ordered evaluation?"

"I would say to discuss anything that you would like to discuss, that does not relate to events that occurred in, I guess, December of '89 that later resulted in me being charged with some seventy-two counts."

"But," Dietz pressed on, "I think you indicated earlier you weren't prepared to talk about the August events related to the tear-gas canister, either?"

Dietz was referring to the bomb that had been sent to the NAACP regional office in Atlanta in the summer of 1989.

"Right," Roy replied.

"Or things leading up to that?"

"Right. That would be the same type of situation where I would not admit having done that in order to pursue a defense, because I didn't do it. Talking about the tear-gas canister as well as the bombs."

"You deny having done any of them?"

"Ri—right."

"Is that likewise true with respect to—do you deny having any motive to wish to intimidate or threaten the Eleventh Circuit Court of Appeals?"

"Well, I would have to say no," Roy answered. Then he added, with a laugh, "But I would also have to say that my attorney has advised me to say no."

"What does that mean?" Dietz went on.

"It means that I did not," Roy replied, again laughing. "And I'm making this admission to you because I think you're a nice guy. My attorneys have told me not to talk to you about it."

"But the admission you're making is that you weren't too happy with that court. Is that—?"

Roy interrupted with a sarcastic laugh, which Dietz ignored.

"Do I understand correctly?"

"Did I say that?" Roy continued. "That's why my attorney doesn't want me to talk to you. You said if I had a reason. I told you no, I did not have a reason. Did not have a motive."

"The question could have been read either way, I suppose."

Roy laughed again.

"What I asked was whether you denied the motive, I think," Dietz went on. "But that's why I'm seeking clarification. So, you're saying no, you didn't have a motive?"

"Right," Roy replied firmly.

At some point during the two days of the Dietz interviews Ed Tolley, apparently acting at Roy's insistence, notified Louis Freeh's assistant, Howard Shapiro, that the insanity plea was being withdrawn. Theoretically, at least, there was no longer any reason for Dietz to continue his evaluation of Roy Moody. Nevertheless, one final interview—the marathon session of May 16—took place at the Atlanta federal penitentiary. This time, Roy arrived in the drab conference room wearing a spiffy sports jacket and tie.

When Dietz asked why he had withdrawn the insanity plea, Roy responded, quickly, confidently, even defiantly, "I'm innocent."

"If the government's as unfair as you think," Dietz persevered, "then you should expect you're going to lose."

"Well, I would prefer to lose," Roy replied. "Being innocent, I would prefer to lose than say I'm guilty of something I haven't done."

"You would rather be a martyr, even if it costs you your life?"

"No," Roy responded. "Being a martyr is not my goal. What I'm saying is that I am not gonna testify that I've committed a crime that I have not committed. Notwithstanding the consequences."

Roy seemed to relish the give-and-take of his interviews with Dietz, but he would grow obdurately uncommunicative when the psychiatrist sought to invade certain areas. He would not even say whether he was familiar with the *American Survival Guide*, a magazine that circulates widely among extremists, or *The Anarchist's Cookbook*, which gave instructions for making booby traps. He refused to comment on Susan's detailed accounts of the odd and onerous missions on which he constantly sent her during the waning months of 1989. He would not say whether he wrote the "Declaration of War" letter that was sent to the federal judges the week following the mail bombings. He refused to say whether he had ever been in Enterprise, the Alabama town where Robert Wayne O'Ferrell ran his junk store. He was especially cautious over any questions about any dealings he had had with his old prison buddy, Ted Banks. And he would not say whether he had once told Susan that he had dumped a typewriter in Lake Lanier, on the Chattahoochee River not far from Atlanta.

Some things he would discuss. He denied he ever made a silencer for a gun. He denied keeping a diary of his daily activities. And he said he was unaware of the existence of the Underground Supply Company in Murfreesboro, Tennessee, even though an order form from that enterprise was found among Moody's papers, which the FBI had obtained.

And yet while Roy steadfastly refused to discuss involvement of any kind in the mail bombings, he did admit, in some detail, recruiting and training Julie Linn-West in concocting the "Gene Wallace" hoax. He maintained that he embarked on the scheme only "after a great deal of thought." Curiously, despite his elaboration of activity that was clearly criminal, he would not admit that he knowingly engaged in anything that was illegal. He did not even see the criminality of having Susan wear disguises and register under assumed names in motels where interviews with potential conspirators were held. This posture led to a revealing colloquy with the psychiatrist.

"Is there a law against perjury?" Dietz asked.

"Well, there's a law against murder, too," Roy replied.

"So that's a 'yes'?"

"Yes. There's a law against perjury."

"Is there a law against paying people to give false testimony?"

"Yes."

"When you were interviewing people to play that role you knew that, didn't you?"

"Yes."

"And isn't that why you told Susan to use an assumed name and wear a disguise?"

"The reason I told Susan to do that and wear a disguise is because in my mind I was justified in what I did because of the extenuating circumstances. I don't think that the people who might have participated—like Julie Linn, who later participated—I don't think they would necessarily care whether it was illegal or not. Some would, some wouldn't."

"Would you care?" Dietz pressed on.

"Would the . . ." Roy replied, pausing for a moment before continuing. "If I had not thought I was justified in doing it, I would not have done it." He then added that there was "no doubt in my mind" that the women regarded their participating as "an attempt to right a wrong. . . . I'm sure Susan felt the same way. . . . She was doing I think what she thought was the right thing and she was doing it because she had a lot of trust and love for me at the time. She certainly had nothing to gain. . . . She essentially did what I told her to do."

Roy also told Dietz that he was aware of the surreptitious video cameras that recorded his visits to Julie Linn-West's apartment in the spring of 1990. He said some of his remarks made at those sessions were designed to let the federal agents know that he knew of their "illegal conspiracy to entrap me."

As the interview progressed, more of Roy's penchant for bizarre ratiocination emerged. He sought to justify his criminal and antisocial behavior as a form of "self-defense"—acts undertaken as an alternative to suicide. In effect, he said, he reacted to injustice by turning his aggressive impulses from self to others. With increasing passion he spoke of "judicial rape"—which he likened to the homosexual rape he claimed to have endured while in prison—and no person more exemplified the rapists than his old nemesis in Macon, Judge Wilbur Owens. Roy repeatedly dredged up the 1972 bombing conviction, which he blamed largely on Owens, even though Judge Gus Bootle had presided over the trial.

"You shouldn't have a man functioning as a judge that says 'Don't file this motion, because if you do you may get rid of Tommy Mann, and Tommy Mann is working for me.'" Roy fulminated. "Or to call an attorney and say, 'Look, if you take this case, I'm gonna give you the time.'

"This type of underhanded bullshit should never occur. And . . . when it results in a person being sent to prison, and when that person does everything within his power in conventional ways—and it was a hell of a lot of work to do that—they read this and send it back: 'No merit.' Without even an evidentiary hearing. Would be—leads me to believe that they don't give a shit about what the truth is. They're interested in covering up a judicial fucking. . ."

Once again he returned to the theme of judicial rape as the justification for his relentless effort to have his 1972 conviction overturned.

"I was—felt it was governed by the same principles that govern any matter involving self-defense," he said in explaining to Dietz why he filed his *coram nobis* case. "You use whatever force is necessary to remove the threat. That's justifiable. If you go beyond that point it's not justifiable."

The Mind of Roy Moody **275**

Then he told Dietz about his spiritual experience that arose from reading Psalm 94—although, in the interview, he appears to have misidentified the biblical passage as Psalm 92.

"I think it's Psalm 92, verses 20 through 23 or 24 . . . talks of the people who use the law to create mischief and the way, I think, this is viewed by God that the—essentially what it says is that it's an intolerable practice and that they will be thwarted in their evil deeds as a result of some, I guess, divine intervention.

"And I recalled also the teachings of John Locke where he expresses the obligations that a person has who is acting in an office of trust and that that person has responsibilities to adhere to. And when they go beyond those responsibilities and when they abuse the powers of their office, they cease to be a judge at that point in time and they become an ordinary man. . . .

"So I view Judge Owens, I view all of the agents that misrepresented the information that got me convicted to begin with, the U.S. attorney that had this information and used it, as well as my attorney—that entire group to me constitutes a criminal conspiracy that violated my civil rights."

As he continued on the theme of relentless persecution, Roy's anger verged into palpable hysteria.

"John Locke," he seethed, "also points out that the disadvantage of such a system that is run by unethical people—like I perceive these people to be—is that in order to get relief you have to go back to the very same people that caused the problem. I did that with the 2255 [a reference to the *coram nobis* petition], and they shoved it up my ass. So you have a situation created where an innocent person has been sent to prison, has experienced traumatic difficulties, has completely fucked up his entire life, has caused various situations with his brother, his sister, and his mother to the point where she is contemplating suicide, all of this has transpired because some son-of-a-bitch did not want to provide me with an investigator to locate Gene Wallace."

In his outpouring of bitterness, Roy expressed what clearly could be taken as a justification if not a confession of sending the mail bombs.

"I think there are circumstances," he told Dietz, "where all of the options have been explored and you have no other options and you're in a life-threatening type situation, under those circumstances, then I would say that the end does justify the means. But I don't think that can be adopted as a philosophy for conducting business per se. You know, it has to be very unusual circumstances."

When he had finished this eruption, Roy seemed to recognize that he had come perilously close to admitting that he had sent the fatal bombs. So he added, "The obstruction of justice charges, this is what I'm talking about, all of those, to me fell in that category."

Dietz pressed on. "That you had to do those things to save your life?"

"Yes," Roy said resignedly. "And I think that eventually, regardless of the outcome of these trials, I think that will prove to be the case . . . The truth of that far outweighs any of the charges against me. And people don't understand that. They say, 'How on earth could you be charged with matters as serious and be concerned with . . .'"

Roy's voice trailed off in a tone of futility, and once again he returned to the theme that he was justified in concocting a tissue of perjury in order to rectify a far graver injustice.

"Why is that?" Dietz asked.

"Because of the fact that I was convicted of a crime that I didn't commit, and that occurred through—if not illegal, immoral and unethical tactics, and essentially has destroyed my entire life. And so, that has much more significance to me than anything else."

"Now," Dietz went on, "whose perjured testimony are you now alleged to have presented?"

"Well, I think really it would be the combination of anything that occurred in the lower court regarding newly discovered evidence because all of that was fabricated. . . . All of the newly discovered evidence was fabricated . . . all of the other information was truthful. So I think the stuff in the Eleventh Circuit that I knew was fabricated would be anything in regard to the newly discovered evidence. . . . it was perjured from the time it was presented to the District Court. . . . In my mind that represents a case where the end justifies the means. Because at that point in time I had done everything that, that I knew that could be done to rectify what I perceived as wrong."

All of this colloquy dealt with Roy's mental condition at the time the crimes were committed. Dietz was also under instructions to determine his competence to stand trial at that particular moment, no matter what his mental state at an earlier time. In pursuing this inquiry, Dietz pressed Roy about his understanding of the nature of the charges against him.

"I'm charged with having made and mailed several explosive devices that has [sic] resulted in the death of two people," Roy said with manifest self-assuredness. He went on to enumerate other aspects of the intricate, seventy-two-count indictment. He showed an intimate familiarity with the criminal-trial process.

"And what," Dietz continue, "are the possible consequences if you were to be found guilty?"

"Probably be executed is what, my guess would be."

Technically, Roy could not receive the death penalty under the federal indictment, so Dietz probed to see if he understood how he might be put to death.

"And how would that occur?"

"They would take the same evidence that they had used in convicting me with the federal government and give it to Alabama, and Alabama would try and convict me and execute me in Alabama."

Clearly Roy had an accurate grasp of the law; he could be tried separately in state and federal courts for the same act.

"And what about Georgia?" Dietz went on.

"Possibly Georgia, too."

"Do you think Alabama is more likely—"

Roy interrupted the question with a mischievous grin.

"They couldn't execute me twice."

"Do you think Alabama is more likely to prosecute on the state charges?"

"Well, I would think so. In view of the fact that the FBI dubbed this the Vance investigation and not the Robinson investigation. I think they are more concerned about the death of a judge than they are Mr. Robinson."

"And because of the FBI's concern you think that Alabama would be more likely to proceed?"

"Yeah."

"Now, if you were not prosecuted on the state charges," Dietz continued, "and I realize this is a purely hypothetical question at this time, what are the possible consequences of the conviction on federal counts alone?"

"I would be sentenced to something like thirty life sentences, I think."

"Do that many counts carry life terms?"

Roy laughed. "It's enough that I wouldn't spend time adding it up."

As Dietz probed, it occurred to him that Roy had grown so paranoid over government that his ability to participate in his defense might be impaired by quixotic expectations.

"What is the role of the prosecutor?" Dietz asked.

"To win," Roy replied.

"And how is that goal furthered?"

"I think any way that would not bring unacceptable disrepute."

"What will the prosecutor do in court?"

"He would present the testimony of various witnesses who have been told if they don't provide the government with the information necessary to put me in prison that they themselves would go to prison. And he will present the testimony, other testimony as well."

"So not all the witnesses will have been subject to that choice?"

"Some of these don't have to be subjected to that. The various government employees would not have to be subjected to that. They are trained to present their information like it's been presented in various affidavits with incriminating innuendos, false statements, that sort of thing."

"Now, what is the role of the defense counsel?"

"The role of the defense counselor, I think, is to present the various defenses to the best of his ability. One would be to point out the things that I've just mentioned. When and where they occur, and any other thing that would reflect upon the innocence of the individual."

"Who is representing you?" Dietz went on.

"Ed Tolley. And Don that you just met," Roy replied, referring to Don Samuel, the Atlanta attorney who had been appointed by the court to assist Ed Tolley. Samuel had met with Roy just before his interview with Dietz at the Atlanta penitentiary.

"What is Don's last name?"

"I knew you were gonna ask me that, and it's hard for me to remember," Roy said with a grin. "I can't recall it right now."

"But you know it?"

"Yeah," Roy said. Then, in a flash of recall, he added, "Samuel . . . It gives me problems because it sounds like two first names."

"Have you been able to communicate effectively with them?" Dietz went on.

Roy laughed. "When I can get them."

"How do they compare to lawyers you've had in the past?"

"They're the best I've ever had."

"Do you trust them?"

"Well, I trust them," Roy replied, and then he began to muse. "They haven't had enough time to prepare the case. It would take—well the government has been working on this for twelve months or more and have spent millions and millions and millions of dollars working hundreds and hundreds of people. And it's simply not realistic to think that two people can counter that type of onslaught."

"Is there a source for those numbers, in millions of dollars and hundreds of people?"

"Well, Ed Tolley has indicated to me that this is the most intense investigation that has ever been conducted in U.S. history. And I know I can recall how Susan and I were followed to an air show down in Florida when they had more agents there than they had spectators watching the air show." Roy laughed again.

"Do you expect your lawyers will do as good a job as could be done under the circumstances?"

"Yes."

"However, you apparently have quite strong reservations concerning whether the government will be fair."

"Yes."

"Well, let's talk some more about that."

"Well, I would use the word 'realistic' rather than 'strong' reservations. And do you want me to give you examples to substantiate why I feel this way? . . . In numerous government documents following the 1972 case, they have disregarded the fact that the jury determined an issue of fact, which was their function; i.e., that I did not make a bomb in 1972. They have repeatedly stated in various memos back and forth to each other that I did in fact make the bomb in 1972, notwithstanding the fact that I was acquitted of those charges. . . . Those are the type of things that gets me concerned. But . . . in addition to that, people telling me that an agent would begin an interview with someone and say, 'We know Mr. Moody committed these crimes, we just wanted to tie up some loose ends, like to ask you a few questions.' That sort of thing."

"Are there some other examples?"

"The intimidation aspect. . . . Telling people that if they don't provide information that will allow them to convict me, that they themselves will be convicted."

"Are there particular witnesses you have in mind—"

"Several," Roy interrupted.

"Would you name them?" Dietz went on.

"No."

"Why is that?"

"I can't think of any reason to give the government that information in advance of the trial."

"Do you think that the government has it in for Roy Moody in particular, or are you one of many . . . ?"

"Well, I've had attorneys indicate that, that I was the closest thing to a political prisoner they had ever seen. So, based upon that, I would have to say yes."

"Do you think the government had it in for you between your release from prison in 1975 and the time this investigation began?"

"No. In 1972 they didn't have it in for me because I was Roy Moody. They had it in for me because I was an easy way that they could resolve that case. Had I been Joe Blow it would have been the same, same type situation. They made a snap decision that I was guilty the day after they searched my house and everything following that was an attempt to prove that rather than an attempt to objectively investigate the case. I was an easy way of wrapping up the case."

Roy went on that the effort to convict him of the Vance-Robinson murders was "almost a replay of what they did in '72. . . . Misrepresenting the interpretation of evidence to the jury in order to achieve a conviction. Standard procedure for them."

"Now, why are they doing this?" Dietz continued.

"Because they want to win the case."

"And anyone whom they could build a case against would do?"

"Absolutely."

"How did you happen to be singled out?"

Roy mused for a moment over Dietz question, then he said:

"I don't think they maliciously pick somebody and target that person and try to convict them out of maliciousness. I think they do it for reasons of expediency, once they have concluded that the person is guilty. And once they suspect that the person may be guilty, I think that comes into play. And even with that in mind, I don't think that results in a large number of innocent people being convicted of crimes. But I think it results in more being convicted of crimes than should be."

Based on this colloquy, Dietz concluded that Roy Moody was not delusional, that he was thinking in entirely rational if somewhat cynical terms.

There was yet one more technical question for Dietz to explore: Was Roy competent, legally and mentally, to reject various options and strategies that might mitigate the harshest application of the law, including the death sentence that might be imposed in potential murder prosecutions in Alabama and Georgia? In effect, was Roy capable of recognizing that it might be in his interest to plea-bargain?

This exploration required delicate questioning based on unspoken assumptions, and the discussion was so sensitive that it was thought to be prudent to have Don Samuel present for the interview. On May 14, the following exchange took place:

"Now, you have in fact weighed the pros and cons of various legal defenses available to you?" Dietz began.

"Yes," Roy replied perfunctorily.

"And you recognize that you could be convicted in subsequent state proceedings?"

"Sure. I indicated that to you earlier."

"And do you realize that there's a substantial case against you?"

Roy paused cautiously, then replied: "I think some people have that impression."

"Do you think," Dietz continued, "you've been able to reflect reasonably on the pros and cons of your options?"

"Yes."

"Have your attorneys been able to help you? . . . Do you accept their guidance and advice?"

"Yes."

"Always?"

"Only when they're right," Roy replied with a mischievous chuckle.

As Roy had anticipated at the outset of the marathon evaluation, Dietz would shortly pronounce the defendant to be "sane" within the parameters of the Insanity Defense Act of 1984.

Working urgently to complete his exhaustive report to Louis Freeh before Roy's trial on the murder indictments, Dietz declared that Roy "gave no indication that he holds any belief that he is being persecuted by the government through the present investigation and prosecution. Rather, he holds the view that the government routinely uses unfair techniques to secure convictions. He does not view himself as a crusader or martyr to the cause of fighting these supposedly unfair techniques, but rather acknowledges that he acts solely out of self-interest when he points to what he believes to be unfair, biased, or unobjective.

"Moody's capacity to be dissuaded from a claim of unfairness by evidence to the contrary, the absence of a personalized sense of persecution, and his acknowledgment of selfish as opposed to grand and altruistic goals all indicate that his perceptions of the government's unfairness arise not from delusional beliefs, but rather from personal values and attitudes toward the government and toward fairness."

On June 11, 1990, Dietz delivered to Freeh his formal report, a document consisting of 161 pages, single-spaced, followed by a thirty-two-page appendix of the impressive "curriculum Vitae of P.E. Dietz, M.D., M.P.N., Ph.D."

In the technical language of psychiatry, Dietz diagnosed Roy as having "dysthymic disorder, . . . paranoid personality disorder, obsessive compulsive personality disorder, [and] personality disorder not otherwise specified with antisocial and narcissistic features."

"Moody's values, attitudes, and beliefs," Dietz went on, "reflect the characteristic distortions of paranoid personality disorder, and their assessment is made all the more difficult because of his habitual falsification of his personal history. Both his paranoid stance and his reluctance to speak the truth no doubt pose problems for his attorneys. I would expect any attorney to find him a difficult client who sought to control every aspect of the investigation, preparation, and trial of the case, who would sometimes reject sound advice, and who would from time to time be on the brink of demanding a new lawyer, demanding to represent himself, or threatening to take action against his own lawyer."

"Despite the challenges these behaviors pose," Dietz went on, lapsing into the boiler-plate language of a skilled forensic psychiatrist, "it is my opinion with reasonable medical certainty that Walter Leroy Moody Jr. is able to understand the proceedings against him and properly assist in his defense."

"The applicable test of insanity," Dietz continued, "is whether, 'at the time of the commission of the acts constituting the offense, the defendant, as a result of severe mental disease or defect, was unable to appreciate the nature and quality of the wrongfulness of his acts.' It is my opinion with reasonable medical certainty that Walter Leroy Moody Jr. does not suffer from a serious mental disease or defect, notwithstanding his personality disorder and the chronic depression resulting therefrom. This opinion reflects not only my psychiatric examination and the formal diagnoses given above, but also the observations of lay witnesses who had contact with the defendant at relevant times and my assessments of his mental state on the basis of his contemporaneous writings."

The evidence was "overwhelming," Dietz wrote, that Roy "had a thorough appreciation of the nature, quality, and wrongfulness of his actions. His actions reflect meticulous planning, experimentation, and implementation of a concerted criminal agenda, and represent the most successfully executed project of his career. The care and planning that went into the construction of the explosive devices and their packaging and into the preparation of the threatening letters show a sustained commitment to achieving the goals of causing death, injury, and terror.

"At every stage," Dietz went on, Roy "took precautions to evade detection, each of which indicates his appreciation of the wrongfulness of his conduct. . . .

"Moreover, there is no evidence that would indicated that Walter Leroy Moody Jr. had an impaired ability to form the intent to commit the crimes charged. To the contrary, there is overwhelming evidence to indicate that he intended to carry out precisely those crimes with which he is charged. . . . In particular, both his use of booby-trap activating devices, instead of timing devices that could have been constructed with greater ease and safety, and his taking extra steps to incorporate fragmentation material into the explosive devices indicate a specific intent to kill the persons opening the packages."

Dietz wrapped up his report to Freeh:

"Although Moody put forth a variety of justifications and excuses for his actions, the one warranting further analysis is his claim that all of his actions since 1972 have been the result of the 'judicial rape' he claims to have undergone that year. In conducting my evaluation I gave careful consideration to the possibility that a delusion or obsession lurked beneath the surface of this claim, and if it does, I have been unable to find it. Instead, I think the claim is based on his distorted perception of personal victimization and the view that this entitles him to sever the social contract.

"Moody is not alone in his perception of injustice and his blame of authority figures for his woes. The most common theme among those who write inappropriate and threatening letters to public officials is to express a grievance over claimed injustice. This is the theme of Moody's signed letters to the president of the United States in 1962 and 1990, of Moody's innumerable communications to the judiciary in the form of letters, briefs, and motions, and of the anonymous threat letters he sent to multiple victims and that he enclosed with three of the four pipe bombs.

"One of the shared features of those who have assassinated public figures in the United States is that they have sent inappropriate and threatening letters to public figures in advance of the assassination, often to a public figure other than the one eventually assassinated. Moody sent inappropriate and arguably threatening letters to multiple public figures for at least seventeen years before he became a public-figure assassin.

"It is probably true that Moody's conviction and imprisonment in 1972 provided a focus for him. He had always blamed others for his failures and troubles, and his imprisonment became for him a badge of injustice that gave substance to his claim to victim status. Each of his many successive failures to exploit the American legal system added bars to that badge, for he has never accepted responsibility for his actions. He blames judges, he blames lawyers, he blames black people, whom he perceives as getting special treatment to which he feels entitled.

"When the Eleventh Circuit affirmed the district court's denial of his petition [for writ of *error coram nobis*] on June 13, 1989, he responded as if it were a call to arms, resolving that he would not be victimized again and developing his 'chemical project.' In the next round, he acted in accordance with Moody's Rule: Do unto others before they do unto you. He fired a preemptive strike against the Atlanta NAACP on the eve of the Eleventh Circuit's expected rejection of his request for a rehearing en banc, declaring war on the Eleventh Circuit and the American public on the same day. Having escaped detection for that round, he raised the stakes for the next round, befitting the importance he accorded his writ of certiorari to the Supreme Court of the United States. Like a college student phoning in a bomb threat to delay taking an examination, Moody launched his package bombs and threat letters *when* he did in the hope that this would buy him an extension on his filing deadline. But this is not *why* he did so.

"His motives are more complex. For Moody, the crimes expressed his sense of injustice, called attention to his claim that courts and lawyers were the source of great injustice, gave him greater power than he had ever known before, demonstrated his skill and determination, and exacted revenge against the groups and institutions he blamed. To Moody, it was poetic justice that the U.S. Postal Service would be his couriers, as it was Postal Inspectors who challenged his mail-order businesses. And if despite his efforts he were to fall under suspicion, he hoped his enemy, Tom Allen, would be blamed."

Dietz ended his report to Freeh with a single paragraph that summarizes, in remarkably succinct form, the enigmatic character of Roy Moody:

"Moody's crimes reflect every aspect of his personality. He used crime as a means of expression and self-definition because he is free of societal constraints. He used remote means of destruction and terror out of cowardice and cunning. He committed the crimes with great attention to detail because of his perfectionism. He committed crimes on a grand scale because of his exaggerated sense of self-importance. Finally, he chose victims who could not be readily linked to him, yet who represented the classes and institutions he blamed for his failures and toward whom he harbored the greatest distrust and hostility."

But the Dietz report was seen only by a few eyes, because before the murder trial began, Roy instructed his chagrined lawyers that under no circumstances was the insanity plea to be entered to the main body of the indictment.

18 "You Have Already Killed Two"

Among Bruce Harvey's last acts before relinquishing Roy's defense, the audacious Atlanta defense lawyer filed an unprecedented motion demanding that all federal judges in the United States disqualify themselves from sitting in judgment on Roy Moody. The more pragmatic Ed Tolley, once he took over the case, did not go so far, but he did seek to have all the federal jurists of the three-state Eleventh Circuit recuse themselves. In the least serious of the charges against Roy, the obstruction of justice case, Tolley's motion was rejected; instead, Judge Wilbur Owens opted only to move the case to the adjoining federal district court for the case to be tried by Judge Anthony J. Alaimo, who had hitherto had no dealings with the tempestuous defendant.

But with the obstruction case wrapped up and the murder case in the offing, all parties knew that it would not be possible for the case to be tried anywhere in the southeast. The federal judiciary is, after all, a small and closed fraternity. The entire Eleventh Circuit in 1990 consisted of only a few dozen judges, all of whom had known Bob Vance on a personal as well as professional basis. None could possibly preside over the trial of his accused assassin without creating the appearance if not the reality of personal bias. Recognizing this, Chief Justice William Rehnquist in February 1991 designated Judge Edward Devitt of St. Paul, Minnesota, to try the case.

Edward James Devitt was already a legend in his time, an authentic folk hero in the Twin Cities of Minnesota. He called himself "a four-cornered Irishman" because all four of his grandparents had immigrated to America from the Emerald Isle, and on St. Patrick's Day he was given to bursting into a good rendition of "Danny Boy."

The son of a struggling railroad roundhouse foreman, Ed Devitt grew up in St. Paul. Among his classmates at the Van Buren Grade School were Warren E. Burger, later to become chief justice of the United States, and Harry Blackmun, who would become an associate justice of the Supreme Court.

In the middle of the Great Depression, Ed Devitt's father could not send his son to college; the most he could do was to use his connections to get the boy a job cleaning railroad coach cars to enable him to earn the money to go to college, then to law school.

After he passed the state bar examination, Devitt practiced law only briefly before plunging into politics, winning election as a municipal judge in St. Paul. At the outbreak of the Second World War, he joined the Navy and won the Purple Heart for near-fatal injuries when a Japanese kamikaze pilot dive-bombed his ship during the Battle of the Philippines. Returning to Minnesota after the war, Devitt won election to Congress in 1948 as a part of the emerging liberal wing of the Republican Party under the leadership of Minnesota's "Boy Wonder" governor, Harold Stassen. He served just one term before he was defeated by an up-and-coming young Democrat named Eugene McCarthy.

He helped win the Republican nomination for General Eisenhower in 1952 and, two years later, was rewarded for his yeoman service by appointment to the federal distict bench with jurisdiction over the entire state of Minnesota. He was only forty-three.

Over the next three decades Devitt built a solid reputation in his home state as a demanding but fair judge who prized civility in his courtroom. Several times he was quietly approached by the state political establishment urging him to take appointment to the Eighth Circuit

Court of Appeals—a position that led to Supreme Court appointments for his two boyhood companions, Burger and Blackmun. But Devitt liked his community and especially liked the endless drama of serving as a trial judge, even though he did complain quietly to his law clerks about the "onerous duty" of sentencing defendants—a duty that he likened to "playing God." But misgivings aside, he gained a reputation for stiff sentences. Once, when an elderly defendant complained that he didn't think he could complete a sentence Devitt had just given him, the judge replied: "Just do the best you can."

By 1991 Devitt had taken senior status, which gave him more flexibility with his schedule. He had written an encyclopedic legal treatise on federal jury practice, and his decisions were almost never reversed on appeal. By 1980, he had gained such a reputation as an exemplary trial judge that West Publishing Company, the leading producer of law books in the country, established a fifteen-thousand-dollar prize in his honor to be given each year to a district federal judge in the country who seemed to measure up to Devitt's ideal.

On top of these weighty credentials, Ed Devitt, with his leonine shock of white hair, simply *looked* like a federal judge—indeed, bearing a striking resemblance to his old colleague, Chief Justice Burger. He was, in short, the perfect choice to preside over the trial of Walter Leroy Moody Jr.

On June 4, 1991, Judge Devitt called to trial the case of the *United States of America v. Walter Leroy Moody Jr.* Technically, Devitt was sitting as a specially designated judge of the Northern District of Georgia, but the setting was more than 1,500 miles from that location, and the pool of potential jurors, drawn from throughout Minnesota, were as different from Georgians as is Swedish from southern accents.

Devitt introduced the lawyers: For the government, Louis Freeh and Howard Shapiro, now joined by John G. Malcolm, the assistant United States attorney from Atlanta who had been assigned to the case from the start; for the defendant, Ed Tolley and Donald Samuel. Ed Tolley quickly put forward the easy, relaxed manner of a Georgia country lawyer who had somehow strayed far from his natural habitat. He introduced to the court his apprentice, Lance Strickland, as "a law student who is working with us, your honor. We needed a backup, as well as a mime."

On instructions from Devitt, Roy Moody stood to face the jury panel. Tall, handsomely attired in a subdued business suit, his mane of black hair perfectly coifed, he gave a hint of a smile that seemed to suggest that he relished his role as the central character in the drama that was about to unfold.

For a case of such extraordinary background, jury selection proceeded apace, and by noon a dozen men and women and two alternates had been chosen. Judge Devitt issued the standard instructions: Do not talk about the case with anyone, not even your husbands or wives; do not even talk about it among yourselves during recesses or luncheon breaks.

The trial began with Howard Shapiro making the opening argument for the prosecution. In sober tones he spoke of the gravity of the crime of assassinating the very symbol of justice, the impartial judge. In dramatic detail he described how an unsuspecting Bob Vance opened the deadly package on the early afternoon of December 16, 1989.

"In opening that box," Shapiro said slowly, "he detonated a pipe bomb packed with explosives and wrapped with nails. Fragments of metal and deadly nails erupted into the room with the speed of bullets, destroying everything in their path, ripping into Judge Vance's body, seriously injuring his wife with the flying debris. Within seconds, Judge Vance was dead. . . .

"Two days later, on Monday, December 18, 1989, a horrifyingly similar scene took place just four hundred miles away in the old seaport city of Savannah, Georgia. NAACP civil rights attorney Robert E. Robinson returned to his office after a day in court. Awaiting him on his desk was a neatly wrapped package." In chilling detail Shapiro described the carnage that ensued when Robinson opened the package.

Then Shapiro began to focus on Roy Moody. He traced Moody's career as "a man who specialized in subverting, undermining, and abusing the legal system." When his capacity for mischief reached the end of the road, Shapiro went on, "he declared an actual war against the court. This was no quiet, covert action, not simply a letter-writing campaign, but a full-fledged publicly announced war. . . .

"Over time, Moody convinced himself that he had been unfairly convicted, and that the conviction had ruined his life, well beyond the three years he spent in prison. . . . He spent an extraordinary portion of his life suing anyone he ever got into a dispute with, using the courts as a method of retaliating against his attorneys, against his bank, even against his brother and sister. . . . In fact, he even attended law school and he was close to a degree. But he faced one insurmountable obstacle: his 1972 conviction."

Roy Moody, Shapiro pressed on, "does absolutely nothing on impulse. He coolly calculates, he schemes, he plans. . . . So he began by making up an elaborate story, a fiction, a lie, the gist of which another man, a fictional character, had been observed back in '72 placing that earlier bomb in his home. . . . Then he set out to cast his play."

Shapiro related the effort to recruit Julie Linn-West to verify the spurious story. When that effort collapsed of its own inherent contradictions, Moody "became a fixture in certain law libraries" as he pursued appeals, which were systematically rejected. When it became clear that his three years of painstaking work were all for naught, Moody gave up. "He didn't wait for the court to rule. He had seen the writing on the wall. And by early June he was already taking action, taking those first steps towards retaliation, a retaliation that would end with the deadly bombs."

Shapiro continued his dramatic narrative. Thereafter, Moody worked alone in June and July of 1989 in home at Rex in rooms his wife couldn't enter and in a makeshift laboratory in the crawl space under his home. The young prosecutor spoke of Roy's "extensive knowledge of chemistry, mechanics, and physics." He related how he sent Susan out "across the Southeast" on mysterious missions to gather such diverse materials as boxes, chemicals, dry ice, plastic pipes, charcoal.

Susan, he went on, "was entirely dominated by, subservient to, and intimidated by Roy Moody to such an extent that she would simply obey his every command."

In late July, perplexed and frustrated by his inability to manufacture a certain type of chemical bomb, Moody abandoned the project and immediately turned to a backup plan: He retrieved a tear gas canister that he had acquired from old prison pal, Ted Banks. Using this device, Roy "carried out a dress rehearsal for the main event" by sending, on August 20, the tear gas bomb to the southeastern regional NAACP office in Atlanta—"an organization that epitomized for Moody the double standard he felt pervaded the court system. For years he had made the racist complaint that while there was no justice for the average white guy, what he saw as black pressure groups like the NAACP received preferential treatment. In his rage Moody had come to see his failure to overcome his own conviction as a symptom of what he perceived as a deeper societal problem, a problem symbolized for Moody by the NAACP, and most of all, by the Eleventh Circuit Court of Appeals."

The practice scheme "worked perfectly," Shapiro went on. Now "confident and puffed up by his success," Moody began to stalk his ultimate prey. In October 1989 he began preparing bombs, identifying human targets. "He saw Judge Robert Vance as an eloquent champion of black civil rights in a series of well-publicized decisions."

With dramatic flair, Shapiro described the frenetic intensity with which Moody pursued his dark mission—the gathering of the materials, the nocturnal meeting with Ted Banks in the boat-building shop in Florida, the purchase of the gunpowder from the Shootin Iron gun shop in Griffin.

Shapiro concluded his opening summation, the sketch of what the government intended to prove, with Roy's secretive journey to Newnan, Georgia, from where the bomb that killed Bob Vance was mailed.

When Ed Tolley rose to give his opening statement, it quickly became apparent that he was a lawyer facing almost certain defeat. He was out of his milieu, and he had no way of knowing how his folksy country-lawyer manner, honed to perfection before Georgia juries, would play before a jury of whose mores still reflected the dour folkways of Scandinavian farmers struggling to survive in the harsh climes of America's north country. And indeed Tolley seemed uncertain as he made puzzling, gratuitous allegorical references to the literary works of Thor Heyerdahl. Perhaps he was grasping for some link to his jury's Nordic heritage.

When he finally got to the business at hand, he strove to make Roy Moody seem more like the trim, middle-aged man who sat in the courtroom than the diabolical figure accused of committing the heinous crimes that had just been outlined, in merciless detail, by Howard Shapiro.

He spoke of Roy's upbringing in "the tiny, rural town in deep South Georgia called Fort Valley. He was an engaging, bright, athletic young man, very, very intelligent as the son of a mechanic and has a very sweet sister and brother."

He spoke of Roy's childhood dream of becoming a doctor, a dream that was frustrated by his family's lack of means. He spoke of Roy's eclectic interests in flying, in gerontology, in mechanical invention.

As he got his bearings in the uncertain venue, Tolley began to speak directly to the jurors, calling them "folks," in the endearing vernacular of South Georgia.

Then he turned serious; he lobbed a small preemptive strike at what was to come in the trial. "The ladies," Tolley said in lamenting tones, "were perhaps his Achilles' heel, because of a number of ladies that he's known over the years will come to court and all of whom, we expect, will offer some type of damaging testimony against him."

"He had a family at one time," Tolley went on, "a wife and a little boy named Mark. He had a small publishing business that seemed to be going pretty well until one Sunday in 1972 when took his son Mark down to visit his mother. He was living in Macon at the time. His wife, Hazel, went into the front bedroom he used as the office and detonated a bomb.

"He was acquitted of building the bomb, but was subsequently found guilty of possessing an illegal explosive device. He was sentenced to five years in the federal penitentiary—a tough place, one they called the jungle.

"That experience became the fulcrum of his life. Here is where the odyssey begins."

At this comment Tolley drifted off once more into an odd diversion about the hero of Homer's great epic poem, *The Odyssey*.

Then the lawyer returned to his case. Roy discovered upon his release from prison, Tolley went on, that everything had collapsed. He struggled to get his life back together, taking up where he had left off at the John Marshall Law School in Atlanta.

Then it was time for another preemptive warning. "You will learn that he is a very litigious person, the kind of person you probably wouldn't like." But Tolley went on, in what was to be the closest allusion he could make to an insanity defense, Roy was beset by "an obsessive desire to get his conviction overturned." It was this uncontrollable impulse, this burning sense of injustice, that led him to resort to perjured testimony. The irony was, Tolley said sadly, that he had already served his time.

Among the witnesses who would be called, Tolley forewarned the jurors, was Ted Banks, Roy's old prison buddy. "Banks," he said with a trace of disgust, "is a career con man. He served time for securities fraud and counterfeiting. He made his living by cheating and swindling, folks."

And then there was Roy's former wife, Susan. At the mention of her name Tolley became cautiously circumspect, saying only that she had been "a willing participant" in everything Roy had done.

And then there was the other victim Roy was accused of killing. "Robbie Robinson," Tolley said gravely, "was a fine man. He was just ahead of me in law school."

But in the end, Tolley could only plead with the jurors to listen closely, and that they would see that the government's case was built entire on "circumstantial evidence."

"Roy Moody had no reason to kill Judge Robert Vance," Tolley declared. "Judge Vance had even issued a favorable opinion in one of his cases."

With the closing statements concluded, Louis Freeh called the first witness—Lloyd Erwin, the forensic chemist with the Bureau of Alcohol, Tobacco, and Firearms who had, within days after the bombs had been mailed, first suggested Roy Moody as a suspect. In meticulous detail Erwin described the similarities between the bomb that exploded at the Moody home in Macon in 1972 and the four that had been mailed from the Atlanta area in 1989. The similarities, notably the threaded rods that held the plate-caps onto the ends of the powder-filled pipes, were like none he had ever seen before. He related how the uniqueness of the bombs had led him to sketch out, on a restaurant napkin at a meeting with other explosives specialists, the striking similarities in construction. "They were made by the same individual," Erwin firmly asserted.

Ed Tolley's cross-examination was perfunctory, seeking only to raise the possibility that the similarities Erwin found were entirely coincidental. Erwin held his ground; Moody had created "a signature bomb," he declared.

Having virtually placed the bombs in Roy's hands, Freeh turned to the task of establishing a motive—Roy's obsession with getting his 1972 conviction overturned so that he could become a lawyer. Freeh called Julie Linn-West, who struggled on her crutches to the stand to relate, as she had done in Brunswick a year before, how the "Gene Wallace" hoax had been created and staged. She related how Roy had given her a five-hundred-dollar bonus "for doing so good in court." She told the wrenching story of how, even after the bombings, she had begged Roy for a small loan to pay off her delinquent electric bills and get her power turned on again. Roy told her that he "had a lot of money tied up in attorneys' fees right now but that he would see what he could do and get back." Several days later, he sent her three hundred dollars by Susan, and cautioned her that she didn't have to talk to any federal agents who might approach her.

It was a prescient caution, because ATF Agent Bill Grom and several others showed up at her house on March 20, 1990. At first she refused to answer any questions, then, in panic, she called Roy, who told her to keep quiet, that he would get in touch with his attorney to advise her. But the following day, when the federal authorities returned, and once more began dropping cryptic hints that she might be confronting five years in prison for perjury, Julie Linn-West said "I threw up my hands and said 'I lied. I lied in Macon for Roy Moody.'" She agreed to allow the secret recording equipment installed in her cramped apartment.

She went on that Roy apparently got wind of her cooperation with the investigators, and sent her a cryptic message by Susan suggesting that he had Mafia connections and that her family members' lives were in danger if she did not agree to plead the Fifth Amendment to any questions, even if she were summoned to a grand jury.

Even after she had begun to cooperate with the government, Roy visited her, along with his attorney, Michael Ford, on March 29, to make another payment for her "services." Roy took care that his fingerprints did not remain on several crisp hundred-dollar bills that he passed to her—unaware that the incriminating transaction was being recorded on videotape.

Almost always, Linn-West testified, Susan accompanied him, and became discernibly "childish" when she was in Roy's presence.

Julie related Roy's offhanded remark about his first wife, Hazel, who was nearly killed by the 1972 bomb: "The bitch deserved what she got."

"He had told me," Julie continued, "that she and him had been in an argument that day so he had gone to his mother's house and she went snooping around in his office and found the package in his file cabinet and got it out and opened it up and it blew up on her and she deserved what she got because she was snooping around where she shouldn't have been."

Once more, Roy's lawyers were defenseless against the powerful testimony, which was reinforced by the videotapes. In his cross-examination, Don Samuel could do little more than force Julie Linn-West to confess that she had repeatedly lied at the *coram nobis* proceedings in 1988. It was a frail hope of persuading the jury that Julie Linn-West was not to be believed under any circumstances.

With a major part of the indictment now proven beyond a reasonable doubt, Freeh turned to establishing Roy Moody's contentious and dangerous nature by exploring his exotic past. In a cryptic piece of testimony, the relevance of which would become known only later, Timothy Williams related how he had worked for Roy Moody's company, Superior Sail Drives, as a design engineer in 1982. He and two fellow employees, Williams said, got their jobs through classified ads Roy had placed in southeastern newspapers; their role was to help Roy build an auxiliary sailboat motor. The three were paid $250 a week, and worked out of a makeshift office located in Atlanta.

Timothy Williams's testimony was laid aside for the moment as Freeh called Tracey Williams, a comely female agent of the Atlanta FBI office who specialized in evaluation of documents. Assigned full time to the VANPAC investigation from the outset, Williams spent much of 1990 poring over ten thousand pages of court documents that formed the footprints of Roy Moody's litigious life—altogether, some twenty-four separate lawsuits in state and federal courts, ranging from his divorce and custody battle, his efforts to block his sister and brother from inheriting their mother's estate, the criminal proceeding of 1972, and the most massive file of all, the obsessive *coram nobis* pursuit that so relentlessly fueled Roy's paranoia and that ultimately brought him to grief.

Williams's painstaking examination even picked up such obscure information as Roy's lying about his felony conviction when he registered to vote in 1986.

To reinforce the picture of Roy as a compulsive litigator, Freeh called various lawyers who had handled his range of lawsuits over the years. Although testifying under the constraints of lawyer-client confidentiality, most of these lawyers managed to convey the impression of a difficult, vengeance-bent man.

As the trial entered its second week, Freeh began to focus on the main charge in the indictment. The FBI's James Eckel described the assorted terrorist paraphernalia seized in an old trunk Roy had stored in a warehouse in Titusville, Florida. Among the items seized, Eckel testified, was *The Anarchist's Cookbook,* with its prodigious and ingenious recipes for making deadly booby traps.

Then Freeh called Ted Banks, Roy Moody's prison buddy. Banks, a slight, wiry man who seemed permanently stamped with the brutal poverty of Kentucky into which he had been born more than six decades earlier, testified hesitantly, even painfully. As he spoke softly and perfunctorily, he avoided the static glare of his old friend. Banks clearly spoke only under the duress of facing yet another term in prison if he did not cooperate. He said sadly that Roy had been "like a brother," but at sixty-four, and spent beyond his years, he easily could have been mistaken for Roy's father.

Under Louis Freeh's questioning, Ted Banks went through his sad life—basically, a life of nonviolent crimes of cheating and swindling. One sensed that had he had a little more than the eighth-grade education he received before he fled the squalor of Appalachia, he might have been a modestly successful businessman, maybe even a lawyer.

As Banks testified, it was easy to see how the natural affinity developed between him and Roy during their time in prison in the mid-1970s at the Atlanta penitentiary. As a streetwise con man who was serving a sentence for counterfeiting and dealing in stolen securities, Ted needed a lawyer. He noticed that Roy spent a lot of time in the prison library, so the younger prisoner seemed to fill the bill perfectly. Flattered by the savvy older man's attention, Roy coached Ted in the bureaucratic procedures to assure his release, which came on November 10, 1975.

Ted left prison determined to go straight, so he got a job as a shop worker for Thompson Trawlers, a boatbuilder in Titusville, on the Atlantic coast of Florida.

Roy was released about the same time, and he kept up his friendship with Banks in occasional visits to the small marine village that lay just a few hours' drive down the Interstate highway from Georgia.

One day in the early 1980s, Ted Banks testified at the St. Paul trial, Roy came seeking help. He was suing a bank in Atlanta, and if Ted would help him fabricate a story about how the bank had ruined Roy financially, they might both get a windfall, probably a settlement so that the bank could avoid the costly litigation of contesting the lawsuit. Roy even established a bogus residence in Titusville, on Alabama Sreet, in order to establish standing to sue in the courts of Florida.

By this time, Ted noticed, Roy was already talking about becoming a lawyer, and he even claimed to know more about the law than the professionals who represented him. Ted also observed that Roy had become obsessed with racial matters and his conversations often contained gratuitous remarks about "niggers." When Ted indicated a discomfort with the racist talk, Roy replied, "Well, they took over Atlanta; they ought to lead them back on a boat and send them back to Africa."

Roy also tried to get Ted and others involved in a scheme to create a phony title to a boat, insure it, then claim it sank.

Some years later, Ted testified, Roy remarked that his mother died and that he had gotten an inheritance of thirty thousand dollars.

In the summer of 1989, Ted went on, his relations with Roy took on a mysterious, even sinister aspect. Roy asked Ted to store several footlockers, explaining only that he was "having trouble with Susan" and wanted to secure a few things. It was about this time that Ted and Roy spent much of an August night cutting and welding several pieces of two-inch pipe. When Ted got cold feet and tried to back out, Roy kept assuring him that the items were not to be bombs but rather were some piece of equipment needed for one of Roy's inventions.

It was only when he saw a television diagram of the four bombs that had been mailed in December 1989, Ted testified in hushed tones, that he became convinced that he had helped assemble the fatal explosives.

As the trial proceeded in the desultory pace befitting the approach of summer in St. Paul, the major players at the time seemed merely to be plodding perfunctorily through the requisite steps of a criminal trial. To be sure, the Minnesota jurors, so distant from the scene of the crime, showed rapt attention as the bizarre drama of race and violence played out, in the accents of the Deep South. But to the throng of attorneys, investigators, witnesses and, least of all, the defendant himself, there were no surprises as Louis Freeh painstakingly built the case against Roy Moody.

At times the witnesses seemed mere bit players with walk-on roles. Thomas Gray, a former Delta Airlines pilot, related that he had done some consultancy work for Roy Moody. A subdued Lewis Morgan, known as "Pete" to his friends ever since his days at the University of Georgia law school in the 1930s, took the stand only to relate that he had served as a federal judge for more than thirty years and lived in a small town near Atlanta called Newnan. Richard Singleton, an elderly man who lived in the Atlanta suburb of Chamblee, testified that he had rented Roy Moody some storage space in his house for ten dollars a month for much of the 1980s.

Karlene Shiver, a comely woman in her mid-thirties, related her brief but stormy relationship a decade earlier with Roy Moody—whom she described, with lowered eyes, as "quite a charmer and a very nice-looking man." But her wariness grew as she learned that he considered George Wallace a "hero," that he spoke frequently of "the corrupt federal judiciary," that he tended to lash out against "niggers and government Jews." When she objected to his coarse epithets, he would tell her that she "just didn't understand." She related how she had pleaded with Roy not to use his publishing scam to swindle a paraplegic Vietnam veteran and he ignored her. When she discovered that the postal authorities were "trying to shut him down," Karlene figured it was time to look for another boyfriend. But, she went on, escaping Roy's clutches wasn't so easy; he sued her for embezzlement.

The drama quickened as Louis Freeh began to call witnesses who had suffered injuries from exploding mail bombs in 1989. Murlene Murray, the longtime office secretary of the NAACP's Atlanta regional office, described her terrifying experience of opening a seemingly innocuous package that suddenly filled her office with tear gas.

But no witness was more riveting than Helen Vance. In calm and composed responses, Helen related the events of December 16, 1989, which took her husband's life, and very nearly took hers as well. She finished her testimony by saying that she had spent two weeks in the hospital before returning to the home in which she and Bob Vance had raised their two sons. When Judge Devitt called on Ed Tolley to begin his cross-examination of Helen Vance, Tolley rose and said in a soft voice, "I have no questions, your honor."

George Pare, an FBI agent for nearly twenty-five years, told matter-of-factly how he was getting ready to go to a Christmas party in Birmingham when he got an urgent call to go directly to the Vance home in Mountain Brook. He remained there all night, and by Sunday morning the place was swarming with dozens of investigators, including explosives experts sent from Washington.

As a cautious lawyer, Michael Ford was a reluctant witness. He testified of his representation of Roy Moody in several of his most recent cases. He was impressed at Roy's ability to draft legal documents. He also noticed the submissive woman, Susan McBride, who always tagged along with Roy but very much preferred to sail paper airplanes with Mike and Dianne Ford's ten-year-old son, who often spent his afternoons in his parents' law offices.

But, Ford testified, he also observed Roy's sudden shift into a dark, fatalistic mood when he finally accepted that he would never get his 1972 conviction overturned, that he would never be a lawyer.

Ford went on that Roy continued to maintain contact even after he had become the prime target of the bombing investigation. Once in the spring of 1990, Ford testified, he received a bewildering letter printed on a letterhead that read, "Moody Motion Pictures." The letter simply said: "Dear Mike: Smile. I am going to make you a star. Sincerely, Roy Moody, president."

When he was cross-examined, Ford conceded that he had never heard Roy express racist attitudes, or reveal a tendency toward violent behavior.

Michael Sussman, a young Harvard-trained lawyer with the NAACP Legal Defense Fund, told how he had won a major desegregation case, in which Judge Vance wrote a scorching opinion about the slow pace of desegregation in Jacksonville, Florida.

Then it came time to relate the circumstances of Robbie Robinson's death. As this phase of the testimony began, Barbara Pulliam, who was attending the trial as the Robinson family representative, quietly got up to leave the courtroom. Helen Vance instinctively knew the reason: The description of Robbie Robinson's final hours was simply too ghastly for a loving sister to endure. Unobtrusively, Helen rose and followed Barbara Pulliam out into the hall. There, on a bench, two daughters of the South, so dissimilar in their backgrounds and yet so linked by common tragedy, sat silently, occasionally holding hands, while the muffled testimony proceeded inside the courtroom.

Joyce Tolbert, Robbie Robinson's secretary, told of receiving the box, wrapped in plain brown paper, which contained the bomb that killed her employer on December 18, 1989. Even more chilling was Dr. Emerson Brown's detailed description of the mortally wounded Robinson lying in confused terror amid the rubble of his bombed law office on Abercorn Street in the twilight of the fateful day.

A paramedic named Christopher Scalisi related the grisly account of getting the portly Robinson to the hospital. And Paula DeNitto, an intern surgeon at that hospital, told of her feverish but vain efforts to save Robinson's life.

As the trial progressed the coolly professional Freeh came to resemble a man methodically putting a jigsaw puzzle together—one piece here, another piece there, until gradually the picture became clear. After presenting the Savannah witnesses, Freeh called Steve Grant from Atlanta. As a security guard at the Eleventh Circuit Court of Appeals building in Atlanta, Grant related how a hastily beefed-up x-ray surveillance system, early on the morning of Monday, December 18, depicted the unmistakable outlines of a battery-activated pipe bomb inside a shoeboxsized package wrapped in plain brown paper and secured by twine. From Grant's outwardly blase account, one could sense the tension on that chilly gray December morning in Atlanta when someone accidentally set the mail conveyor belt into motion, and terror-stricken security men watched what they knew to be a powerful bomb fall three feet to the concrete floor of the building's drab mailroom. "Everyone was somewhat startled," Grant testified in an extraordinarily euphemistic statement from a man who must have known that he faced imminent obliteration.

But the packaging of the bomb was so proficient that even such a heavy thump did not set the bomb off.

Next, Peter McFarlane, an FBI agent in Atlanta, related how his bomb squad "suited up" with protective gear to remove the deadly device. Despite the painstaking care with which the team worked for two tense hours, McFarlane testified, the nails inside the box could be heard rattling as the package was gingerly placed inside a five-thousand-pound double-lined steel bucket. Thus sealed, the bomb was removed to a distant location, which McFarlane, citing security reasons, declined to identify. For the remainder of the day, the team worked meticulously to deactivate the bomb. Only at the end of the exercise, McFarlane went on, did he realize that the suits he and his men had worn in the removal were wholly inadequate to the task; if the bomb had gone off, anyone close by would have been killed.

McFarlane concluded his testimony by reciting an inventory of the parts of the disassembled bomb that were so mundane they might have been a shopping list for a trip to the corner hardware store: glue, common nails, rubber bands, insulated wires, paper towels, flashlight batteries, the barrel of a ballpoint pen, cutout pieces of aluminum pie pans. The gunpowder, he said, was readily obtainable at any one of the numerous gun stores in that part of Georgia.

Next, Miguel Cortez, the clerk of the Eleventh Circuit Court of Appeals, gave a general description of the nature of the work of the court. Each year the court received, mostly by mail, some 4,500 appeals from the three southeastern states that constitute the circuit. This prodigious annual flow of mail included, he went on, about a dozen letters that are deemed threatening. Generally these are crude, handwritten missives. Because it was a little out of the ordinary, Cortez had a special recollection of the letter he received on August 23, 1989—the carefully typed letter, which began with the ominous words, "DECLARATION OF WAR," and which warned of "widespread terror" spread by chemical weapons because of what was deemed "the court's callous disregard for justice."

Then Willye Dennis took the stand to relate how she had received a package bomb at her NAACP office in Jacksonville on the very day that Robbie Robinson was killed. Although threats were common, this was the first time she had actually come close to being killed.

"Do you do anything in response to those threats?" she was asked.

"Pray," Willye Dennis replied with aplomb.

As the puzzle-picture grew inexorably more vivid under Freeh's commanding direction, the weakness of Ed Tolley's defense grew commensurately apparent as he engaged in little more than perfunctory cross-examination. Increasingly he would end up his questioning by asking plaintively, but it is a fact, is it not, that you do not *know* that this defendant, Roy Moody, had anything to do with what you describe? It was a feeble effort to implant in the jury's mind the remotest flicker of the "reasonable doubt" over "circumstantial evidence" that Ed Tolley knew he would stress in his closing argument at the end of the trial.

The desultory pace of the trial changed abruptly on the morning of June 13 when Susan McBride took the stand. By then approaching thirty, but still evoking the appearance of a timid high school girl, Susan began to testify in such soft voice that Judge Devitt frequently had to gently admonish her to speak louder. At once it became apparent that she avoided the cold, intense gaze of the man at the defense table—the man whom she had met in the most randomly casual manner and with whom she lived for nine tumultuous years.

Susan softly described how she met Roy at the suburban Atlanta restaurant called the Waffle House where she was working as a waitress in 1981; how she began living with him shortly thereafter, even though he was nearly thirty years older than she; how she gradually took over the day-to-day management, for virtually no pay, of Roy's scam businesses that were by then producing around $180,000 a year, even though the Post Office had tried to shut him down; how she worked amid filth and clutter in a house that was always unkempt, inside and out; how Roy isolated her, first from her few black friends, then from all other friends, ultimately even from her parents; how she discovered, only accidentally, that Roy had been married once before and had served a term in prison; how he began to punish her with "the silent treatment" for unfathomable reasons for which she blamed herself.

With a sense of deep shame, she related how she surrendered totally to Roy's heavy sexual demands, having relations several times a day, activity that Roy often recorded with video cameras. She testified that he made no effort to conceal the fact that he was seeing other women, some of whom were contacted through "personals" advertisements in the Atlanta newspapers.

She told how, toward the end of their relationship, Roy became violent, on one occasion, choking her and "beating my head against the floor."

Why, Louis Freeh gently asked, did she stay with Roy?

"I didn't have anything," she replied softly. "I had very low self-esteem, and I knew that if I did leave he could find me. . . . I was afraid."

In curiously detached detail, Susan told of Roy's constant preoccupation with various lawsuits, with his elaborate schemes to make money through fraudulent lawsuits.

Then Freeh patiently guided Susan through the fateful summer of 1989, when Roy retreated to the privacy of his "laboratory" to work on arcane projects. She described his increasing obsession with secrecy as he sent her on mysterious missions to collect materials he needed for his work. He seemed especially haunted by the fear that she might leave a fingerprint somewhere.

With scrupulous attention for dramatic impact, Freeh led Susan to the climax of her testimony: On December 21, 1989, four days after Bob Vance was killed and two days after Robbie Robinson died, Susan and Roy saw on the evening television news the report that a judge in Maryland had been gravely injured by a bomb delivered as a package to his house.

"And he made the comment," Susan began haltingly, "—he said, 'That one is not mine,' or either he said, 'I didn't do that one.' I can't recall which statement it was."

Tolley instantly recognized the power of Susan's testimony, but there was little he could do to blunt its impact. In his cautious cross-examination, he could only seek to implant a tiny seed of doubt in the jury's mind by portraying Susan as a vengeful woman who had been eagerly involved in every nefarious scheme Roy Moody might have concocted and was now only trying to save her own neck by cooperating with the government, saying whatever they instructed her to say. In his heart he believed that Susan was an accomplice in the two murders, but he also knew that he was severely limited in how far he could press this theory. He knew that if he proved Susan was a murderer, he would have proved too much: He would prove that Roy was a murderer.

After Susan's dramatic testimony, the workaday routines of a trial in process returned to the courtroom. Judge Devitt, near the end of his distinguished career and serenely secure in his ability to conduct a criminal trial without the kind of misstep that would result in a reversal, occasionally added a moment of decorous levity to the proceeding.

In the throes of the investigation, Howard Shapiro had become so immersed in the pursuit of the prey that he had not been present when his wife, Shirley, gave birth to their first baby, whom they named Zachary. But Shirley understood the necessity of the absence, and by the time the trial got underway, the baby was old enough that she could take him to Minnesota. Sometimes she would slip quietly into the courtroom, take a seat on a back row, and cradle the dozing infant in her arms. On such occasions, Judge Devitt would furtively summon Howard Shapiro to approach the bench, then tell him, in a whisper loud enough to be heard throughout an amused courtroom, "Your baby just came in." In one touching moment, Helen Vance, who was attending the trial on a daily basis, offered to watch Zach in order to give Shirley a closer view of her young husband in action.

At considerable length, James "Tom" Thurman, head of the FBI's explosives laboratory in Washington, described the parts of the four bombs, which he called "carbon copies." Thurman's technicians found nearly a thousand similarities between the 1989 bombs and the bomb that had exploded in Hazel Moody's hapless hands in 1972. Essentially, all Thurman was doing was fleshing out and verifying the crucial early recognition of Roy's "signature bomb" by the keen-eyed ATF agent, Lloyd Erwin, within days of the murders.

Andrew Bringuel, an FBI agent based in Atlanta, related how he was shopping at Kroger's supermarket one Sunday for supplies for a routine home repair job when, to his amazement, he spotted on a shelf packages of nails that appeared virtually identical to those that the mail bombs had contained. Laboratory analysis showed that the nails had indeed come from the same factory—thus confirming a crucial piece of Susan McBride's testimony that Roy had shoplifted the nails from the supermarket.

William Bodziak, the FBI documents specialist, testified that the letters in the bomb came, unmistakably, from the same typewriter that Robert Wayne O'Ferrell had used to type his peevish letters appealing his lost case in the Montgomery federal district court.

But here, the government prosecutors confronted a difficult problem. Mary Ann O'Ferrell had identified Susan as the person who had bought the typewriter in the summer of 1989. Yet, Susan adamantly insisted she had never been to Enterprise, and she had no reason to lie about that aspect of the case. Louis Freeh could only speculate as to the contradiction: In all likelihood, some other woman had been with Roy Moody when the typewriter was purchased, and Mary Ann had confused this woman with Susan, whose photograph she had seen in the newspapers. It was a simple case of mistaken identity, but under the circumstances, he could not afford to put Mary Ann on the stand. But Freeh knew, of course, that neither could Ed Tolley risk calling Mary Ann; after all, she probably would put Roy on the scene as well.

To show Roy's obsessive hostility to the federal courts, Freeh called Jackie Stanford Davis, the Atlanta woman who had responded to Roy's classified ad seeking female companionship. Jackie testified that Roy's obvious anger at the "crooks" on the court made her so uncomfortable that she eventually broke off the relationship.

Kathy Burks, a waitress who often served Roy on his frequent breakfast trips to the Po' Folks restaurant and occasionally went out with him, testified about Roy's preoccupation with "uppity niggers." She related how Roy ostentatiously left the restaurant when a well-mannered black family came in to order a meal; Kathy apologized to the customers. She described the bizarre incident in a restaurant parking lot when Roy became so enraged because someone had parked too near his car that he vowed to wait there all night to confront the offending parties; she caught a cab home.

Next Roy's prison-cell mutterings were described by Robert Lennek, an FBI wiretap expert who had monitored the surveillance. Lennek repeated Roy's incriminating murmur, "You have already killed two."

Testifying only under his objection on grounds of lawyer-client privilege, Tommy Mann related his representation of Roy at the 1972 trial, telling how the bomb had been addressed to "a Mr. Downing" at an Atlanta car dealership after Roy's car had been repossessed because he gave a bad check in payment. Mann told of his astonishment at Roy's raising the "Gene Wallace" matter for the first time during the course of the 1972 trial. Mann said he made a mental note that the newspaper article reporting on the explosion that injured Hazel appeared on the same page of the *Macon News* with a story about George Wallace running high in the polls in the 1972 presidential election. The page had been introduced into evidence, and was lying on the counsel table when Roy blurted out his contention that "Gene Wallace" had concocted the whole scheme to send the bomb to Downing.

After two weeks of testimony, Louis Freeh announced that the government rested its case. At that point Ed Tolley rose to make the obligatory motion to dismiss on the grounds that the government had not sufficiently established a case to be submitted to the jury. But the motion was entirely perfunctory, as was Judge Devitt's swift ruling: "Motion denied."

Guilty on All Counts

As Ed Tolley anticipated from the outset, he now stood virtually defenseless. If he called any witnesses at all on Roy's behalf, he would only be opening himself up to yet another onslaught of rebuttal testimony about his client's eccentric past, which would only further add to the certainty of conviction. Tolley would simply rest his case without presenting any defense.

Then the trial suddenly took a bizarre turn: Roy Moody demanded that he be allowed to take the stand in his own defense.

Based on a year of dealing with the impulsive and unpredictable client, Tolley was prepared for anything, but this maneuver caught him so much off guard that he suddenly found himself opposing his own client in open court. He rose to announce: "I veto his right to testify."

"His testimony will be entirely against my legal advice," Tolley told Judge Devitt. Now arguing in grave, almost desperate terms, Tolley said he had told Roy that he still faced murder prosecution in Alabama and Georgia, each of which could impose the death penalty if he were convicted. "Any statement he makes here," Tolley argued, "can certainly be used in those subsequent proceedings. . . . It is very clear that there is not a double-jeopardy bar, and therefore I have so warned him.

"His testimony is not advisable and further I will sayeth not about that issue." If Roy were permitted to testify, Tolley declared, he would do no more than tell Roy to relate whatever he wished in narrative form; there would be none of the customary procedure of a lawyer carefully guiding his witness through testimony.

Tolley was not being merely crabby over his dispute with Roy. He was acutely aware that he had a serious problem of his own: The lawyers' ethical code explicitly forbids attorneys from knowingly aiding a client in committing perjury. And while lawyers can play fast and loose with that stricture, Ed Tolley was not about to pursue a course that would in effect implicate himself in Roy's crimes. Yet he had an equally compelling ethical obligation as a lawyer to represent his client "zealously within the bounds of law." He could have, of course, resolved his dilemma by withdrawing from the case for unstated reasons, but he knew Judge Devitt would not likely permit this course at this late stage of the trial. Such a course would, after all, play directly into Roy's infinite mischievous capacity for throwing monkey wrenches into the legal system.

Despite Tolley's strenuous objection, there was clear precedent for permitting defendants in criminal trials to testify in their own behalf, even over the objection of their own lawyers. After all, Roy already had been declared, following careful evaluation by competent mental health professionals, to be capable of standing trial and participating in his defense. Judge Devitt called Roy to the bench and asked in careful words if he wanted to testify against Tolley's advice.

"Your honor," Roy said with self-assurance, "I have made the decision that I would like to testify."

Without further ado, Devitt directed Roy to take the stand. But he also implicitly recognized Ed Tolley's dilemma; it would be quite satisfactory, Devitt said, for Tolley to forgo the customary direct examination and do no more than lead his client through a narrative account of whatever he wished to say.

Then the jury, which had been out of the courtroom during these dramatic exchanges, was called back, and on June 19, Roy launched into three days of testimony.

He began with a rambling account of his life, beginning with his birth and childhood in Fort Valley, his military service, his fitful attendance of various colleges amounting to what he confessed was "an undistinguished academic career."

In wistful tones he related what began as an ordinary, mundane course of life—his struggle to work his way through college, his marriage to Hazel Strickland, the arrival of their son, Mark Bryan Moody. He related how he would often care for Mark during the day in order to enable Hazel to work at her job as a clerk for a local manufacturer of livestock feed.

Then, he continued, his life took a turn for the worse. The automobile he had to have to make a living was repossessed, unjustly, by a cunning, avaricious used-car dealer in Atlanta. Then he was drawn—innocently, he implied—into a mysterious scheme by a law school classmate named Gene Wallace to get back his car. Only later, he went on, did he realize that Gene Wallace was "a part of the hippie subculture, one of those who was bombing the Pentagon and planes and so on." But before he saw the truth, Roy went on, the portentous encounter resulted in his conviction for "constructive possession of an unregistered firearm," for which he was sentenced to five years in the federal penitentiary. His conviction, he maintained, resulted from a chain of willful dereliction or blundering incompetence on the part of lawyers and court officials. His frantic mother had hired a lawyer named Manley Brown, paying him many thousands of dollars up front, but the man did so little that eventually the court appointed Tommy Mann to represent him as an indigent. This tangle of legal action ultimately resulted in a prison term that, he said gravely, traumatized him and permanently changed his life.

Despite this, he went on, when he regained his freedom he prospered in his small business of publishing anthologies of poems and short stories by promising writers from around the country. He related his encounter with the youthful Susan McBride at the Waffle House, and how she ultimately took over the day-to-day management of the business while he devoted most of his time to the pursuit of his eclectic projects as "an amateur inventor."

With Ed Tolley firmly holding to his resolve not to question his client, Roy entered into as bizarre a spectacle as has ever been witnessed in a federal courtroom. For three days, hour after hour, he rambled through often-incoherent testimony, full of paranoia about lawyers and judges and "Gene Wallace," about the horrors of his life in prison, about his experiments in "cold fusion," about the time Susan told him that she thought she was pregnant and wanted to get an abortion, about his trips to see his old friend Ted Banks at Titusville.

At times his discourse seemed to range far afield, as when he spoke of how his father and mother had been avid hunters and fishermen, how his mother was an excellent shot with a rifle. He related in moving terms his final conversations with his dying mother—conversations about how she wished to have her earthly belongings divided after she died.

But nothing in his testimony was more dramatic than Roy's account of a time when, in the thrall of suicidal depression, he turned to the Bible and his eyes fell upon the Ninety-fourth Psalm. It was almost as if the ancient words were being addressed directly to him; in an instant of blinding recognition, he understood that venal, corrupt, or incompetent public officials had been grinding the common man since time immemorial. But there was hope: God would not permit injustice to continue into perpetuity; wrongdoers would get their just deserts. And the Word of God had justified his fabrication of evidence to overturn an unjust conviction.

He compared himself to Jacobo Timmerman, an Argentine Jewish dissident who was held political prisoner for many years but who never stopped criticizing governmental tyranny.

He declared that it was Susan's perverted idea to videotape their sexual activities in the hope of marketing these as X-rated movies.

Then he dropped a bombshell: He claimed that he'd never heard of Robert Vance or Robbie Robinson until his attorney, Mike Ford, told him that the Ku Klux Klan had sent the deadly bombs as a retaliation for the racial strife in Forsyth County, a rustic area just north of Atlanta in the Georgia mountains.

Despite the Alice-in-Wonderland quality to the testimony, Roy proved to be such a convincing witness that Helen Vance, sitting in the courtroom all the time, was amazed to find herself wondering:

Is it possible that we have the wrong person?

But soon Helen recovered her sense of reality, and once, when Roy appeared overcome by tearful emotion as he related a lifetime of struggle against injustice, Helen stormed out of the courtroom in a calculated manner that could not escape Roy's notice.

Roy's lachrymose testimony continued for two days, ending on Friday, June 21, when Judge Devitt recessed the proceeding for the weekend. But this field day of self-indulgence came to an abrupt end when court reconvened on the following Monday with Louis Freeh starting his cross-examination.

No one knew better than Ed Tolley that Roy was now in for a battering at the hands of a master of the courtroom, and there would be little Tolley could do to protect his client; it is a given of courtroom procedure that attorneys are allowed the broadest latitude in cross-examination, that it is in this phase of the trial more than any other that the truth will emerge, that a witness's account will stand or fall before the withering assault of sequential logic.

At times Freeh's interrogation resembled that of the psychiatrist, Dr. Park Elliott Dietz, whose massive report lay on the counsel tables of the lawyers but unseen by any other eyes. But Freeh had a distinct advantage in that if Roy sought to dissemble, Judge Devitt could always compel an answer. Moreover, Roy was keenly aware that his earlier jousting with Dietz was just a dress rehearsal for the main performance, which was now taking place before that most crucial audience, the jury.

When, Freeh asked, is a person justified in lying under oath, as Roy conceded he had done in the *coram nobis* fabrication?

"I think," Roy began, "in a situation where there has been a deliberate attempt to deny an individual constitutional rights, where this is not an error but where it is a contrived act by a group of people who are sworn to uphold the law, who are . . . ."

His voice trailed off, and he added weakly, "when people are driven to suicide."

But Freeh systematically pressed the line of questioning until, through the defendant's own words, he had enmeshed Roy in a clear pattern of self-serving lies.

Moreover, as Tolley had feared, Roy's testimony served only to open the door for another devastating round of rebuttal testimony. Roy's attempt to implicate Michael Ford in a Ku Klux Klan-engineered bombing enabled Freeh to call the Atlanta attorney to the stand for testimony that otherwise would have been precluded by lawyer-client confidentiality.

Testifying reluctantly, Ford told of his turbulent relationship with Roy. This account included Ford's anguished description of a telephone call he received from Roy, at a time when it was known by both that the line was tapped by the FBI, inquiring as to where Ford bought his gunpowder.

"That was the most bizarre thing we could imagine," Ford said softly. "He was doing that to try to involve me in his—in this case."

This, Ford said, occurred well after he had concluded that Roy was "uncontrollable as a client."

Roy's references in his direct testimony to his Writers Guild also gave Freeh the opening to call new witnesses to testify to the fundamentally fraudulent nature of the enterprise. Still other witnesses reinforced Roy's attempt to murder his three employees in the turbulent, shark-infested seas of the South Florida coast in 1982.

And finally, the rebuttal testimony included the account of Glen Hunter, an FBI agent who specialized in white-collar crime, detailing the extravagant lifestyle Roy enjoyed on his ill-gotten profits from his mail swindles.

Freeh's cross-examination had been devastating. When both sides rested their case on June 26, Ed Tolley knew that Roy's testimony had rendered any chance of acquittal, always slim, virtually impossible.

Closing arguments are crucial in criminal trials because they afford the opposing lawyers to make a fabric of the tangled skein of testimony that constitutes the body of evidence presented. On June 26 Louis Freeh took his hour of closing argument to weave that fabric in the Roy Moody trial, masterfully and mercilessly. He began with a firm assertion: "One person, acting alone, made and mailed those bombs."

Why? That, declared Freeh, "is a very interesting question, and a very important question, because we are all human beings and we like to know why. And I suggest that there's compelling evidence as to why Mr. Moody made and mailed those bombs."

But however intriguing the question may be, Freeh went on, there was no necessity for the jury to arrive at any conclusions as to motive or motivation, "because to do that, you have to get inside the brain of Walter Leroy Moody."

All that was necessary, he said, was that the jury believe that Moody had done the deed, and that had been proven "beyond dispute" by "a mountain of evidence."

Roy Moody was, Freeh went on, "a stealth bomber. His bombs are made, designed, and delivered with great stealth, great cleverness, great caution, because he doesn't want to get caught." Roy chose the Christmas season to send the lethal devices, Freeh speculated, because he knew that the increased mail volume of the season would make detection less likely.

Freeh used Roy's own words, his two days of rambling testimony, to reinforce the case against him. "He effectively saw the end of his life in 1972. He blamed the court, the witnesses, the prosecutors, his lawyer, everybody but himself. He blamed Gene Wallace." And he developed an obsessive passion to seek revenge by stealthy retaliation. He became a person "who has for twenty years played by his own rules: The end justifies the means."

This brooding culminated in the mid-1980s with Roy's desperate effort to get his 1972 conviction overturned, a pursuit that became "a matter of life or death."

He invested thousands of hours into that pursuit, and when he saw this tremendous expenditure of financial resources and emotional energy going down the drain, Roy "declared war" on the courts of America. "It is as simple as that."

He referred to Roy's "130 IQ genius level." In his evil mind, the prosecutor went on, the NAACP and Robbie Robinson became mere "diversions" to throw investigators off track. "He wanted to make this look like a race crime," Freeh said gravely. "He blew that man to pieces . . . so these guys sitting here wouldn't look at Walter Moody."

Make no mistake, Freeh added, "he is a racist. But he is not an ideological racist. He wouldn't go to a Klan rally. He is too good for that. He considers himself much more clever. But he is a racist. Mr. Robinson's life had absolutely no meaning to him." Robbie Robinson was merely a disposable figure, like a piece on a chess board sacrificed for tactical purposes and, in all likelihood, because he had been associated with Mike Ford in the past.

As he reached the conclusion of his closing argument, Freeh's voice softened as he related how Roy Moody, in his increasing habitation of law libraries, came upon Bob Vance's opinion in the Jacksonville school case, in which the jurist had declared emphatically that the mere passage of time could be no bar to denial of fundamental rights—no matter that judges on the same court had denied *his* rights on the basis of passage of time.

"Can you imagine the rage," Freeh said softly. "Quiet rage—he is a very quiet man, very charming—the quiet rage when he read that, Judge Vance telling black plaintiffs that remoteness in time is *not* a bar? And his judge telling him, remoteness in time *is* a bar? The perfect target becomes Judge Vance."

Then Freeh added a touch of irony that Bob Vance's friends had ruefully but silently considered for more than two years. "Maybe," Freeh said, "it was because his home address was listed." Most federal judges don't list their telephone numbers in the public directory as a measure to avoid threats or crank calls; but such privacy was inimical to the nature of a warm, outgoing man like Bob Vance, who enjoyed keeping in touch with his friends. "Maybe," Freeh continued ominously, "it was because a long time ago Mr. Moody read that Judge Vance was an arch enemy of Governor Wallace, who was his hero."

"These are not the crimes of a madman," Freeh said somberly. "There is another word for the person who commits these crimes: It is called *terrorist.*" Indeed, Roy himself had already put the courts on notice that if he were denied his demands to overturn his 1972 conviction, there would be "profound social consequences."

With dramatic flourish, Freeh described the moment of the explosion, eighty nails, "traveling at thirteen thousand feet per second, like bullets." It was, he said, "a coward's crime," but one that was consistent with Roy Moody's lifelong penchant. "Everything he has done in life," Freeh said, "is to deny responsibility." Freeh recalled Roy's feigning mental illness as early as 1967 in order to get free college tuition. "Feigning is a very big part of this man," Freeh said with contempt, "and when he's up there crying and cajoling, I suggest that's an absolute fraud, a con, it's what he's been doing his whole life." The same was true, Freeh went on, of Roy's claimed "religious experience" after reading the Ninety-fourth Psalm. "It's a fraud, a scam. It's his last con. He is a master of deceit, the absolute, ultimate con man."

With the jury rapt as he neared the end of his presentation, Freeh once more returned to the evidence. He recalled Lloyd Erwin's immediate recognition of Roy's "signature bomb." He spoke of Roy's familiarity with the mails, because "he's been in the mail fraud business for his whole adult life."

He recalled the testimony of the girlfriend who said that in 1981 Roy remarked that "the perfect crime would be to build a bomb and when everything exploded there wouldn't be anything left to investigate."

He spoke of Susan as a piteous figure, a woman "whom he brainwashed, whom he tormented, whom he kept in captivity for ten years, reduced her to nothing but a subservient woman who spoke to him in a childlike voice, who acted as a child, who did everything to please him, who couldn't understand why he wouldn't speak to her for a week."

He recalled the embarrassing episode of the O'Ferrell investigation, saying that it was "a fluke, an absolute fluke," that Roy bought the crucial typewriter from O'Ferrell on his way back to Atlanta from the Florida panhandle in the summer of 1989.

Once more he reminded the jury of James Paul Sartain's devastating testimony that he had urged the absurdly disguised Roy Moody to buy four one-pound cans of gunpowder rather than one four-pound can, and that Roy had stated flatly, "No, I'm going to use it all at once."

This gunpowder, Freeh said, killed Bob Vance—and killed Robbie Robinson solely because Roy Moody "wanted to protect his butt when he had to."

"Retaliation is a way of life to Mr. Moody, and the court was only the last target, this time a deadly target."

At long last, almost exactly a year after he had first met Roy Moody, Ed Tolley rose to make his final defense of his enigmatic client. In the course of that year, he had missed the first birthday of his first-born son, he had gained thirty pounds in weight, he had forfeited at least a hundred thousand dollars in legal fees he might have received for work that would have been more productive as well as more profitable. And yet, he had a curious sense of satisfaction in having completed, with honor, the most difficult assignment a lawyer can get: Defense of a man accused of a lethal attack on the very foundation of the legal system, the impartial judge. He knew that he had won the respect not only of the organized bar but also of his chief courtroom adversary, Louis

Freeh, and of the eminent jurist, Edward Devitt, who was presiding over the trial.

He also knew that he was undertaking a hopeless cause in asking the jury to acquit Roy Moody. There might have been the slimmest chance for acquittal had Roy only listened to him and pleaded insanity. Conceivably, given the occasional erratic vicissitudes of American juries, there might have been a mistrial—brought on perhaps by one lone obdurate holdout—if Roy hadn't insisted on one final grandiose act of narcissism in taking the stand in his own behalf.

But no matter how hopeless the cause, Ed Tolley still had to go through the motions of making his closing argument. In fact, there was so little to say that he had to wander, just to take up his allotted time. He began with a little discourse on the role of lawyers in an adversarial system of justice. He spoke of the functionary in Roman times called the "pontifex," who mingled his priestly duties with advocacy on behalf of the accused, and even judicial tasks. Cicero, he said, was such a figure. "Even today," he said, "in certain parts of rural Georgia, lawyers oftentimes double as preachers. In the early days almost all of your lawyers served as preachers."

Out of this great tradition, he said, came the lawyer's professional sense of idealism, duty, and public service. "In the final analysis," he said with a convincing solemnity, "that is what we are supposed to be about. Our profession . . . is not about carrying bags of money on Wall Street. Even the damned . . . in this system of justice that we operate under are entitled to a lawyer."

This allusion led Tolley to speak of Clarence Darrow, the great advocate of the early twentieth century who was often called the "attorney for the damned." Roy Moody, he said, "represents the class that Clarence Darrow might have represented: the class of the damned, the man who comes to you accused of the most heinous crimes." Thus, he went on, it had been for him "a privilege to do these things that our profession requires us to do. . . . I hope we have done so honorably."

With his time now nearing its merciful end, he turned to the specific case that was about to be submitted to the jury. It was the government's ploy, he said, "to shift the focus from the lack of evidence to the man himself." He hammered on the most cherished belief of criminal law, that every person is presumed to be innocent at the outset of a trial, and it was the government's heavy duty to overcome that presumption; he bore down on the necessity for every juror to convince himself "beyond a reasonable doubt" that Roy was guilty. He knew he had to overcome Roy's own damning testimony, and he fell back, weakly and somewhat cryptically, on a Georgia colloquialism: "If you set out to beat a dog, you can always find a stick."

And finally he resorted to the old standby that the government had presented only "circumstantial evidence" of guilt. He alluded to the biblical story of Joseph, whose bloody clothing was submitted as proof that he had been murdered, as a case of circumstantial evidence that was in fact false. Then, his labors over, Ed Tolley took his seat beside the man whom he knew was about to be convicted of crimes he knew he had committed.

Judge Devitt's charge was brief. Paying passing obeisance to Ed Tolley's argument, he spoke of "the hallowed principles" of proving guilt beyond a reasonable doubt. But then he added that this does not mean "beyond all possible doubt." He described spent a little time describing the legal term, "malice aforethought," which basically meant premeditated commission of an illegal act. Then he sent the jury into seclusion to decide the case.

No matter how strong the evidence, a seventy-two-count indictment requires a few hours of deliberation. As the courtroom functionaries waited, there was a festive atmosphere. Judge Devitt announced that there was a visiting judge from Washington, named MacKinnon, who was an amateur pastry chef and who had brought in a batch of his own molasses cookies. Judge MacKinnon passed around a plateful of the delicacies to anyone who wished to sample them; Roy Moody took one.

After a few hours the jury returned its verdict: Guilty on all counts.

Two months later, after the perfunctory formality of reading a history of the defendant's criminality, Judge Devitt passed what would be among his final sentences after forty years on the bench; the old jurist would be dead in a few months.

The sentence was seven life terms, plus four hundred years.

Then Roy Moody was taken, in shackles, from the courtroom for the return trip to the Atlanta penitentiary, which he had entered almost twenty years earlier, to begin spending the remainder of his troubled life behind bars, with virtually no hope of ever again being a free man.

In ritualistic completion of his appointed task, Ed Tolley filed an appeal of Roy Moody's conviction, and because all of the judges of the Eleventh Circuit had been friends and colleagues of Bob Vance, the case was assigned to a panel of three judges from the neighboring Fourth Circuit Court of Appeals. The chief judge was Sam J. Ervin III, the son of the North Carolina senator of Watergate fame.

Tolley was fully aware that Judge Devitt was almost never overruled by the appellate courts, but he still went through the motions, basing his appeal on three alleged "errors" at the trial. He maintained that Judge Devitt should not have allowed the jurors to hear tape recordings of Moody's jail-cell mutterings, nor see evidence seized on the basis of flawed search warrants. These were boilerplate appeal grounds; Tolley knew the law was so settled in this area that Judge Devitt would hardly make a simple blunder.

So in the end the appeal rested on something of a contradiction: Tolley argued that Judge Devitt should never have permitted Moody to testify—never mind the defendant's own insistence in taking the stand.

On November 6, 1992, just under three years after Moody had initiated his orgy of violence, the court rejected his appeal. After a dry, point-by-point recitation of the law, Judge Ervin concluded: "Moody received a fair and impartial trial before an able and experienced district judge. He was represented at that trial and on these appeals by very competent and diligent counsel. . . . [W]e affirm his conviction."

A few weeks later, the United States Supreme Court quietly and summarily upheld the appellate court's conclusion; Roy Moody's sentence was now upheld.

But this was not the end of the matter for Roy. Ed Tolley had warned his troublesome client at the St. Paul trial that Roy's theatrical testimony might expose him to an even graver danger than ever. Under federal law, the harshest punishment he could receive would be a sentence of life imprisonment. But the federal conviction did not preclude prosecution for murder under state law, in both Alabama and Georgia, for the Vance and Robinson murders, and both states had death-penalty statutes—statutes that juries showed no reluctance to apply.

The federal trial had barely ended when Alabama Attorney General Jimmy Evans, Bob Vance's old political ally, secured a capital-murder indictment against Moody in Birmingham. Georgia authorities indicated an indictment might be forthcoming in Savannah as well.

Early in 1992 Roy was transported from the federal penitentiary in Merion, Illinois, to the Birmingham jail to await trial and to continue his contentious pastime of filing lawsuits. Among those he sued was L. Dan Turberville, the Birmingham attorney who was appointed to represent him. By this time, though, everyone had had his fill of Roy Moody's incessant litigation; the judge summarily threw the case out of court.

As four years passed, one delay followed another, and Jimmy Evans, Bob Vance's old Democratic Party ally, lost his bid for reelection as state attorney general—to a New South Republican. In the fall of 1996, Roy at last went to trial in the Circuit Court of Jefferson County in Birmingham. Now he was without a lawyer at all; he had fired—and sued—yet another lawyer, and had defiantly refused to accept any other attorney that Judge William Rhea offered to appoint for him.

Despite this history, as the proceedings began Roy announced that he was hiring new lawyers and demanded a delay in the trial. Judge Rhea summarily refused the eleventh hour request. As the trial got underway, the only other person sitting at Roy's counsel table was a young female paralegal who was reported to have fallen in love with him.

Roy's "opening statement" consisted of shrieking at the judge that he was the victim of an FBI "setup." Then, he got into a shouting match with prosecuting attorneys, but his tirades ceased when he observed jurors laughing at him. Thereafter, for most of the week-long trial, Roy sat in sullen silence, not even responding when asked if he wished to cross-examine the witnesses whose collective testimony systematically and inextricably enmeshed him in the mail bomb murders.

On November 5 the case went to the jury, which deliberated for only twenty minutes before returning the verdict: guilty as charged. The recommended sentence was death by electrocution. Under Alabama law, the judge may, upon finding mitigating circumstances, reject the jury's recommendation and instead impose a sentence of life without parole.

After yet more delays, on the clear, crisp winter afternoon of February 10, 1997, Judge Rhea called Roy Moody to court to hear his fate. Moments before he entered the courtroom, Roy had filed a document in which he maintained that a bomb expert who had been helping with his defense was, in fact, an FBI informant. For the better part of an hour, Roy read a rambling statement, claiming that his conviction had been "fraudulent," and that indeed, Judge Rhea himself had been part of the pervasive conspiracy against him.

The jurist listened patiently, then began to intone his sentence. The court was aware, Judge Rhea said, that Roy had been diagnosed as suffering from a paranoid personality disorder, and he had carefully considered this diagnosis as a mitigating factor.

"But," Judge Rhea went on, "it is the judgment of the court that the aggravated circumstances [of the murder] far outweigh the mitigating circumstances." The death sentence was pronounced on a subdued Roy Moody. The unheeded implicit warnings of Ed Tolley, and even Park Dietz, were fulfilled.

Helen Vance was not in court for the grim proceeding. Bob Vance Jr. was there, and as the shackled condemned man was led back to his jail cell, the murdered man's son said simply, "He hung himself."

Whether Roy will ever be put to death remains to be seen; as a practical matter, few foresee that the sentence will be carried out. After all, Moody is now in his sixties, and by the time all appeals—which he has vowed to pursue—are completed he could be an old man. It is unlikely that even in Alabama an aged man would be placed in the electric chair to be put to death for a crime committed many years earlier.

In Savannah, Robbie Robinson's widow, Ann, fell into financial distress and had to sell the suburban bungalow in which she and her husband had lived. She has since remarried.

The Robinson family has established a small scholarship fund to honor Robbie by helping a needy student attend college to pursue a degree in a field of public service.

Since the events of 1989, it has become increasingly clear that Walter Leroy Moody Jr. represents a particular type of criminal—an individual who nurses a profound sense of injustice, who harbors a willingness to act out of a sense of "higher purpose" even when innocent blood must be shed in the process, and who has the perverse intelligence to carry out his dark deeds.

And there is no indication that the successful prosecution of Roy Moody has dissuaded others from continuing to spread this particular form of terror. In the four years after Roy mailed his deadly packages in 1989, the number of bombing episodes in the nation has more than doubled to nearly three thousand a year. Controlling such activity is all but impossible, given the fact that bombs can be assembled in secrecy, from readily available materials, by any person of average intelligence.

Most illegal bombs that are detonated in America each year are the vengeful handiwork of men settling petty scores; most of these bombers are apprehended and prosecuted. But others are much like Roy Moody, acting out of some amorphous grievance or generalized malignant malice against "the system." This propensity, at least at this time, was grievously demonstrated in the bombing of the federal building in Oklahoma City in 1995, resulting in the loss of 168 lives in the deadliest act of terrorism ever committed in America. A similar bomb attack on the World Trade Center in New York two years earlier might have taken a far greater toll had it not been for the clumsy execution of the plot by the terrorists responsible for that episode.

And the elusive Unabomber—once briefly suspected of perpetrating the Vance and Robinson murders—was arrested in the summer of 1996 after an eighteen-year reign of terror that killed three men and wounded doubled to nearly three thousand a year. Controlling such activity is all sixteen others—in the name of a "war" against society in general.

These are the kindred souls of Walter Leroy Moody Jr.

Note on Sources

This book is drawn from many sources, but it would not have been possible without the cooperation of numerous individuals who generously shared with me the bits and pieces of the story that they possessed.

Bob Vance's surviving brother, William Vance, and his sister, Martha Vance Cameron, were the chief sources for the early life of their younger brother. Vern M. Scott of the Talladega County Historical Association supplied an excellent outline of the history of Talladega, the town in which Bob Vance was born and spent his early years. Dr. Taylor Littleton of Auburn University shared his reminiscences as a boyhood playmate in the Woodlawn section of Birmingham in the 1940s.

Helen Vance provided not only the details of her life with Bob Vance but also her own painful account of the events of December 16, 1989, which took her husband's life and very nearly her life as well. For a filial view of the happy home life of the Vance family, I drew from an eloquent, poignant, and witty tribute to his father delivered by Robert S. Vance Jr. at a ceremony in 1990 at the federal courthouse in downtown Birmingham for Judge Vance. The picture was completed through an interview in 1992 with Charles Vance, the younger son, at Durham, North Carolina, where he was completing his medical training.

The account of Bob Vance's political career draws heavily upon my own coverage of Alabama politics during the 1960s and 1970s. But I am also indebted to many of his political allies, all close personal friends, who granted interviews or supplied memoranda. These include the late Clifford Fulford, Max Pope, Chris Doss, Al LaPierre,

Jim Klinefelter, Bill Baxley, Jimmy Evans, Judge Truman Hobbs, Mary Texas Hurt Garner, Alex Newton, Marie Jemison, and Charles Morgan Jr.

Griffin Bell, who was attorney general of the United States at the time Bob Vance was nominated in 1977 for a seat on the United States Court of Appeals for the Fifth Circuit, supplied me with an excellent account of the considerations that went into that choice, culminating with an account of the Oval Office meeting at which President Jimmy Carter settled on Vance from the list of nominees.

For the account and analysis of Judge Vance's twelve years as a member of the United States Court of Appeals for the Fifth and Eleventh Judicial Circuits, I read many of his opinions as carried in official court reports. For an excellent summary overview, I relied heavily on "Footprints of a Just Man: The Case Law of Judge Robert S. Vance," an article written by eight former law clerks in the Spring 1991 issue of the *Alabama Law Review*. That issue also carried an article by another Vance law clerk, Michael Mello, that poignantly stated the anguish of a federal judge in deciding death-penalty cases. Also helpful was Judge Ed Carnes, who succeeded Bob Vance on the Eleventh Circuit Court of Appeals. To complete my assessment of Judge Vance's years on the bench, I interviewed two of Judge Vance's former law clerks, Michael Waldman and Jefferson M. Gray.

For the family background of Robert Edward Robinson, I am indebted to his sister, Barbara Robinson-Pulliam, who not only supplied records tracing their ancestry to antebellum times but also provided the details of her brother's early years in Savannah. Ann Robinson gave me a moving account of the final days of her husband's life.

Professor Robert Strozier of Armstrong College in Savannah provided me with not only valuable suggestions as to contacts but also an excellent overview of social and political currents in Georgia's most historic city during the lifetime of Robbie Robinson. More specific information about Mr. Robinson was provided by many of his personal, professional, and political associates. Among them were former Savannah Mayor John Rousaikis, Fletcher N. Farrington Jr., Clarence Martin, Bobby Hill, John Alexander, Steven Scheer, W. W. Law, Joyce Tolbert, and Lester Johnson. The *Savannah Morning News* graciously allowed me to use its files.

For the history of Fort Valley, I relied largely on a monograph now on file in the town library and thought to have been written in 1938 by Mrs. W. J. Braswell. Professor Donnie D. Bellamy gave me his own insights and provided written materials on the vital role of Fort Valley State College in that community's life during the first half of the century. My information on the role of Fort

Valley's industrial mainstay, the Blue Bird Body Company, came from Albert and Joe Luce, from the files of the *Atlanta Journal-Constitution,* and from an authorized history of the firm by Bernard Palmer, published privately in 1977.

For reasons that require no explanation, Roy Moody's sister, Delores Moody Cummings, and brother, Bobby Moody, did not wish to discuss the most painful chapter of their family's turbulent history. They did, however, refer me to their uncle, William Oscar Moody, who was only eleven years older than Roy and who proved to be an invaluable source as a meticulous family historian. The files of the *Fort Valley Leader-Tribune* also provided useful information on Roy's parents as well as an overview of Fort Valley during his youth.

The most useful information about Roy Moody's early life came from the former Joyce Law, who, as a childhood neighbor, in many respects became Roy Moody's first victim. Many others in Fort Valley shared their recollections of Roy Moody or the ambience of the town during the time in which he grew up there. These included Dr. Margaret Howard Drubig, Paul Spahos, Albert Luce Jr., Joseph P. Luce, Georgeann Harris Seymour, Henry Harris, Judge George Culpepper III, Jeanette Wheaton, and Ray Allen.

Probate Judge William Self of Macon shared with me his recollections as the lawyer who represented Roy Moody's first wife, Hazel. I also found many small threads of this period in the files of the *Macon Telegraph and News,* as well as from documents on file in the Macon public library.

My account of the investigation of the Vance-Robinson murders was drawn from contemporary newspaper accounts, from the official trial transcript, from internal documents gathered by the chief prosecutor (and subsequently FBI director) Louis Freeh, and from interviews with a wide range of individuals who were involved in what was then called "the largest manhunt in history." These include former Attorney General Richard Thornburgh, former Assistant Attorney General Robert Mueller, former FBI director William Sessions, and Chief Judge Gerald Bard Tjoflat of the Eleventh Circuit Court of Appeals. Especially valuable was the cooperation of Lloyd Erwin, Tom Stokes, and David Hyche of the Bureau of Alcohol, Tobacco, and Firearms. Others from the FBI who shared their accounts of the investigation included Assistant Director Larry Potts, Charles Archer, Bill Baker, William Hinshaw, Oliver "Buck" Revell, and Allen Whitaker. Earl Shinhoster gave me an account of Roy Moody's smoke-bomb attack on the Atlanta NAACP office in 1989.

My account of the diversionary investigation into Robert Wayne O'Ferrell in the weeks that followed the Vance murder came chiefly from contemporary newspaper accounts, from court records, and from an interview with O'Ferrell in Enterprise.

For my account of the trial of Roy Moody in St. Paul in June 1991, I relied primarily on the official trial transcript, but I also drew heavily from newspaper coverage, especially the excellent reporting of Peggy Sanford of the *Birmingham News*. For background on Judge Edward J. Devitt, I relied chiefly on the files of the *St. Paul Pioneer Press*.

An invaluable source for insights into the mind of Walter Leroy Moody Jr. was a report dated June 11, 1991, prepared by Park Elliott Dietz, a forensic psychiatrist, for use by government prosecutors in the Moody trial in St. Paul. Dietz was engaged to conduct a psychiatric evaluation of Moody in anticipation of an insanity-defense plea. Dietz's evaluation included a thorough examination of FBI internal investigation reports and prior court records, interviews with Moody's associates, and most important, twenty-five hours of videotaped interviews with the defendant. Because Roy Moody forbade his attorneys to enter an insanity-defense plea, Dietz was never called to the stand, and his report was never made public.

Additional insights into the psychological makeup of Roy Moody came in interviews with Dr. Sheldon Cohen, an Atlanta psychiatrist who was engaged by the defense team to evaluate the defendant.

The imperatives of attorney-client confidentiality created delicate problems for the many lawyers who represented Moody at various times during his litigious life. Despite this potential impediment, several of these lawyers granted interviews. Especially valuable was the insight of Edward Tolley, the court-appointed lawyer who defended Moody at his St. Paul trial. As a lawyer myself, familiar with the ethical constraints of attorneys with regard to client confidentiality, I can state emphatically that never once did Tolley cross that ethical threshold in the interviews he granted to me. The same can be said of Bruce Harvey, Michael Ford, and Tommy Mann. All acted in the highest traditions of professionalism.

Because of pending appeals and state prosecutions, federal attorneys were likewise circumscribed in discussing the case. The most valuable inside account was provided to me by Howard M. Shapiro, who, at the time of our interview, had left the Department of Justice to become a professor of law at Cornell University. He provided an excellent personal perspective on the preparation for the Moody trial that could not have been reflected in the official transcript.

Miriam Walmsley Duke, an assistant United States attorney in the Middle District of Georgia, shared her experiences as the lawyer who represented the government in Moody's prolonged effort to have his 1972 conviction for possession of explosives overturned.

For the dramatic account of Susan McBride's crucial decision to testify against her former husband, I am indebted to McBride's court-appointed attorney, Sandra Popson of Macon. Subsequently, Susan McBride gave me her own tortured account of her eight years with Roy Moody.

Newspaper colleagues who assisted in steering me to sources included David Johnston and Peter Applebome of the *New York Times* and Ronald J. Ostrow of the *Los Angeles Times*. Professors John Brumbaugh and William Reynolds of the University of Maryland Law School helped me on some legal aspects. Professor Patricia Romero of Towson State University read much of the manuscript and made suggestions, as did my wife, Bettina C. Jenkins. Peggy Obrecht gave me useful guidance on some of the more obscure aspects of Roy Moody's "theology."

A major source was the official transcript of Walter Leroy Moody Jr.'s trial in St. Paul, Minnesota, in June 1991. The document covers more than three thousand pages and, when stacked, measures a yard high.

Jimmy Evans, Bob Morrow, Mary Ann Melko, and Dan Turberville all gave guidance on Roy Moody's pending trial in Alabama after his conviction on federal charges.

I am especially indebted to Professor Dan T. Carter, the Kenan Professor of History at Emory University, for reading the manuscript and making valuable suggestions.

The books on southern history, sociology, and culture from which I drew generally are too numerous to mention, but there were several of considerable value. C. Vann Woodward's *Tom Watson: Agrarian Rebel,* first published in 1938 by the Macmillan Company of New York, was the source of my view of the political climate in Georgia the early part of the century. Equally valuable was *The Wild Man from Sugar Creek,* a superb account of the political career of Eugene Talmadge by William Anderson, published by the Louisiana State University Press in 1975.

To buttress my own twenty-five years of first-hand observation of Alabama politics, I relied especially on the following books: *Dixiecrats and Democrats: Alabama Politics, 1942–1950,* by William D. Barnard (Tuscaloosa: University of Alabama Press, 1974); *One Man, One Voice,* by Charles Morgan Jr. (New York: Holt, Rinehart and Winston, 1979); *Lister Hill,* by Virginia Van der Veer Hamilton (Chapel Hill: University of North Carolina Press, 1987); *Bull Connor,* by William A. Nunnelley (Tuscaloosa: University of Alabama Press, 1991); *The Transformation of Southern Politics,* by Jack Bass and Walter DeVries (New York: Basic Books, 1976); *The Two-Party South,* by Alexander P. Lamis (New York: Oxford University Press, 1984); *Elephants in the Cottonfields,* by Wayne Greenhaw (New York: Macmillan, 1982); *Alabama: The History of a Deep South State,* by William W. Rogers, David Ward, Leah Atkins, and Wayne Flynt (Tuscaloosa: University of Alabama Press, 1994).

Index